Data Warehousing

Edited by SCN Education B.V.

HOTT Guide

Edited by SCN Education B.V.

This series of books cover special topics which are useful for a business audience. People who work or intend to work with Internet - at a management, marketing, sales, system integrating, technical or executive level - will benefit from the information provided in the series.

These books impart how new technologies and sales & marketing trends on Internet may be profitable for business. The practical knowhow presented in this series comes from authors (scientists, research firms and industry experts, a.o.) with countless years of experience in the Internet area.

The HOTT Guides will help you to:

- Enlarge your knowledge of the (im)possibilities of Internet and keep it up-to-date
- Use Internet as an effective Sales & Marketing tool by implementing new technologies as well as future-oriented strategies to improve your business results
- Facilitate decision making on a management level
- Reduce research costs and training time

These books are practical 'expert-to-manager' guides. Readers will see a quick 'return on investment'.

The Publishing department of SCN Education B.V. was founded in 1998 and has built a solid reputation with the production of the HOTT Guide series. Being part of an international IT-training corporation, the editors have easy access to the latest information on IT-developments and are kept well-informed by their colleagues. In their research

HOTT Guide

activities for the HOTT Guide series they have established a broad network of IT-specialists (leading companies, researchers, etc) who have contributed to these books.

SCN Education B.V., Newtonstraat 37C, 3902 HP Veenendaal, The Netherlands,
tel. +31 – 318 – 547000, fax +31 – 318 – 549000, www.scnedu.com,
www.hottguide.com.

Books already in print:

Webvertising
Mobile Networking with WAP
ASP – Application Service Providing
Customer Relationship Management
Electronic Banking

Data Warehousing

The Ultimate Guide to Building Corporate Business Intelligence

Edited by SCN Education B.V.

Die Deutsche Bibliothek - CIP-Cataloguing-in-Publication-Data
A catalogue record for this publication is available from Die Deutsche Bibliothek (http://www.ddb.de).

Trademarks
All products and service marks mentioned herein are trademarks of the respective owners mentioned in the articles and or on the website. The publishers cannot attest to the accuracy of the information provided. Use of a term in this book and/or website should not be regarded as affecting the validity of any trademark or service mark.

1st Edition April 2001

Vieweg is a company in the specialist publishing group BertelsmannSpringer.

Printing and binding: Lengericher Handelsdruckerei, Lengerich
Printed on acid-free paper
Printed in Germany

ISBN 3 - 528 – 05753 – X

Preface

Data: from acquisition to interpretation

Historically, the major challenge for organizations was capturing data. Years ago, businesses were able to leverage the information they could get, but weren't very good at getting detailed information across a range of business processes.

In the business environment of today, virtually every transaction and minute business data is recorded in databases to enable better, more effective decision making throughout the organization. Most of the technology emphasis has been on storing data, with less attention paid to tools for transforming data into meaningful information which can be easily accessed and shared by executives.

A data warehouse system can take meaningless data and, using intense analytical processing, offer insight into changing market conditions before they occur. The capability to optimize customer interactions and supply chain operations is becoming a source of great competitive advantage.

This HOTT Guide will give you access to all the essential information about the newest was to store and interpret data: through articles by expert trendwachters on strategic considerations, how-to reports defining the various ways to extract the data needed for critical business decisions, technical papers clarifying technologies and tools, business cases and key concepts that will provide the reader with a comprehensive overview of a business solution that is already indispensable.

The Editors

Acknowledgements

Many people and professionals have contributed directly or indirectly to this book. To name them all would be practically impossible, as there are many. Nevertheless the editors would like to mention a few of those who have made the production of this book possible.

Executive Editor for SCN Education B.V.: *Robert Pieter Schotema*
Publishing Manager: *drs. Marieke Kok*
Product Manager: *Martijn Robert Broersma*
Editorial Support: *Dennis Gaasbeek*
HOTT Guide Online: *Rob Guijt, Richard van Winssen*
Interior Design: *Paulien van Hemmen, Bach.*

Contents

Contents

Contents

Introduction to Data Warehousing

The Sales and Marketing Imperative: The Impact of Technology on Business Strategy

Title: *The Sales and Marketing Imperative: The Impact of Technology on Business Strategy*

Author: *IMT Strategies, Inc.*

Abstract: *IMT Strategies explains how technology is radically changing business strategies and the role of sales and marketing professionals. They help you understand and anticipate the technology trends for your business.*

The Forces of Change

In the early 21st Century, dramatic business change, disruption and innovation will define sales and marketing strategy. Sales and marketing leaders must capitalize on the potential of technology, anticipate changes in customer buying behavior and create innovative selling models to survive and grow sales. Rapid advances in technology will create opportunities and risks that will profoundly impact most aspects of sales and marketing strategy and management, including:

- Resource planning and allocation;
- Sales and distribution channel management;
- Product and market planning and development;
- Customer behavior and expectations;
- Customer service and support;
- Demand chain planning and partner management;
- Sales and marketing mix;
- Performance measurements and incentives.

In the next decade, businesses that can build highly efficient selling systems that successfully develop high levels of growth, customer intimacy, and competitive differentiation will dictate market leadership. To achieve aggressive revenue growth objectives and establish market leadership, sales and marketing leaders at Global 2000 companies must:

- Maximize the return on their sales and marketing investment dollars;
- Anticipate rapid changes in customer buying behavior;
- Capitalize on powerful new interactive, database and communication technologies;
- Stay ahead of rapidly evolving demand chains, changing business models and a new breed of virtual competitors.

Selling More With Less
Product commoditization, e-business and new competition are putting pressure on already thin margins, forcing organizations to reduce sales and marketing budgets. At the same time, revenue growth targets

remain aggressive, forcing companies to find new ways to increase their sales with fewer resources. To grow "more for less," companies must maximize the return on their sales and marketing investments.

Changing Customer Buying Behavior
The broad-scale adoption of new technologies has empowered consumers in previously unimagined ways. As a result, customers are adapting to advances in these new technologies faster than many marketers can keep up. For example, customers will migrate from one selling channel to another, moving from the "high touch" appeal of shopping at face-to-face retail outlets to the 24-hours-a-day/7-days-a-week access of call centers and self-service electronic commerce.

Figure 1

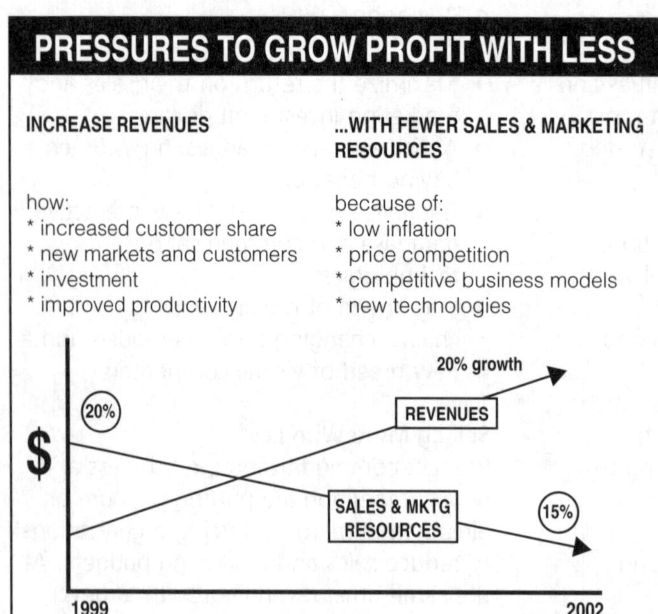

Also, customers will expect "seamless" service from businesses, whether they are interacting with a salesperson, a telemarketer, a shipping clerk, a Web site, an ATM or a retail kiosk. And, these customers will expect more customized and personalized products, services and relationships. As technology lifecycles shorten and the pace of innovation explodes, customers will expect better quality, personalized service and access to more information, creating new markets while making others obsolete. Businesses must anticipate and respond to these new market segments and deliver products and services that meet customers' needs, or they will lose market share.

The Sales and Marketing Technology Revolution
The rapid adoption of technology by suppliers, customers, partners and competitors presents both an opportunity and a threat. Advances in database, communication and interactive technologies are fueling a rapidly maturing menu of sales and marketing solutions. Investments in electronic commerce, sales and marketing automation, Internet marketing, customer interaction centers and customer data warehouses have the potential to create significant corporate value. They provide businesses the

opportunity to dramatically improve the efficiency and productivity of sales and marketing programs while enabling new levels of customer intimacy and market differentiation. Companies that can incorporate these technologies into their sales, marketing and service processes faster and better than the competition and ahead of customer expectations will thrive. Those that wait too long or make the wrong decisions will pay a price.

New Business Models
The wave of technology-driven sales, marketing and distribution innovation is enabling the creation of new business models, markets, and services that were impossible as little as two years ago. This new breed of business will have far-reaching impacts on the way business is conducted by radically reducing transaction costs and margins, providing competitors and partners direct access to customers, minimizing customer switching costs, building higher levels of intimacy.

Figure 2

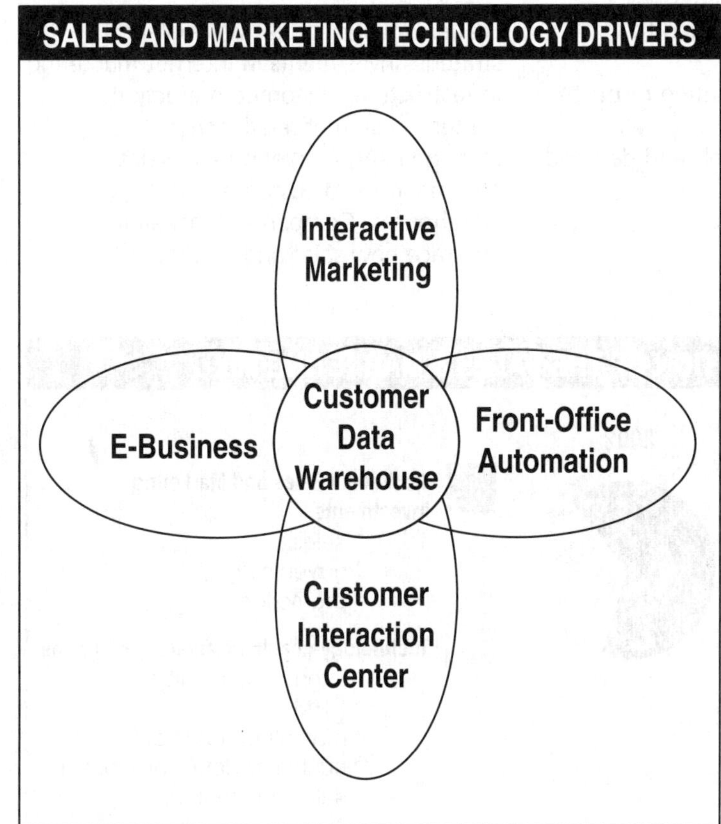

Sales and Marketing Leadership on the Line

Technology is radically changing sales and distribution strategies and redefining the traditional "4 Ps" of marketing—product, pricing, promotion and placement. Pressures to improve growth, productivity and customer intimacy with limited resources will force companies to reconfigure their selling systems to maximize returns on their sales and marketing investment dollars. The potential of technology to create selling leverage, enhance customer relationships and increase competitive differentiation will drive dramatic shifts in the sales and marketing mix.

Bottom line: to remain competitive, sales and marketing organizations will significantly increase investment in selling technologies and technology-enabled marketing programs.

Market leaders will successfully adapt to changing customer needs, pre-empt new competition and capitalize on the potential of technology to create competitive advantage. Sales and marketing organizations will be challenged to:

- Optimize sales and marketing resource allocation;
- Manage complex channels and demand-chain networks;
- Adapt to changing branding, direct marketing and pricing models;
- Create world-class customer-centric organizations.

Optimize Sales and Marketing Resource Allocation

Sales and marketing budgets will shift dramatically as businesses reorient their selling systems to react to competition, adapt to changing customer behavior and leverage technology. Spending will be reallocated from traditional sales, marketing and promotional tools to technologies that can improve customer loyalty, sales productivity and growth.

Leaders must prioritize and balance strategic investments in Internet marketing infrastructure, customer interaction centers, customer relationship management, marketing and sales automation and customer data warehouses. Companies that fail to embrace new sales and marketing

Figure 3

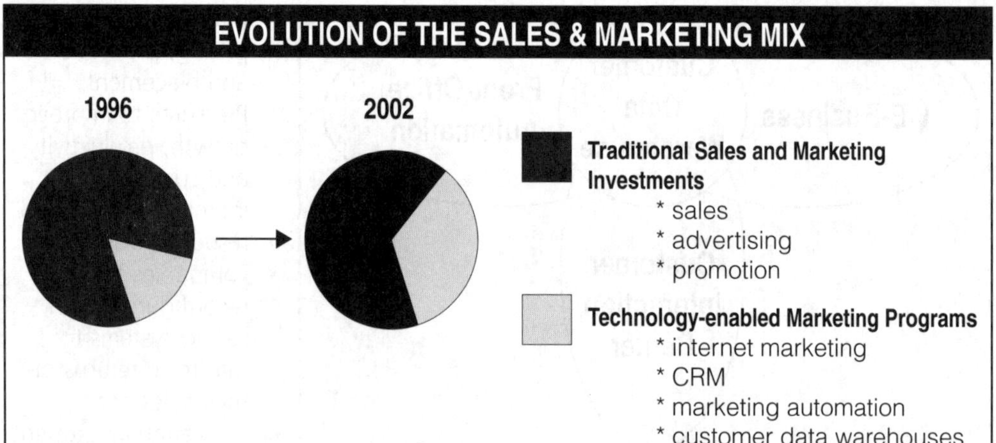

technologies risk losing their competitive advantage and customers. However, companies that invest aggressively in such technologies without strategic insight and understanding risk sinking millions of dollars into the wrong solutions, resulting in minimal return on investment.

Manage Complex Channels and Demand Chain Networks

The nature of selling channels and business partnerships is changing radically. To grow sales and improve market coverage, companies are building complex hybrid distribution systems that combine field sales, partners, electronic and tele-channels as well as multiple customer access points like retail outlets, call centers, and the Web. Executives must develop policy, planning and measurement tools to manage these complicated systems. Companies should actively plan to deliver products through diverse "routes to market" and define clear product "channel readiness" requirements for pricing, transaction costs, service and intimacy. Businesses must re-examine their position in the supply and demand chains to ensure that they are not "disintermediated" from access to customer data or eclipsed altogether by a new breed of competitors. Additionally, it is imperative that companies identify new ways to improve their market position by developing relationships with new kinds of partners, such as Web portals, dynamic trading communities, virtual logistics providers, and e-commerce outsourcers.

Adapt To Changing Branding, Direct Marketing and Pricing Models

Technology is also transforming corporate brand, pricing and promotional strategies. Sales and marketing leaders must navigate through these changes and find new ways to build customer retention and brand loyalty. They will struggle to manage the impact of buy-side and sell-side technologies as well as electronic trading communities on margins and pricing. Businesses will be challenged to build brand equity in e-channels, virtual communities and across multiple selling partners, channels and points of interaction. Companies will seek to maximize the return on marketing dollars by finding ways to capitalize on highly targeted and personalized interactive and

Figure 4

IMPACTS ON SALES AND MARKETING ORGANIZATIONS

- ☞ Reduced Switching Costs
- ☞ Changed Marketing Mix
- ☞ Increased Reliance on Technology
- ☞ Hybrid Distribution Channels
- ☞ Demand Chain Remediation
- ☞ Changing Brand, Pricing and Direct Marketing Strategies

direct marketing tools. They will experiment with new approaches and strategies for anticipating or influencing the way customers buy. Product and marketing staffs will work to develop economic approaches to mass customizing products for individual customers, channels, and partners.

Create World-Class Customer-Centric Organizations and Processes
To better integrate with a growing number of partner, channel and customer relationships, businesses will have to become more externally focused. Organizations will be recast to reflect this customer focus with increased functional management of customers, their issues and the processes that touch them. These customer-centric organizations will provide better management of customer segments, customer care processes, customer relationship management (CRM) processes and customer data warehouses. To effectively manage customer processes that span the entire company and many functions, businesses will have to create new job descriptions and develop a new breed of executive. These executives will be challenged to direct this transformation by defining business requirements for customer collaboration, including customer relationship management infrastructure, e-care processes, and enhanced customer management policies. To ensure access to world-class skills, improve flexibility and drive down costs, leaders must establish and increasingly rely upon strategic outsourcing relationships with a new breed of sales and marketing utilities, service providers and e-channel partners.

The Changing Role of the Sales and Marketing Professional

The emerging business environment will significantly change the role of the sales and marketing professional and will present a new set of management challenges, market opportunities and business risks. What worked in the past will not necessarily work in the future. Success will require new vision, new skills and new disciplines.

Today's sales and marketing executives should anticipate that:

- Budgets will be dramatically reallocated or outsourced;
- Incentives and compensation will change significantly;
- Conflicts will arise between organizations and partners over control of brand, customer relationships, and market access;
- Markets may suddenly vanish due to channel disintermediation or customer migration.

Sustained competitive advantage and corporate value will not come simply from the deployment of a corporate Web presence, call centers or a sales force automation package. To achieve true marketing differentiation, customer intimacy and selling channel efficiency will require new, innovative approaches. Sales and marketing professionals must develop marketing strategies that capitalize on marketplace changes and strategically deploy technology to enhance sales, service and support processes.

To survive, tomorrow's sales and marketing leaders must:

- Manage inevitable channel conflicts;
- Learn new, cross-functional skills;
- Prioritize and justify investments in new technologies;
- Gain tighter control over customer data within the demand chain;
- Understand patterns in customer buying behavior better;
- Manage complex, hybrid selling channels and multiple customer points of interaction;
- Build stronger customer relationships with higher levels of intimacy and new switching costs;
- Develop mass-customized, channel-ready products;
- Redefine brand, pricing and direct marketing strategies;
- Develop "end-to-end" e-care and customer service processes that span departments, selling channels and the entire customer lifecycle.

How To Take Action

Sales and marketing professionals will be charged with anticipating change, focusing on the most important business issues and taking action to capitalize on market opportunities and manage risks. To succeed, professionals will need foresight and insight into critical advances in technology, new business models that materially change the competitive landscape and how their customers will behave in the future. They must focus their activities on the top opportunities to build competitive advantage and market differentiation: tighter customer relationships that build customer loyalty and more efficient sales and marketing systems that accelerate revenue growth.

The risks to sales and marketing management are clear: fail for doing nothing, fail for doing the wrong things, fail for doing the right things too late. The business implications are significant:

- Lost customers through disintermediation and customer migration;
- Diminished brand equity and marketing effectiveness in new selling channels and business models;
- Eroded margins and reduced switching costs due to e-commerce and dynamic pricing technologies.

To capitalize on opportunities and manage risk, sales and marketing professionals must balance strategic planning and timely action. To do so requires an understanding of the short- and long-term management implications of changes in technology, customer behavior and business models. Leaders will focus on prioritizing the most significant business issues and putting in place the right strategies, structures, processes and people necessary to succeed.

Sales and marketing professionals must take leadership in specific areas:

Business Models
To articulate business impact and prioritize resource reallocation, leaders must develop better ways to understand and assess the business impact of new technologies, dynamic buy-side and sell-side pricing, sales and marketing outsourcing, better

customer data analysis, alternative branding approaches and demand chain remediation.

Investment Priorization and Selection Criteria
To establish technology investment priorities and budgets, sales and marketing executives must be able to identify and prioritize strategic technology investments that will support the enterprise's growth strategy and business model and fit with the unique characteristics of markets, channels and products.

Resource Allocation
To optimize returns on sales and marketing investments, leaders must redefine the sales and marketing mix and reallocate investment to selling channels and marketing programs that demonstrate the greatest "bang for the buck."

Business Requirements
To align and integrate more closely with information technology (IT), leaders must find ways to develop clear, cross-functional business requirements for mapping technology strategy to growth and market coverage strategies.

Establish New Measures
To realize top-and bottom-line impact from investments in technology and process changes, leaders must redefine measures to better manage end-to-end processes, optimize selling resource productivity, dynamically assess the value of customers and decipher customer buying behavior.

Define New Rules
Leaders must redraft product, channel and pricing policies to economically and efficiently manage more complex channel systems, partnerships, market segments and customized products, as well as to stay ahead of changing customer buying behavior.

Figure 5

LEADERSHIP KEYS

- ☞ Define New Business Models
- ☞ Establish Technology Investment Priorities
- ☞ Optimize Resource Allocation
- ☞ Establish Clear Cross-Functional Requirements
- ☞ Establish Strategic Operational Measurements
- ☞ Define New Rules
- ☞ Evolve Organizational and Functional Models

Evolve Organizational and Functional Models
To integrate better with a growing number of complicated partner, channel and customer relationships, leaders must recast organizations to become more externally focused and install hybrid management for enterprise-wide leadership of cross-functional issues such as e-care, e-commerce, and customer relationship management.

The Top 12 Impacts of Technology on Sales and Marketing

IMT Strategies tracks technology's top 12 impacts on sales and marketing operations. Our service helps executives understand and anticipate these trends, focus on the most significant implications to their business and take action quickly to capitalize on market opportunities and actively manage risks.

The following trends serve as the backbone of IMT Strategies' research agenda and represent strategic imperatives to sales and marketing management over the next decade.

Operational Imperatives

Collaborative Customer Relationship Management (CRM)
Assembling and integrating CRM systems that enhance customer collaboration and build customer loyalty and switching costs.

Outsourcing Sales and Marketing Functions
Increasing outsourcing of sales and marketing budgets to a new generation of businesses including marketing agencies, e-commerce utilities/service and e-channel partners to obtain specialized talent, technical expertise and cost efficiencies.

Customer-Centric Organizations
Recasting organizational and functional models to become a natural extension of customer segmentation, enterprise selling processes and complex demand-chain partnerships.

Operationalizing E-Care
Establishing enterprise-wide management of the customer care processes to ensure seamless service and enhanced intimacy across multiple channel interfaces and throughout the customer lifecycle.

Channel Imperatives

Hybrid Distribution Systems
Building multi-channel, hybrid distribution systems that leverage low-cost, high-touch technologies to improve cost efficiency, market coverage and overall selling performance.

Value-Added Direct Sales
Changing the role of direct sales to better align high-touch, face-to-face selling interactions with high-value and high-margin products and services.

Demand Chain Remediation
Restructuring demand-chain relationships to maximize value creation and customer access while leveraging costs and value-added channel partnerships.

Customer Interaction Centers
Consolidating and integrating call centers, Web, email, fax and marketing technology assets to better manage selling resources, technology infrastructure and customer interactions.

Market Imperatives

Mass Customized Products
Designing modular, "channel-ready" products optimized for specific sales channels, partners and customer segments, and improving personalization, ease of doing business and transaction costs.

Dynamic Pricing
Managing the impact of buy-side and sell-side technologies and trading communities on margins and pricing.

Changing Role of Branding
Building brand equity in e-channels, virtual communities and across multiple selling partners, channels and points of interaction.

New Age Direct Marketing
Developing new tools, approaches and strategies for anticipating and influencing the way customers buy.

Managing Intelligence

To fully grasp and understand new technologies and their business impact, sales and marketing executives require market intelligence, foresight, and insight. They face two obstacles to obtaining this critical information:

- Rapid change—Business innovation and new learning occur on a daily basis;
- Information proliferation—Executives have hundreds of legitimate sources of information.

Existing sources of information are generally fragmented, biased and not focused on the needs of sales and marketing executives. Traditional business partners can provide some answers; however, consultants, marketing agencies, systems integrators and technology vendors provide only part of the picture and often have a stake in a particular technology, strategy or decision. Media and IT advisory services are numerous and are generally focused on specific technologies rather than on the issues and solutions relevant to the sales and marketing function.

Focus, relevance and context are lacking. Making decisions based on the glut of available information about developments in technology, customer buying behavior and best-practice technology deployments can be overwhelming. There is too much information, while too few sources of comprehensive, objective, strategic and actionable insight.

About IMT Strategies

IMT Strategies, Inc., is an advisory firm that helps business leaders understand and anticipate the impact of rapidly maturing sales and marketing technologies, changing customer buying behavior and emerging technology-enabled business models. We help executives focus on the most important management implications, risks and opportunities of the new business environment and help them take action with the best strategies, structures, processes and people necessary to differentiate, grow and win.

- IMT Strategies provides retainer-based advisory services, strategic publications, research and training to help companies build high-performance selling strategies that allow them to grow more for less.
- IMT Strategies analysts are internationally renowned experts in developing high-performance selling strategies that leverage technology, including e-business, inter-active marketing, customer interaction centers (call centers, Web and email "e-care"), customer relationship management (CRM), front office automation (sales force automation (SFA) and marketing automation and customer data warehouses.
- IMT Strategies is an affiliate and close strategic partner of META Group, a world leader technology research, analysis and advisory services.
- IMT Strategies' management team has over 15 years experience developing high-growth, technology enabled sales and marketing strategies for leading marketers such as IBM, American Express, Citibank and GE.

IMT Strategies, Inc. provides a unique solution for business executives. Our services are geared to provide a centralized, objective, on-call resource for clear insight and answers. Our analysts are at the forefront of tracking the key developments that will impact sales and marketing strategies and interpreting their implications to sales and marketing organizations, including:

- The core technologies that will enable new high-growth selling systems;
- Innovative technology deployments by marketing leaders that establish "proof of concept";
- Changes in customer buying behavior and service-level expectations.

IMT Strategies helps business executives focus on what is important by highlighting the most critical management implications and identifying the strategic, structural, process and organizational actions necessary to create competitive advantage.

Data Warehousing - adopting an architectural view, and maximizing cost benefits

Title:	*Data Warehousing - adopting an architectural view, and maximizing cost benefits*
Author:	*Ian Manning*
Abstract:	*A data warehouse environment can offer enormous benefits to most major organizations if approached in the correct way, and if distractions from the main goal of delivering a flexible, long-term information delivery environment are placed in perspective.*

Biography: A consultant specializing in data integration and decision support, Ian has been an IT professional for over 20 years. Industry experience includes banking, energy, pharmaceuticals, telecomms, and insurance.

Data Warehousing – what exactly is it?

Heralded as the solution to the management information dilemma, the term "data warehouse" has become one of the most used and abused terms in the IT vocabulary. But ask a variety of vendors and professionals for their vision of what a data warehouse is and how it should be built, and the ambiguity of the term will quickly become apparent.

To a number of people, a data warehouse is any collection of summarized data from various sources, structured and optimized for query access using OLAP (on-line analytical processing) query tools. This view was originally propagated by the vendors of OLAP tools. To others, a data warehouse is virtually any database containing data from more than one source, collected for the purpose of providing management information. This definition is neither helpful nor visionary, since such databases have been a feature of decision support solutions since long before the coining of the term "data warehouse".

The concept of "data warehousing" dates back at least to the mid-1980s, and possibly earlier. In essence, it was intended to provide an architectural model for the flow of data from operational systems to decision support environments. It attempted to address the various problems associated with this flow, and the high costs associated with it. In the absence of such an architecture, there usually existed an enormous amount of redundancy in the delivery of management information. In larger corporations it was typical for multiple decision support projects to operate independently, each serving different users but often requiring much of the same data. The process of gathering, cleaning and integrating data from various sources, often legacy systems, was typically replicated for each project. Moreover, legacy systems were frequently being revisited as new requirements emerged, each requiring a subtly different view of the legacy data.

Data Warehousing - adopting an architectural view, and maximizing cost benefits

Based on analogies with real-life warehouses, data warehouses were intended as large-scale collection/ storage/staging areas for legacy data. From here data could be distributed to "retail stores" or "data marts" which were tailored for access by decision support users. While the data warehouse was designed to manage the bulk supply of data from its suppliers (e.g. operational systems), and to handle the organization and storage of this data, the "retail stores" or "data marts" could be focused on packaging and presenting selections of the data to end-users, often to meet specialized needs.

Somewhere along the way this analogy and architectural vision was lost, often manipulated by suppliers of decision support software tools. Data warehousing "gurus" began to emerge at the end of the 80s, often themselves associated with such companies. The architectural vision was frequently replaced by studies of how to design decision support databases. Suddenly the data warehouse had become the miracle cure for the decision support headache, and suppliers jostled for position in the burgeoning data warehousing marketplace.

Despite the recent association of the term "data warehousing" with OLAP and multi-dimensional database technology, and the insistence of some people that data warehouses must be based on a "star schema" database structure, it is wise to restrict the use of such designs to data marts. The use of a star schema or multi-dimensional / OLAP design for a data warehouse can actually seriously compromise its value for a number of reasons:

(a) such designs assume that all queries on the warehouse will be of a quantitative nature - i.e. queries on aggregated numeric data. This overlooks the fact that data warehouses can also offer enormous benefit as repositories of text-based or qualitative data - e.g. the provision of a 360° view of customers by collecting profile information from a range of sources;

(b) such designs require the pre-aggregation of data in the data warehouse. In doing so, and eliminating much of the original transactional data, much information can be lost. If information requirements change, requiring alternative aggregations from the transactional data, a star or multi-dimensional design will quickly become obsolete. A normalized design, on the other hand, which accommodates transactional level data would be able to support any number of alternative aggregations. While capacity and/or performance constraints may preclude this as an option for some data, the storage of low level transactional data in a data warehouse should not be ruled out, as this is often the only way of ensuring maximum flexibility to support future information needs;

(c) optimized models such as star schemas are, in general, less flexible than normalized designs. Changes to business rules or requirements are generally more easily accommodated by normalized models.

Data marts provide the ideal solution to perhaps the most significant conflict in data warehouse design - performance versus flexibility. In general, the more normalized and flexible a warehouse data model is, the less well it performs when queried. This is because queries against normalized designs typically require significantly more table join operations than optimized designs. By directing all user queries to data marts, and retaining a flexible model for the data warehouse, designers can achieve flexibility and long-term stability in the warehouse design as well as optimal performance for user queries.

Why is it so expensive?

While the data-warehousing concept in its various forms continues to attract interest, many data warehousing projects are failing to deliver the benefits expected of them, and many are proving to be excessively expensive to develop and maintain. For this reason it is important to have a clear understanding of their real benefit, and of how to realize this benefit at a cost which is acceptable to the enterprise.

The costs of data warehousing projects are usually high. This is explained primarily by the requirement to collect, "clean" and integrate data from different sources - often legacy systems. Such exercises are inevitably labor-intensive and time-consuming, but are essential to the success of the project - poorly integrated or low quality data will deliver poor or worthless management information. The cost of extracting, cleaning and integrating data represents 60-80% of the total cost of a typical data warehousing project, or indeed any other decision support project.

Vendors who claim to offer fast, cheap data warehouse solutions should be asked to explain how they are able to avoid these costs, and the likely quality of the results of such solutions must be carefully considered. Such vendors typically place the emphasis on tools as a solution to the management information problem – OLAP tools, data integration technology, data extraction tools, graphical user query tools, etc. Such tools resolve only a fraction of the management information problem, and represent a small proportion of the cost of a successful data-warehousing project.

Focus on technology rather than data quality is a common failing among data warehousing projects, and one which can fatally undermine any real business benefit.

How can the cost be justified?

Given the high costs, it is difficult to justify a data-warehousing project in terms of short-term benefit. As a point solution to a specific management information need, a data warehouse will often struggle to justify the associated investment. It is as a long-term delivery mechanism for ongoing management information needs that data warehousing reaps significant benefits. But how can this be achieved?

Given the above facts about the loading of costs on data warehousing projects, it is clear that focus must be on the reduction of the ongoing cost of data extraction, cleaning and integration.

A number of years ago I conducted a study for a multi-billion dollar manufacturing and services organization. The purpose of the study was to identify why previous data warehousing projects had failed to deliver the expected benefits, and to make recommendations for how future projects could rectify this.

The study resulted in a number of significant findings, including the following:

1. 80% of the data used by the various data warehouses across the corporation came from the same 20% of source systems.
2. Each new data-warehousing project usually carried out its own process to extract, clean and integrate data from the various sources, despite the fact that much of the same data had been the subject of previous exercises of a similar nature.
3. The choice of data to be populated in the data warehouse was usually based on needs of a specific group, with a particular set of information requirements. The needs of other groups for the same data were rarely considered.

Experience of other organizations showed a very similar pattern to the above. From these findings alone it is clear that there is scope for economies of scale when planning data warehousing projects; if focus were to be placed initially on the 20% of source systems which supplied 80% of the data to decision support systems, then an initial project which simply warehouses "useful" data from these systems would clearly yield cost benefits to future MIS projects requiring that data. Rather than targeting a specific business process or function, benefits should be aimed at the wider audience for decision support. Such a project would form an invaluable foundation for an evolving data warehouse environment.

When building a data warehouse the use of multi-dimensional, star-schema or other optimized designs should be strongly discouraged, in view of the inherent inflexibilities in these approaches as outlined above. The use of a relational, normalized model as the backbone of the warehouse will ensure maximum flexibility to support future growth. If user query access is then strictly limited to data marts, the data warehouse needs only to support periodic extracts to data marts, rather than ad-hoc query access. Performance issues associated with these extracts can be addressed in a number of ways - for example through the use of staging areas (either temporary or permanent) where relational table structures are pre-joined or "flattened" to support specific extract processes.

Once this initial project is complete, emphasis can be placed on the growth of the warehouse as a global resource for unspecified future decision support needs, rather than as a solution to specific requirements at a particular time. In subsequent phases of the warehouse development, new data, which is likely to play a major role in future decision support needs, should be carefully selected, extracted and cleaned. It can then be stored alongside the existing data in the warehouse, hence maximizing its information potential. As new information needs emerge, the cost of meeting them will be diminished due to the elimination of the need to perform much of the costly extraction, cleaning and integration functions usually associated with such systems.

Over time, this environment will grow to offer a permanent and invaluable repository of integrated, enterprise-wide data for management information. This in turn will lead to massively reduced time and cost to deliver new decision support offerings, and hence to true cost justification.

The effort required to achieve this must not be underestimated, however. Identifying which data is "useful" requires a great deal of experience and insight. The way in which the data is modeled in the warehouse is absolutely critical - a poor data model can render a data warehouse obsolete within months of implementation. The process used to identify, analyze and clean data prior to loading it into the warehouse, and the attendant user involvement, is critical to the success of the operation. Management of user expectations is also critical. The skills required to achieve all of the above are specialized.

Once in the warehouse, data can be distributed to any number of data marts for user query access. These data marts can take any number of forms, from client-server databases to desktop databases, OLAP cubes or even spreadsheets. The choice of user query tools can be wide, and can reflect the preferences and experience of the users concerned. The wide availability of such tools and their ease of implementation should make this the cheapest part of the data warehouse environment to implement. If data in the warehouse is well-structured and quality-assured, then exporting it to new data marts should be a routine and low-cost operation.

server database to desktop data marts, OLAP cubes or even spreadsheets. The choice [illegible] they [illegible] provide [illegible] of the users [illegible] wide availability of solutions and ease of implementation should make this the cheapest [illegible] of the warehouse [illegible] data in the warehouse is well-structured and quality assured, then [illegible] should be [illegible] operation.

ments should be carefully selected [illegible] and [illegible]. It can then be stored alongside the existing data as the warehouse [illegible] potential. As new information needs emerge, the [illegible] will be diminished due to the elimination of the need to perform [illegible] extraction, cleaning and integration functions usually associated with such systems.

[illegible]

[illegible]

[illegible]

What is Data Warehousing?

Title: *What is Data Warehousing?*
Author: *David Heise, Andrews University*
Abstract: *David Heise explains what a data warehouse is, why we need it and how to get it.*

1. What is it?

The Oracle database used by Banner is designed for OnLine Transaction Processing (OLTP). A data warehouse is designed for a different purpose. It is designed to support ad hoc data analysis, inquiry and reporting by end users, without programmers, interactively and online. This is called OnLine Analytical Processing (OLAP), or Multi-Dimensional Analysis. It is more than just a better set of reports. Mostly for performance reasons, a data warehouse is held in a separate database from the operational database, usually on a separate machine.

2. Why do we need it?

The Banner database is designed to be efficient at processing online transactions, and this kind of design is quite inefficient at processing analytical queries and ad hoc reports. This gives frustrating performance for the person making the inquiry, as well as having a significant impact on the performance of the system for regular Banner users.

But there is an even more important reason for building a data warehouse. The structure of the OLTP database is almost incomprehensible to anyone but a programmer. Rules of OTLP database design are broken in a data warehouse to make navigation through the subject areas and data elements correspond to business functions, thus making a data warehouse more intuitive to use.

This results in at least the possibility of being able to ask questions about the data that can be answered without calling on a programmer.

The table on the next page summarizes some of the main benefits that are possible through data warehousing.

Table 1: Benefits of Data Warehousing

- Has a subject area orientation
- Integrates data from multiple, diverse sources
- Allows for analysis of data over time
- Adds ad hoc reporting and inquiry
- Provides analysis capabilities to decision makers
- Relieves the development burden on IT
- Provides improved performance for complex analytical queries
- Relieves processing burden on transaction oriented databases
- Allows for a continuous planning process
- Converts corporate data into strategic information

3. How do we get it?

Some of the key factors to consider when building a data warehouse are listed in table 2:

Table 2 Key Ingredients for Data Warehousing Success (2)

- Be Ready for the Data Warehouse
  Develop an understanding amongst senior administrators of the potential role of IT and data warehousing in achieving the institution's goals.
- Choose The Right Project Team
- Have a Training Strategy
  Take appropriate training, and/or hire selected consultants
- Choose the Right Architecture
  Start small, using a phased approach, but within the framework of a system-wide architecture.
- Have a Project "Mission Statement"
  Feasibility study
  Project Charter
  Project Plan
- Show Early Business Benefits
  Choose strategically important subject areas, (i.e. areas that are linked to the Strategic Plan), that have high visibility and fast return. (remember the 80-20 rule).
- Ensure Scalability
  Evolve the data marts iteratively, constructing the architected data warehouse as you go.
- Understand the Importance of Data Quality
- Be Wary Of Vendor Claims
  Choose the data repository, data warehousing tools, and desktop tools with care.
- Use a Proven Data Warehouse Methodology
- Define and Manage Data Ownership Issues
- Don't underestimate the Difficulty of Implementing Change

There is a process for choosing strategically important subject areas that starts with the mission statement of the institution, and the goals and objectives. Critical success factors are then identified, as well as the steps for achieving success as outlined in the strategic plan. Indicators are found that can be measured and that can be used to monitor the success of the plan, especially in the areas deemed critical, and also adherence to the plan. These are called key performance indicators, and these form the basis of analytical data models that are provided in the data warehouse.

Endnotes

1) Heise, D. Data Warehousing at Avondale College. p15 http://www2.andrews.edu/~dheise/dw/Avondale/ACDWTOC.html

2) Crofts, S.A. You Can Create the Perfect Data Warehouse: Key Ingredients To Data Warehousing Success. (Adapted) The Data Warehousing Institute. Data Warehousing Buyer's Guide. p26

Data Warehousing Solutions. High-Availability, High-Performance Networks Support Superior Business Decisions.

Title: *Data Warehousing Solutions. High-Availability, High-Performance Networks Support Superior Business Decisions.*

Author: *3Com*

Abstract: *A data warehouse is an integrated, multi-subject repository containing highly detailed historical data; it accepts and processes queries for a group of end users. It is a complex system requiring a distinct architecture to successfully deliver sophisticated support for business decisions. This paper examines the business environment and the drivers that have given rise to the data warehouse. It describes the various types of end-user data warehousing applications, as well as some network implications for organizations preparing to implement or upgrade data warehousing capabilities.*

Business Environment

The business environment continues to be volatile and intensely competitive. Organizations today must constantly acquire and lever-age information to survive. Indeed, the widespread shift away from paper-based systems to software-driven, automated business processes has been driven largely by a need to streamline operations through better information management and flow.

Historically, the major challenge was data acquisition. Years ago, businesses were able to leverage the information they could get, but weren't very good at getting detailed information across a range of business processes. But this situation has now reversed. Businesses now collect orders-of-magnitude more information than they can process and leverage in a meaningful way.

The inability to effectively leverage information arises from the way it is gathered. Numerous, non-integrated systems engage in purpose-directed collection of data based on differing, myopic business data models. This leads to the creation of numerous data silos with very limited capability for synergy. A data warehouse taxonomy defines architecture, tools, and processes that enable a business to develop and exploit synergistic opportunities among these operational data silos. Data warehouses integrate and transform disjointed data into meaningful information that provides insight into the various aspects of the business.

Business Drivers

To remain competitive, today's leaner, more empowered organizations demand consolidated information at all levels to achieve strategic objectives. After years of downsizing, rightsizing, reengineering, and continuous improvement, organizations find themselves in a permanent state of flux. Increasing productivity demands require that analytical information be distributed widely throughout the organization.

For example, a fundamental change is occurring in the approach to managing customer relationships and supply chains. The key to success in both areas lies in a company's ability to respond quickly and appropriately to changing market conditions and requirements. A data warehousing system can take meaningless data and, using intense analytical processing, offer insight into changing market conditions before they occur. The capability to optimize customer interactions and supply chain operations is becoming a source of great competitive advantage.

A range of business drivers can push the need for data warehousing to the fore:

- Mergers and acquisitions. Data warehousing can be used to isolate core reporting and decision making from the chaos of buying and selling companies; some acquisitions may start with financial consolidation, while others are used to provide uniform procurement and human capital management. A data warehouse could be used to "roll up" this information from an enterprise resource planning (ERP) or financial reporting system.
- Customer intimacy. Data warehousing can be used to effectively gather, cleanse, position, and disseminate external and internal customer data, improving value orientation and intimacy. For example, customer relationship management (CRM), the provision of a single enterprise-wide customer view, is better enabled when all relevant customer information such as order history, profile, and interaction history is consolidated for comprehensive analysis. A data warehouse can be used to house the potentially large amount of customer information gathered from numerous data sources.
- Electronic commerce. Data warehousing can be extended forward and backward via the Web. From data collection to data dissemination, e-commerce initiatives can receive strategic support beyond simple order management.
- Business performance management (BPM). Data warehousing provides the needed subject breadth and historical depth of data required to support BPM, avoiding problems of using data silos for decision support.
- Supply chain planning. Through all phases of the product cycle, organizations must develop synergy and create visibility both internally, for costing and efficiencies, and externally, for service levels and relationship building. Inventory and order information from suppliers and distributors can be stored in a data warehouse as part of a supply chain planning system.

Data Warehousing End-User Applications

There are three general categories of end-user applications that rely on data warehousing:

- Deductive (query/online analytical processing). The process of applying specific -though probably ad hoc- questions against the available data. This well-established category includes "what-if " analysis and decision support.

- Inductive (data mining). The process of interrogating the available data before a specific question has been formulated. This category is relatively new but growing rapidly, and substantial offerings are already available.
- Reporting. The process of generating reports about the available data based on one of the above activities.

The sections that follow describe each application type in more detail.

Deductive Applications

Deductive applications, the traditional mainstay of data warehousing end-user applications, fall under the umbrella term online analytical processing (OLAP). The OLAP Council defines OLAP as "a category of software technology that enables analysts, managers, and executives to gain insight into data through fast, consistent, interactive access to a wide variety of possible views of information that have been transformed from raw data to reflect the real dimensionality of the enterprise as understood by the user."

Recently, OLAP has both competed with and been integrated with data mining tools (see "Inductive Applications"). Data mining and OLAP solutions are increasingly packaged as horizontal and vertical applications—emphasizing third-party data sources, data service providers, and database marketing. These intelligent agent solutions will increasingly promote real-time, closed-loop "decision implementation systems."

Inductive Applications

The area of inductive tools is the heart of data mining. Data mining is the process of automatically unearthing information from databases; this information ore, thus mined from the data lode, is smelted into predictive information that can be used for crucial business decisions. Data mining tools search for non-obvious patterns and indicators in data that shed new light on business conditions. Some look at data mining as a way to help users formulate their questions. Data mining is subdivided into two parts:

- Micro-mining. Data mining and statistical tools for analysts with advanced skills; typically used for hypothesis discovery using various methods for pattern discovery and forecasting.
- Macro-mining. A data mining development environment that supports a data analysis framework (DAF), including an advanced modeling workbench and support for integration with production systems (for a closed-loop solution).

Inductive knowledge discovery tools (data mining/micro-mining) support semi-automated pattern discoveries, but are often designed to perform specific tasks (segmentation, clustering, binning, and prediction) using standard algorithms. Statistical tools are still necessary to develop custom models and perform analysis specific to line of business (LOB) and industry requirements. Both deductive and inductive solutions are required to maximize data warehousing value, and both must be part of any data warehousing implementation.

The challenge to users in accessing these massive amounts of information in a data warehouse is that of information overload. Information access (OLAP, query, and reporting) tools provide access to the data warehouse, but finding patterns and trends in a large body of information pushes the limits of human comprehension. Micro-mining or desktop data mining tools that are focused on ease of use for pattern discovery offer a new view of the information. On the low end, however, they are typically based on "black box" solutions that prevent customization. To develop specific LOB and industry models and enable the analyst to work without boundaries, custom statistical models and applications are needed.

Historically, statistical models were designed to understand trends in large volumes of data. Recently, statistical suite vendors such as MathSoft, SAS, and SPSS have evolved products to enhance ease of use, reduce skill requirements, and address issues of data warehouse scale. Even with the proliferation of desktop micro-mining tools (such as those from Cognos and Business Objects), applied statistics continue to have a place in either the data warehouse or statistical data mining for finding patterns and trends for use in custom models and analytical applications.

A statistical workbench can be used to develop a model that has the same properties and functionality as a data mining algorithm, or to apply specific mathematical models to the problem. Most industry-standard algorithms are available in the statistical workbench, and the analyst can develop, train, tune, and apply a statistical model to address a specific business problem.

The statistical workbench offers a fundamental advantage: portability. While most micro-mining tools are limited to the desktop interface, a model developed in a statistical workbench can be applied and shared with other applications for integration and deployment. Macro-mining solutions for specific marketing applications (for example, one-to-one, campaign management, response systems, or attrition management) that require integration with production systems remain viable across large organizations, but their high cost limits their use for smaller departmental projects.

Reporting Applications

These tools allow users to produce sophisticated, graphics-intensive reports, whether prepackaged or customized. In years past, organizations maintained large staffs of COBOL programmers to write and maintain proprietary report-generation programs. These programs rarely used graphics for data visualization, and produced lengthy, sometimes impenetrable reports. Fortunately, today's reporting tools can provide considerably more concise and intuitive presentations of data using sophisticated visualization techniques. Organizations can now rely upon a few individuals skilled in tailoring these tools to meet the business demands. There are generally two classes of reporting functions:

- Operational reporting. Static batch operational reports (such as exception reporting), often incorporating agents that reside in data warehousing or operational systems to monitor key performance indicators.

- Interactive reporting. Predefined reports with the option for some light interaction (using, for example, filters, sorts, drills, pivots) supporting data navigation to help the non–power user interact with the data.

Scope of Deployment

End-user applications can also be viewed in terms of their scope of deployment (Figure 1). On one end of the spectrum are business analysis-driven tools that tend to be restricted to a small number of users who have large, customized data reporting requirements. On the other end are tools that make standardized reports available to a large number of users (for example, Web-based customer account management, or portals).

Figure 1: Scope of Deployment of End-User Data Warehousing Applications

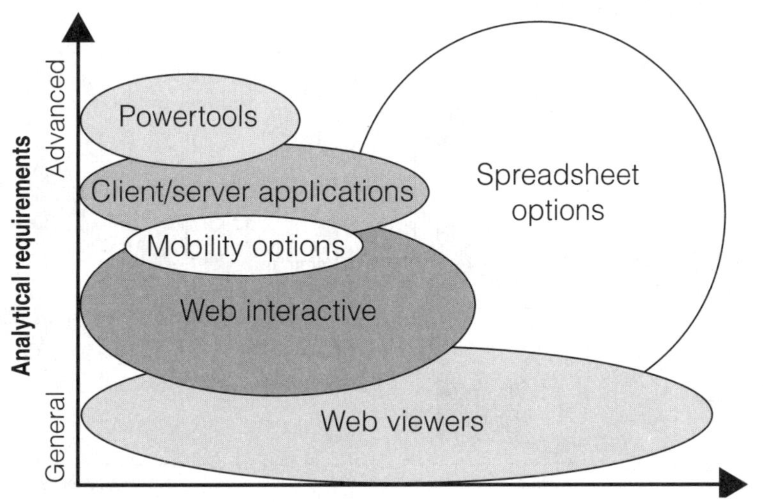

Data Warehousing Architecture

Figure 2 depicts current "best practice" in data warehousing architecture. This "hub-and-spoke" data warehouse architecture provides specific constructs to meet the challenges encountered in building modern data warehouse systems. A hub-and-spoke architecture provides a cost-effective foundation to efficiently handle metadata administration, simplify con-figuration management, and facilitate data movement. Monitoring and control is facilitated by the unidirectional nature of information flow, while costs are relatively easy to observe and manage. The hub-and-spoke data warehouse architecture provides specific constructs to meet the challenges encountered in building modern data warehouse systems:

- Sources. These are the sources of the data that goes into the data warehouse. Often separate databases, these sources can include the databases supporting ERP (such as those from SAP, Baan, and PeopleSoft), order entry, point-of-sale, or other business applications.

- Staging area. The extract, transform, and load (ETL) zone; its function is to extract information from operational data sources, transform extracted data in accordance with the metadata repository; and load new information into the enterprise data ware-house and updates into the operational data store.

- Enterprise data warehouse (EDW). An integrated, multi-subject structure containing highly detailed historical data. While flexible for different purposes, it is not typically used for processing end-user queries, but rather as a source for feeding more purpose-specific data marts.
- Metadata repository. A consolidated corporate data model; it contains universal definitions of all corporate data (such as descriptions, source mappings, calculations, date/time last updated, etc.).
- Operational data store (ODS). Similar to the EDW, but it contains current operational data. Frequently updated from operational sources, it supports analytical usage within the context of the current state of the business. Consequently, the ODS tends to be normalized and geared toward mission-critical applications.
- Data mart staging. Performs subsetting, summarizing, customizing, indexing, merge/joining, categorizing, etc.; this component maintains the linkage between the EDW and the numerous data marts (DMs) required by various departments by periodically updating the contents of respective DMs with information from the EDW. Immature data warehouse initiatives will have DM-EDW linkage.
- Data mart (DM). A subject-narrowed structure (for example, single-subject, single-department/ function focus) that contains a subset of EDW information, processing actual end-user queries and supporting end-user tools. Mature data warehouse initiatives have several DMs integrated back to a common EDW; immature ones have numerous, disjointed DMs with no synergy.

Figure 2: Data Warehousing Architecture

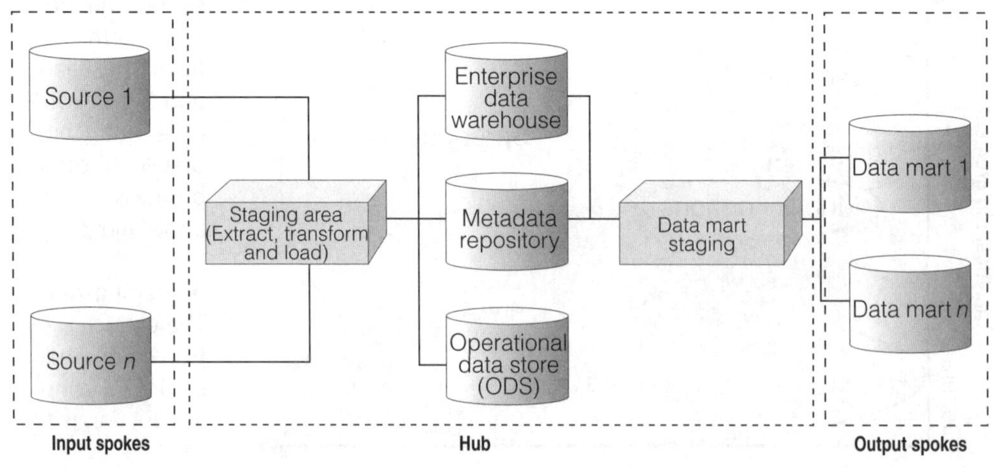

In practice, every data warehouse component can be located on physically separate databases (separate database servers) or all on the same machine with separate database instances or partitions. The actual distribution depends on many factors, including the volume of data processed, the amount of massaging that needs to be done to the source data, and the transactional requirements of the system. Typically, the data sources are located on separate machines (such as ERP servers), while most of the data warehouse is located on a few high-powered servers.

Network Implications of Data Warehousing
The networking implications of data warehousing primarily arise from two dimensions:

- Data warehouse storage
- User tools

The issues arising from user tools are not unique to data warehousing environments; however, the data warehouse storage architecture does raise some new issues.

Linking operational data sources to the data warehouse hub can be done over LAN, WAN, or storage area network (SAN) links (Figure 3). Physical distribution of the operational data stores may require data to be fed into the data warehouse front end via WAN links. On the other hand, aggregate data volumes may demand a dedicated SAN subnet. The data warehouse hub itself, internally, will preclude the use of WAN links because of performance requirements. This is typically not an issue, since the data warehouse core is located in a consolidated data center. Performance demands also make data warehousing an excellent candidate for a SAN solution. Finally, LAN or WAN links will generally work for linking data marts to the central data warehouse hub. The interaction between the various data warehouse components usually relies on a database access protocol (such as SQL or ODBC) running on top of IP. The nature of these interactions can be highly intensive, with hundreds if not thousands of exchanges occurring over a few minutes or

Figure 3: Data Warehouse Connectivity Options

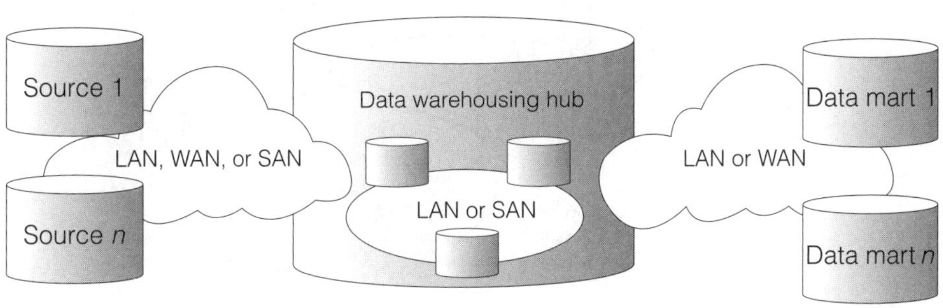

less. If the system is used for highly transactional purposes, the interactions will also be very frequent. Large amounts of data (100 MB or more) might be extracted just once a day from several different ERP systems into the data warehouse, where it could be analyzed a few times daily. On the other hand, inventory information from several data sources could be continuously pulled into the ODS so that real-time transactions could be performed against it. Depending on how the data warehouse is used and what the volume of data is, the network must provide appropriate flexibility and bandwidth.

Regardless of how the data warehouse is used, its core should be interconnected with high-speed, low-latency network links if the components are distributed across several machines (Figure 4). The interaction between the staging area and the EDW can be intensive if the data requires a lot of formatting. A powerful network management application, used in conjunction with RMON-1 and RMON-2 capable devices, will help provide an understanding of the real-time and historical traffic flows and network behavior. Using this information, the data warehouse infrastructure can be tuned to provide the most efficient service possible. The flexibility of Class of Service (CoS) or other policy enforcement tools allows administrators to groom traffic flows according to type of conversation, requested destination, or even time of day.

Figure 4: High-Speed Links at the Network Core Support the Data Warehouse

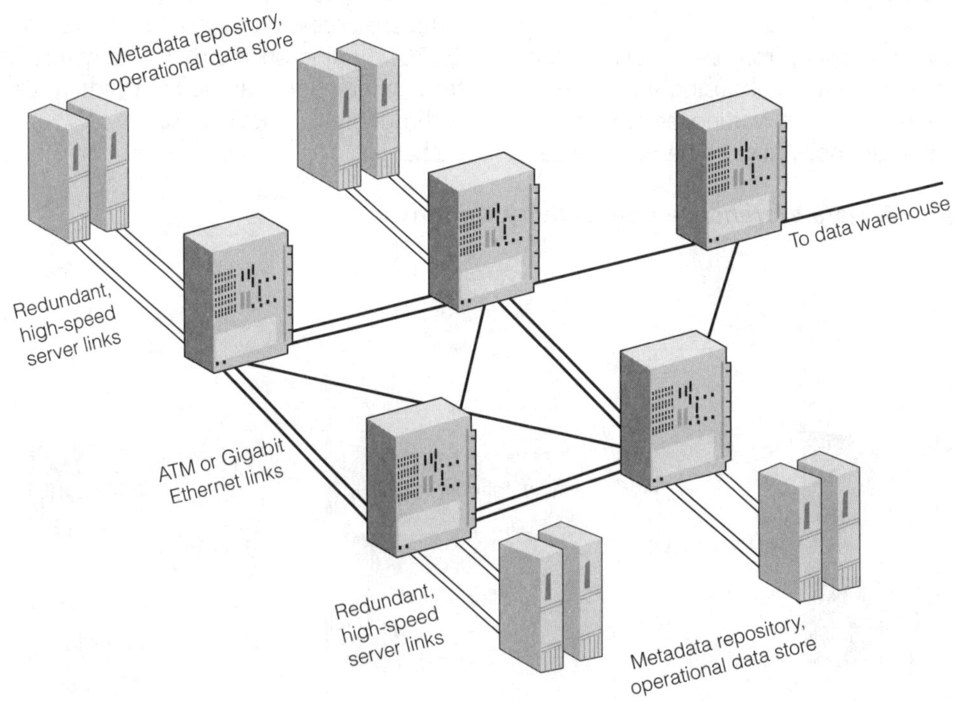

Data Warehousing Solutions. High-Availability, High-Performance Networks Support Superior Business Decisions.

The best way to provide a flexible, high-speed data warehouse is to upgrade away from contentious, shared LAN topologies or high-latency, routed connections to dedicated high-speed connections by deploying switching. Removing shared topologies and high-latency connections reduces the impact of other network applications on the data warehouse traffic. Layer 2 or Layer 3 switching solutions, such as those available in 3Com's CoreBuilder® and SuperStack® II products, can greatly increase the efficiency of the network and subsequent bandwidth availability to the data warehouse. By offering CoS and RMON capabilities, these 3Com products provide options for flexibility and visibility into the network. These features become especially crucial as the data warehouse application and query functions increase in complexity and use.

Bandwidth availability can be further increased and latency in the campus or building environment reduced by migrating to high-speed network technologies such as Fast Ethernet, Gigabit Ethernet, or ATM. Fast Ethernet desktop connections, corresponding riser/backbone links (that is, Fast Ethernet, Gigabit Ethernet, ATM), and high-speed server network interface cards (NICs) can significantly increase the bandwidth available to data warehouse components. For optimal network efficiency and throughput, a single-vendor, end-to-end solution such as 3Com's high-performance series of CoreBuilder and SuperStack II switches and broad family of NICs should be used.

Furthermore, to increase the availability and reliability of the data warehouse, critical network links between such components as the staging server and the EDW should be fault tolerant with redundant links between them. Two or more 3Com NICs with Resilient Server Link (RSL) in each server can achieve this redundancy. RSL is a DynamicAccess® software feature that enables a standby NIC to take over following a primary NIC connection failure. For added reliability, these NICs should be connected to redundant switches connected in a mesh topology to ensure NIC and switch fault tolerance. Furthermore, 3Com's server Ethernet cards also come with Self-Healing Drivers (SHDs) that add a high level of robustness to the server link by continually monitoring the state of the connection and the NIC for error conditions that could lead to link failure.

If the data warehouse is used for more analytical purposes, data in it may be "refreshed" infrequently but the data transfers may be substantial. It is not uncommon to see nightly uploads of greater than 300 MB per data source into the data warehouse. In these situations, high-speed WAN links with CoS/QoS features should be used to ensure that other critical business applications or systems management functions (such as system back-ups) are not negatively impacted. 3Com pro-vides a robust solution for this environment (Figure 5). By using the NETBuilder ® family of routers, the administrators can specifically set which protocols and traffic types are given high priority into and out of the data warehouse core. The PathBuilder ™ family of WAN access switches extends this capability by providing multiqueue CoS options. They also enable cost-effective WAN transfers by allowing virtual private network (VPN) tunnel termination, generation, and management.

Conclusion

This paper has provided an overview of data warehousing and the network implications for organizations seeking to leverage data warehousing solutions. 3Com's industry leadership continues to deliver superior solutions to address important business initiatives such as data warehousing. For more information on 3Com's solutions in this area, contact your local 3Com representative.

Figure 5: High-Performance Data Warehousing WAN Configuration

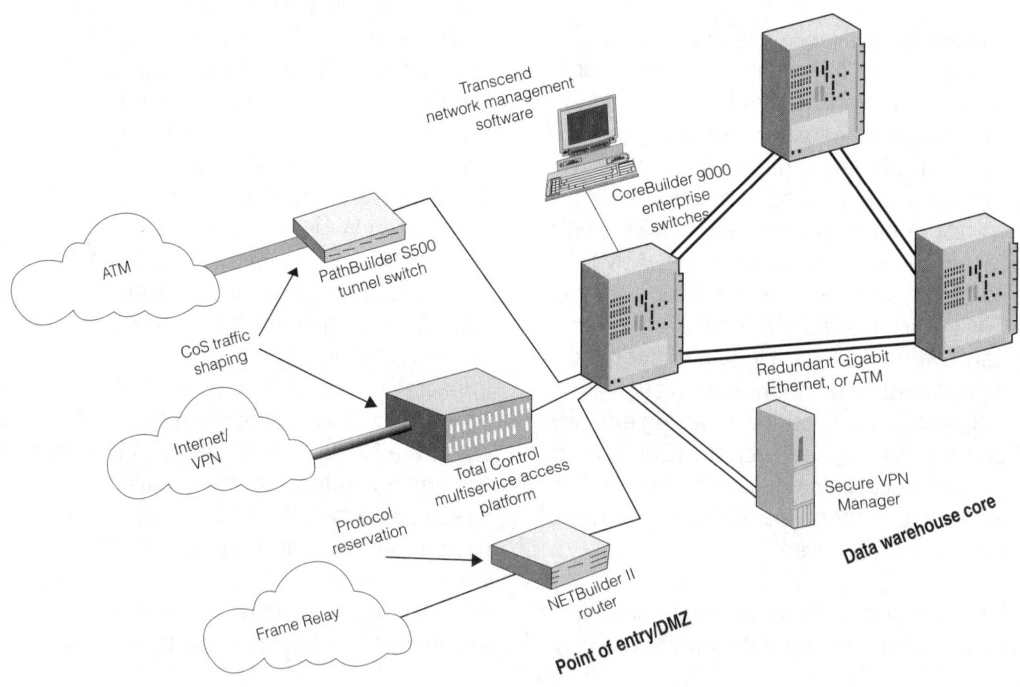

Getting Started - Building the Scalable Warehouse the Right Way

Title: *Getting Started. Building the Scalable Warehouse the Right Way*

Author: *Michael Meltzer, NCR Corporation*

Abstract: *Many managers have been inundated with information about the benefits of a Data Warehouse but little has been written to help the banker navigate through some rather treacherous waters. Where and how to start, why bother and what about all the hype? Isn't it all about databases? We have them, so what's the big deal!? This article introduces some of the ways to move towards your very own knowledge repository (your own data warehouse) and how it can help you better understand your business and support your decision-making. I will also look at some of the benefits and some of the ways other banks have moved forward successfully. Yes there have been failures but these are often the result of not getting the best advice you can and accepting that everything is a technology issue - it's not!*

Building A Data Warehouse For Competitive Advantage

Ask any senior banker today whether they are considering building a data warehouse, or have one already and the answer you will probably get will be yes! Is it that they have one, don't have one or don't know? Once again the answer is probably yes! This article will look at how a bank can go about developing a data warehouse, some of the technology issues that must be faced and how to continue the iterative building process that constitutes the data warehouse concept within a competitive banking environment.

The Answer Will Probably Be Yes!

The early adopters of the data warehouse are continuing to roll out their systems to more and more end users. They can say: " yes we do have a data warehouse and are successfully reaping the rewards of our investment." Many others, although implementing a data warehouse are still testing the water and have not told the rest of the bank yet. Whilst some banks believe they are "doing something" by continuing to evaluate alternatives, there are still a few banks who believe that any questions that relate to the use of information and computers should be answered by their Information Technology specialists alone (big mistake). However, the biggest problem for banks that are now ready to take the plunge relate to understanding where to start and how they can justify a strategic rather than an operational investment.

Some Basic Truths

You want the advantage of a Data Warehouse and the benefits it can offer you. You want to know which customers to treat in different profit building ways and who will be the most likely to respond to your latest direct marketing campaign. You might even consider that customer profitability, derived from transaction detail and agreed apportionment rules, is a good place to start. To cut a long story short you want to: market the right products to the right customers at the right time, and at the right price. Many firms outside banking have seen the trends in their market (stiffer competition, shrinking profit margins, diminishing brand loyalty, and increasingly short product life-cycles) and joined the DW (data warehouse) revolution some time ago. Lets look at some basic truths surrounding a data warehouse that Irwin Konopolsky has put forward:

How and Why Data Warehouses Are Used

1. The most frequent use of a data warehouse is to analyze historical data, discover trends and correlations and project events forward into the future (before your competition does).
2. The most valuable insights are almost always the result of "analytical expeditions" whose beginnings, routes taken, and endings could not have been predicted. In other words, the questions asked of the data are truly situational.
3. While it is always possible to assemble sets of numbers, such as sums or averages, the level of detail (granularity) of the stored data in your data warehouse limits how accurately you can dissemble it.
4. Data warehouses are also constructed to bring data from diversified sources together in one place so that data can be matched, merged, or compared. In order to accomplish this, the different sources of data must have consistent business definition, must be refreshable at the same interval, and must be at the same level of granularity.

Basically nobody really knows what questions you are going to ask, of your data warehouse, when you will ask them and how you will ask them. So how do you get started in building that granular data warehouse? First we must consider some of the technology issues including the reasons why your current processing systems cannot provide you with the business intelligence you need.

A lifeboat in a sea of data

Banks see themselves drowning in a sea of data. What they demand is business information that can support their business decisions and operational activities. Current bank systems support the day-to-day running of the business although this often only can create an operational parity with other banks, yet there have been some notable exceptions. The bank needs systems that can help it compete and alter the level of the playing field in it's own favor.

The data warehouse is a proven means of improving a banks competitiveness. That is if the DW (data warehouse) is designed in partnership with IS (information systems) from day one. The business user must drive the development, the DW must be implemented in an iterative manner and to maximize its benefit, it must be used "creatively". Oh yes, there have also been some failures but very few people talk about those. My remit in this article is to enable your bank to successfully build (not to have a failure) and/or extend a DW to continuously create and extend the potential competitive advantage you gain. To begin you must understand the need for different technology based architectures and processing systems as well as some tried and tested methods for effectively constructing a successful data warehouse.

Enterprise Information Architecture

Some suggest that before you embark on any IT related project that could impact the whole organization you must consider an enterprise wide information technology plan that is aligned to the business plan. Undertaking such a task would put a damper on your enthusiasm to do anything for the next 12-18 months as the IS organization and its consultants create the plan. However most plans that attempt to be all encompassing - rarely if ever are. They are often out of date by the time they are completed and just don't meet business needs.

The true cost of implementing a full blown enterprise rebuilding programme would put it outside most bank's IS budget anyway. You do need to let IS consider an enterprise information architecture but it must be in the form of an umbrella set of standards rather than a straight jacket. You need the benefits of guidance and some form of harmonization that can meet your changing needs. You don't need a set of standards and rules that are supplied as tablets of stone delivered from on high for you to follow blindly.

An umbrella information architecture can be considered as a framework (potentially Zachman's) and is required before the organization pulls itself apart by building even more systems that will not operate together. You need a structure an architecture that enables the planning and development of computing, communications, data and systems to happen in a coherent manner. "... coherence involves retreats and rethinks as much as thrusts and blueprints" (Michael J. Earl)

Data Warehouse Architecture
"As an integrated subject-oriented collection of data, the data warehouse brings together common information from various sources. As a non-volatile, time-variant collection of data, the data warehouse provides a stable source of information gathered over a period of time. The supporting metadata provides a map into its contents. Thus, a business analyst can use the data warehouse to discover what current and historical information is available on a particular subject and then to obtain it based on business data retrieval needs, without being confined to the limitations of individual systems which were built to improve the efficiency or effectiveness of business processes."
(Inmon, Zachman and Geiger)

The Tower Of Babel

Most departments have built systems and applications that meet their particular needs. This has lead to a proliferation of different islands of data and definitions. In a bank a customer's identity could be recorded five or more different ways in five or more different applications.

The DW is part of the solution/buffer to the problem of legacy systems and is a means to improving a banks competitiveness. A DW integrates data from the operational systems the bank uses. The data in the operational systems is held in a way to enable efficient transaction processing not search and retrieval. Traditional OLTP (Online Transaction Processing Systems) systems, designed for automating day-to-day operations, are very good at putting data into databases quickly, safely, and efficiently but are not very good at delivering meaningful business information in return.

Retrieval of useful information takes too long -- content for a typical new report can take days to specify and convey to an IS group with a wait that can stretch into months to get to see the report. Furthermore, data stored in OLTP databases is inconsistent and can change almost moment by moment. Often there are multiple records or reversing entries which get in the way of the business analyst who needs a stable environment to work from. Historical data is missing from the OLTP database which makes analysis a non starter. The DW is tuned to enable search and retrieval. This is at the heart of the difference between operational and analytical systems. Bill Inmon the father of DW suggests:

- The data serving operational needs are physically different data from those serving informational or analytic needs.
- The supporting technology for operational processing is fundamentally different from the technology used to support informational or analytical needs.
- The user community of operational data is different from the one served by informational or analytical data.

The processing characteristics for an operational environment and a informational environment are fundamentally different.

Horses For Courses

You therefore separate operational from informational processing. Data warehousing is the process of extracting and transforming operational data into informational data and loading it into a central repository or DW. The task that architecture fulfils is: to get the right information to the right place, in the right form, at the right time. Given the sheer size of the potential DW even the technologies (underlying computer systems) used differ. Initially you might start with a small SMP (symmetrical multi-processing) server and grow to use an MPP (massively parallel processing) system.

Consider the SMP server to be a small/medium computer that is powerful and often used for many applications but one that has limitations in dealing with ad-hoc queries on a large DW. Whilst the MPP (although not physically large) is almost exclusively used to run large DW's and can handle those potential "queries from hell" that some managers (knowledge workers) can come up with. To answer many questions you need to hold the data at lowest level so that you have the greatest flexibility. This granularity in the warehouse enables you to summarize to any level knowing you can go back to the base data.

The ROI On A Data Warehouse

You now know that an ordinary operational system is not the answer and can believe that PC solution despite its potentially clever statistical modeling capabilities will not cut it. You must now decide to invest time in figuring out which business area could justify your first DW. In 90% of organizations embarking on their first DW, marketing is the chosen area for their deployment. How we define marketing implementations is open to debate as some have started to form the base of customer profitability whilst others have started with direct marketing applications and grown from there. So what sort of ROI (return in investment) could you expect to get?

In a recent study IDC analyzed the mean return on data warehousing investments (ROI) for some 62 study participants. Those sampled achieved an impressive 401 percent, with a mean payback period of 2.31 years. Over 90 percent reported a three-year return on investment exceeding 40 percent. Half reported returns of greater than 160 percent, and one quarter over 600 percent. European companies averaged 340 percent ROI, compared with 440 percent among North American firms. Only eight companies reported negative ROI results, which they attributed to either extraordinarily high costs, low warehouse usage, or a large undertaking requiring longer than three years for payback. "Yet these numbers only scratch the surface of a warehouse's true value. A successful data warehouse leads to many qualitative, as well as quantitative, benefits".(IDC)

Another use of the DW, its access tools and potential Data Marts is to improve share prices explicitly. After Chase demonstrated their latest profitability analysis system to a number of security analysts in New York, a number of favorable comments were made. Tom Hanley of UBS as an example said "Chase Manhatten has developed a state-of-the-art retail profitability system which allows the company to generate reports on a number of different categories including by product, pricing relationship, channel of delivery organization, financial, or customer segment." Statements like these made by analysts often help to increase shareholder wealth through talking up the share price. However all that glitter may not be gold!

I assume that you have overcome the political hurdles and created a business case to justify the expenditure (see Business Case Blues) then the next step is to identify exactly which strategic business opportunities you will pursue. Your IS group/team must be involved or you could produce another point solution that cannot grow to meet the whole banks needs. The idea is to think big but start small.

External Support

To build a successful DW you must have a good team of potential user, IS and a committed senior management steering committee. You need to work with IS but you will require additional external support to bring the opportunity to life. The reason often sited why a competent banks with good IS departments bring in outside consultants to help is "experience". Few IT specialists can truly represent the business side of the bank. They are not close enough to the actual banking coal face. They have difficulty in translating the business problems the bank faces into an information based DW. If the IS department builds the DW in isolation on the basis that "build-it-and-they-will-come" then you are likely to have an expensive failure on your hands.

Some banks believed that buying a packaged solution was the answer - "buy this off the shelf solution and in 'N' months you too will have the DW of your dreams"!! Simplistic solutions in the highly competitive worlds of banking and technology are dangerous. This type of approach comes back to the problem of not really understanding the real business requirements and tries to make your bank fit the solution providers business model not your own. The package solution looks for banks that fit it's capabilities - there must be one somewhere - maybe it is yours, then maybe it's not!

You Could Do With A Champion

The business users who including perhaps a deeply committed champion to drive the project through must be deeply involved in the DW development often require external consultants as sounding boards that have in pertinent depth business knowledge of their own. This external knowledge enables the bank to build on the shoulders of others that have gone this way before and not feel that they are part of an experiment or an organizational learning experience.

In addition there is the need to facilitate team building. Given that communication between divisions and departments within most organizations spans the continuum from difficult to impossible, there is a need for someone non-partisan to bridge that gap.

Data Warehouse Readiness Assessment?

Many DW solution vendors will help your bank to take those first tentative steps towards building your very own DW. Some organizations believe that a DW readiness study should be carried out. This study tries to assess if the organization is ready to build and can use the DW effectively. This appears to be a good money-spinner for the consulting houses as few ever say that a firm could not make use of a DW. Oh and of course any development should be assisted by the firm that carried out the DW readiness assessment.

Yet as part of an overall set of actions the readiness assessment can validate the impact of an identified solution within your environment. Elements necessary to support the implementation, such as data readiness, technology readiness, functional readiness, support readiness and infrastructure readiness are studied. Then a roadmap for implementation is created based on these findings.

The Data Warehouse Feasibility Study?

Another group of consultants offer a DW Feasibility Study that asks and answers the questions you need to know before you start planning, building, or buying a DW. Through this study you will understand why you need a data warehouse; learn whether the solution to your business issues is a data warehouse or whether another type of database is more appropriate to your business requirements; and, most importantly, discern how you will achieve a data warehouse, as well as what it will take to acquire, support, and maintain it.

This study may help the project but it really just puts off taking any action. You could die before all the possible types of analysis could be applied to a potential DW project. I believe your money would be better spent working with your own IS group and seeking input from a solution's vendor who has a vested interest in a successful DW implementation.

Business Discovery Methodology

Another method that has worked well for many banks involves a process of uncovering business opportunities/needs/ problems. The idea is to get you thinking through some of the business questions you can't answer now or an application (that is derived from those questions) that is impossible to run without history. Those answers must help you improve your business and the way you do it. This will the help define the type of data you should put in the warehouse.

This method uses in-depth interviews with the business users and IS to gain insight and consensus. It also uncovers high-impact business opportunities, either across the bank, or within specific departments. This methodology leads to the development of a logical data model that would then lead to a physical data model for implementation.

The specific objectives of the this process are as follows:

- Problem Diagnosis - working with executives to understand the bank's business strategies, business objectives, information systems, and financial objectives, and uncover opportunities as well as the issues blocking the achievement of these objectives and identify the current business issues and challenges impacting the bank.
- Decision Analysis - Develop the business "questions" that must be answered to solve current challenges.
- A shared perception by all parties of how they will benefit from the

implementation of this application and information model.

- Information Availability - Identify the informational requirements to solve these business opportunities.
- Prioritization and quantifying value - Gain agreement on the priority of the issues and the use of the information (as if it were available), obtain agreement from all participants, and assign value metrics for the potential business impacts of solving these business opportunities and questions.

Bank of Montreal

The opportunities then get prioritized and qualitative "value metrics" defined for several of the top priority applications. These metrics are then used in the final documentation to define the pay-back value of the entire project. The whole approach culminates in one or more workshops and a final report that tells all. This type of approach really works and enables a bank to get off to a good, fast and effective start in implementing a DW.

Rita Nayar, manager, database management services, Bank of Montreal said: "The first step in the development process was to conduct business discovery sessions where IS could learn the data needs of the end users. Once the target information was identified, IS had to extract credit, consumer and product data from 10 different operational sources — a formidable task. This was complicated by the fact that top management wants to see business benefits quickly".

Benefits:

The Process:

- Helped the bank to discover new opportunities that would create competitive advantage.
- Provided a shared vision of what could be done, what needed to be done, and the priorities for doing it
- Provided a basis for developing a technology plan that satisfied cross-functional business needs
- Improved co-operation and understanding between the business users and the Information Systems (IS) organization

Their implementation was to gain competitive advantage and better asset management. Bank of Montreal is now reaping many other benefits from its data warehouse investment. Management is able to obtain corporate information in a timely manner, helping them to accurately gauge the state of the corporation and make sound business decisions. Financial managers are able to execute ad hoc credit risk exposure analysis, and avoid bad credit risks that could cost the bank millions of dollars. Product and account managers look at customer and market trend information to identify new product and lending opportunities.

Overall, using the information now available through its DW, the Bank of Montreal is better positioned to manage its assets and take advantage of market fluctuations for greater profitability.

Information Discovery?

Some solution vendors suggest a method of gathering the information requirements of a bank together to identify the banks - specific functional requirements for the data warehouse. It uses as a foundation the business discovery process that prioritized business opportunities and applications. It builds an initial logical data model and initial high level data warehouse architecture. It adds detail data requirements, initial data sizing, data sourcing and transformation issues, and addresses requirements from the user and application perspective. It establishes objective criteria for evaluating various technology solutions and assists in recommending a technology framework and operational organization environment.

The end result is the compilation, prioritization, and quantification of the data, user, application, and operational requirements for your bank. A high-level project plan (road map) for the design and Implementation phases can also be created during this step.

Scaleable Technology

You could use some form of map (this could come out of the business discovery process) to get you from where you are now to where you want to be. You need to know that any developments you undertake today are sufficiently scaleable to grow to meet your needs tomorrow. Certain technologies and software will lock you into a costly reinvestment in few short years if you are not careful.

Some banks that have started on the route thinking that data mining is the answer. A few access tools and some statistical applications and "hey presto" they start getting results they can use. There are many data mining myths and magic can that baffle brains. Their failure is to grasp that the real benefits lie in the granular data the bank has accumulated not in samples of that data.

Building a data warehouse is simple in theory. It goes like this:

1.Extract data from the relevant operational systems in the bank.
The data can be identified from the logical data model that you will develop with your supplier (Solution vendor and or consultants). These may include, channels transactions, accounting information, account/customer detail files, marketing and so on. Each bank division will probably have its own systems and applications although you may be lucky enough to have one central accounting system (some "lucky" banks are still using account centric systems decades old). The goal is to bring all the relevant information together into one place. Data stored in different formats with multiple definitions available across multiple platforms doesn't make decision making very easy.

2.Clean and integrate the data from multiple sources.
Reformat, recalculate or key structures so that you have consistency. Time dimensions may have to be added and default values identified. If it's customer information, you must create the consistent spelling of

customer names, addresses and other pertinent information. The goal is to make it usable, raw data. Clean data is void of corrupted fields and inconsistent naming. This data is for complex analysis and must be accurate.

3.Bring all of your clean accurate data into the data warehouse.
Loading initially can sound easy, but you must consider data volumes and frequency of updates. A means of supplying a logic to choose between multiple data sources will have to be applied. And an efficient and effective way will have to be found for summarising, totalling and merging data from multiple sources.

4.Provide users access to the data in the warehouse.
This is the pot of gold at the end of the rainbow. There are tools that let you do this. The most commonly used tools range from general query languages to OLAP (On-line Analytical Processing (see Data Mining Dispelling the Myths) systems specified to meet your company's needs. Set them up for specific applications, jobs, job levels and expertise. The vendor you work with to implement your warehouse should be able to support your exact needs.

Adapted from Axciom

Rapid Development Is Important

The time the project takes is very important. A project spanning years is of no use in the banking world today. With new products and new entrants trying to cherry pick your best customers you need to invest in quick returns. A DW enables you to get that quick return whilst building a solution that will go bank wide.

Banks such as Chase, Bank of America, Barclays and Lloyds TSB started off small and built up their usage through iterative projects. The idea is to build the DW through short iterative projects that show business benefits at each stage. How long should each stage take? Some promise a fully implemented DW in 90 days. You need to see what they promised other customers and what their track record is like.

How do you measure the success of a DW project?

There are some direct measures such as reduced costs or increased response rates (direct mail and campaign management). Other measures relate to the effective use of information, better decisions, knowing customer behaviors, understanding customers value to the bank and so on. The ultimate test of a successful DW project will be a positive impact on the bank's bottom line.

If you found this article interesting then you might like some of the other articles in this series that covers: the Business case, customer profitability, retention, development and acquisition plus many other aspects of SDW in banking.

Chapter 2: How to Integrate Data Warehousing in your Business

Data Marts: Key to Reviving the Enterprise Data Warehouse

Title: *Data Marts: Key to Reviving the Enterprise Data Warehouse*

Authors: *Joe Brown, product manager for data warehousing at Microsoft, and Paul Hill, Cognos, senior vice president, BI Solutions Marketing*

Abstract: *This article discusses how the use of data marts can help you to implement the traditional enterprise data warehouse.*

Have delays in implementing an enterprise data warehouse put your business at a competitive disadvantage? Managers today can't run a business blind. They need information—business intelligence—about the company, customers, competitors, markets, and more, and they need it quickly and easily. The enterprise data warehouse was intended to be the cornerstone of an organization's business intelligence strategy, promising business intelligence on demand.

The enterprise data warehouse—the storehouse where all manner of information from a wide range of sources is collected and made available to users enterprise-wide—sounds like the ideal solution for business intelligence. But the reality is often quite different. In practice, the traditional enterprise data warehouse has proven slow and costly to build. With implementations taking two, three, or more years and costing millions of dollars, the payoff from the enterprise data warehouse is pushed too far into the future. Business managers who need business intelligence now have been forced to wait, missing opportunities in the meantime.

In addition, some business managers have raised concerns about the nature of the information ultimately delivered by large, traditional enterprise data warehouses. In an attempt to make the data warehouse serve the broadest number of users, organizations fill it with general data of the lowest common denominator. This general information, however, is unsuited for the ambitious business intelligence efforts required for success in today's business environment.

Instead, business managers need specific quality information now if they are to pursue the kind of business intelligence initiatives that translate into competitive and strategic advantages. This information fuels a wide range of information-based management strategies, including business intelligence, comprised of decision support, online analytical processing (OLAP), and data mining. Business intelligence is where most businesses receive their return on investment (ROI) from their data warehouses.

For example, managers need to view sales by product and region and make correlations with advertising campaigns and marketing promotions. Or, they want to analyze groups of customers and purchases and identify relevant patterns. All areas of the organization; such as finance, sales, marketing, purchasing, production, customer service, and human relations, are ripe for business intelligence initiatives. The opportunities for valuable information analysis are endless. Given the urgency of the need and the disappointment with conventional enterprise data warehouses, organizations are turning to data marts as their primary business intelligence storehouse. Think of a marketplace where small shops specialize in particular products versus a warehouse club which seems to carry everything but often doesn't have an extensive inventory of any particular item or even a wide variety of different brand names. Data marts are streamlined, highly focused, smaller scale versions of the enterprise data warehouse. Data marts, unlike their larger enterprise cousins, don't try to be all things to all people. Instead of delivering lowest common denominator information, they provide detailed information focused on a single area, such as marketing, sales, production, or finance. Packed with information critical to the particular area of interest, data marts give managers in each area access to the kind of specific data that is not readily available in an enterprise data warehouse.

Compared to the conventional enterprise data warehouse, data marts are faster, easier, and less expensive to build, due to the use of low cost, readily available, off-the-shelf products. For example, data marts typically are built on PC servers running operating systems such as Windows NT and use flexible, full function, relational databases like MS SQL Server. Business managers access and manipulate the data mart through easy-to-use desktop tools, such as Cognos' Impromptu or PowerPlay.

The end result is an information storehouse that can be delivered easily, inexpensively, and quickly, in weeks or months. The data mart provides access to critical data sooner than the enterprise data warehouse, allowing business managers to initiate business intelligence strategies and reap the rewards sooner. The payback comes not years down the road but within months, with many companies achieving valuable results in 90 days.

Given the speed, ease-of- use, low cost, and high payback of data marts, the idea quickly spreads throughout an organization, with each functional area putting up a data mart of its own. The result amounts to a virtual enterprise data warehouse (albeit one which actually contains the special information necessary to informed decision-making) with each individual data mart maintaining its specialized information. The success of data marts and their proliferation throughout the enterprise is leading many organizations to reconsider the role and definition of conventional enterprise data warehouse and the relationship between data marts and data warehouses.

Despite their proven effectiveness, however, data marts won't replace enterprise data warehouses. Instead, Gartner Group, in a recent report, heralds data marts as a valuable subset of the enterprise data warehouse. Organizations will adopt both data marts and data warehouses, using them in several complementary ways.

For instance, the development of multiple data marts can become a stepping stone to an enterprise data warehouse. While linking multiple data marts to form a seamless virtual enterprise data warehouse still presents some technical challenges, the information modeling, transformation, and data organization embodied in the data marts, at the least, can provide a powerful jump start for the building of an enterprise data warehouse.

Or, as Gartner Group suggests, the individual data marts operate as subsets of the enterprise data warehouse. Here the data warehouse assumes the role of supporting the data marts. It feeds data to each data mart and simplifies the process of gathering data from source production systems. For example, rather than having each data mart individually download data from each production source, the enterprise data warehouse downloads the data once and distributes appropriate segments of the data to each data mart.

While many conventional enterprise data warehouses have failed to fulfill the promise of business intelligence on demand, the data mart has emerged as a practical alternative within the reach of any organization today. Through the success of the data mart, organizations will evolve a new enterprise data warehouse. This new breed of data warehouse will join the IS organization, as manager of the data warehouse, and business users, as the consumers of business intelligence provided through specific data marts, in a cooperative effort where data warehouses and data marts complement each other to deliver business intelligence.

Enterprise IT Value: Beyond Data Warehouse and ROI

Title: *Enterprise IT Value: Beyond Data Warehouse and ROI*

Author: *Hummingbird*

Abstract: *The benefits of data warehousing projects are often so great that the temptation may be to rely too heavily on the business benefits and not enough on implementation disciplines — project economics and project management. A search for project metrics and implementation best practices regarding this class of solution has revealed there is a heavy reliance upon long-term ROI based planning that weigh benefits and costs equally. This white paper proposes a renewed focus on project discipline and project economics as a means of driving implementation success, and from this organizational value.*

Biography: see end article

Introduction

Much has been written in recent years about data warehouses, data marts and analytical applications, and the value that this class of solution brings to the intelligent organization. From research papers to white papers, articles to seminars, investing in these solutions has been hailed as a guarantee to drive competitive advantage and generate top and bottom line value for the enterprise. Having spent considerable enterprise resources on implementations, senior management is now asking the tough questions about quantifiable benefits and return on investment (ROI). Too often, organizations examine the ROI issue from the perspective of future cash flows, often ignoring project economics and increasing the risk of time and budget overruns. Failure to manage project risk, coupled with achieving lower than expected benefits (post-implementation), can wipe out some or all of the anticipated ROI.

This situation most often arises because there is no clear owner of the expected ROI. Business management should own the benefit, and IT management should own the implementation and cost targets. If this accountability is clearly split between these two stakeholder groups, there is a greater likelihood of ownership and positive outcomes in both instances.

Project Economics Best Practices

Make no mistake about it — data warehousing and related solutions (i.e. analytical applications) are yielding tremendous value for organizations. There are two key challenges in delivering this value — accurately identifying business benefits that are likely to be achieved, and employing project management disciplines to reduce project risks and ensure on-time and on-budget delivery. ROI metrics and measurements must focus on both.

Once business benefits are clearly identified and ownership is assigned, the organization should immediately focus on project-level disciplines, minimizing project risk and maximizing value of the IT infrastructure. Deploying best practices at the project level is an excellent way for delivering projects on time and on budget, and to yield IT value.

There are four key best practices that are relevant to delivering such value. The first two are project management focused and policy-oriented, while the last two speak to the critical opportunity within technical architecture and the technology selection.

1. Clear Delineation of Scope and Objectives
Once the project is set to move forward, it is critical that project scope, objectives and mandate be clearly defined. Without this guide, the project can be quickly derailed by focusing on non-value add work to its central premise.

2. Bring Experience and Competence to the Delivery Process
There is no replacement for experience and skills in the delivery process. Seek out the brightest and best within your organization, and/or hire consultants with the relevant experience who will not only lead the project, but can coach and mentor your organization so you can build self sufficiency for future projects.

3. Design the Architecture for Openness and Neutrality
In every implementation, there are a series of architectural layers that need to be considered. From data and technical architecture to metadata and user access, there must be a focus on constructing a solution which is architecture neutral and open architecturally, as well as supportive of current investments in technology. The choices of hardware, operating systems and software need to be considered from this perspective.

Some key considerations of this best practice include:

- Ability to achieve bi-directional Data Exchange — there is an increasing requirement to achieve bi-directional data movements for application integration needs within this class of solution, which needs to be properly measured.
- The design should deploy an open metadata repository, storable on any major RDBMS and capable of both metadata exchange with other repositories and the ability to browse all enterprise metadata.
- Deploy technology products that are Architecture Neutral, enabling the organization to leverage value from its current IT investments, or change its IT strategy and direction.

4. Select Technology that Supports Cost Effective Deployment
Over the past 20 years, IT departments have evolved from application developers to solution implementers. In this new world, organizations have heterogeneous platforms, databases, and operating systems. Technology has advanced and business requirements and expectations have changed. It has become critical in this complex world to implement technologies that deliver cost effective implementations. Some of the key dimensions to consider here include:

- Scalability — the ability to accommodate growing volumes of data, increased demands for throughput, increasing numbers of end-users.
- Ease of Reuse — the ability to easily share and reuse components and modules within the development organization.
- The ability to work smarter (do more with less) — the ability to build more transformation processes with less effort.
- Capturing the vast majority of transformations in the native design environment (with metadata) — the ability to build all data exchange processes, including the most complex transformations, without having to exit and build outside the product.
- Low cost of maintenance (on a per change basis and aggregate cost of ownership) — the ability to build data warehouses and transformational capabilities that are very easy and inexpensive to maintain.

Traditional ROI Methods

There are a variety of tools and techniques that organizations have leveraged over the years as they sought to measure the financial impact of data warehousing and other project investments. While there are more than five basic methods of conducting the financial analysis, these are the core methods most often associated with and appropriate for the due diligence process:

Payback Analysis
The length of time it takes to recover the initial cost of a project, without regard to the time value of money. Given the increasing pace of technology change, shorter and shorter payback cycles are the expectation.

Return on Investment (ROI)
Indicators of profitability, where net new revenues or operational cost reductions exceed the investment. This is typically used to compare projects (investments) to ensure that the maximum enterprise benefit is achieved.

Net Present Value (NPV)
The present value of the expected future cash flows minus cost. This technique is useful for comparing alternative projects.

Internal Rate of Return (IRR)
The discount (interest) rate at which net present value (NPV) is zero. Usually an organization will set a benchmark rate, such as 25%, so that only the highest value add projects get considered.

Economic Value Add (EVA)
A relatively new concept — over the past fi ve years, companies have converted to the concept of economic value added (EVA). The concept is simple but rigorous. Profitability should account for the cost of equity capital as well as debt and other means of capital acquisition. Companies should invest only in projects that promise to return more than the total cost of capital.

Successfully measuring and prioritizing IT investments is critical for organizations that are looking to build new sources of revenue and reduce operating costs to make themselves more competitive. Without exception, these ROI measurement techniques are based on a comparison of benefits to costs. However, they miss the opportunity to apply a rigorous set of cost management guidelines to ensure the technology and related expenditures are within acceptable norms for the project outcomes, and that long term maintenance costs are minimized.

ROI Models for Technology Projects

The five techniques outlined above are used by organizations to determine whether technology investments and projects will add value to their bottom line, and answer the question — should this investment be made? In many cases, such measurements are used to prioritize projects and investments, enabling senior management to pick the highest value add projects. These measurements alone are not enough; companies need ROI models or methods within which these techniques are used.

There are two widely used ROI models that help organizations assess and prioritize project investments — Enterprise ROI and Productivity. As an alternative approach, a third type is being introduced here — IT Value/Utilization — which specifically addresses implementation issues to ensure efficient and effective deployment. Each are examined below.

Enterprise ROI

With Enterprise ROI, the objective is to identify new revenue sources or hard cost reductions attributable to the investment and compare that with the allocated project costs. Business management is accountable for identifying benefits, and owns these financial targets. Senior management needs evidence that the financial investment has generated net new revenues or operational cost reductions.

- The value of this approach is derived from the fact that there is a context for making resource investments or allocation decisions and a basis for a post-implementation audit to ensure that the benefits promised were achieved.
- The difficulty of using this method is that benefits may not appear as anticipated. For example, if a distribution data warehouse is built to reduce inventory costs, but the ability to achieve these results is still based on manual human effort of running reports and changing or altering product orders, the actual benefits may prove elusive. Often, such results are predicated on a business process re-design in parallel to the project implementation.
- This category tends to work well in capital and labour intensive industries, such as telecom, manufacturing and retail.

Productivity

A second category of ROI measurement is Productivity, where the project and business re-design is justified on the basis of employees doing more with less. It is a less tangible measurement with a reduced likelihood that any gains can be directly attributable to the investment. However, it is likely that such investments will contribute to and improve competitiveness. For example, key information consumers (knowledge workers, managers and executives) may spend less time searching for information, and therefore will be able to do 10% more work in the same time period each day. Such changes translate to improved organizational agility and an enhanced ability to detect new opportunities.

- The value of this approach is that it better supports organizations in their efforts to leverage the value of information in the e-economy.
- The challenges associated with this approach are that it is extremely difficult to both audit and measure the actual benefits achieved. In a consulting firm, for example, there may be the perception that stiff competition affects their ability to land contracts. A method of differentiating themselves from competitors may be to prepare and equip their consultants with a data warehouse of appropriate industry information for significantly better analyses than other fi rms. However, it is extremely difficult to measure the impact of such an investment.
- This category tends to work well in service and knowledge intensive industries, such as management consulting and business services.

IT Value/Utilization
An alternative approach to the above full-business case modeling of ROI is IT Value/Utilization, a measurement model based on project-level economics and managing controllable factors at the implementation level. The opportunity here is that, once the business benefits have been committed to, the focus should be only on the project economics and maximizing IT value. The technologies deployed must align with the organization's IT strategy and contribute to a low-cost maintenance cycle.

- This category of measurement is designed for any project-oriented work. The focus is on generating cost-effective outcomes for the organization deploying data exchange solutions.
- Solutions in this category must do a wide range of things — build complex transformations within the Universal Data Exchange product, share and easily re-use components, support complete impact analysis to minimize maintenance costs, easily leverage the investments you have made within your IT infrastructure and protect against loss of personnel. Measurements must account for these solution requirements.

The question of which ROI model is most appropriate is connected to the same broad issue — the fundamental need for an IT Value/Utilization Framework. Here, the intention is to measure the effectiveness of the technology product to be deployed.

The IT Value/Utilization Framework

There are three key elements to project economics — Architecture (technical infrastructure), Project Management Approach and Methodology, and the comprehensiveness of the IT skills available to work the project. Of these three, only Architecture is within the scope of this white paper. As with the discussion around Best Practices above, the last two components, while important topics on their own, are outside the scope of this white paper. The opportunity here is to identify a set of risk factors that can be used to gauge the likelihood that a particular solution can yield the expected results, from the perspective of cost and time deliverables. With this perspective, alternative solutions can be compared.

There are seven architectural (technical infrastructure) dimensions listed below. These are required elements for assessing the ability of the technology solutions to withstand the rigours of a disciplined project process and IT investment model. These seven elements apply as much to ETL and Data Exchange as to the Business Intelligence and analytical portion of the aggregate solution.

- Scalability — the ability to accommodate growing volumes of data, increased demands for throughput, increasing numbers of end-users.
- Ease of Reuse — the ability to easily share and reuse components and modules within the development organization.
- The design should deploy an open metadata repository, able to be stored on any major RDBMS and capable of both metadata exchange with other repositories and the ability to browse all enterprise metadata.

Figure 1: IT Value//Utilization Framework

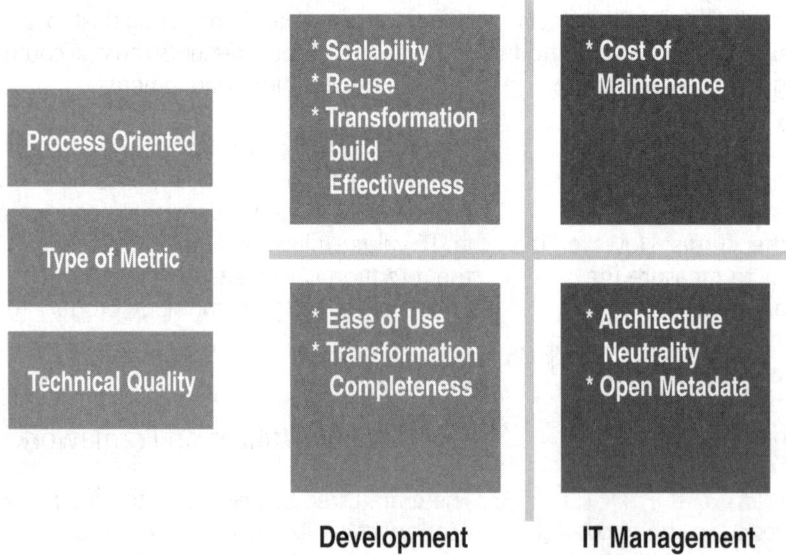

Adapted from a GIGA Information Group, Selecting Metrics and Using them Effectively. May 1999

- The ability to work smarter (do more with less) — the ability to build more transformation processes with less effort.
- All transformations captured natively (with metadata) — the ability to build all data exchange processes, including the most complex transformations, without having to exit and build outside the product.
- Low cost of maintenance (on a per change basis and aggregate cost of ownership) — the ability to build data warehouses and transformational capabilities that are very easy and inexpensive to maintain.
- Ability to achieve bi-directional Data Exchange — there is an increasing requirement to achieve bi-directional data movements for application integration needs within this class of solution, which needs to be properly measured.
- Architecture Neutrality — the ability to conform to industry standards, enable the organization to change its IT strategy.

For each of these risk factors, it is not enough to just identify them — there must be owners for each, and a means of categorizing and managing them. Figure 1 below is an adaptation Giga Information Group report on selecting and using metrics. Along one dimension are measurement owners — IT Management (including Project Management) is one owner, and developers (such as the Architect) are the second. A second dimension differentiates between two types of metrics — process and technical quality.

Placing the above eight dimensions in this framework provides a means for assigning ownership, identifying the measurements that may fi t within these dimensions, brain-storming about additional dimensions that may make sense for a specific implementation, refining specific metrics, and prioritizing the importance of the measurements. For this model to work, it is critical that the list of metrics be comprehensive.

Opportunities in Data Warehousing ROI

A well-known rule of thumb in data warehousing is that 80% of the cost lies in the extract, transform and load (ETL) portion of the overall process. Historically, this 'information value engine' — the data management practice of turning raw data into value-add information — has been the most complex and difficult deliverable within the entire end-to-end process. Specifically, the two most significant expenditure groups here are the data exchange software, and the consulting services/people costs that build the ETL processes and build valuable, business-relevant information.

The key difference between successful implementations and those that fall short is how the project team can deploy these solutions efficiently. Beyond the project scope — at CIO level where technology investments are managed for the enterprise — there is also the opportunity to fi nd re-usable technologies and processes that can be easily leveraged in downstream projects, thereby substantially increasing the payback on current investments.

Hummingbird Genio Suite Solution

Genio Suite is an enterprise scaleable Data Exchange product that enables IT professionals to implement data exchange and information sharing across enterprise-wide decision support and operational systems. Offering more functionality than current data transformation tools and greater productivity than point-to-point and hard-coded data exchange routines, Genio helps eliminate the difficulties associated with mixed-system computing environments and inconsistent data nightmares. Genio's single platform, component-based architecture addresses simple and complex data exchange processes within a procedure-driven graphical environment. Genio automates many data exchange tasks that normally require tedious programming. This allows IT professionals to rapidly develop data transformation routines for an immediate return on investment.

Hummingbird Genio Suite is comprised of a tightly integrated set of components including: Engine, Designer, Repository, Scheduler, Met@Data Studio, Met@Data Explorer, Met@Data Web Server, Data Links, and MetaLink.

Genio Engine

Genio Engine is a scalable, multi-threaded transformation engine that brokers information between source and target systems. The scalable architecture supports the distribution and synchronization of data transformation and exchange processes over multiple Genio Engines. This is critical as data volumes increase in size and transformation processes grow in complexity. Additionally, this scalability enables Genio to leverage the power of existing distributed computing resources within user environments.

Genio Designer

Genio Designer provides a graphical scripting environment, enabling users to easily create and administer data transformation and exchange processes. Data structures can be imported directly from source and target systems. User defined business rules, functions, and procedures created in designer are stored as objects within the Genio Repository and are completely reusable. The unique graphical scripting environment provides a complete and powerful procedural language to design complex data transformation processes. Genio processes can be triggered by external events such as file modifications or table updates. Conversely, Genio processes can trigger external events such as file transfers or e-mail. Essentially, Genio Designer is the nerve center for the data exchange solution, enabling the efficient and effective design of transformation and exchange processes within a familiar and intuitive environment.

Genio Repository

The Genio Repository stores all aspects of data transformation and exchange processing metadata. Housed in any RDBMS, Repository treats and stores each component as an object. Genio automatically identify es any change made to metadata, provides an impact analysis report, and requires every object affected by the change to be addressed before the next data transformation and ex-change process is executed. This ensures information quality and consistency across the entire universal data exchange solution.

Genio Scheduler
Genio Scheduler is the control center of the universal data exchange solution. Administrators schedule, deploy, and manage Genio processes using Scheduler. Processes can be scheduled to execute on an event or calendar basis. Process scheduling may also include dependencies. Genio Scheduler provides real-time control and monitoring of process executions, full history and audit trail reporting, and detailed log file analysis.

The IT Value of Genio Suite to a Data Warehouse Implementation
Numerous analyst reports have recently suggested that organizations need to focus on acquiring technologies that can reduce the cost of implementing this class of solution, and support real ROI in less than a 24 month period. Genio Suite is ideally suited to generating IT value (and therefore ROI) within the first project or within 6 months of initial use.

- Scalability — Genio Suite's Data Access Methodology allows for full control of transformation processes across the source RDBMS, the Genio engine and the target RDBMS, enabling full optimization of the available network and CPU resources. As data volumes and processing demands increase, Genio Suite is fully capable of scaling up to handle this. Since it is an architecture neutral product, it can scale up as quickly as the RDBMS and network are extended.
- Ease of Re-Use — Genio can easily share and support the re-use of all components and objects from within the product. In addition, it supports multiple developers and full versioning.
- Open Metadata Repository — Genio Suite's repository can be stored on any major, ODBC compliant RDBMS. It is open, able to exchange metadata with Business Objects Universes and Cognos Catalogs, export Genio Metadata for import into a variety of BI Tools, and will soon be able to browse most major metadata repositories in the industry to provide a user-centric view of all enterprise metadata.
- Capture 100% of the ETL processes within the native design environment — Due to the procedural scripting approach of Genio Suite, all interface requirements within the data-warehousing environment can be addressed using the native functionality of the product. This provides a significant productivity gain, as only one product is needed for the data scrubbing, transformation and transportation needs.
- Low cost of maintenance — Given that Genio is so cost effective to deploy, it is even more cost effective to maintain. With all of the ETL processes captured natively for full metadata capture and exceptional impact analysis, the cost of maintaining the environment is significantly reduced over products that cannot capture as much metadata natively.
- Genio Suite's unique Hub-and-Spoke based architecture accommodates bi-directional Data Exchange to achieve data movement in support of

application integration needs within this class of solution.

- Architecture Neutrality — Genio Suite is architecture neutral, in that it can operate with any major RDBMS, with an engine that runs on NT and virtually any flavour of Unix (Solaris, AIX and HP-UX). As well, there is a Metalink for SAP R/3 product (certified at two levels) that enables direct access to SAP R/3 data to facilitate data warehousing solutions with SAP R/3 and external data. As well, Genio's architecture promotes flexibility within the installed environment regarding IT strategy. An NT to Unix migration for operational applications would not be an impediment.

Given that Hummingbird has over 200 installations world wide, there are a number of real-world examples of how significant IT value (i.e. ROI) has been generated in these situations. The following case studies are excellent examples of generating an ROI from the initial implementation project.

Telecommunications
A large North American telecommunications manufacturer wanted to build a financial analysis application. It was decided that the platform would be Hyperion Essbase, and a Tier 1 consulting organization was invited to give estimates on the data exchange and transformation component of the project. The preliminary estimate, based on hand coding the extraction, transformation and load processes, was 120 workdays of effort to build and load the analytical processes from the operational sources. When the project implemented using Genio Suite, with its native multidimensional database support, the entire project was completed in 20 days. The total budget remained the same but the project was delivered quicker and the maintenance costs were estimated to be only 10% of the original estimate.

Communications
A large private TV station in Europe needed to build a consolidated view for the management of its commercials. The problem was that most data was scattered among various AS/400 machines, several different databases and mainframe files. The project was planned for implementation using internal IT resources using a 4GL tool like Microsoft Visual Basic. The final choice was Genio Suite, and the reported timesavings were up to 75% of the original estimate using a 4GL. As the project manager expressed, "We saw a return on our investment almost immediately."

Migration Toward Application Integration: Another Consideration

Data warehousing, as a practice, has matured over the past few years. There are better ETL products, significantly improved metadata integration, enhanced reporting and analysis capabilities, and a solid understanding of implementation practices. As well, there are tremendous resources and expertise (free and otherwise) available through consultants, web sites, analysts and industry associations.

Organizations that have implemented this class of solution are now looking downstream to bi-directional data movement and application integration. From a Data Warehousing context, the opportunity is to close the loop between the informational and operational worlds. Businesses are starting to demand that information generated for the data warehouse is loaded back into one, or more, operating systems.

For example, a Marketing VP for a Bank may be interested in cross selling to current customers who have only one or two financial products. To assist in this process, there may be a regular set of reports generated that segment customers based on dimensions such as geography, demographics, number of products and loyalty. This may be valuable information to have at the disposal of the call center staff so they can better understand the customer and potentially advance cross selling opportunities.

With data exchange functionality, organizations can expect that standardized electronic interfaces between operational systems can be managed with this product. Such interfaces can be centrally managed within this solution suite using the appropriate metadata. This means reduced time to build and improved maintenance abilities through impact analysis now that these interfaces are registered to the metadata.

In Summary

Choosing an ETL/Data Exchange product over the more traditional hand coding or using code generators is a significant step towards ROI in the project but it is as important to choose the right tool.

The key issues to consider are those raised previously:

- Scalability
- Ease of reuse
- Doing more with less
- Capture all transformations natively (with metadata)
- Low cost of maintenance
- Achieve bi-directional data exchange for application integration
- Open and neutral architecture

If these risk factors are centrally considered within the implementation project for product choices and architectural design, there is an increasing likelihood that the project will be able to claim a return on investment.

The bottom line is that choosing an ETL tool significantly increases the likelihood that the data warehouse will be successful.

Biography: Hummingbird is a leader in the development of enterprise software solutions that provide access to all business-critical information and resources. The Hummingbird EIP™ (Enterprise Information Portal) leverages the company's core strengths in network connectivity, data integration & reporting, and document & knowledge management to connect users to all the business information they need, aggregated and categorized through a single user interface. With a diverse product portfolio, Hummingbird offers complete global enterprise solutions from advanced host connectivity, through sophisticated data exchange, business intelligence and analytic applications, to powerful information management at the desktop or on the Web. Headquartered in Toronto, Canada, the company offers its products, along with related consulting, education, and support services, in more than 50 countries around the world.

Building Corporate Business Intelligence: From Datamarts to the Enterprise Data Warehouse

Title: *Building Corporate Business Intelligence: From Datamarts to the Enterprise Data Warehouse*
Author: *Daphnesoft*
Abstract: *What is a data warehouse? What kinds of data warehouses are there? And what about datamarts? These are just some of the questions answered in this white paper.*

The Information Advantage

Access to information is a prime requirement in any organization that wants to have a competitive edge in today's fast changing markets. Executives need clear and meaningful answers to any hard, complex questions off data. And they need it quickly.

In the corporate environment of today, virtually every transaction and minute business detail is recorded in databases to enable better, more effective decision-making throughout the organization. Most of the technology emphasis has been on storing data, with less attention paid to tools for transforming data into meaningful information, which can be easily accessed and shared by executives.

Therefore, today's business managers are often forced to spend more time navigating the myriad sources of enterprise data than analyzing the information. Often, these efforts are channeled through IS departments, where precious time is taken away from maintaining and improving enterprise-wide technology systems.

Challenges in accessing the information

- Retrieving facts takes too long and is often too late
- Analysis disrupts daily operations and interferes with transaction performance
- Data is raw and unrecognizable, not in an easily understandable format
- Data is subject to constant change and is seldom consistent
- Ad-hoc queries are difficult to support

The simple reality is that these highly specialized systems cannot obey two masters at the same time. There is a clearly identified need to separate the data capture systems from the data access systems. The requirements of an enterprise-wide Decision Support System (DSS) can only be met by a system optimized for data access.

The Decision Support Systems have the ability to:

- Provide a multi-dimensional, conceptual view of data
- Create complex criteria sets, which allow pinpoint access to required information
- Provide rapid response to queries and the ability to support ad-hoc queries
- Support for hierarchical consolidation of data, and the ability to drill down into detail
- The ability to leverage existing investments in information technology

Large organizations worldwide have recognized the value of Data Warehouses fulfilling the information needs of corporate decision-makers today. A data warehouse empowers decision-makers with business information on their desktop, resulting in faster, better decision-making and a more flexible, responsive organization.

What is a Data Warehouse

A data warehouse, simply stated, is a physical separation of an organization's operational systems from its decision support systems. It includes a repository of information that is built using data from the far-flung, and often departmentally isolated, systems of enterprise-wide computing so that it can be modeled and analyzed by business managers.

A data warehouse has been defined as a:

- Subject-oriented
- Integrated
- Time-variant
- Nonvolatile

collection of data in support of management's decisions making process. A data warehousing solution ensures consistent and cleansed information at a corporate level to plan and to make everyday decisions for smooth functioning of an enterprise.

Table 1

	Transaction Processing	Data Warehouse
Purpose	Run day-to-day operations	Information retrieval and analysis
Structure	RDBMS optimized for Transaction Processing	RDBMS optimized for Query Processing
Data Model	Normalized	Multi-dimensional
Access	SQL	SQL, plus Advanced Analytical tools
Type of Data	Data that runs the business	Data to analyze the business
Nature of Data	Detailed	Summarized & Detailed

The information may be used to manage the enterprise wide business processing to a single business area processing.

In other words, the data warehouse is a database designed specifically to meet the needs of decision-makers or DSS, rather than transaction processing systems.

Data Warehouse types

Given the categories of business requirements, there are two Warehouse types to suite the information requirements. These data warehouses can be categorized as follows.

Enterprise Data Warehouse
An Enterprise Data Warehouse contains data that is drawn from multiple operational systems. The data is cleansed, transformed, integrated and loaded into the separate databases organized by subjects. This Data Warehouse can contain both detailed and summarized historical data ranging from few weeks to many years.

Figure 1

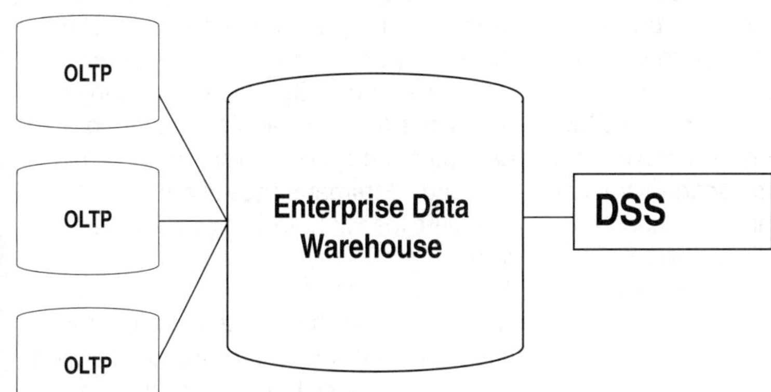

An Enterprise data warehouse supports time-series and trend analysis across the different business areas. It can be used for both every day and strategic decision-making.

Datamarts
Datamarts are subject-oriented databases of each business area. It is a object of analytical processing by the end user. There may be marts setup for pockets of the company, such as finance, marketing, and inventory. They are less expensive and much smaller than a full blown corporate data warehouse.

Datamarts -- the special breed of data warehouses

A datamart has data specific to a business area/department. It contains only a subset of the enterprise data that is value to a specific business unit or department. It can contain both detailed and summarized data for each specific business areas of an enterprise. The data may be captured from operational systems or enterprise data warehouse. The analyzing is only to an extent of a single business area unlike an Enterprise Data Warehouse, which can analyze data across multiple business areas of the enterprise.

Building Corporate Business Intelligence: From Datamarts to the Enterprise Data Warehouse

The industry is moving towards Datamarts
A phenomenal success area of data warehousing is datamarts. They can be built directly from the operational sources or from an enterprise wide data warehouse. Datamarts are essentially designed as a solution specific to business areas and users. The scope of the Datamart is characterized by its functional abilities and not by its size. The size of the datamart seldom increases over 100 GB of data. However, as the usage of datamarts increase, their size is expected to grow rapidly.

Datamarts lead to shorter development cycle
The key to wide spread acceptance of datamarts is its rapid development and affordability. An Enterprise Data Warehouse project can typically cost about a million dollars and can take more than 2 years to implement. On the other hand Datamarts can be built directly from operational sources and can be built in 3 months at a fraction of the cost of an Enterprise Data Warehouse.

Datamarts justify ROI
Datamarts are undoubtedly the cost-effective way to provide information to the users. They can be deployed on low cost Intel based UP or SMP hardware. As datamarts seldom grow more than 100GB of data, Intel hardware with Windows NT as a operating system has become industry standard to host the datamarts. Datamarts because of their low cost and shorter development time start giving an early payback, thus justifying the ROI.

Datamarts are scalable to Enterprise Data Warehouse
Organizations can build a series of datamarts over a period of time, by treating them as test beds before a integrating them to build an Enterprise Data Warehouse. Datamarts allow organizations to start small and are scalable to Enterprise Data Warehouse. Organizations can select one or two business areas to focus on first, define the datamarts required to support them, and start with a manageable project.

Datamarts help provide solutions for smaller businesses, as well as focused segments of company's decision-makers. Organization can get the information required for business decisions in a shorter time period. Their modular nature exhibits a linear cost curve.

Datamarts are a special breed of data warehouse solutions that are driven by the user requirements.

The incremental approach towards a data warehousing solution, according to some, will get data onto the users hands quicker, but may put obstacles in integrating data from various datamarts when organizations move on from datamarts to an Enterprise Data Warehouse. By proper planning of datamarts the problem of integrating datamarts into a Data warehouse can be resolved. Datamarts thus allow for a flexible expansion and growth over a long term.

A data warehousing solution would be imperfect without an efficient data access tool that provides business intelligence.

Business intelligence tools have been there all along and are known as Decision Support Systems. These early business intelligence tools have the ability to give answers to ad-hoc reports but lacked the analysis power. The business intelligence software helps in accessing data from data warehouse. The next generation of business intelligence is OLAP (On-line Analytical Processing).

The data access tools

OLAP is the technology that enables users to access the data multi-dimensionally in a fast, interactive, easy-to-use manner and performs advanced metric computations such as comparison, percentage variations, ranking, and multidimensional ratios against data in the warehouse.

OLAP, On-line Analytical Processing allows users to look at the data in terms of many dimensions. The ability to present ad-hoc reports multi-dimensionally and provide analysis of data differentiates OLAP from other query and reporting tools available.

Two essential architectures exist for OLAP today are Multidimensional OLAP (MOLAP) and Relational OLAP (ROLAP). The analytical ability and the interface of these two architectures are the same, what differs is the way data is physically stored.

In MOLAP, the premise is that, data must be stored in a proprietary multidimensional database to be viewed in a multidimensional manner.

In ROLAP, data is stored in a relational database or a SQL database. MOLAP databases have a limit on the physical database size they can handle. They also have a limited number of dimensions they can handle. Further, a proprietary multidimensional database is essential for MOLAP, which has definite disadvantages leveraging an RDBMS that can handle terabytes of data.
ROLAP has the advantage of being scalable upto several terabytes. It does not have any limit on the dimensions it can handle. It uses relational technology that is a proven and is not proprietary. ROLAP technology is reusable when you move on from datamarts to Enterprise Data Warehouses because of their capacity to handle huge databases and multitudinous dimensions.

Considering various technological issues such as

1. Reusability of the OLAP tool to access the Enterprise Data Warehouse
2. Fast access of information from the datamarts
3. Ability to perform analysis on large data sets
4. Using an open proven technology, which is not proprietary
5. Ability to perform high end metric computations
   ROLAP is best suited for enterprises that are going for data warehousing and are drawn to the long-term strategic advantage OLAP technology promises to deliver.

Selection of products

The organizations contemplating to build a data warehouse solution need to consider certain issues pragmatically before they start implementing this business solution. A end-to-end solution that provides tools for all the phases like designing a Datamart, populating the datamart, managing the datamart, and providing on-line analytical processing is best suited.

General guidelines for product selection:
1. All Data warehousing software should support SMP platform.
2. Open platform – Open systems
3. Easy to use and maintain

Selecting the datamart product

When looking for a datamart product, organizations can evaluate the vendors whose products provide datamart automated solution based on some criteria.

The criteria are:

Ability to take advantage of parallel processing
A datamart tool should take the advantage of parallel processing facilitated by multi CPU architecture such as SMP that serve as the host for many datamart implementations.

Metadata Functionality
Management of information about the enterprise data is as important as the data itself. Metadata is to a data warehouse what road map is to a navigator. It is an integral part of the decision support system, which must be constructed alongside the datamart.

An important aspect of the data warehouse environment is the metadata. Simply stated, Metadata is data about data. Metadata keeps track of what is where in the data warehouse. Typically, the things the metadata store tracks are:
- The structure of data in the transaction-processing environment
- The structure of data in the datamarts
- The source data feeding the datamart
- The transformation information of the data as it passes into the data warehouse
- Extraction information
- Update information in periodically updated datamarts.

A datamart product should naturally have metadata. The metadata should store the definitions of source data, target data, source to target mappings, transformation information and update information.

Extraction
Extraction is the first phase of moving operational data into the datamart. The operational data can be in form of records in the tables of a RDBMS or flat files where each field is separated by a delimiter. The specification of the source and other important information of operational data needs to be given by the user for extracting the data for the next phases of the datamart design.

The Datamart product should selectively retrieve from variety of disparate databases on incompatible RDBMS and file systems.

Datamart tools should make the process of extracting data from the source a simple exercise.

Transformation
This phase of Datamart population changes the structure of data storage. The transformation process is carried out after designing the datamart schema. It is a process that ensures that data is moved into the datamart, it changes the structure of data suitable for transaction processing to a structure that is most suitable for DSS analysis.

Datamart tools should be able to automatically perform complex transformations such as date, arithmetic, character, lookup, encoding, conditional, and multi-step through simple a visual interface.

Load
Loading of the datamart with the transformed data is an iterative process. The datamarts have to be populated continually and incrementally to reflect the changes in the operational system.
The datamart tools should have the ability to automatically load the records in to the target tables, schedule the start and end timings of the load and number of rows loaded into the datamart with the changes in the operational data.

Selecting the data access product

ROLAP (Relational OLAP) products, which can be reused from datamarts to and Enterprise Data Warehouse are best suited to access datamarts and provide Relational On-line analytical processing. Organizations can select the ideal ROLAP product on the following criteria:

1. The ROLAP product should have reusability to data stored in an Enterprise Data Warehouse. It should be capable of retrieving meaningful information from large data sets.
2. A ROLAP tool with a three tier architecture which distributes the workload of analytical processing between the RDBMS, ROLAP Server, and the client application, enabling each tier to perform specific functions for faster performance can enhance the speed of retrieval of information.
3. The design of the ROLAP product should be multithreaded in order to utilize the SMP architecture, which is used for deploying a large scale data warehouse.
4. The metadata will not allow mismatched sets of data to be retrieved from the datamart. It standardizes the presentation of data to the users.

   It describes where the data can be found, names of tables and attributes. A presence of metadata that presents the data instantaneously in natural business terms hiding the complexities of database schemas is necessary for a ROLAP tool.

5. ROLAP tool needs to be time smart. It should allow users to schedule the report generation to be executed at the specified time.
6. The ROLAP server should be able to generate multi SQL against the data warehouse to deliver advanced metric computations such as comparison, percentage variations, ranking, and

multi dimensional ratios.

7. The ROLAP server should provide data surfing and analysis features such as drill down, drill up, pivot, and filter.
8. The ROLAP server should be able to access multiple datamarts and allow users to perform analysis on various business areas to help them in making decisions.
9. A Graphical User Interface based no programming required interface for ad-hoc reporting and multidimensional analysis.
10. ROLAP server should provide RDBMS based processing thus improving the three tier performance. Fat mid-tier degrades the performance as the complex queries demand for advanced analytical computations.

Summary

When business needs and technological innovations converge, they drive major changes in the way businesses are run. Data warehousing technology will help many businesses respond to an ever-shifting competitive environment.

For these reasons most organizations have built data warehouses, or are in the process of doing so. The power of the analytical processing tools has also begun to be felt. Organizations that have taken an aggressive approach to developing a business intelligence solution are finding plenty of ways to make the warehouse payoff.

Now that datamarts can be built and harnessed using business intelligence tools and can be coordinated for implementation of an Enterprise Data Warehouse, their use is spreading to many organizations.

Datamarts can be implemented on standard SMP platforms with Windows NT. Which provides a low cost server platform and easy networking with a GUI.

The ROLAP technology gives you the reusability to access individual datamarts as well as an Enterprise Data Warehouse.

The Four Challenges of Customer-Centric Data Warehousing

Title: *The Four Challenges of Customer-Centric Data Warehousing*

Author: *Carleton Corporation*

Abstract: *With today's ever-increasing competitive pressures, higher customer expectations, and new enabling technologies, customer-centric data warehousing is increasingly becoming an important business opportunity. Yet such customer-focused initiatives have – at least historically – been difficult to implement. This paper will look at the risks and rewards of customer-centric data warehousing, and will specifically focus on four key technical challenges unique to data warehouses that center on customer data. This paper addresses each of these four challenges and shows how — as never before — the benefits of customer-centric data warehousing can be attained today.*

Customer-Centric Data Warehousing - What is it? What are the rewards?

Customer-centric data warehouses are simply data warehouses that require complete, accurate views of customers, with their associated data, to solve important business problems. We are using customer broadly here to mean individual customers, business customers, households, prospective customers, and even vendors and suppliers. While the concept is simple, implementation of customer-centric data warehouses is often easier said than done – as we shall see.

Integrating Customer Data Throughout the Enterprise

The value of the customer-centric data warehouse or data mart is due to its integration, or consolidation, of customer data. The warehouse integrates customer data that is fragmented across multiple sources within your organization. The sources often include various business line systems that support the following functions:

- Order processing
- Customer support
- Inquiry systems
- Marketing
- Various transaction systems, etc.

Businesses' transaction systems are typically designed to deal only with the needs of that transaction process. Therefore, each transaction system has a piece of information about the customer. For example, a bank will typically have these transaction systems (see figure 1).

Data in these transaction systems are often organized around "accounts" or "policies" or other similar transactional concepts, that limit the ability to identify unique customers and their total relationship to the business.

Customer-Centric Data Warehouse Applications

In the customer-centric data warehouse, the customer data from each transaction system will be brought together, or integrated, to provide a whole, unified

Figure 1

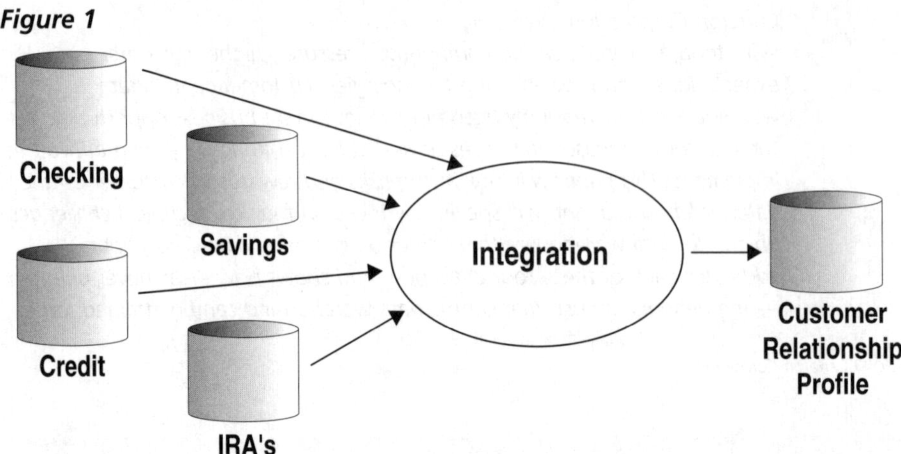

view of the customer. There is tremendous value to businesses in possessing this unified view of customers. Here are just a few examples of the many ways in which integrated customer data may be used to achieve competitive advantage, improve customer service, or reduce operations costs:

- Customer relationship management
- Consolidating customers after acquisitions or mergers
- Greater revenue and profitability from customer retention, cross-selling, and cost management
- Fraud detection
- Reliable data mining results
- Vendor consolidation
- Healthcare Master Patient Index (MPI)
- Healthcare outcomes analysis
- Customer service

External Supplementary Data and Householding

Building a unified customer view may even involve integrating data from outside your organization, such as demographic data, or credit information, to enhance your customer knowledge. Further, a customer view often involves establishing relationships, often referred to as householding. Householding is identifying the individuals who are in the same family, or household, often for marketing purposes. Similarly, business householding is identifying the relationships within a business, such as all those individuals at a particular location of a larger organization.

Building Customer-Centric Data Warehouses Is Challenging

The business rewards for integrating and using customer data are enormous. But customer-centric data warehouses, until recently, have been difficult to build. Why is that so? First, building any data warehouse or mart is challenging. Numerous articles have been written on the benefits and challenges of data warehousing and there's no need to repeat that. Rather, we will focus here on what is particularly challenging about customer-centric data warehouses.

The Four Unique Challenges

There are four reasons in particular that customer-centric data warehouses can be difficult to build and maintain:

1. Customer data requires integration. Rarely is a reliable common key available on which to match up and identify the same customer from different sources, and then merge the data.
2. Names and addresses are difficult. Usually, the matching must include matching on names and addresses, which requires specialized tools (and often specialized knowledge)
3. Update requirements are complex. Customer data warehouses must typically be updated, rather than completely refreshed, or updated in increments (such as adding another week of retail sales). This updating is more complex than a refresh or incremental addition.
4. Requires separate transformation and cleansing tools. Historically, there have not been tools that provide a complete solution for building customer data warehouses.

Let's understand each of these challenges and, most important, how to address them.

Challenge 1: Customer Data Requires Integration to Build a Unified View

As we've seen, a customer-centric data warehouse must combine customer data from internal sources, and may require adding external data. Unique customers must be identified across and within all these sources. And the business needs may require not only identifying the individual customers, but also the relationship between customers, such as household relationships. Let's look at the matching and merging capability required to integrate this customer data.

Fuzzy Matching Required

Since it is very rare that all sources have the same customer identifier (primary key), matching customers across sources is difficult. It requires what is often called fuzzy matching. Fuzzy matching uses algorithms to identify similar records (rows). It is probabilistic, and only records that have a very high confidence of a match should be considered a match.

Several columns of data that in some way identify a customer, that are in common across the systems, are used for matching. For example, fuzzy matches might be attempted on these three columns:

- Phone number,
- Name, and
- Address

Typically, matches are attempted in several different ways, in accordance to a business' rules for what they consider a match. For example, in addition to the above three columns, in order to "catch" individuals who have moved and there-fore have different addresses, one might also match on:

- Credit card number,
- Date of birth, and
- Address

Two records are considered a match when a match was made on either set of data and business rules.

Match Candidates Must Be Clustered

One complicating factor in matching, is that the number of match comparisons to be attempted grows exponentially with the size of the data, if every record is compared with every other record. In fact, the formula is:

(n2 -n) / 2

With even a small number of records, let's say 100,000, the number of comparisons would then be 4,999,950,000! (almost 5 trillion!)

Therefore, records must be clustered into candidate groups, or workunits. The idea is that only records within a workunit are compared with each other. This dramatically improves performance. Careful selection and management of workunits is needed to avoid missing matches.

Matched Data Must Be Merged (Consolidated or Integrated)
Once a match is made between two records (or three or four, for that matter), the records must be consolidated, or merged. After all, that's the whole reason the data warehouse is being built – to integrate the important data about the customer. Different information will be merged from each source, for example:

- Current balances
- Credit status
- Investment activity
- Support contacts
- Direct marketing response

Sometimes the information to be merged, such as personal identification information, is in more than one source. Then, merge rules determine where the data is merged from. For example, a field might be merged by:

- Source priority (e.g., the checking address is considered more reliable than the IRA address)
- Most recent update (the source with the most current date stamp will be used)
- Most frequently occurring (e.g., three of four sources have the same phone number).

Imperative to Business That the Match/Merge Be Done Right
It's important that the match and merge be done as completely and correctly as possible. When matches are missed, a single customer will appear as two or more customers. You will have an incomplete view of your customers, and your customer count will be exaggerated. According to the META group, healthcare organizations implementing master patient indexes have found 5 to 30% of their patient records to be duplicates. Even worse, if two

individuals or companies are matched that shouldn't be, you get a warped view of the customer. Customer matches that are incomplete, inaccurate, and unreliable thereby lead to incorrect business analysis and poor decisions. These decisions can cost the organization losses in revenue and higher expenses, just the opposite of what the customer data warehouse was intended to achieve. It is very important that you or the project sponsors identify and estimate the cost of each incorrect customer match or missed match, in terms of lost revenue, lost profit, or unrealized cost savings.

Examples include:

- Assigning the wrong accounts to a customer and wasting valuable marketing resources and customer goodwill in cross-selling products this customer already has
- Losing a profitable customer because the customer service representative doesn't understand the relationship value
- Targeting prospects based on wrong marketing criteria
- Not recognizing the full credit risk associated with the customer

Challenge 2: Names and Addresses Require Special Attention to Match Customers

Names and addresses are very important to the accurate matching of customers and building a complete, accurate customer data warehouse, for several reasons:

- Unique IDs, SSN, Date of Birth, etc. are often unavailable or inadequate
- Names and Addresses are almost universally available

For effective customer matching, names and addresses must be cleansed. Now let's look at each of these points regarding names and addresses, and customer matching.

Non-Name and Address Data Not Adequate for Matching

There are several highly desirable fields to help identify customers, such as social security number, phone number, date of birth , and DUNS number (Dun & Bradstreet identifier) that are often not available. If the data is available, it is usually available for only some sources or some percentage of records within a source. Furthermore, when the data is available, the data may not be reliable. These are some examples. With area codes bursting at the seams, new phone numbers are too quickly re-assigned to new households. A parent or trustee's social security number is used in place of a child's. Typos of various sorts occur. And the stories of matches made on SSN alone, with thousands of matching 999-99-9999's (or similar "placeholders"), are legendary.

Name and Addresses are Ubiquitous but Messy

Names and addresses, on the other hand, are typically in almost every source and record. And they both have high cardinality, making them excellent personal identifiers. That's the good news. The bad news is that names and addresses are the most difficult type of customer data to work with. Invariably, name and address data must be cleansed in order to be used for matching. Unlike, say, date of birth, there is tremendous variability that can occur even between what are actually the same name and address. Here are examples of how the same individual's name and address can easily vary:

- Nicknames
- Marital status change, and consequent change or hyphenation of last name
- Variation due to formality (A.J. Jones and Dr. Andrew Jones PhD)
- Omitting Jr., Sr., II, or III
- Abbreviations in address (E. and East Ave and Avenue)
- Including or not including apartment #
- Changing to or from PO Box rather than street mail delivery
- Spelling errors and typos can be hard to identify (how do you know if it's 100 Main or 1000 Main?)

Similarly, there is tremendous variability in company name and address data:

- Titles change
- Titles may be entered in name field
- Company names are abbreviated in many ways (PPG, PP&G, PP&G Inc., Pittsburgh Paint & Glass)
- Companies may be identified by division or parent or both (GM, Cadiallac, Cadillac – GM, etc.; the variations are almost limitless)
- Individuals may move frequently within corporate campuses,
- Mailstops, department names, and building identifiers may be mixed in with mailing addresses or company names

Varying Formats Require Parsing
Let's imagine that your data is 100% clean. That is, every instance of the same customer is represented in exactly the same way in the various source databases. All the data is perfectly complete and consistent. Then there would be no need to cleanse the names and addresses, right? Wrong! Invariably, the data from different sources is formatted (fielded) differently. The data from each source must be parsed into consistent fielding. And furthermore, for matching purposes an individual name or a street address, as examples, must be parsed into their finest elements, such as first name, last name, street number, street name, and so on.

Quite often, on close analysis, you will find data has been mis-fielded or mis-entered. The parsing routines of name and address tools can be used to fix this by concatenating fields and re-fielding them from the tools' results.

Capabilities of Typical Name/Address Processing Software

For all these reasons, it requires a special-purpose solution to cleanse name and

Figure 2: Name parsing

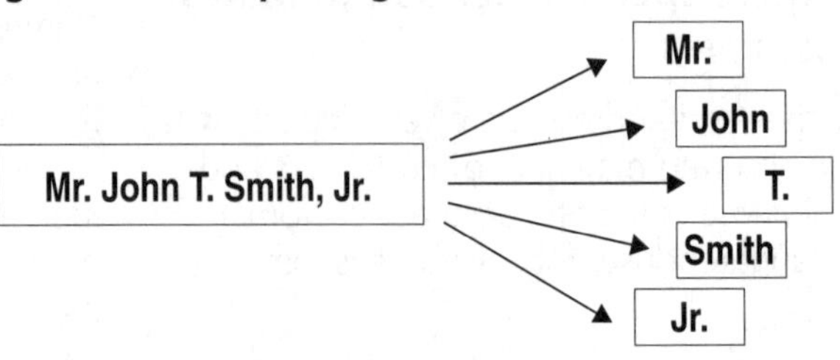

address data. Name and address processing software typically will:

- Parse name and address information into the individual elements for improved correction and matching
- Standardize (consistently represent) names and addresses for improved matching
- Correct address components, such as street names, city, and zip code for greater accuracy
- Augment with new data elements for better target marketing or other purposes
- Reformat for merging the data and populating the warehouse

Here are some examples of these above functions, for name and address processing respectively (see table 1):

Name/Address Pre-Processing Has a Huge Impact on Accurately Identifying Customers

This parsing and cleansing of name and address data dramatically improves the quality of matching, resulting in:

- Fewer missed matches
- Fewer erroneous matches

When matching on names and addresses, specialized processing tools are an absolute must, and will contribute more to quality matching, and data warehouse quality, than the most sophisticated matching algorithms and rules.

Table 1

Function	Name	Address
Parse	Individual, Company Name, plus title & "firm location" (dept. mailstop building name, etc.)	Mailing addresses
Standardize	Doctor to Dr, Vice Pres to VP, Bill, Billy, etc to William, etc.	Street or Str to St. East Main to E Main
Correct	NOT APPLICABLE to names	Street names, city names, ZIP codes
Augment	Add gender codes	Add ZIP4, county codes, etc.

Challenge 3: Update Complexity to Maintain the Unified Customer View and Add New Customers

The maintenance of customer data warehouses is different, and more challenging, than the maintenance of most other types of data warehouses. Customer data warehouses must be incrementally updated, rather than completely refreshed (re-loaded). Let's look at why this is so, and what the implications are.

Customer Data Warehouses Require Incremental Updating

Why is customer data usually an update situation rather than a complete batch refresh? A customer warehouse or mart contains all customers (or vendors, prospects, etc.) depending on the purpose of the warehouse or mart, and generally a long history of data. This means that totally rebuilding the warehouse at each update period is usually not an option, for two reasons:

- The historical data is no longer available on the source systems.
- The amount of processing to totally re-match and rebuild each time you up-date is not feasible within the batch update window (overnight or over the weekend).

Therefore, since it is not practical to re-build and refresh with each update period, the customer data warehouse must be incrementally updated. This means that new data from each update period must be added to the data warehouse, while preserving existing data. More specifically:

- New data must be identified as belonging to a new or existing customer
- New customers must be given a unique ID, and new rows inserted
- Existing customers must have their data updated, on a column-by-column basis (to reflect additional purchases, change in service status, or whatever other data is stored in the data warehouse about the customer and their activity)

Contrast the update requirements of a customer data warehouse to that of a warehouse of retail sales data, containing no customer information. Each week new sales data is added to the warehouse. But there is no need to match incoming data with existing data. There is no change to the existing detail data. There are no field by field incremental updates. It's true that some of the data is also rolled up by sales season and by day of week, for example. But that is typically handled as a complete refresh with the rolling up occurring before getting into the database. So, the maintenance of this type of database involves a complete re-load. This is significantly simpler to maintain than the updating of the customer database.

Incremental Updating is More Complex Than Refreshing and Often Poorly Supported

From the above description of what needs to be done with a periodic update of a customer warehouse, we can derive that the system or tool doing the update must have these capabilities:

- Match incoming (source) data with warehouse data to distinguish whether the incoming customer is new or existing.

- Create Unique IDs for new customers
- Conditionally insert
- SQL update on a column-by-column basis
- Updates may involve calculations using values in existing columns (for example, total sales history for an individual, or total value of all accounts)

The first point, matching incoming with existing warehouse data, deserves a closer look. To understand the issue, let's consider an example where the data warehouse contains 10 million customers, and it is updated nightly with information on an average of five thousand customers. Some tools and systems will require you to unload all the customer identification information tables in order to match up the incoming and existing customers. With batch update window time constraints, and matching being an inherently processing-intensive activity, this is usually not feasible. Instead of unloading all the data, only true candidates for matching should be read from the warehouse. This dramatically reduces the processing time required. This type of periodic updating and matching is called synchronization. It synchronizes the incoming and existing data efficiently without totally redoing the initial processing. Because of architectural constraints or relational I/O limitations, many tools cannot synchronize.

As you can see, customer data warehouses have some inherent complexity in the nature of their updating that many other types of data warehouses do not.

Challenge 4: Separate Tools to Build and Maintain the Customer Warehouse

Data Prep Processes in Customer-Centric Data Warehouses

Before looking at the tools that have been available to prepare the data, let's first look at the data-preparation processes needed to build and maintain a customer-centric data warehouse. From our discussion of the special challenges of customer data warehouses, we know customer-centric warehouses have several processes not usually encountered in data warehousing data preparation:

- Match & merge
- Name and address processing
- Synchronization and incremental updating

Figure 3: Functional Requirements for Customer Data Warehouse Preparation

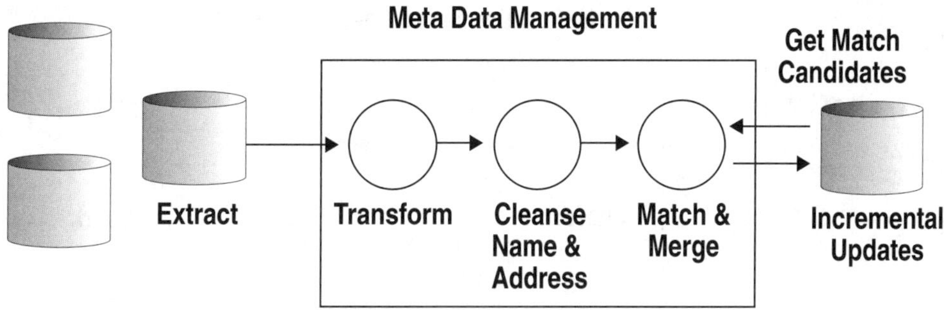

In figure 3, see how the name and address cleansing is a necessary precursor to matching. Note how not only do we have to process the source data, we also need to get candidates of possible existing customers to match against. When the match and merge is complete, then updating is done (not a load). Keep in mind that sub-processes are shown to help you conceptualize the process. The sub-processes are not separate batch processes, involving files to disk. Rather, they should actually be done in memory, for performance.

Two Types of Tools Needed in the Customer Data Warehouse

Now that we have an overview of the processes needed, let's look at the two types of tools that are used to prepare the data in customer-centric data warehouses:

- Data warehouse transformation tools
- Cleansing products

We will see that though there has been some confusion about these tools, because there is some overlap in functionality, they are for the most part quite different. Both are needed to build and maintain a customer data warehouse.

Transformation Tools Meet Generic Data Warehousing Needs Not Special Needs

Over the past several years, transformation tools have become widely used to build and maintain the data warehouse. The primary functions of these tools are shown in figure 4.

Note how these tools don't include all the processes that we identified as necessary:

They lack:

- Name and address cleansing
- Fuzzy matching and merging

And, typically, their synchronization with the target database and update capability is weak. The reason for this is that these transformation tools, with one exception, were not designed for customer integration. They were designed for simpler extraction, aggregation, and loading. These tools are oriented to OLAP analysis of summarized data, not granular customer-level data.

Figure 4: Capabilities of Transformation Tools Incomplete

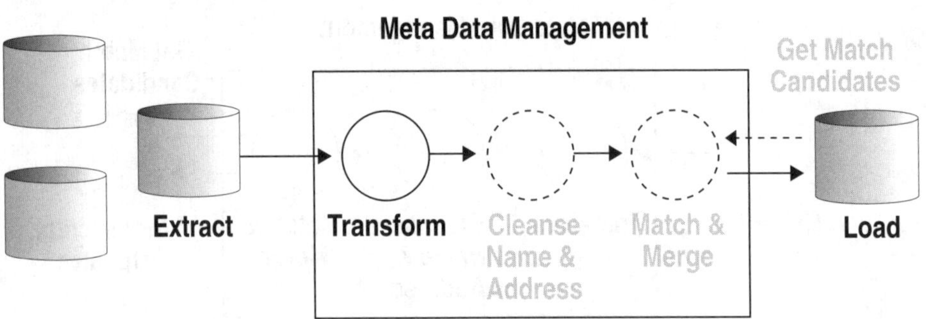

Cleansing Products Meet Special Needs but Don't Provide General Data Warehousing Needs

Cleansing products, as the name implies, primarily cleanse and match. All of the most commonly used products focus on names and addresses. They can perform the name and address processing previously described, to some extent. And they perform the matching and merging described earlier, again to varying degrees. On the other hand, they do not provide:

- Extraction
- Load or update
- Metadata management

Where they overlap with transformation tools, is in their transform/validation capability. The cleansing tools vary widely in this regard. They vary, with non-name and address data, from no capability to very extensive data discovery capability beyond what some transformation tools can provide. But mostly, the core focus of the cleansing tools is just that, cleansing and matching.

The cleansing tool's name-and-address focus is easy to understand when you understand the origins of these products. Whereas transformation tools were designed specifically for data warehousing, the origins of cleansing products are:

- Mailing/direct marketing
- Mainframe customer consolidations (acquisitions/mergers) or customer application conversions, such as in banking

Consequently, all of these products are flat file in/out oriented, though some are available as I/O-less libraries. They do not have RDBMS read/write capability. They didn't need this since mailing services bureaus work on a tape in/out basis. And mainframe system conversions are batch processing oriented. Furthermore the mainframe conversion products are written in COBOL and thus not well suited to the open-systems oriented data warehousing tasks.

Figure 5: Capabilities of Transformation Tools Incomplete

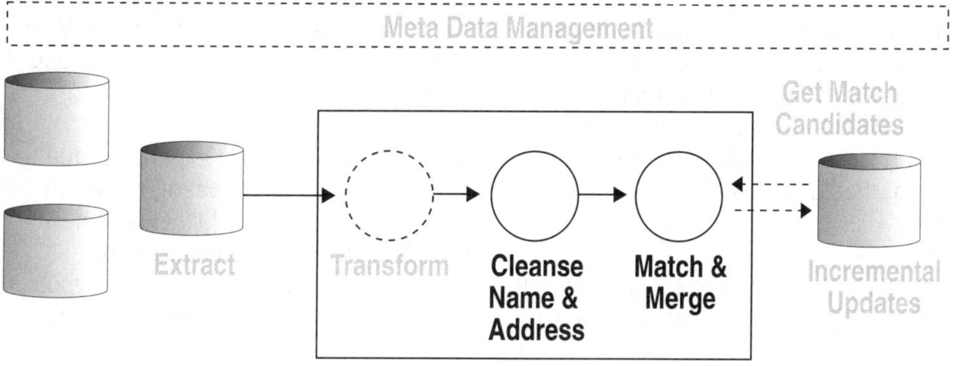

Not All the Cleansing Products Provide the Same Functionality
The mailing/ direct marketing products tend to be especially strong in the address correction, whereas the consolidation/conversion products lack the ability to correct or validate street-level data because they lack the United States Postal Service address database and do not go through the accuracy certification process of the USPS. All these products tend to work well with cleansing names. The other variation in the cleansing products is their sophistication with non-name and address data and their ability to merge. Again, this is due to their heritage. Since in mailing the only data typically handled is names and addresses, sometimes the products have limited matching flexibility and limited ability to work with a variety of data that can be identifying (Date of birth, SSN, credit card, account numbers, etc.). Their field-by-field merge capability tends to be even more limited. This is often not realized, in part because in mailing these products are called merge/purge products, which makes it sound as though they're designed to merge. However, merge – in mailing – means something very different. In mailing, merging means that matching records from various mailing lists are purged out except for the one survivor to be mailed, whereas in data warehousing data from the matching records are merged together. Furthermore there ability to carry along or work with large amounts of data (such as sales info) that is not used for identifying, is limited.

To summarize the cleansing tools, they tend to be very strong in processing and matching names and addresses, but - alone - are not geared towards data warehousing. This is because they can neither source nor load / update relational databases, nor provide the metadata management environment that is especially important for maintenance, and often lack adequate transformation/mapping functionality.

Customer-Centric Data Warehousing Demands an Integrated Cost-Effective Transformation & Cleansing Tool

As you can see, transformation and cleansing tools overlap slightly, but for the most part are almost completely complementary. Both types of products are needed.

So buy both, right? But there been two problems with that approach:

- The tools are not integrated together.
- Both types of tools are expensive (often $150K - $200K each)

The integration effort for a user is time-consuming and costly. Integration at both the data and metadata level is needed. And often the architectures of the two products do not fit well together into the overall data warehouse architecture. With the integration effort also comes increased project risk.

Since both products are expensive, due to budgets, and to some extent, confusion about overlapping capability, users have sometimes found it hard to get the justification to purchase both. The result has been serious data quality problems, often leading to failure of the data warehouse when cleansing tools were not purchased. Or when transformation tools were not purchased, extensive and expensive hand coding required to fill in the gaps, and resulting in a very difficult and costly system to maintain, also due to poor metadata management.

What is needed is a transformation tool that integrates the features of both transformation and cleansing tools and addresses the unique challenges of customer data warehousing. Wayne Eckerson, previously of Patricia Seybold and now with The Data Warehousing Institute, has written of exactly the need for the complementary functionality of transformation and cleansing tools to be integrated, and to be provided as a cost-effective product. Such a tool would completely handle the data preparation processes previously described (see table 2).

Very recently such an integrated solution has become available. It provides transformation and cleansing in one product. This saves integration cost and effort, reduces licensing costs, reduces risk, and increases the likelihood of project success. This is a significant development in the data warehousing industry and a milestone in dealing with the data quality issues that are so critical to data warehouse success.

A Tool Evaluator's Checklist - What to Look for

Let's summarize the key points we've identified regarding the customer data warehouse challenges as it applies to the tool needs for data preparation. When evaluating such solutions, as we've seen, here are the some checklist requirements:

Table 2

	Transformation Tools	Transformation Tools	Integrated Tools
Meta Data Management	a		a
Transformation	a	limited	a
Name & Address cleansing		a	a
Fuzzy matching and merging (integration)	Usually not	a	a
Relational I/O (source, read DDL, load, update)	a		a

- An integration of transformation and cleansing capabilities
- Single source for implementation and service of integrated product
- Consulting or implementation services experienced with the challenges to successfully building customer data warehouses
- A more cost-effective solution than buying the two products separately
- An architecture designed for integration – for fuzzy matching and merging
- The ability to synchronize with and intelligently update the data warehouse
- Sufficient flexibility and sophistication in matching and merging to implement your business rules for matching and merging
- "CASS" level data (street correction) in the address processing (in Canada, look for "SERP" data, from Canada Post). Specifically look for CASS data but you do not need generation of a "CASS certificate" as that is needed only for submitting mailings.

Conclusion - Complete, Integrated Transformation and Cleansing Tool Is Essential to Success

Customer-centric data warehouses — data warehouses that integrate customer data — have tremendous business value. We've seen that there are four technical challenges characteristic of customer data warehouses that differ from other types of warehouse projects:

- Customer data requires integration since sources rarely have a common key. Fuzzy matching, and an architecture to enable that matching and merging, is required.
- Usually, the matching includes names and addresses, which requires specialized tools to parse and cleanse the data to facilitate high-quality matching
- Customer data warehouses typically require synchronization and incremental updating, rather than simpler refreshes (re-loads).
- Historically, two tools have been needed to prepare the customer data – transformation and cleansing tools. They provide complementary functionality, both of which are needed. Only recently have integrated cost-effective tools that combine the functionality of both become available.

Integrated customer integration tools for data warehousing simplifies all the challenges, reduces the risks, and increases the potential rewards of customer-centric data warehousing.

ERP and Data Warehousing in the Intelligent Enterprise

Title:	*ERP and Data Warehousing in the Intelligent Enterprise*
Author:	*Informatica*
Abstract:	*This white paper explores the methods and alternatives for merging ERP and data warehousing that are available today, and details the role of Informatica's product family in supplying key services — from data integration to customized application deployment — to facilitate the merger of ERP and data warehousing.*

ERP and data warehousing: the two would seem inextricably linked, yet they're miles apart.

For most large companies today, Enterprise Resource Planning (ERP) serves within the core set of day-to-day transaction processing applications. From General Ledger to Human Resources, ERP systems do the central work of running, tracking and reporting on business data processing.

Just as ERP is critical to business transactions, so is data warehousing central to analysis of those transactions. Through data warehousing, product managers, marketing managers, communications specialists, human resources recruiters, financial executives, CIOs and CEOs formulate analytical queries and obtain reports; with these, they are able to make tactical and strategic business decisions — faster and better than ever before, thanks to their analytical resources.

But operational and analytical systems have always been somewhat at odds with each other.

Operational systems — including but not limited to ERP systems — are meant to operate, not report. They typically work full time, shutting down only for maintenance or upgrades. Their internal data structures are optimized for reporting, not for analysis.

As for analytical systems, including data warehouses, data marts and even direct reporting tools, in order to do their jobs, they need to intrude on the operational systems long enough to take "snapshots" of data, data they can cleanse, reorganize, and assess. IT managers and database administrators know too well how easily the needs of operational and analytical systems can conflict. Analytical systems may want to pull more operational data, at more frequent intervals, in order to expand analytical scope or improve accuracy. This can place greater burdens on operational planning. At the same time, analytical systems (and their users) may be frustrated by the arcane data structures of operational systems, data structures that make it exceedingly difficult to determine basic information about company operations.

In the midst of this conflict, however, there's a growing quantity of good news. Vendors from the ERP and data warehousing/decision support industries are working hard to develop solutions to these conflicts, and to bring ERP and data warehousing closer together.

ERP and Data Warehousing: Information Partners

Over the past decade, the disciplines of ERP and data warehousing have been moving ever closer together.

ERP systems from vendors such as SAP ® and PeopleSoft have secured their central place in large companies across all industries, with today's worldwide ERP market estimated at $39 billion. The reason ERP has succeeded so thoroughly: ERP systems represent a close-to-off-the-shelf solution set for handling the most important business-process applications, from manufacturing planning to finance and human re-sources, of companies today.

In some cases, companies rely on a single-vendor's ERP product family; in many other cases, companies pursue a best-of-breed strategy, selecting operational applications based on product performance and application coverage. And in most cases, the companies' ERP systems take their places among various other operational systems — from UNIX and NT-based client-server systems to legacy mainframe implementations — to complete the operational topology.

Analytical systems have gained their foothold, too, among the world's businesses. Many of today's analytic applications originate from the concept of the Executive Information System, or EIS. The concept was valid: give company executives the ability to analyze any and all operational activities, and at a variety of levels, from macro to micro. But the implementation was daunting: many EIS and DSS (decision support) initiatives collapsed under the weight — actually the scope and cost — of the galactic data warehouse that was needed to support enterprise-wide analytic tools and applications.

Today, some companies still maintain their "top-down" data warehouses. But many more have come to rely on the newer, bottom-up, component-based approach made possible by distributed data mart architectures and analytic applications. Data warehousing technology is still used to store, organize and consolidate raw operational data, but it is designed and employed in a more focused fashion, typically at a business-unit level. This permits rapid, cost-effective creation of data marts, and, when used with products such as Informatica's PowerCenter and PowerMart software families, makes it possible for companies to synchronize and share resources of multiple data marts that draw from a single staging area built with clean, consistent corporate data.

ERP: Analysis Challenges

If corporate data is the lifeblood of most large businesses today, ERP systems form heart of the typical organization, turning raw input into data, and data into valuable information. Within today's ERP systems a wealth of information exists, and users are now realizing that through data warehousing/analytical technologies, that data can be selected, shaped, analyzed and turned into insight worthy of an intelligent enterprise.

As effective as they are at processing transaction data, however, ERP systems with proprietary internal data structures can present substantial challenges to companies attempting to deploy in-house developed data warehouses or analytic applications. The major challenges are:

- Identifying data to be analyzed — proprietary ERP systems employ unique logical structures that shield the physical tables from end user access. Moreover, these structures are frequently oddly named, and there is no centralized mechanism for interpreting or understanding their contents.
  For instance, an ERP system might contain thou-sands of tables, each with various interrelationships, and each named with an acronym that doesn't reveal the table's contents. Here, it's nearly impossible to determine which and how many of the tables might be pertinent to, say, a "Customer ID" query.
- Extracting the data — the unique logical structures of proprietary ERP systems also require that analytical programmers use special programming languages or proprietary access tools to extract operational data. Such languages and tools are intended for operational-system coding, however, and not for designing the large data transformations that must take place as part of the extraction process. As a result, at best they are unwieldy to work with; at worst, impossible.
  Further compounding this problem is the fact that proprietary ERP vendors typically make changes to their internal logical-to-physical mappings with each new software release. Their operational users are protected from these changes by the logical-structure "middleware," but this process makes it even more difficult for analytical developers to perform changed-data capture, a technique that reduces extraction time.
- Reconciling developer differences — not only do ERP and data warehousing technologies come from different origins, but the programmers who support these systems must be reconciled and coordinated in order to integrate analytical components with operational ERP systems. The challenge is that basic differences in underlying designs and terminologies are reflected in the programmers themselves; although they are experts in their own field, ERP and data warehousing developers rarely delve into each other's field of expertise.

User Alternatives

Today, solutions to these problems are coming from a range of vendors, and in a range of forms. Users are encouraged, yet they are also frequently bewildered by the widely varying alternatives. Essentially, the alter-natives to homegrown analytical development and ERP integration are these:

- ERP-vendor tools and initiatives — A growing number of ERP vendors are producing tool sets and pre-programmed extraction routines that users can employ to identify and extract raw ERP data. The primary benefit to this approach lies in the potential for tight integration between analysis and ERP; for example, this benefits maintenance of changed-data capture currency.
  A major disadvantage is that the tools themselves tend to be proprietary; as a result, they may not be effective at accessing data from other operational sources, then merging it with the ERP data for ultimate analysis. This is problematic because incomplete data can cause faulty analysis.
  Another disadvantage: the ERP tools are not likely to feature the same functional or performance robustness as do tools from established data warehousing/ analytical vendors; this can again result in less than complete analysis.

- ERP-oriented niche packages — Also available are off-the-shelf packages for building and/or populating data marts with ERP data. These products come from vendors with experience in ERP systems, so they too carry the potential advantages of tight integration with the ERP systems they support.
  However, they lack the capacity, functionality and stability of production data warehouses/data marts, so they typically fall short in important areas such as transformation processing performance and metadata synchronization and sharing capabilities. Also, as with the ERP tools, they tend to be weak at accessing data from other operational sources.

- ERP interfaces from traditional data warehousing vendors — Traditional data warehousing vendors bring a different expertise to the problem: they understand the issues involved with mapping, extracting, transforming and loading large volumes of complex data from source systems to target platforms. However, they lack an in-depth knowledge of the programming techniques necessary to identify and manipulate the varying data structures of the large, proprietary ERP systems. As a result, they carry a disadvantage in that they may have trouble identifying and extracting ERP data; moreover, they will likely have greater difficulty in extracting and consolidating data from multiple ERP and non-ERP operational sources.

Informatica: A Different Approach

Informatica believes that each of these alternatives may be effective for some users. For instance, ERP-designed or ERP-oriented tools may work well in single-vendor applications, and simple ERP interfaces may suffice for relatively simple applications, say, for populating large, existing data warehouses with minimal, non-complex ERP data.

But for most companies, each falls short of the central challenge today: to optimize analytical capabilities across multiple operational sources in a typically complex and dynamic information environment, they type worthy of an intelligent enterprise.

Meeting the Needs of the Intelligent Enterprise

Informatica defines the Intelligent Enterprise as:

An organization that:
1) has timely access to all the critical information it needs in order to gain insight into its performance at any given moment; and
2) is able to deliver effective decision support services across a full spectrum of user demands, from the simplest to the most complex analytical requirements.

Beyond this definition, most industry experts agree that today's — and tomorrow's — intellectually ambitious enterprises will continually stretch out, toward more types and sources of operational information, and toward an ever-growing, ever-changing catalog of best-of-breed analytic tools and applications.

In addition to finding an effective tool for identifying and extracting ERP data, such an enterprise will exhibit certain obvious needs:

- To collect data from diverse operational sources — The intelligent enterprise will likely glean input from several ERP systems, as well as from other sources, internal and external. Finance and manufacturing information may come from SAP, for instance, with Human Resources and Compensation Management residing on a PeopleSoft ERP system. To this data, the enterprise would add data from legacy mainframes — these are still handling business-critical processing for a majority of large businesses — as well as other data, say, for research purposes, from sources as nearby as the departmental UNIX server,

Figure 1: Informatica is helping companies transform data from every corner of their enterprise into valuable business insight

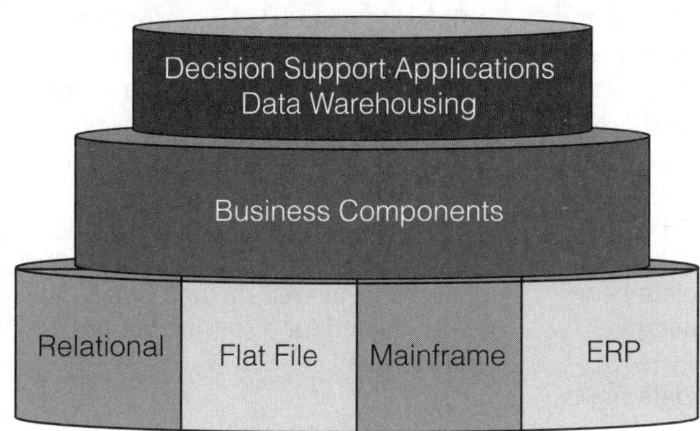

and as distant as a remote former merger partner or an Internet-based resource. In addition to tightly-bound interfaces to these sources, the intelligent enterprise will need an effective mechanism for capturing and aggregating only changed data, thus minimizing the "load window" necessary for each source transaction.

- To speed movement of that data to best-of-breed analytical resources — Because of the volume and range of source data, high speed is important in performing the necessary extraction, transformation and loading functions necessary to populate the data warehouse and feed the analytic applications. Performance is even more critical if some system components are located remotely.
  Also vital is metadata-level (command-level) compatibility among the key infrastructure components. This helps maximize efficiency and analytical accuracy, since inter-component instructions don't have to be re-set or re-interpreted.

- To respond quickly to changing market and competitive conditions — Unlike the days when data sources were stable and analysis routine, intelligent enterprises today need to be able to respond quickly to price cuts, market changes, competitive moves and other conditions. They thus need to be able to gain fast access to new operational sources, and they need to be able to formulate new analytical resources — by building "disposable" data marts, for instance — rapidly and easily. Disposable data marts depend on yet another dimension of metadata performance, that is, the ability to synchronize metadata within a distributed data mart architecture.

PowerCenter, PowerMart and PowerConnect: Extending Enterprise Intelligence

Informatica's product families bring to enterprises with ERP source systems a comprehensive solution for automating the extraction and mapping of complex source data, as well as for applying Informatica's traditional strengths in creating high-performance, metadata-driven data warehouses that support wide-ranging analytical options.

Key product elements are:

- PowerCenter and PowerMart — These products power the intelligent enterprise through a basic "hub and spoke" architecture. At the hub, PowerCenter serves as an enterprise-wide data integration platform, managing data transformations and movement through the analytical infrastructure, and employing metadata to synchronize and integrate data marts and data warehouses with source systems and analytic applications. For deploying and customizing data marts, PowerMart gives users powerful, intuitive tools to design and build any number of fully synchronized line of business functional data marts, as well as "one-time" data marts created for a specific business analysis need.

- PowerConnect — The PowerConnect family consists of specialized interfaces for extracting native data from complex sources, from IBM's DB2 to SAP and PeopleSoft ERP systems. Not only does PowerConnect hide the complexity of source extraction from the user, it makes possible the integration of multiple source extractions into a central staging area that can feed the enterprise's analytic applications.

- Business Components — These are source-and-target application templates that make up a business abstraction layer between the user and the native data formats. Business Components are invoked during the data warehouse and analytic application design process, and insulate developers from the inherent complexity of source systems and target applications. Business Components also enable analytic systems to be built and maintained easily by personnel who are not familiar with internals of the transaction systems, and insulates entire decision support systems from disruptive change in the IT environment (eg: mergers & acquisitions, software upgrades, new product introductions).

Figure 2: PowerConnect for PeopleSoft provides Informatica's PowerCenter customers with high-speed data extraction from PeopleSoft's ERP system

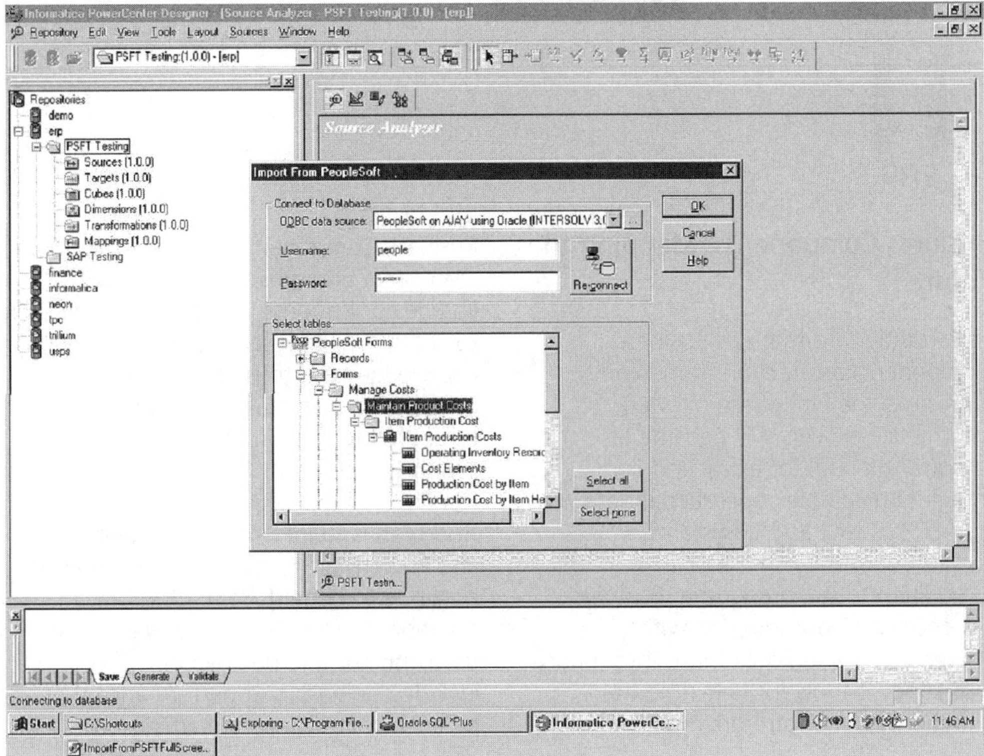

Chapter 2: How to Integrate Data Warehousing in your Business

Figure 3: Business Components accelerate the development and deployment of ERP data warehouses and analytic applications

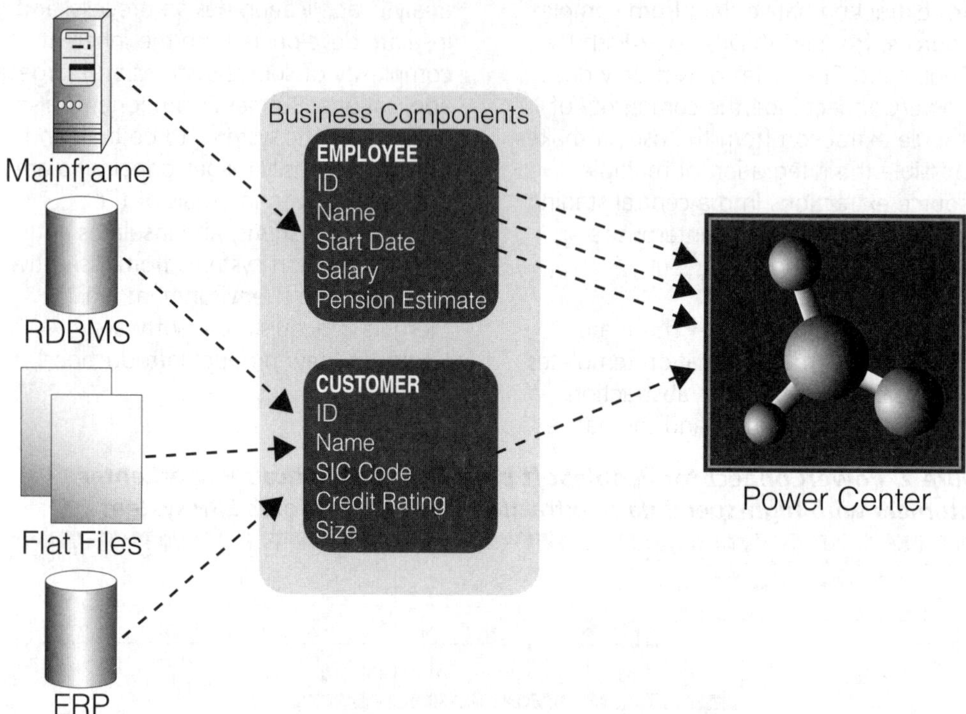

Business Components: Mapping the Future

Importantly, Informatica's Business Components abstraction framework represents the first phase of what Informatica expects will become an important model for extracting and integrating complex operational data, from non-ERP as well as ERP systems.

In addition to the pre-written Business Components now shipping with PowerCenter and PowerMart, Informatica also supplies tools for helping data warehouse administrators modify existing Business Components or create their own. Over time, enterprises can thus build libraries of Business Components that serve to capture and preserve their collective knowledge, and thus enhance the competitive advantages they achieve through information analysis and decision support.

And thanks to Informatica's PowerCenter and PowerMart families, enterprise users continue to benefit from Informatica's traditional strengths in data warehouse development and deployment. These include engine-based performance that permits source data "streaming" by overlapping the extraction, transformation and load functions normally executed in serial fashion, as well as wide metadata-level data exchange capabilities with different vendors' analytical resources.

These capabilities are designed to help enterprises extend their intelligence from today's tactical decision support endeavors to more strategic initiatives in the future. Initiatives such as these will place more far-reaching demands on source extractions and analytic capabilities, and they will add new dimensions of complexity to the underlying tasks that are hidden within Informatica's Business Components and other automation features.

For Informatica users, the future will ultimately promise greater competitive advantage, thanks to an ever-increasing ability to make the most of the growing world of information sources, and the analytical capabilities to turn that information into business knowledge, and better decisions.

Tightening the Sales Cycle

Title: *Tightening the Sales Cycle*
Author: *Jon-Paul Contreras, Neovation*
Abstract: *This paper describes how data warehousing can effectively leverage a company's transactional data to get a better return on investment from its sales force*

Biography: As a senior consultant Contreras oversees the implementation of Data Warehousing software and OLAP functions to support a variety of business areas such as quality and production information analysis across several industries, including financial, hotel, and manufacturing. Contreras' works extensively with SAP Business Information Warehouse™ and is a certified SAP BW' Application consultant. Contreras' technical expertise encompasses several operating environments including ABAP and HTML programming languages.

The Need

There is a commonly held belief that 80 percent of a company's business comes from 20 percent of its customers. Are you willing to give your competitors a chance at one of these customers, especially when what causes customers to look elsewhere is directly under your control?

There is a trend toward companies trimming overhead by reducing inventory levels. This presents a significant business problem for their suppliers. Inventory management practices for today's companies do not allow for a large amount of excess reserves. Companies must be able to obtain raw materials quickly in order to continue the manufacturing process. Therefore, if their suppliers cannot supply the needed raw materials, companies are more likely to move on to the next supplier. Companies cannot sacrifice production by waiting for supplies.

A supplier that looks to partner and integrate with its customers will constantly want to improve customer service. Suppliers can take a proactive approach to customer service by analyzing trends in its data, which will allow a sales force to review, analyze and make recommendations for the betterment of customer service.

A few key questions can help suppliers evaluate their standing with their core customers.

Key Questions

- Which customers have significantly decreased order volume this quarter?
- How many shipments were not completely filled due to products on backorder?
- Which products are currently on backorder?
- Which customers have the highest order-to-cancellation ratio?
- How long do customers' orders remain on backorder before they are cancelled?

To keep pace with today's business trends, the sales force needs the ability to access the answers to these questions quickly. This information will enable them to handle current customer concerns before they become major problems, or even cause the loss of a customer. This type of forward thinking allows companies to stay ahead of the game.

Key questions like these can be answered quickly through the use of Data Warehousing. Data Warehousing can provide a supplier's sales force with the information they need in a fast, reliable manner, allowing them to manage their customers better. With this tool, the sales force is able to address the questions at the heart of managing customer relationships.

The Tools

Information Technology (IT) has enabled companies to store information on a wide variety of subjects. With regard to sales, Information Technology allows for storage of information on orders, shipments and billing. As companies engage in these transactions with customers, suppliers or even internally, a wealth of information is captured. With all this information, the question then becomes how to harness it. The answer: Data Warehousing.

The term "Data Warehouse" has often been used to describe the consolidation of operational data into a common repository and represents the means to extract and analyze that data. Data Warehouses have often been developed as a means to achieve the goals of information access systems.

With the advent of Data Warehousing and online analytical processing, companies can query their data stores and return information on such topics as revenue and units and any calculations derived from these figures in a timely, easy-to-use manner that makes sense to business users. For example, users can query orders received by customer, product, geographic location or any combination of these or other characteristics.

The development of a Data Warehouse is a complex undertaking, involving one or more years of design and development and several million dollars. Few companies can afford to wait years or spend millions of dollars before realizing the benefits of a Data Warehouse. For this reason, many companies use data marts, which typically require smaller amounts of source data, fewer data elements to define, fewer business rules to develop and simpler data models – making data marts a quick, iterative solution to accessing and analyzing corporate information. The overall framework, strategy and technology for an enterprise Data Warehouse can be implemented with incremental, subject-oriented data marts.

In order to successfully implement a Data Warehouse and achieve its stated goals, an incremental data mart approach is followed in this document. The data mart approach is:

- Responsive
  The data mart is targeted directly to clearly defined business needs. It has a focused audience and a tightly defined scope.

- Scalable
  Because the data mart is built within an information architecture, it is scalable to any size, up to and including evolving into the Data Warehouse itself.

- Flexible
  Because the data mart is built using proven architectures and design techniques, it can be quickly modified to reflect rapidly changing environments and requirements.

- Quick impact
  Data marts can be constructed and implemented quickly, providing immediate impact on business challenges.

- Low cost
  Data marts can be constructed incrementally, at a fraction of the cost of a Data Warehouse.

All these characteristics add up to a fundamental building block of decision support in the modern business enterprise. The data mart is now the key component in meeting the needs for information access and delivery.

Aspects of Implementation

System Integration
One of the biggest challenges in getting the correct data into a Data Warehouse is extracting information from many different source systems. Companies can have orders, billing and inventory on different systems. Some have many packages that are customized to meet the needs of the different functional areas of the business. While others have packages integrated with custom developed systems. Some IT departments have all systems custom developed, but these systems were developed using different databases or on different operating systems. The integration of these environments takes time and money.

A growing trend in the IT industry has been the use of Enterprise Resource Planning (ERP) systems to eliminate the heterogeneity and create one large platform for all company systems. System integration through ERP can save companies the time of integrating data from disparate systems.

SAP™ Environment
The historical leader in the ERP industry is SAP™. With modules that allow customization to many companies' needs, SAP has created one system on which an entire company can operate. After a large boom of ERP implementations in the 90s, companies are now stabilizing and realizing they need to extend their systems through their supply chain. Many companies are integrating their ERP systems with back-end supply chains, CRM and Data Warehousing systems. SAP is developing their own line of software that extends through the supply chain for companies that have implemented R/3. The foundation for SAP's new software is called Business Information Warehouse (BW).

BW Standard Delivered Content
Whether or not you use R/3 as a source system, BW provides many benefits, including the reduction of development

time as a result of its standard business content. Business Application Programming Interface (BAPI) source systems and custom flat file developed interfaces provide limited flexibility to BW, and allow it to interface with systems other than R/3.

InfoSources and InfoObjects

While BW provides benefits in many environments, its biggest return, based upon the current release, is that it interfaces with R/3. BW provides pre-developed extractors that allow it to interface natively with R/3, enabling it to extract data from logistics, sales and distribution, controlling and other modules that a company has implemented in R/3. BW makes use of the existing business models operating in R/3 and builds upon each of the application-specific models. The amount of time that is saved with these pre-developed InfoSources is a major benefit and they can be used in their delivered form or can be modified to add additional data into the pipeline flowing into the BW system. After some minimal work has been done to set up the environment for data extraction in R/3, InfoObjects, which are the equivalent to fields in a database, can be aligned with the fields in R/3 to map data from one system to another. Based upon field name, domain or data element, one of approximately 1,400 InfoObjects can be selected to map to fields in R/3. Each of these objects is re-usable over any amount of InfoSources, which means additional time is saved during development.

BW provides additional business content through the release of delivered InfoCubes. InfoCubes are the multi-dimensional data stores that BW uses to query for reporting. InfoCubes can be filled with data that is specific to a functional area or they can contain data from many functional areas. InfoCubes can be custom built, or existing InfoCubes operating in business content can be modified to add InfoObjects and dimensions.

Updating InfoCubes

Sitting between the InfoCube and the source of the data are structures that define the data flow through the BW system. Update rules are created when the data is ready to be written into an InfoCube from a specific InfoSource. Therefore data from the same source system can be stored in many different InfoCubes, based upon requirements and aggregation needs. These update rules can be created to add data into as many InfoCubes as exist in the BW system. Within the update rules, data can be modified through the use of ABAP code to add values, restrict the amount of data being populated in the InfoCube, or carry out currency conversions. The update rules can also be used for time conversions to aggregate data being written to the InfoCube, especially if the transactional data is stored at a daily level, but the needs of the users require data at a monthly level. For access to a daily level of data coming from R/3, an operational data store (ODS) is available to store detailed data that can be accessed through drill-through functionality (with release 2.0). Therefore the smaller percentage of users that have the need to see daily level data can access it through the same reporting tool without sacrificing the performance of the reports being run for the larger group of users.

While the ODS will be updated and more functional in release 2.0, BW's current problem is that if the data you want to analyze does not fit into a multi-dimensional data store, the reporting and system integration issues are multiplied. A Data Warehouse should be able to report on relational tables as well as multi-dimensional tables. In the future, BW will provide drill through functionality to the ODS as well as all the way back to specific R/3 transactions.

Addressing Sales Cycle Problems with Sales and Distribution InfoSources

By combining and querying multiple sources, Data Warehousing can give you answers to the key questions mentioned earlier, and thus lead the way to solving your business problems. For heterogeneous systems, loading data from disparate sources can be time consuming. BW provides the developed interface and the business content to make combining this data a quicker, more manageable process.

A fair amount of work must be done before this type of solution can be effective. BW has a building block approach. First, business users must be competent in building queries with BW's querying tool in order to get the right level of data from the InfoCube. Users must be able to use the OLAP functionality BW provides to get the necessary calculations to answer questions. To get data in the InfoCube quickly, a system design needs to be put in place.

Systems that allow information to be accessed quickly must be put in place.

Companies are finding that the best way for the sales force to access data is through a thin-client, Web-enabled solution. This allows the sales force to access reports remotely without having to pass the records of the query over a long distance. Instead, all that moves over the line is HTML code. All record processing is centrally performed on the server before the HTML code is sent.

Currently BW does not have its own thin client solution on general production release, but it does support the use of OLE DB for OLAP so that queries can be accessed through other Web servers. BW will be packaged with thin client functionality starting with release 2.0. This functionality will provide a great help to BW's ability to extend information to the sales force, as well as other entities of the supply chain.

Answering the Key Questions

Having explored the more technical aspects of how Data Warehousing and SAP can help answer tactical business questions, it should be mentioned that Data Warehousing addresses more over-arching business issues as well, because it has the ability to report on data and aggregated levels of business.

For example:

- Which product line sales have been below budget this year?
- What is my projected revenue for the year?
- Which customers order various product lines, driving general marketing versus customers that order specific product lines?

- What percentage of sales revenue is attributable to vendors?

Once these questions have been answered, Data Warehousing can also be used to generate reports on more specific issues, including:

- What have been the buying trends of my top five customers over the year?
- Which customers have seasonal versus non-seasonal demand?
- Which invoicing periods generated the revenue that increased my margin over plan?
- What orders does this customer currently have open?

Specific BW InfoSources can be used to address the key questions. Within the sales and distribution area, InfoSources exist to extract transactional data from the R/3 core tables of orders, shipping and invoicing.

InfoSource Description	Technical Name
SD – Sales Order	2LIS_01_S260
SD – Delivery	2LIS_01_S261
SD – Billing Document	2LIS_01_S262

These InfoSources pull data from R/3's sales information system. Within these InfoSources, data is captured in relation to the customer, materials purchased and other dimensions that characterize the units and dollars associated with each document. Within the records of the documents, orders, shipments and invoices are captured along with the returns and cancellations. Therefore, users can query the InfoCube to determine which customers have had cancellations in the past month. With this information sales representatives can address the account and its issues.

The ability to answer questions in real time, as well as over specific time periods, like quarters or months, can be valuable for both the sales representative and the customer. The company's performance regarding specific customers can be used not only as a sales tool for add-on sales, but also as a marketing tool when looking to attract customers that have similar buying patterns.

As a company learns the advantages of BW and its reporting capabilities, the company's focus can start to move from that of a reactive position, to a proactive position. As recognition of patterns set in, the company can change to meet the needs of its customers to increase the level of service. This higher level of customer service can go a long way toward keeping competitors away from your clients.

SAP and Data Warehousing

Title: *SAP and Data Warehousing*

Author: *W. H. Inmon, Kiva Productions*

Abstract: *SAP's BW is not a real data warehouse. Its intended purpose is to provide an infrastructure for developing specific management reporting applications. In contrast, a true data warehouse architecture will support a complete range of decision support functions. The true data warehouse architecture will leverage the business investment in best of breed query, OLAP and business intelligence tools without limiting their capabilities. Business that requires the robust and valuable amount of information that resides in a data warehouse will implement a true data warehouse outside of SAP by pulling data out of SAP and integrating the data, or will build a true data warehouse along side the SAP cubes.*

Kiva

In the beginning were applications. Then these applications were maintained. And the maintained applications were merged with another company and had to interface with their maintained applications that were never before imagined or designed for working with other applications. And these applications aged and were maintained some more. Then application packages appeared and were added to the collection of applications. Soon there was a complex mess of epic proportions.

More maintenance, more requirements, more time passing, more mergers, more small applications and trying to get information out of the stockpile of applications was an impossibility.

Into this arena came ERP applications such as SAP, BAAN, J D Edwards, and a host of other players. The ERP applications offered to take the Gordian approach and smite the applications stockpile a mighty blow by creating new applications sensitive to current requirements, which were also integrated. The appeal to the businessperson was enormous and soon ERP applications were everywhere. Indeed, as time passed, ERP applications began to make a dent in the older applications stockpile.

Figure 1 shows the appeal of unifying older applications into an ERP framework.

Figure 1: Individual transaction applications are consolidated into ERP

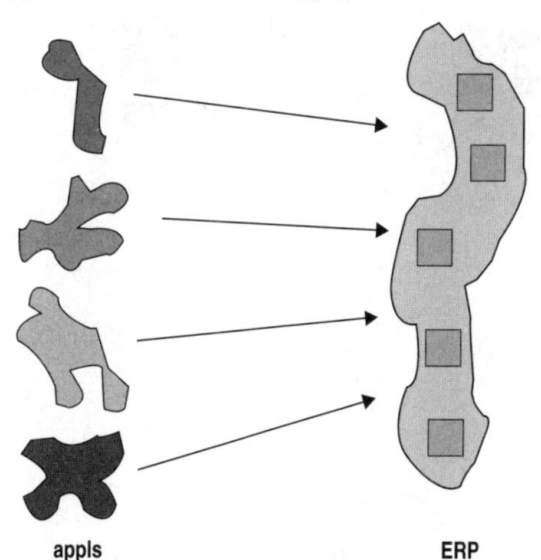

The appeal was such that many corporations around the world began to buy into the ERP application solution, even when it was known that the ERP solution was not cheap or fast. The odor of the older legacy applications stockpile was such that, coupled with the threat of the year 2000, many organizations could not resist the appeal of ERP, whatever the cost.

The Corporate Information Factory

At the same time that applications were evolving into ERP, the larger body of information systems was evolving into a framework known as the corporate information factory. The corporate information factory accommodates many different kinds of processing. Like other forms of information processing, the ERP solution fits very conveniently into the corporate information factory. Figure 2 shows the relationship between the corporate information factory and ERP.

Figure 2: Where ERP fits into the corporate information factory

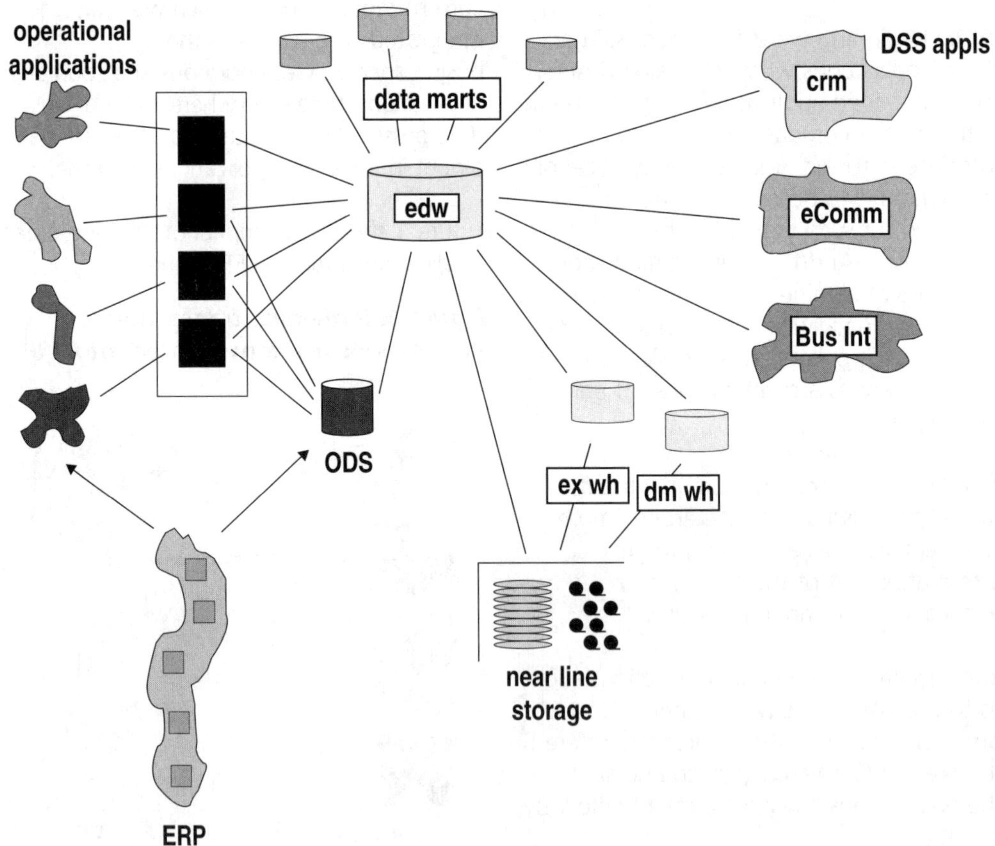

ERP fits into the corporate information factory as either another application and/or as an ODS. In the corporate information factory, ERP executes transactions which then generate data to feed the ODS and/or the data warehouse. The detailed data comes from the ERP application and is integrated with data coming from other applications. The integrated data then finds its way to and through the different part of the corporate information factory. (For an in depth explanation and description of the various components of the corporate information factory, please refer to THE CORPORATE INFORMATION FACTORY, W H Inmon, Claudia Imhoff, John Wiley, 1998.)

The advent of ERP was spawned by the inadequacies and the lack of integration of the early applications. But after implementing part or all of ERP, organizations discovered something about ERP. Organizations discovered that getting information out of ERP was difficult. Simply implementing ERP was not enough.

Figure 3: Getting information out of ERP is difficult

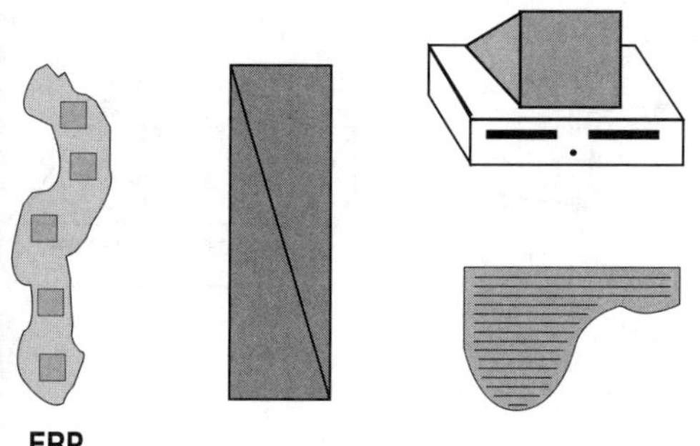

Frustration With ERP

Figure 3 shows the frustration of organizations with ERP after it was implemented.

Many organizations had spent huge amounts of money implementing ERP with the expectation that ERP was going to solve the information systems problems of the organization. Indeed ERP solved SOME of the problems of information systems, but ERP hardly solved ALL of the problems of information systems.

Organization after organization found that ERP was good for gathering data, executing transactions, and storing data. But ERP had no idea how the data was to be used once it was gathered.

Of all of the ERP vendors, SAP was undoubtedly the leader.

Why was it that ERP/SAP did not allow organizations to do easy and smooth analysis on the data contained inside its boundaries? There are many answers to that question, all of which combine together to create a very unstable and uncomfortable information processing environment surrounding ERP/SAP.

The first reason why information is hard to get out of SAP is that data is stored in normalized tables inside of SAP. There are not a few tables. There are a lot of tables. In some case there are 9,000 or more tables that contain various pieces of data in the SAP environment. In future releases of SAP we are told that there will be even more normalized tables.

The problem with 9,000 (or more!) tables storing data in small physically separate units is that in order to make the many units of scattered data meaningful, the small units of data need to be regrouped together. And the work the system must do to regroup the data together is tremendous. Fig 4 shows that in order to get information out of an SAP implementation, that many "joins" of small units of data need to be done.

The system resources alone required to manage and execute the join of 9,000 tables is mind-boggling. But there are other problems with the contemplation of joining 9,000 tables. Some of the considerations are:

- are the right tables being joined?
- do the tables that are being joined specify the proper fields on which to join the data?,
- should an intermediate join result be saved for future reference?
- what if a join is to be done and all the data that is needed to complete the join is not present?
- what about data that is entered incorrectly that participates in a join?
- how can the data be reconstructed so that it will make sense to the user?

In short, there are many considerations to the task of joining 9,000 tables. While performance is a big consideration, the integrity of the data and the mere management of so many tables is its own large task.

But performance and integrity are not the only considerations. Life and the access and usage of information found in SAP's 9,000+ tables is made more difficult when there is either:

- no documentation, or
- significant portions of the documentation that exists is in a foreign language.

While it is true that some documentation of SAP exists in English, major important aspects of SAP do not exist in English. For example, the table and column names of SAP exist in what best can be described as "cryptic German". The table and column

Figure 4: The performance implications of doing joins on 9,000 or more tables is tremendous

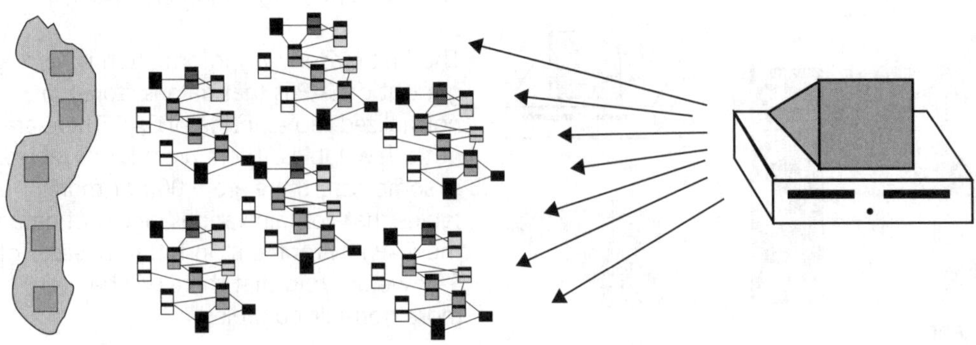

names are mnemonics and abbreviations (which makes life difficult). And there are thousands of table and column names (which makes life very difficult). But the mnemonics and abbreviations of the thousands of table and column names are of German origin (which makes life impossible, unless you are a German application programmer). Trying to work with, read and understand cryptic German table and column names in SAP is very difficult to do.

Figure 5 shows that when the documentation of an ERP is not in the native language of the users of the system then the system becomes even more difficult to use.

But there are other reasons why SAP data stored internally is difficult to use. Another reason for the difficulty of using SAP lies in the proprietary internal storage format of the system that SAP is stored in, as seen in Figure 6.

In particular the data found in pool and cluster tables is stored in a proprietary format. Other data is stored in packed variable format. And furthermore, different proprietary formats are used. There is one proprietary format here, another

Figure 5: Important parts of the documentation are not in English

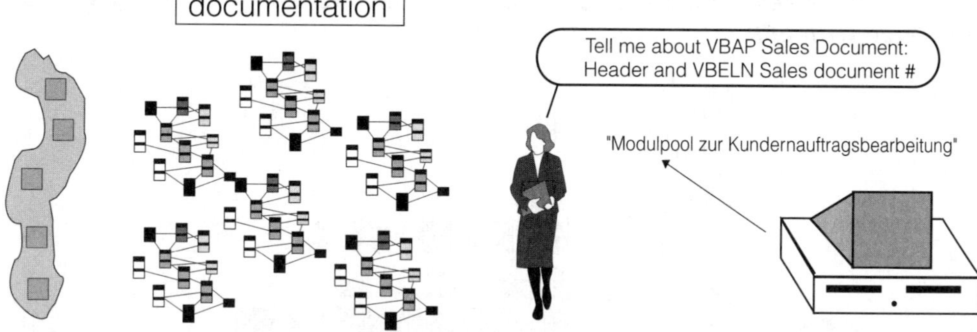

Figure 6: The internal format is proprietary

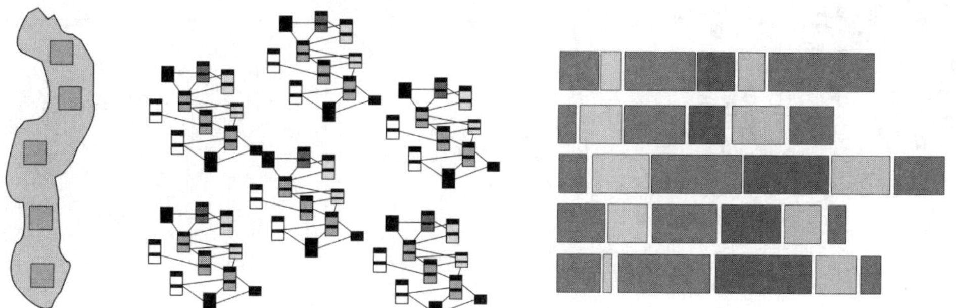

proprietary there, and yet another everywhere. Coupled with the multiple proprietary formats are the proprietary structures used to store hierarchies (such as the cost center hierarchy, which are critical to multi dimensional analysis).

The interrogator or the analyst needs some way to translate the proprietary formatted data and proprietary structured hierarchies into a readable and intelligible format before the data can be deciphered. The key to unlocking the data lies in the application, and SAP has the control of the application code. Unfortunately SAP has gone out of its way to see to it that no one else is able to get to the corporate data that SAP considers its own, not its customers. In short, SAP has created an application where data is optimized for the capture and storage of data. SAP data is not optimized for access and analysis, as seen in Figure 7.

The problem is that it is not sufficient to capture and store data. In order to be useful, data must be able to be accessed and analyzed. There is then a fundamental problem with SAP and that problem is that in order for the SAP application to be useful for analysis, the data managed under SAP must be "freed" from the SAP "data jail".

Figure 7: ERP design is optimized for the capture of data and the storage of data, not the access or the analysis of data. No wonder end user analysts are so frustrated with ERP

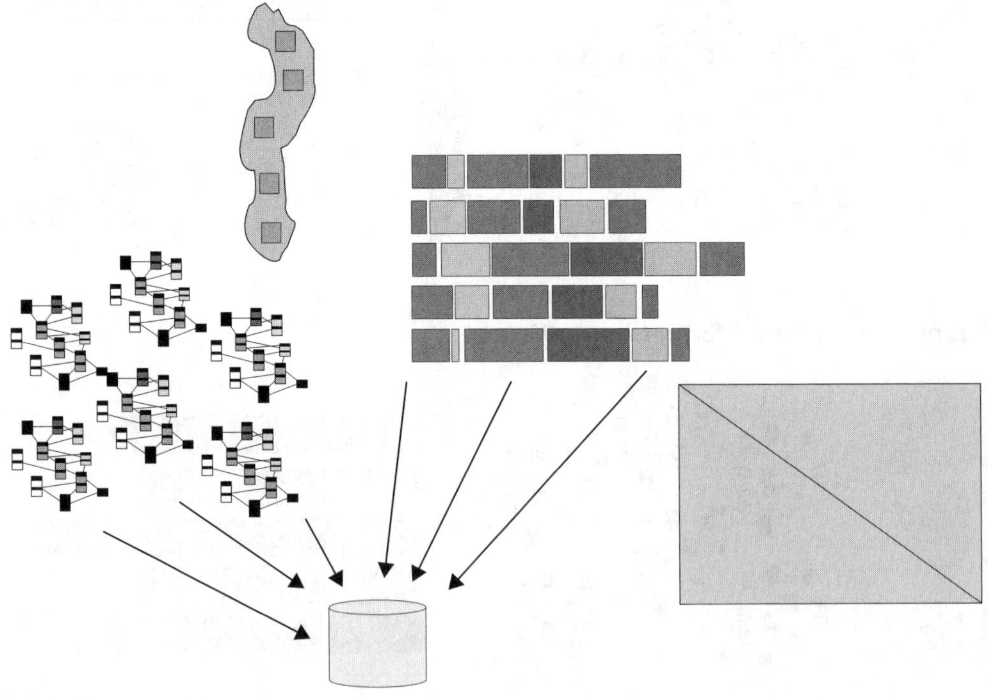

The problems that have been described are not necessarily limited to any one ERP vendor. The problems that have been described are - in small or large part – applicable to all ERP vendors. The only difference from one ERP vendor to the next is the degree of the problem.

Figure 8: Now comes SAP's BW

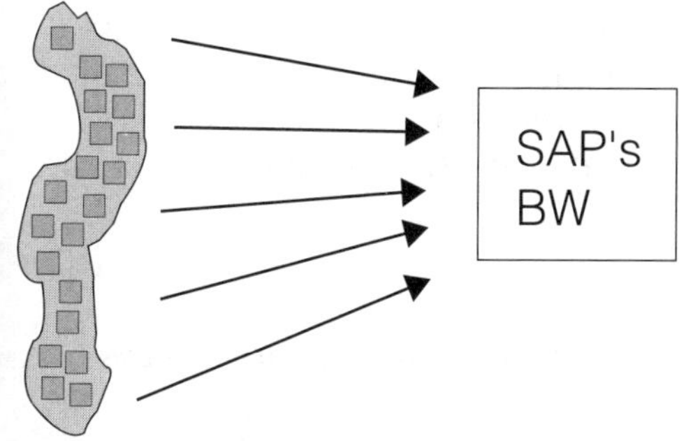

Figure 9: What SAP calls a data warehouse is a bunch of cubes.

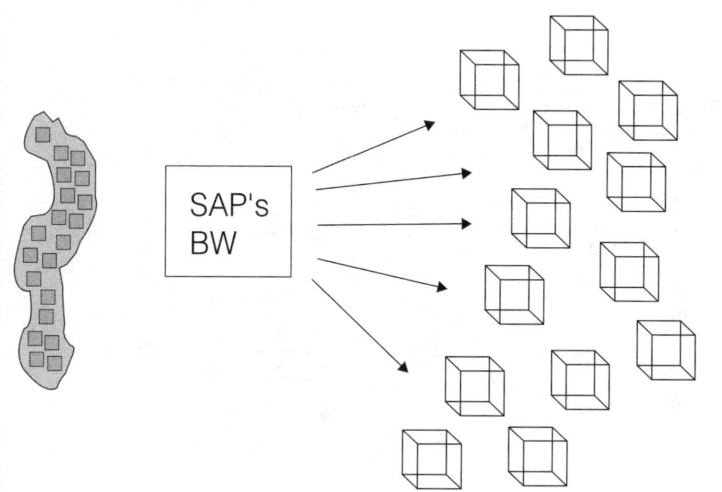

SAP, The ERP Leader

SAP, the leading ERP vendor certainly recognizes the problems that have been created by the placing of data in the SAP "data jailhouse". In response to the need for information that is locked up in the ERP jailhouse, SAP has created what it calls the "Business Information Warehouse" or the "BW". Figure 8 shows that SAP has created the BW.

While it is certainly encouraging that SAP has created a facility for accessing and analyzing data locked up in SAP, whether the form and structure of the BW is really a data warehouse is questionable. SAP has created a collection of cubes (i.e., OLAP like structures where the multi dimensionality of data can be explored.) Figure 9 shows the structures that SAP has created.

There is no doubt that the cubes that SAP has created are welcome. Cubes make the information available within the structure of the confines of the cube. Indeed, given the lack of SAP reports, these cubes provide a partial replacement for that essential part of the SAP architecture that does not exist.

Do Cubes Make A Data Warehouse?

But do cubes constitute a data warehouse? The experience of data warehouse architects outside the SAP environment strongly and emphatically suggest that a collection of cubes - however well designed and however well intentioned - do not supplant the need for a data warehouse.

There are many reasons why a collection of cubes are not a replacement for a data warehouse. This paper will go into some of the more important of these reasons. But it is suggested that there are plenty more reasons why a collection of cubes do not constitute a data warehouse than will be discussed in this white paper.

A Data Warehouse

In order to be specific, what is a data warehouse? (To have a complete description and discussion on data warehousing, please refer to BUILDING THE DATA WAREHOUSE, 2ND EDITION, W H Inmon, John Wiley.) A data warehouse is the granular, corporate, integrated historical collection of data that forms the foundation for all sorts of DSS processing, such as data marts, exploration processing, data mining, and the like. A data warehouse is able to be reused and reshaped in many ways. The data found in the warehouse is voluminous. The data warehouse contains a generous amount of history. The data in the warehouse is integrated across the corporation.

Figure 10: The interface from the many SAP tables to the staging area to the cubes is circumspect

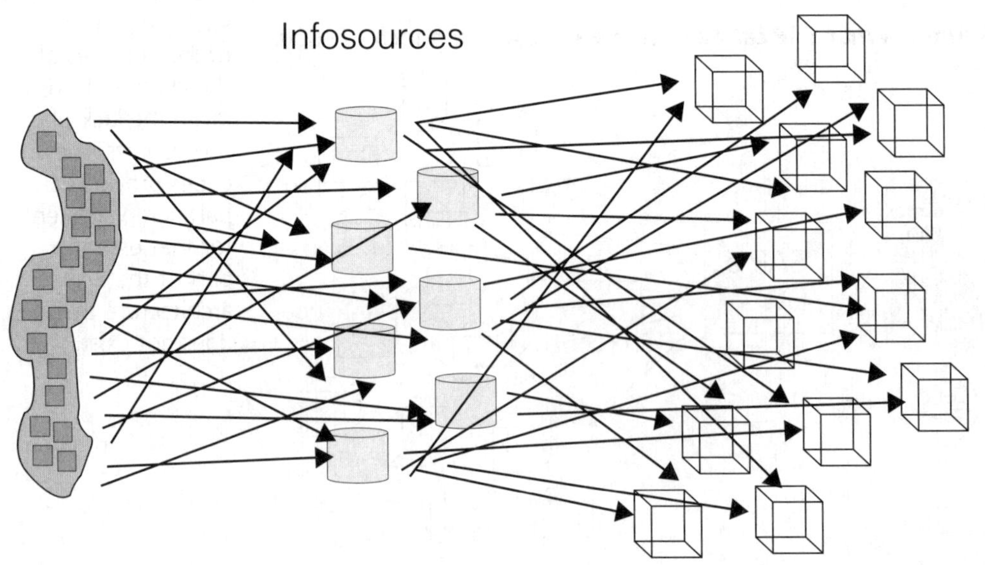

The first reason why a bunch of cubes do not constitute a data warehouse is because of the interface from the cubes to the application. Figure 10 illustrates the problem.

The ERP application contains a lot of tables. The cubes are built from those tables. Each cube must be able to access and combine data from a lot of tables. In order to accomplish this, SAP has created a staging area (in SAP parlance called an "ODS"). The staging area is an intermediate place where data is gathered to facilitate recoverability and the loading of cubes. While a standard data warehouse functionally does the same thing, there are some very important reasons why SAP's staging area is not a data warehouse:

- the granularity of the data inside the staging area is not consistent. Some data is detailed at the transaction level. Some data is weekly summary. Some data is monthly summary. In short the staging area consists of a bunch of tables which have different levels of granularity. Trying to mix data from two or more tables of different granularity is an impossibility, as DSS analysts have found over the years.
- the data inside the staging area is not directly accessible nor comprehensible to anyone using a non SAP OLAP access and analysis tool. While the staging data exists in Oracle, its structure and content is such that it is not useful for direct access by a standard tool such as Brio, Business Objects, or others. In order to access the SAP data, the OLAP vendor must make the third party software work on top of the SAP OLAP engine using an OLE DB interface. The problem with this approach is that the third party OLAP vendor is subject to the limitations of the SAP OLAP engine. It is fair to say that the third party OLAP tools are much more sophisticated than the SAP OLAP tool. Furthermore, if a third party OLAP vendor does not have an OLE DB interface, then the third party OLAP tool cannot access the SAP data at all. By creating a roadblock to the access of the data, SAP has grossly limited the functionality that can be applied to SAP data. In addition, the ODS does not contain dimensional data (master data) and transactional data cannot be joined with dimensional data.
- the tables (InfoSources) in the staging area are segregated by source or destination and data elements (InfoObjects) need not be consistent across InfoSources.
- there is no consistent and reusable historical foundation that is created by the cubes. In a data warehouse, not only is a stable foundation created, but the foundation forms a historical basis of data, usually transaction data. From this historical foundation of data, many types of analysis are created. But there is no such historical foundation created in the staging area of SAP. It is true that SAP can store data historically. But the storage of historical data is done so that there is no compatibility of structure or release across different units of storage. In other words, if you store some data on Jan 1, some more data on Feb 1, and yet some more data on Mar 1, if the structure of data or the release of data has changed, then the data cannot be accessed uniformly. In order to be

historically enabled, historical data must be impervious to the moment in time and the release of the storage of data.

In short, SAP staging area does not provide a basis for access to data by third party tools, does not provide integrated data, does not provide a historical foundation of data, and does not provide transaction level data. Instead, a web of cubes is created that require constant refreshment.

If there were only a few cubes to be built then the complexity and size of the interface would not be an issue. Even if a cube can build off of data that has been staged, the interface is still very complex.

Every cube requires its own customized interface. Once a corporation starts to build a lot of cubes, the complexity of the interface itself becomes its own issue.

Furthermore, over time, as the corporation continues to add cubes, the interface becomes more and more complex. One way to calculate how many programs to be created is to estimate how many cubes will be required.

Suppose m cubes will be required.

Now estimate how many individual programs will be needed in order to access ERP tables. Suppose on the average that 36 tables need to be accessed by each cube. Now suppose a program can reasonably combine access to tables by doing a four way join. (If more than four tables are joined in a single program, then the program becomes complex and performance starts to really suffer.)

Furthermore, suppose that a staging area serves ten cubes. In this case the ten cubes

Figure 11: The number of interfaces and the lack of consistency of granularity is daunting

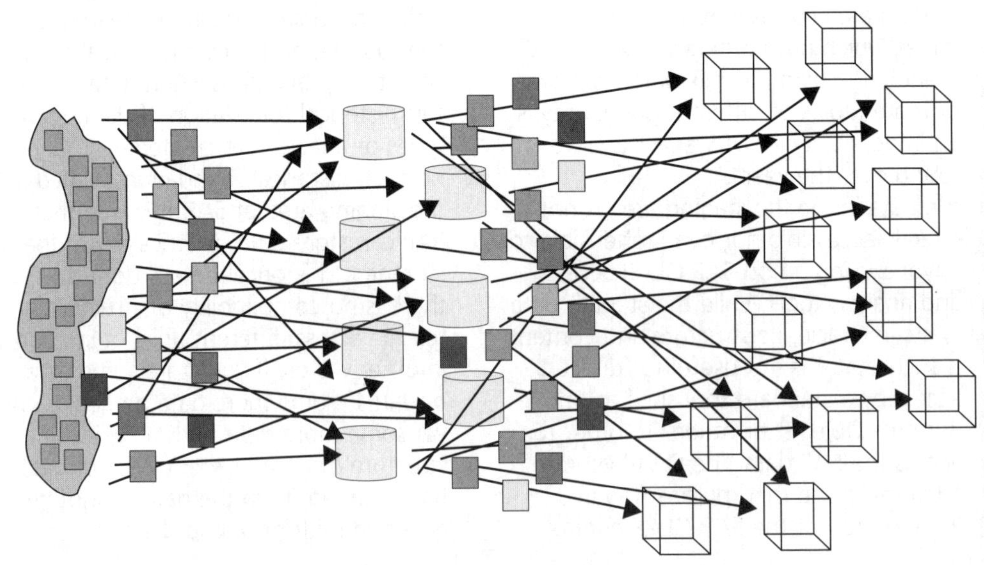

would all have the same level of granularity.

Under these circumstances, the number of interface programs that need to be written and maintained are:

((36 / 4) x m) / 10 = (9 x m) / 10

If there are 25 cubes then (9 x 25)/10 = 22.5 programs need to be written. But if the SAP installation is large and there are a lot of cubes, then as many as 200 cubes may need to be created. The number of programs that need to be written and maintained in this case are:

(9 x 200) / 10 = 180 programs

It does not require a vivid imagination to see that the interface between the cubes and the SAP tables can become its own bottleneck. Both the initial creation of the interface and the ongoing maintenance of the interface present challenges.

Figure 11 shows that the complexity of the creation and maintenance of the interface between the SAP tables and the cubes is its own consideration.

But the creation and the maintenance of the interface programs is not the only issue. The next issue is that of the resources needed to keep the cubes up to date.

Figure 12 shows that significant hardware resources are required in order to keep the cubes in synch with the latest version of data in the transaction environment.

Every time the world of transactions changes, the staging area that the cube

Figure 12: The sheer amount of hardware resources required for constantly maintaining the cubes is tremendous

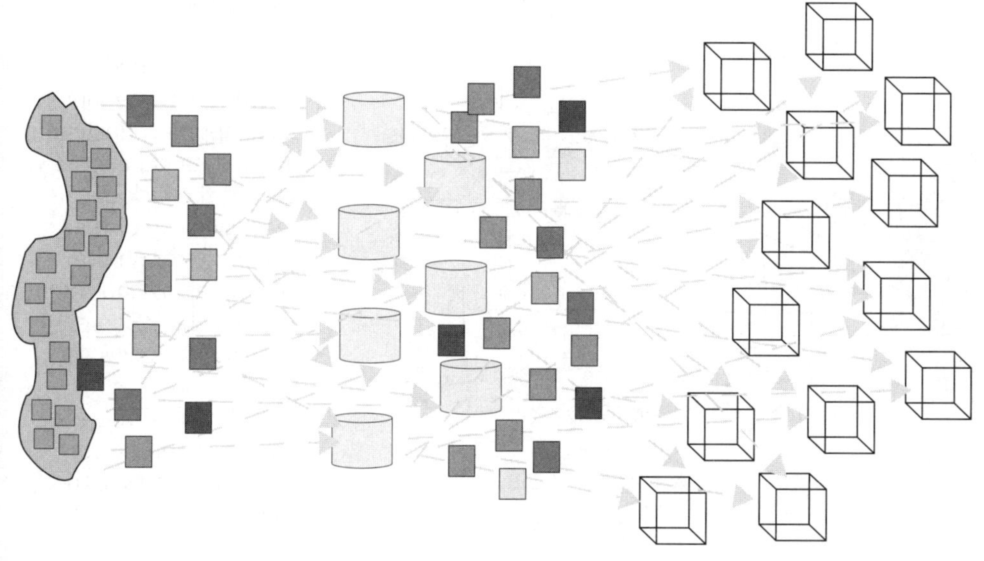

accesses needs to be changed. Then the cubes that emanate from the staging area that depends on data from the transaction that changed each require update. If update is not done, then one cube will be operating on and reporting on data from a different point in time than other cubes. In doing so, the consistency of reports coming from the cubes will vary, and in some cases vary considerably.

Hardware Resources

But updating one or more staging areas and then the cubes the staging area services every time a change is made in the transaction environment is a very expensive thing to do. The sheer number of resources required for constant creation and recreation of cube data is intimidating.

Keeping constantly moving data in synch is only one aspect of the problem of managing multiple cubes without a real data warehouse. Another challenge is that of keeping the structural semantics of the data in the cubes in synch as well. For example, suppose the definition and structure of a table in the ERP environment changes. The change has the potential for rippling throughout the staging environment and the cube environment, requiring the alteration of the structure of each cube (or at least many cubes). Each cube that is affected must be destroyed and rebuilt. In some cases this is not too much work. But in other cases this is an enormous amount of work. And in yet other cases the rebuilding of significant portions of the staging areas and the cubes is out of the question.

Figure 13: The ripple effect of making a single change in the SAP environment on the cubes is intimidating

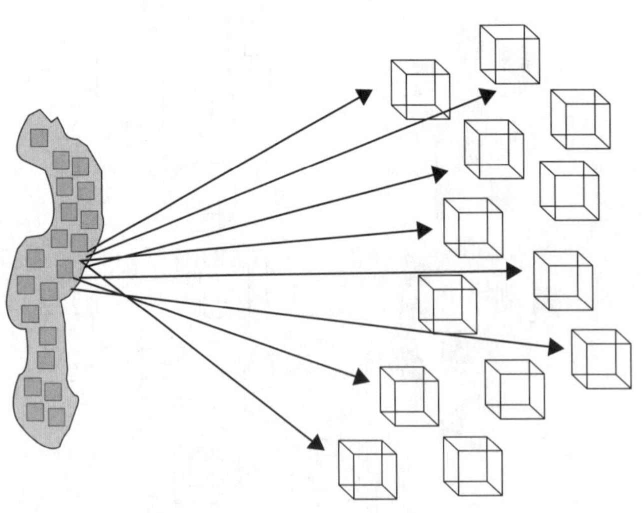

Figure 13 shows the ripple effect of structural changes throughout the cube environment.

Another very bad downside of the multiple cube approach instead of a real data warehouse is that of the lack of reconcilability of data coming through the staging areas and through to the cubes. Figure 14 shows this downside.

Fig 14 shows that each cube is different from each other cube and yields different results when queried. The cubes are shaped by the requirements of the different members of the end user community. The cubes are different in many ways:

- different granularity,
- different dimensions,
- different calculations of roll ups of data,
- different volumes of data, and so forth.

It is not surprising that cubes are constructed differently because different cubes serve different communities. But this inherent difference in the structure and content of cubes leads to a problem with the lack of integration and the lack of consistency of data found in each cube.

Not surprisingly, one cube provides management with one answer and another cube supplies management with another answer. What is management to do? Who is management to believe?

Furthermore, the ability to reconcile results across cubes is circumspect. There is no "single point of truth" on which to make decisions. When viewed from the organizational perspective, no wonder the organization is so frustrated with the multiple cube approach to making decisions.

But inconsistency of information across cubes is not the only problem. There is no basic interchange of information across cubes as well. One of the powerful uses of OLAP technology has long been the ability to do drill down and drill across processing. But SAP's OLAP product builds and treats each cube as if it were a singular entity, with no ability to communicate or coordinate analysis across multiple cubes.

Figure 14: Reconciliation of information across cubes is impossible

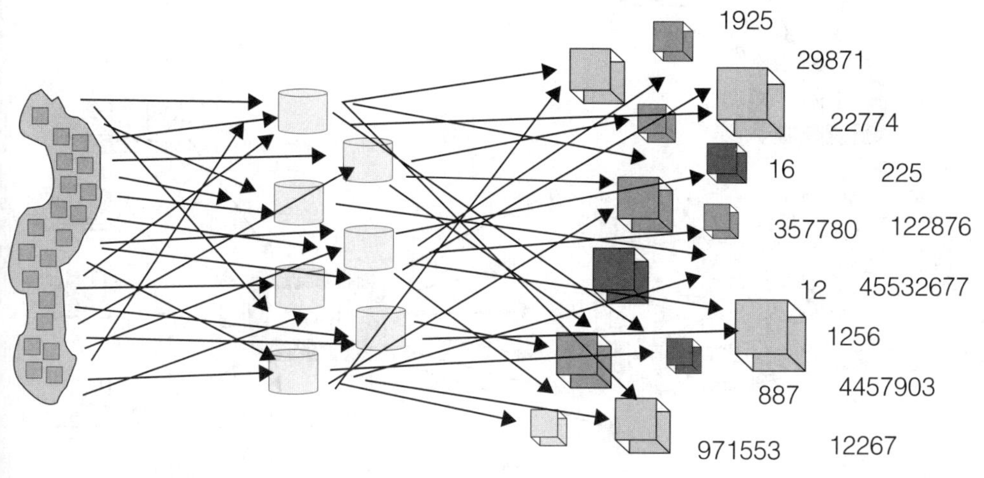

Other SAP Problems

But there are other problems with the SAP multiple cube approach to DSS processing. The problem is that many organizations already have a major investment in third party OLAP tools. The problem is effectively that SAP only allows its OLAP tool to access the cubes. Third party OLAP tools can access SAP data but only at a very superficial level. If third party tools could get at the transactional data or the cube data found in SAP cubes or staging areas then there would not be a problem. But, for the most part, SAP bars standard third party tools of access and analysis from getting to the SAP staging area or cube data. Figure 15 shows that the SAP solution is a highly proprietary solution.

SAP will say that third party OLAP tools can access SAP data. This is true in the sense that SAP allows access through SAP interfaces. But the third party OLAP tools have to access the SAP data through an SAP interface. Stated differently, the third party tools have no direct and independent access to the SAP data. In short, the third party OLAP tools outside of ERP are out of luck. Unfortunately for SAP, the community of third party OLAP access and analysis tools are well entrenched and are already well accepted. There is a mature audience of users of third party OLAP access and analysis tools that cannot directly use SAP data. Many corporations have a significant capital and intellectual investment made in these third party OLAP tools and would like to see a constructive interface to SAP, if SAP would allow it.

Figure 15: Third party tools for access and analysis of SAP data are used awkwardly if at all

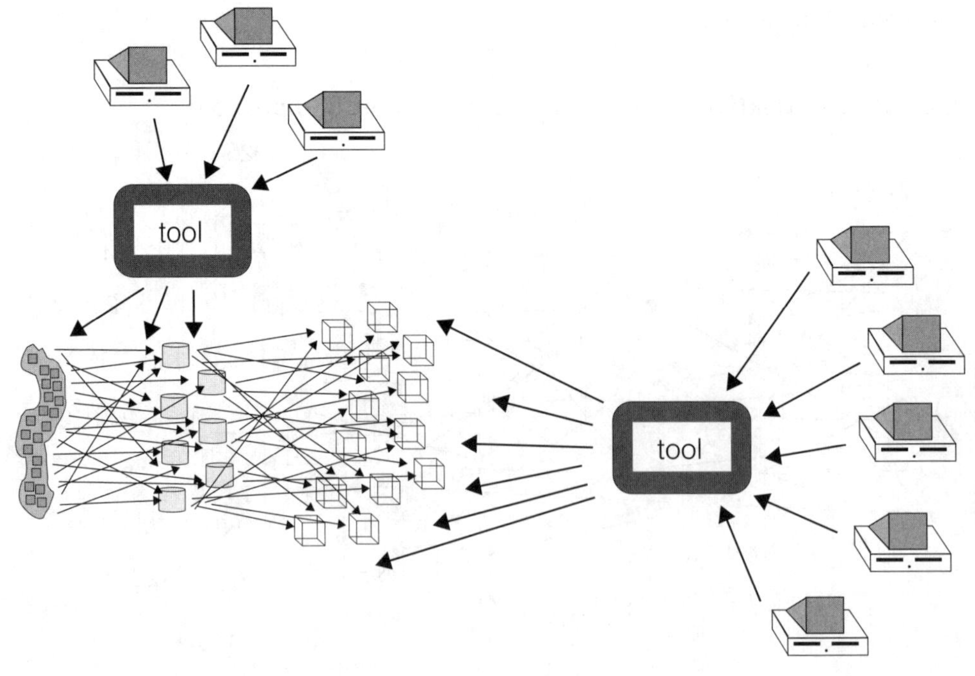

Redundant Data

But there are other reasons why the SAP multiple cube approach instead of a real data warehouse is expensive. There is a tremendous amount of redundant data across the cubes that are created. Figure 16 shows this redundancy of data.

The redundancy of data occurs because each cube must effectively capture, restructure and store the same data that each other cube stores. (Strictly speaking this may not be true. Under some circumstances for a small number of tables, there may not be much redundancy of data. But over many tables over normal circumstances, it is normal for much redundant detailed data to be repeated in cube after cube.) The creation of redundant data implies that the cubes are much larger and much more expensive than they have to be.

The Challenge Of Including Non SAP Data

Another problem of the SAP multiple cube approach is that of what to do about non-SAP data that needs to be included in DSS analysis. Figure 17 shows this dilemma.

Fig 17 shows that there are two choices. One choice is to integrate the non-SAP data into the R/3 portion of SAP and then include this data into the SAP cubes.

The second choice is to try to incorporate non-SAP data directly into BW without bringing that data into SAP R/3 at all. This direct approach is very appealing. The problem is that in order to do this, customers must write complex ABAP programs to reconcile SAP and non-SAP data. This may be able to be done for some very simple sorts of data, but for the

Figure 16: The amount of redundant data is enormous

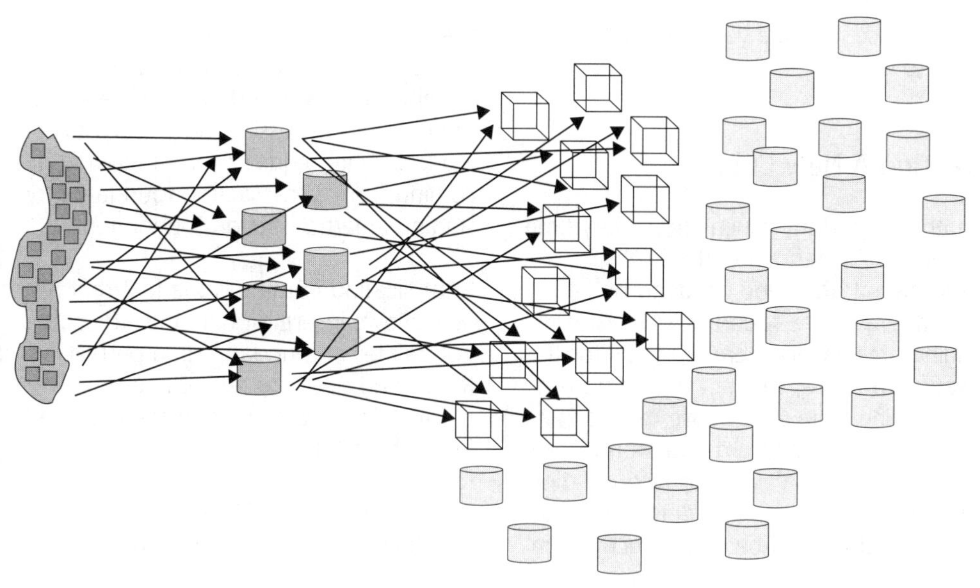

Figure 17: Integrating non SAP data into the DSS architecture is a real trick

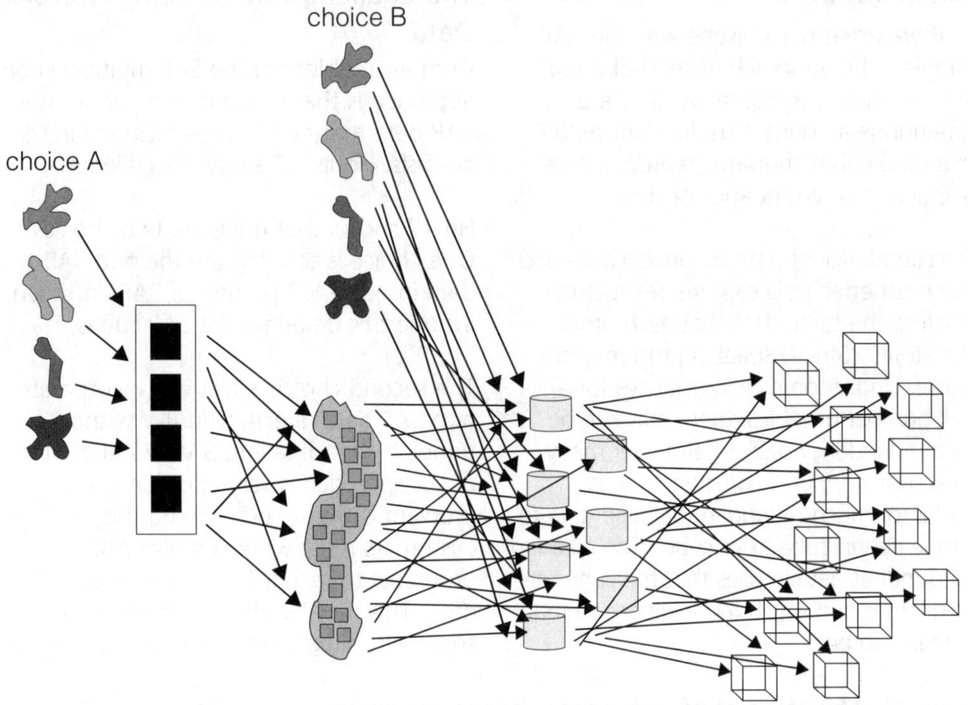

choice B

choice A

general case, this is a very, very difficult thing to do.

Creating A New Cube

Another important issue is that every time a new cube is defined in the SAP environment, the cube needs to be fed from the raw data found in SAP or from a staging area. While there are tools for the creation of cubes, the fact that there is no intermediary data warehouse means that all cubes must start from scratch if a staging area doesn't exist as a foundation. If in fact there were a real data warehouse, the new cube could be built directly from the data warehouse, not from the raw transaction data. By using a data warehouse as a foundation for new cubes, the designer bypasses huge amounts of work that are required for integrating data coming from a transaction foundation or a staging area/transaction foundation.

Complicating matters is the fact that SAP only allows inserts of data into the cubes, not deletes and updates. In a perfect world there is no need for periodic refurbishment of data. But in a real world there is need for such activity.

A final issue of the SAP cube approach is that there is no satisfactory place for historical data. Figure 18 depicts this shortcoming of SAP.

The SAP R/3 application is good for holding a modicum of historical data. But when it comes to years and years of historical data, the SAP application is hardly the optimal place for historical data. Holding significant amounts of historical data in the SAP application impairs the running of day-to-day transactions.

And holding large amounts of historical data in the cubes created by SAP BW is not the thing to do either. A cube is limited in its ability to optimize the structure of data for more than one client at a time. For this reason a cube may be good for one user and useless for another user. If historical data were to be placed in the cube environment, the historical data would have to be placed in many cubes. The problem is that placing historical data in many cubes costs a lot.

A second problem with placing historical data in cubes is what to do with the historical data when the cube must be reconstructed. It is one thing to reconstruct a cube when the base data is all in one place to begin with. It is quite another thing to reconstruct a cube when only part oft he data is available for reconstruction. And reconstructing a cube when there is a lot of data already residing in the cube is not a pleasant prospect either.

One approach to the management of historical data is that of putting the historical data in the staging area. But there are many problems with this approach. The first is that the staging area contains data at many levels of granularity. A data warehouse bypasses this problem by placing historical data in the warehouse at the most granular transactional level.

Figure 18: Another issue is that there is only a handful of historical data that is available

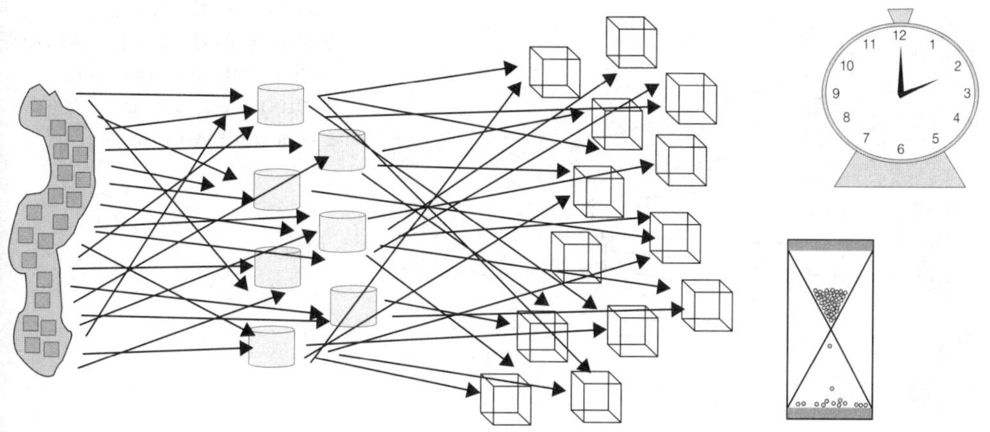

What Does The Multiple Cube Approach Do?

What then does the SAP multiple cube approach do? In order to answer this question, there must be a discussion on management reporting. There are many facets to and types of management reports. Management reporting can be done for:

- "what if " analysis,
- exception reporting,
- critical factor analysis,
- statistical analysis,
- exploration analysis,
- data mining,
- periodic standard reports, and so forth.

Management reports serve many different levels of the company, from the president to the newly minted MBA. The reports that are available from SAP barely scratch the surface for management's needs for information. The multiple cube approach barely provides a sliver of the spectrum of reports that are needed.

Figure 19: A much more rational approach is to pull the data out of SAP and into a real data warehouse

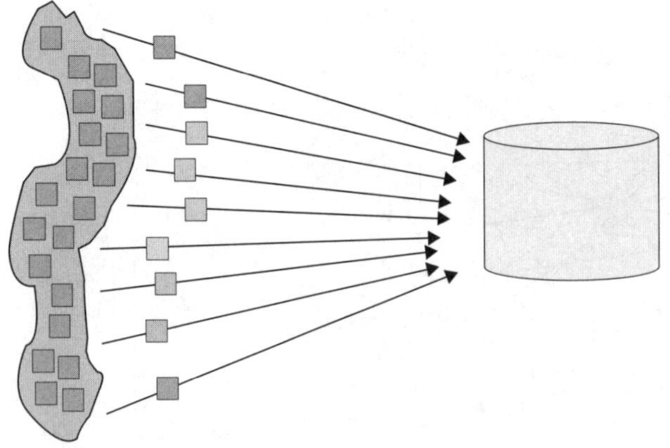

Given that SAP R/3 effectively has no operational reports (as opposed to management reports), the multiple cubes offered by SAP BW make a first attempt at providing the necessary information.

In order to be most effective, SAP's transaction detailed data needs to be stored in an integrated, historical manner where easy access can be made by any tool desired by the end user. SAP's current solution is light years away from this structure.

A More Rational Approach

A much more rational approach for the execution of informational processing is to create a proper foundation of integrated, detailed, historical transaction data. In order to create this foundation, it is necessary to pull detailed data out of SAP and create a real data warehouse, not a multiple cube imitation of a data warehouse. Figure 19 shows that a real data warehouse can be created from data pulled from the SAP environment. Fig 19 shows that the detailed transaction data is pulled out of SAP, integrated and/or reintegrated, and placed into a real data warehouse.

Once the real data warehouse is built:

- the detailed foundation of data can be reused by many users,
- can be reconciled,
- can have detailed data stored in a single place,
- can have historical data stored,
- can have non-SAP data easily integrated into the data warehouse,
- can be accessed by standard tools, and so forth.

In other words, the problems of the multiple cube approach espoused by SAP are solved by pulling the data out of SAP into a real data warehouse, not a multiple cube facsimile.
The multiple cubes of information that SAP has created can easily be created from the data warehouse, as seen in Figure 20.

Figure 20: The cubes of information are easily built and easily accessible

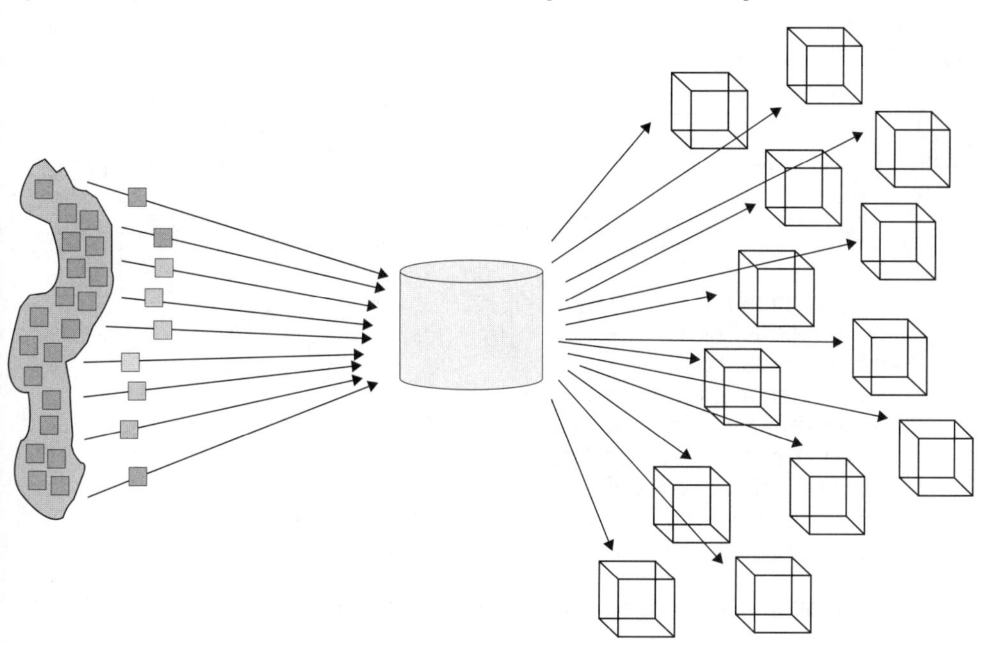

There is no loss of functionality by going to a real data warehouse outside of SAP.

The environment that is created is shown by Figure 21.

Figure 21: Building a real data warehouse with SAP data outside of SAP

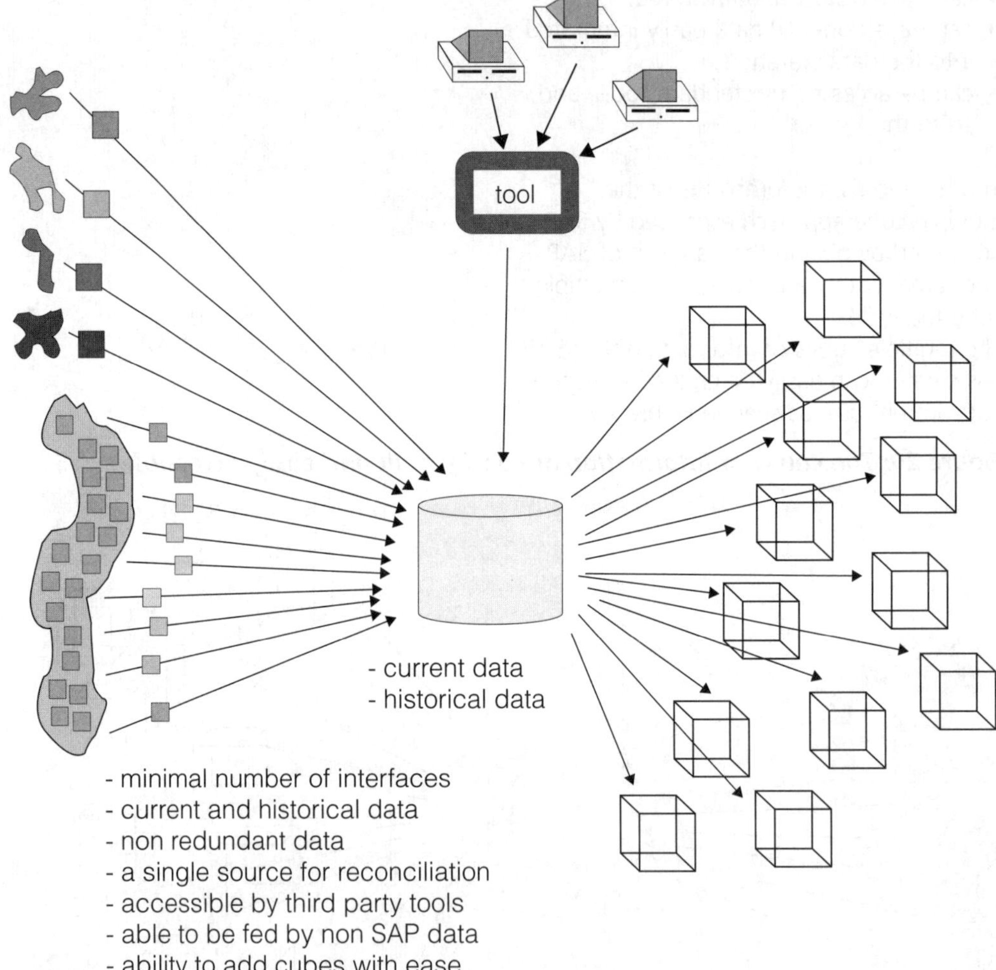

Building a real data warehouse with SAP data ourside of SAP.

Another way to contrast the differences between a real data warehouse and the cube approach shown by SAP is illustrated by Figure 22.

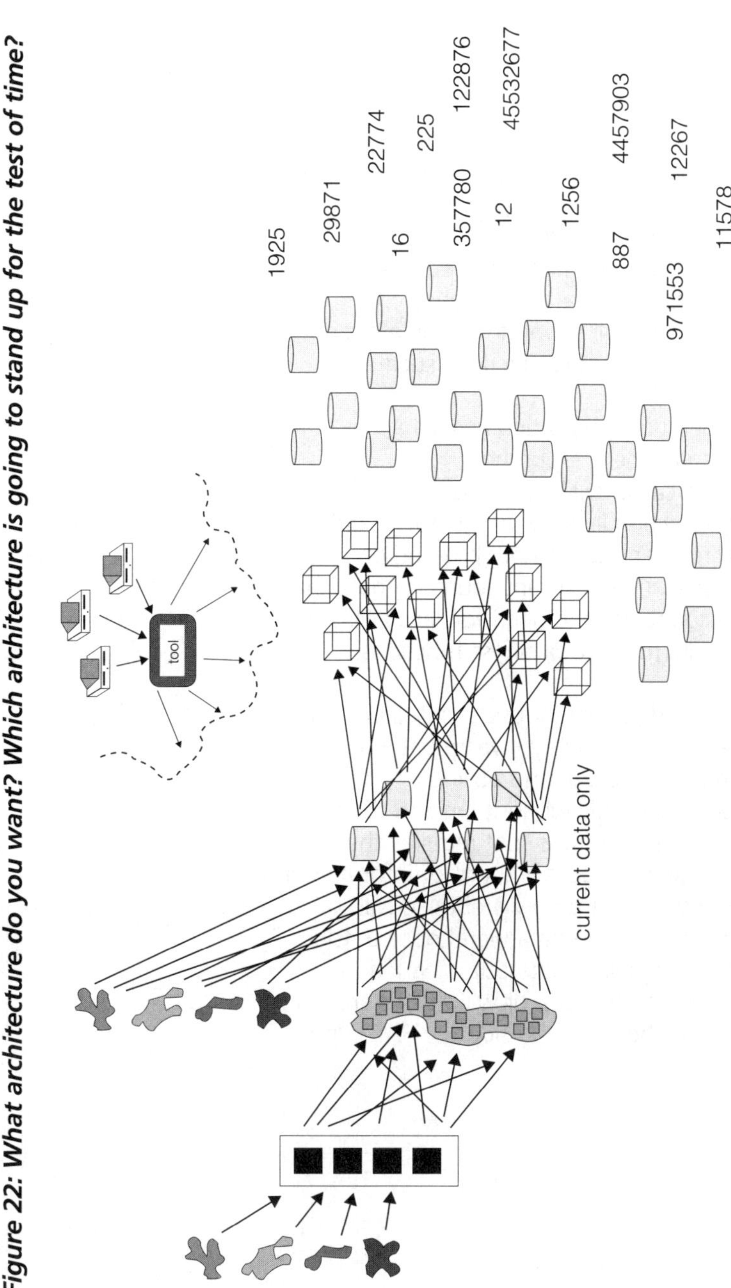

Figure 22: What architecture do you want? Which architecture is going to stand up for the test of time?

Figure 22 shows that there are major architectural differences between the two approaches.

Conclusion

SAP's BW is not a real data warehouse. Its intended purpose is to provide an infrastructure for developing specific management reporting applications. In contrast, a true data warehouse architecture will support a complete range of decision support functions such as:

- Operational reporting as well as management reporting,
- Root cause analysis at the detailed transaction level with drill down, drill across, and drill through based on a single and consistent source of data that accounts for the need for reconciliation across multiple business functions.

The true data warehouse architecture will leverage the business investment in best of breed query, OLAP and business intelligence tools without limiting their capabilities. Business that requires the robust and valuable amount of information that resides in a data warehouse will implement a true data warehouse outside of SAP by pulling data out of SAP and integrating the data, or will build a true data warehouse along side the SAP cubes.

SAP R/3 Data Warehousing and Application Integration

Title: *SAP R/3 Data Warehousing and Application Integration*
Author: *Hummingbird*
Abstract: *Hummingbird Genio Suite is a leading solution that enables IT professionals to access and exchange data and metadata on an enterprise basis regardless of hardware or database technology.*
This white paper is one in a series that provides insight into Genio Suite, its core components and the solutions it enables, as well as related technological issues.

Introduction

Organizations today fi nd the SAP R/3 application suite invaluable for running day-to-day operations. With SAP R/3, they manage operational areas such as fi nancial accounting, human resources, manufacturing, logistics, sales, and distribution. However, for a host of reasons, these organizations have critical data stored in other business applications spread throughout the enterprise. These applications typically reside on heterogeneous platforms and in dissimilar database technologies than those driving the SAP R/3 system.

In order to further competitive advantage through faster, better decision making, organizations must fi nd ways to include SAP R/3 in their data warehousing strategy. Addition-ally, to facilitate an e-commerce ready environment — to e-enable the enterprise —organizations need to exchange SAP R/3 data with other mission critical applications. Essentially, there is a rapidly growing need for a single solution capable of handling the SAP R/3 data exchange requirements for warehousing and application integration.

This paper explores the opportunity presented by successfully integrating SAP R/3 data with other business applications throughout the enterprise. Moreover, it addresses the challenges of SAP R/3 integration and the requirements for overcoming those obstacles. Finally, this paper discusses how, with the right solution, organizations can simultaneously achieve seamless SAP R/3 application integration as well as fulfi ll the need to include SAP R/3 data in their data warehousing strategies.

E-enabling the SAP R/3 Enterprise

Currently, organizations are changing the way they think about business. Bill Gates' idea of "Business at the Speed of Thought" is now a reality and organizations are taking steps to recast themselves as e-businesses. They are altering business models, opening up new opportunities in previously unthinkable regions, and introducing innovative applications that enable unparalleled collaboration between themselves, their customers, and business partners.

At the core of this exciting time is the need for robust universal data exchange solutions. For SAP R/3 driven organizations universal data exchange provides seamless integration of their ERP system data with other applications spread throughout the enterprise. Moreover, a comprehensive universal data exchange solution simultaneously manages the complexities of including SAP R/3 data in organizational data warehousing initiatives. It is with this ability to combine the wealth of information housed in the R/3 System with analytical applications and application integration strategies that the real opportunity lies for e-enabling the SAP R/3 enterprise.

Architectures

SAP R/3 Architecture

Enterprise Resource Planning (ERP) systems can be thought of in terms of three layers of logic — the presentation logic, or front end access layer, the business logic, or application layer, and the data logic, or the database layer that drives the system.

Presentation Layer
Used for browsing SAP R/3 data, this layer, commonly referred to as the user interface or GUI, can be thought of as a window to an organization's SAP R/3 system. Additionally, data entry (OLTP) is carried out via the presentation layer.

Application Layer
Business rules and logic for SAP R/3 applications, such as those designed for human resources, fi nance, and sales and distribution, are stored at this layer. They work with data that they fetch from the database layer and write the resulting new data back to that layer. SAP R/3 system application enhancements, or customization work (performed using the SAP ABAP Workbench) is carried out at the application layer. The application layer manages much of the data integrity involved with the R/3 System. Because of this, any data access (e.g. directly accessing tables via the metadata layer) should be

Figure 1: SAP architecture

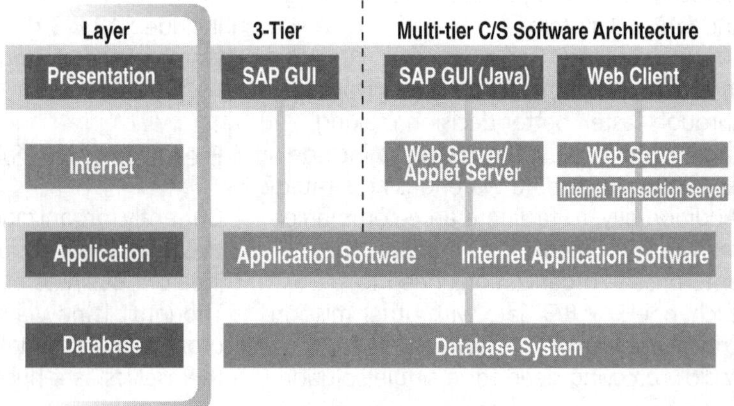

limited to read-only as allowing write capability may lead to inconsistent, unreliable, or corrupt data in the system.

Database Layer
The database layer manages an organization's operational or transactional data. It also manages the metadata maintained in the R/3 System that describes the database structure. The database layer, run by industry standard relational database managementsystems (RDBMS) harnessing structured query language (SQL) for defi ning and manipulating all data, drives the SAP R/3 system.

Challenges Presented by the SAP R/3 Architecture
This three tier architecture, and the underlying data structure, delivers maximum performance. The SAP R/3 data structure is designed in such a way as to optimize operational effi ciency in the system. However, in accomplishing this, the resultant data structure does not easily lend itself to data warehousing projects or application integration initiatives.

There are more than 50,000 logical tables in the most recent release of SAP R/3. It is not diffi cult to see how this may cause some "navigation" problems in fi nding, getting at, and extracting desired information. On top of this, the normalized data structure poses additional challenges in that a thorough knowledge of the way in which data is stored within SAP R/3 — in transparent, pool, and cluster tables — is required in order to locate appropriate and complete information for extraction. An additional obstacle that the SAP R/3 architecture presents is the proprietary naming convention of tables. For example, a table may be called "KNA1" in the R/3 system, but might actually be a "Customer Master" table. Understanding this naming convention is extremely diffi cult at best and getting at and deciphering SAP R/3 metatables is not an easy task either. Again, a thorough knowledge of SAP R/3 data structure is required to know what information is stored where as well as what tables the related information or dependent data is kept.

SAP Business Information Warehouse Architecture
SAP Business Information Warehouse (SAP BW) enables organizations to create data warehouses from SAP R/3 operational sources. SAP BW can also be broken down into three layers:

- A top layer made up of the Business Explorer, comprising Business Information Warehouse's client components for the end user,
- A middle layer representing SAP BW Server, and
- A bottom layer made up of the OLTP systems from which data is extracted.

Business Information Warehouse is designed to automate a good portion of the data warehousing process, to minimize implementation time, and to require the least amount of administration. Three major components make up SAP BW: Production Data Extractors, Staging Engine, and Administrator's Workbench.

Production Data Extractor
The Production Data Extractor is a set of technologies designed to extract data from SAP R/3 OLTP applications. Initially, a

complete refresh of the data warehouse is required, loading all OLTP data from the R/3 System. Subsequent updates of SAP BW involve subset data loads, or incremental change (delta updates) replenishment.

Leveraging the SAP Intermediate Document format (IDOC), the Production Data Extractor is designed to optimize the extraction of SAP R/3 data into Business Information Warehouse. Non-SAP data sources are connected using certifi ed third party solutions, such as Genio MetaLink for SAP R/3, or through hard coded extraction programs.

Staging Engine
The Staging Engine is employed to implement automated data mapping and transfor-mation.Application Link Enabling (ALE), SAP's persistent messaging middleware, is used for data transport from OLTP platforms to the SAP BW server.

The Staging Engine initiates and extracts from OLTP systems based on a defi ned schedule basis. Typically, an extract job will be based on a selected, fi ltered set of data. Following extraction, production data undergoes a series of mapping and transformation processes prior to being loaded into InfoCubes — the central data containers of Business Information Warehouse. Once there, business logic can be applied, ranging from aggregations to arbitrary calculations on key performance indicators.

Administrator 's Workbench
The Administrator's Workbench is a set of tools driven by a graphical interface to specify and maintain InfoCube defi nitions as well as all technical metadata (such as connected source systems and their sources with the corresponding mapping and transformation rules), and the business logic for InfoCube updates.

Basically, the Administrator's Workbench provides effective support not only for setting up SAP BW, but also for monitoring performance and usage, and for accommodating changing update scheduling, requirements and such administrative tasks as access privilege assignment and report catalog maintenance.

InfoCubes — The information foundation of SAP BW
Business Information Warehouse is designed to provide end users with the ability to look at data from many different perspectives, to transparently combine data from various sources and to drill down from one level of detail to another. To enable this, SAP BW stores data in a star schema format.

InfoCubes are the central containers of data used in analysis and reporting. They contain two types of data: key fi gures, or metrics, and characteristics, or dimensions — key fi gures being quantifi able values such as revenue, while characteristics are elements needed to compute and present key fi gures. Characteristics for revenue, for instance, would include the corresponding product or customer.

Essentially, an InfoCube is a set of relational tables arranged in a star schema — one large fact table at the center and several surrounding dimension tables. Fact tables hold key fi gures at the lowest level of granularity while dimension tables store the necessary characteristics for reporting and analyzing the key fi gures.

Challenges Presented by the Business Information Warehouse Architecture
As stated in a recent MetaGroup report, when most — greater than 80 percent — of operational data is handled by SAP R/3, the Business Information Warehouse is the platform of choice for data warehousing. However, if operational data handled by SAP R/3 is 20 percent or less, a platform neutral approach is considered the best method for data warehousing. In between these two extremes, organizations are left to a preferential decision.

Regardless of the chosen data warehousing strategy, there are some issues that organizations must consider, the most important of which being that data from ot sources must be included in warehouse tables.

If SAP BW is chosen as the data warehousing platform, data from non-SAP systems must be included to provide knowledge workers with a complete view of the business reality. Loading and replenishing Business Information Warehouse environments with non-SAP data requires SAP certifi ed solutions to ensure that information housed in the system is reliable.

Figure 2: SAP Business Information Warehouse Architecture

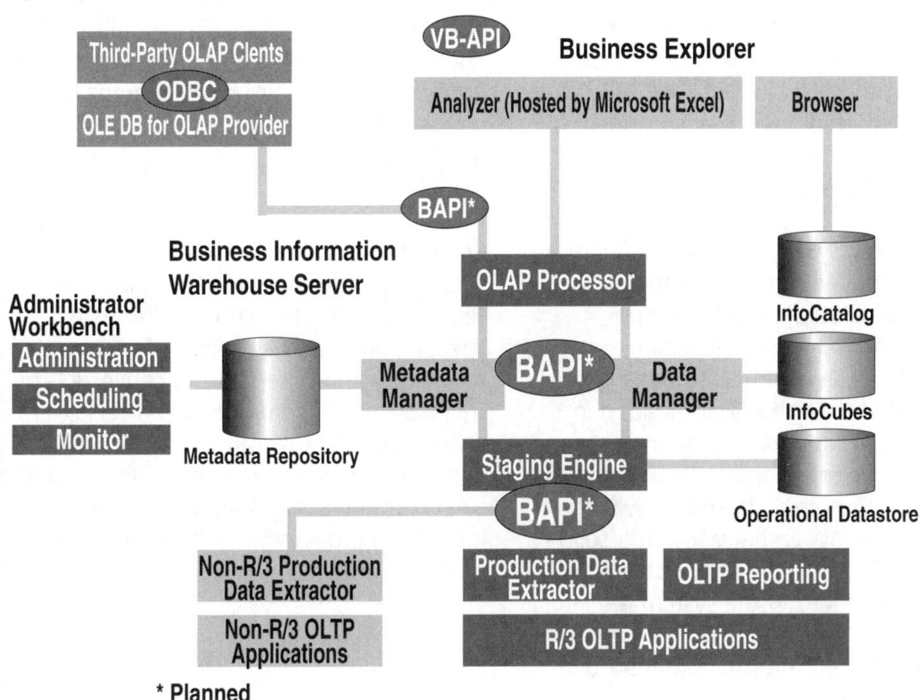

Including SAP R/3 Data in Platform Neutral Data Warehouses

Organizations may elect to warehouse enterprise data, including that stored in ERP systems, based on a platform neutral strategy. For SAP R/3 driven organizations this means having to get at and extract desired data, transform it into appropriate formats, and load warehouse tables with the resultant information.

Extracting SAP R/3 data for exchange with external systems has traditionally been a complex task involving custom coded processes. Given that more than 50,000 tables comprise the SAP R/3 system, just locating desired information can pose a signifi cant challenge. While transparent tables are more readily accessible as they conform to standard relational database table structures, pool and cluster tables present unique obstacles due to the complexity of the dependency relationships involved with them. In fact, SAP R/3 extract projects require the work of seasoned SAP consultants which can mean incurring considerable costs.

Moreover, costs will continue to mount as any future data extract requirements would demand additional consulting fees. Without SAP R/3 data integration, organizations are not free to dynamically choose what data they want loaded into their decision support system and, therefore, cannot provide a complete view to their decision makers and knowledge workers. The fact is that without a solid understanding of the SAP R/3 structure — how data is stored in the system — organizations will require skilled personnel to extract desired information and build the processes for transforming and loading that raw data into warehouse systems.

Enterprise Application Integration

By defi nition, SAP ALE (Application Link Enabling) technology for distributed application systems permits effi cient, reliable business communications to achieve a high degree of integration between technically separate systems.

ALE technology is based on the controlled and timely exchange of business messages, with synchronous and asynchronous communication mechanisms allowing demand-driven application integration. SAP R/3 has pre-confi gured distribution scenarios to provide proven templates that organizations can customize to suite their own solutions.

ALE Architecture

The open ALE architecture allows non-SAP applications and third-party systems to be connected up to a distributed system architecture.

Business messages are generated by ALE application services, and ALE distribution services link the business level with the technical level, including, for instance, specifi ca-tion and checking of message recipients, and fi ltering and conversion of messages. ALE communication services ensure that data is transmitted reliably, with intermediate documents (IDOCs) and BAPIs (Business Application Programming Interfaces) providing the basis for smooth data exchange.

SAP Intermediate Documents (IDOCs)
IDOCs, developed by SAP, are the basis for smooth, reliable exchange of data in integrated distributed application environments. They are data containers designed to ensure reliable, seamless exchange of messages between SAP systems or between SAP R/3 and non-SAP systems. IDOCs have a neutral data structure, independent of the application data to enable the free exchange of SAP R/3 data with non-SAP applications and vice versa.

Messaging Technology — Message Oriented Middleware (MOM)
Message Oriented Middleware (MOM) is an enabling software layer residing between the business applications and the network infrastructure that supports high-performance interoperability of large-scale distributed applications in heterogeneous environments. Technologies such as enterprise application integration (EAI) tools and message brokers qualify as message oriented middleware.

MOM supports multiple communication protocols, languages, applications, and hardware and software platforms. It also can reside between applications themselves, depending on the implementation. For instance, SAP R/3-driven organizations could implement IBM MQSeries for SAP middleware and connect with the J.D. Edwards system of a recently acquired organization. MOM refers to the process of distributing data and control through the exchange of messages. SAP R/3 systems use IDOCs as the standard message container. That is, MOM technologies queue IDOC messages and handle their transmittal between SAP R/3 systems and other applications. Message oriented middleware also serves as the receiver for incoming IDOC messages from external systems.

Figure 3: SAP ALE Architecture

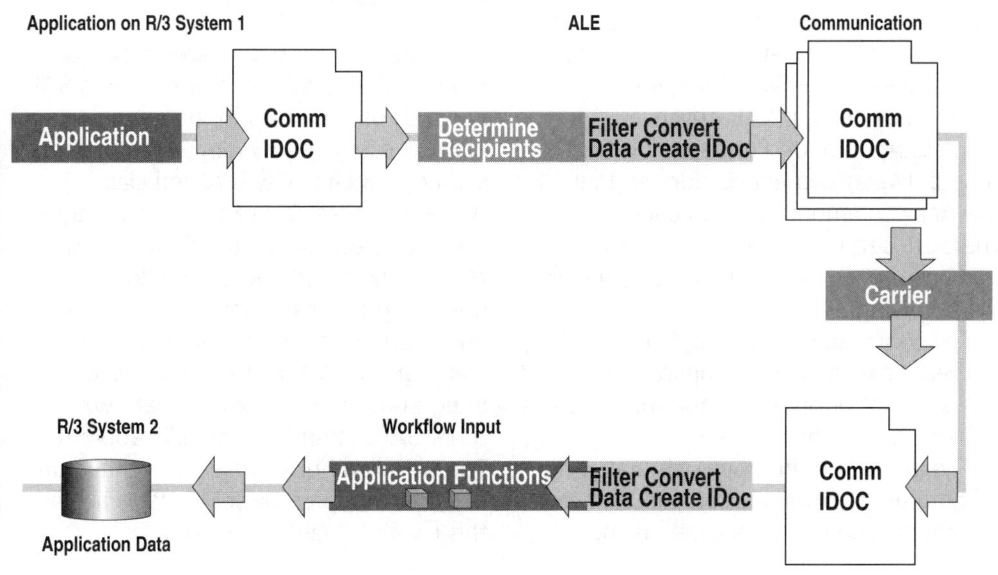

MOM lends itself to event-driven rather than procedural processing. Time-dependent and time-independent processing, as well as memory and disk-based systems are all available. A key technology for change data capture (CDC), MOM is an enabler of near real-time data exchange.

While representing a highly efficient solution for process automation (banking, telecom-munications industry applications), MOM technologies often lack the ability to transform data content. In other words, MOM is ideally suited for carrying business messages between applications (format interpretation and conversion) but lacks the sophistication required to transform messages from raw data to valuable information, a fundamental requirement of data warehousing.

Challenges Presented by SAP R/3 Application Integration

The majority of SAP R/3 data integration projects make use of homegrown point-to-point connections between applications. That is, developers write low-level communica-tions or SAP Advanced Business Application Programming (ABAP) code between two applications so that they may communicate with each other. There are several problems with this traditional handcrafted approach, including the following:

- The connection is hard-coded so that every time there is an application, system, or business change the code has to be rewritten;
- The point-to-point approach makes the integration extremely complex and very time-consuming. Over time, as the number of applications and connections between them proliferate, an organization ends up with an unmanageable jumble of code holding the business system together.
- There is no impact analysis, so changes to existing programs or applications that effect the integration interfaces are not indicated to administrators. This means that the low-level code built to enable data exchange may be broken without programmers or administrators knowing it.

Given the complexity of many integration projects being undertaken today, especially by organizations driven by SAP R/3 systems, investing in a universal data exchange solu-tion to overcome these obstacles will prove to be a sound, cost effective investment.

Functionality Overview — The Real Requirement

With the case for both warehousing SAP R/3 based data as well as integrating SAP R/3 with other enterprise operational systems established, a discussion of the solution functionality is benefi cial.

A true Universal Data Exchange solution is one that, because of sound architectural framework, is capable of simultaneously managing the extraction, transformation, and movement requirements of data warehousing R/3 data as well as seamlessly integrat-ing SAP application data with other SAP systems or non-SAP applications. The so called hub-and-spoke architecture has been adopted by solutions to achieve this level of dual-functionality.

The Hub-and-Spoke Data Exchange Architecture

Solutions based on the hub-and-spoke architecture are ideally suited to organizations looking to maximize their investment in SAP R/3 systems by including it in their data warehousing strategy and application integration initiatives. For data warehousing projects, a central engine, or information broker, serves as the hub of the solution. Its role in the solution is to automate and manage the fl ow of data — all extraction, transformation, and loading processes. The hub can be thought of as a traffi c controller of sorts, controlling the movement of data from disparate sources and ensuring the safe, reliable arrival at the data warehouse destination. Moreover, the engine serves to transform raw source data into valuable information to be used by knowledge workers, decision makers, and other decision support system users.

For SAP R/3 data-level application integration initiatives, a central hub-and-spoke-based architecture facilitates the controlled exchange of business messages between the R/3 system and other enterprise operational systems. Essentially, the engine serves as a data format mediator. In other words, the hub intercepts messages from the SAP R/3 system in the form of IDOCs and ensures that any desired transformation is carried

Figure 4: Hub-and-Spoke Architecture

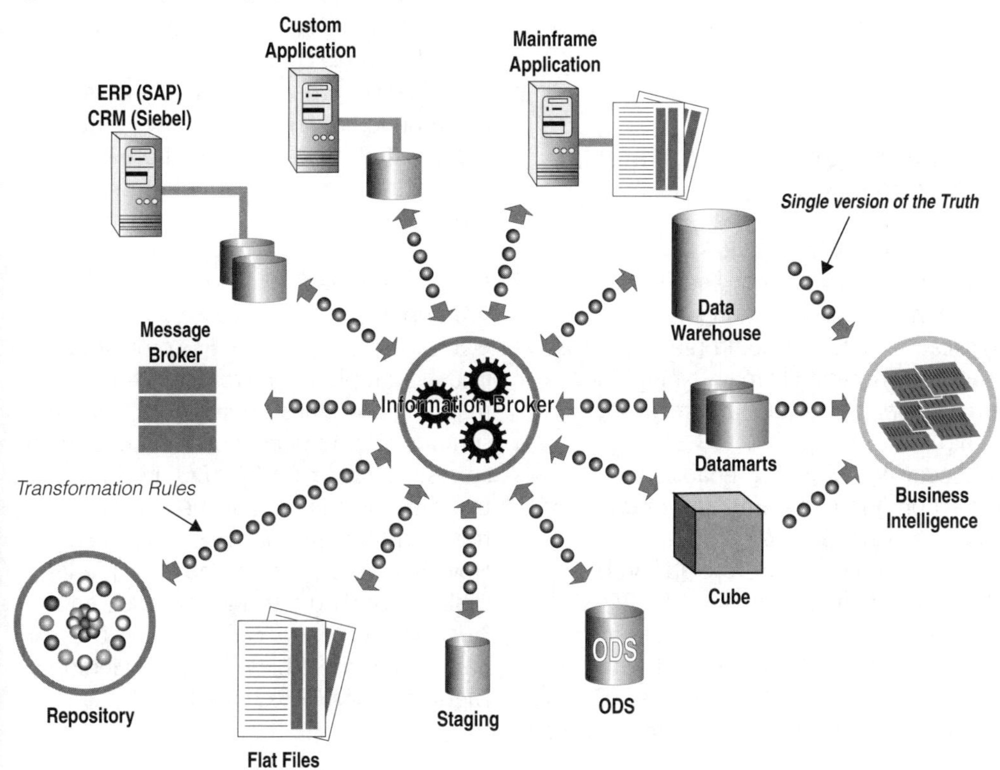

out on the affi xed data prior to passing the message on to target systems.

The alternative to the hub-and-spoke based data exchange solution, as discussed, is for organizations to develop separate hard-coded point-to-point interfaces that patch together systems for data integration or extraction, transformation, and loading pro-cesses for data warehousing. As outlined, maintaining and modifying these band-aid solutions to meet changing organizational requirements becomes unwieldy. The hub-and-spoke based solution ensures effi cient application integration by providing reliable delivery of business messages in required formats while simultaneously managing the extract, transformation, and load processes demanded by data warehousing projects.

The Hummingbird Genio MetaLink for SAP R/3 Solution

Genio MetaLink for SAP R/3
Extracting, transforming, and sharing data between enterprise resource planning applications and metadata repositories is crucial to successfully maintaining an organization's operational effectiveness. Genio MetaLink for SAP R/3 is a connectivity bridge that enables the extraction and transformation of data and metadata from SAP R/3 applica-tions. This gives organizations the ability to access information stored in SAP R/3 applications, combine it with data from other sources, and then share it with other systems throughout the enterprise. Genio MetaLink for SAP R/3 allows direct access to SAP R/3 data, SAP intermediate documents, and the population of SAP Business Information Warehouse environments.

Genio MetaLink for SAP R/3 Data Warehousing
Extracting and transforming SAP R/3 data for use in a data warehouse has traditionally been a complex and time-consuming task. To reduce the effort involved, both SAP and third party vendors are producing a variety of different packaged solutions for building data warehouses based on SAP R/3 data. Additionally, SAP itself has implemented a proprietary data warehousing environment called the Business Information Warehouse (SAP BW). However, loading and replenishing this environment with non-SAP R/3 data is critical.
For instance, organizations may have external demographics or legacy data sources that need to be integrated with SAP data to provide a complete customer profile.

Loading and Replenishing non-SAP BW Warehouses
Genio MetaLink for SAP R/3 provides an intuitive graphical environment for mapping and transforming data from R/3 systems to data warehouses or other data stores. MetaLink for SAP R/3 achieves this by accessing the data at the logical level by traversing the internal SAP meta-tables. However, access is provided for all SAP tables, including transparent, pool, and cluster tables. Users can also view the SAP data within the tables using the Genio MetaLink for SAP R/3 interface.

Figure 5: Genio MetaLink for SAP R/3 Functionality

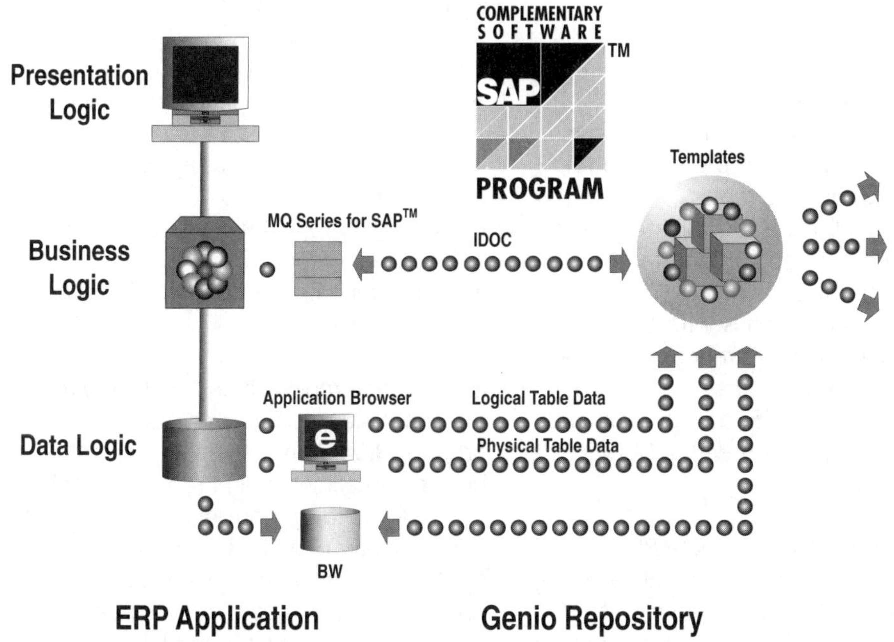

What is involved with this process? Essentially, Genio understands the SAP R/3 data structure, enabling it to locate, fi lter, and extract appropriate information and share it with external analytical environments. From a logical data table standpoint, this means the ability to recognize the complex storage structure, locate, and extract information, decipher any proprietary naming conventions or codes, traverse logical data relation-ships, and load and replenish external tables with valuable information. Often, this involves "unclustering" SAP cluster tables, "unpooling" pool tables, and combing them for appropriate or desired data through the use of ABAP remote function calls (RFC).

Transparent tables are more readily accessible as they conform to standard relational database table structures. Genio extracts and shares data with SAP transparent tables and other physical tables as it would with any other supported data source.

By enabling this seamless SAP R/3 data level integration with external analytical envi-ronments, Genio offers organizations the ability to generate real competitive advantage. Within Genio,the process for loading and replenishing non-SAP data warehouse tables is very straightforward. Essentially,by following the steps below,organiza-tions can have ef o cient and effective SAP R/3 data integration:

- Use Genio MetaLink for SAP R/3 interface to display and identify the necessary objects (tables and IDOCs)
- Copy them into the Genio Suite Metadata Repository
- Build required transformation objects around the objects in preparation for loading warehouse tables
- Start Genio Engine to facilitate process of loading and replenishing target warehouse tables
- Note:For organizations with the need for transactional level warehouse updates (e.g.near real-time data warehousing),Genio can run IDOC pro-cesses in conjunction with IBM MQSeries for SAP R/3.

Loading and Replenishing SAP BW
The ability to aggregate external (non-SAP R/3) and internal data and convert it into useful information in real-time is critical to enabling organizations to respond with speed and accuracy to market changes. The SAP Business Information Warehouse is a new-generation data warehousing solution that combines state-of-the-art data warehousing technology with the business expertise of SAP.

The SAP Business Information Warehouse closes the loop between business processes and decision support and enables context-based demand management for supply-chain planning and optimization. It comes pre-loaded with business content, allowing com-prehensive data analysis covering numerous environmental conditions. Genio MetaLink for SAP R/3 enables ef o cient staging of data for inclusion in SAP Business Information Warehouse environments.The following steps are carried out using intuitive Genio and MetaLink interfaces to accomplish this:

- Identify data models in source systems using Genio Suite Designer
- Create SAP BW staging area in Genio Suite Designer
- Connect to SAP BW using Genio MetaLink for SAP R/3
- Drag and drop SAP BW staging objects into Genio repository
- Start Genio Engine to load SAP BW staging area

Loading and replenishing SAP BW with external data presents a challenge to organiza-tions.While there are several business intelligence and reporting tool vendors providing front-end access to SAP BW, very few provide the external data feed that is crucial to the environment's acceptance within corporate enterprises. It is this role that Hummingbird Genio Suite takes on. Certifi ed by SAP under the Complementary Software program (SAP Certi o cation ID – STA BW – Business Informa-tion Warehouse – Data Staging), Genio is classifi ed as a data staging tool for the Business Information Warehouse. Essentially, Genio harnesses the power of SAP Business Application Programming Interfaces (BAPI) that include methods for updating and retrieving metadata as well as sending data extracts to the SAP Business Information Warehouse. By using these BAPIs, Genio can connect its metadata repository and powerful extraction and transformation engine to SAP BW.

Genio MetaLink for SAP R/3 Application Integration

With Genio MetaLink for SAP R/3, organizations achieve robust data exchange between SAP R/3 and non-SAP applications through the use of IDocs. Technically, Genio Suite creates IDoc messages and passes them between the IBM MQSeries for SAP message broker technology and vice versa. After this, the SAP R/3 application layer takes care of the message, which may require information from or pushing data to the system. Genio enhances the concept of data exchange between SAP R/3 and other operational systems and data stores by using direct program-to-program communication instead of a fi le interface to transfer IDocs. An additional benefi t is that it is possible to build interfaces that allow Genio to recognize the format of any interface structure of a non-SAP system and not simply standard formats. This greatly broadens the range of data sources and targets that Genio can exchange data between. The concept of the SAP application link enabling (ALE) involves using external converters to connect non-SAP systems to the SAP R/3 system. External converters are generic format conversion programs. In addition to SAP certifi cation for populating the Business Information Warehouse, Hummingbird Genio Suite qualifi es as an ALE converter in accordance with SAP guidelines (SAP Certi o cation ID -CA-ALE – Cross-Application – Application Link Enabling Interface).The following converter functions are covered by SAP ALE certifi cation:

- The transfer of R/3 intermediate document (IDoc) formats straight into the Genio repository so that these data descriptions can be used as source or target structures when assigning data fields. IDocs are a set of standard message containers can be used to read and write data from and to SAP R/3's different versions.
- Adoption and conversion of intermediate documents from SAP R/3 systems via the ALE interface — a remote function call that can be called up using a normal transaction.
- Conversion of any data format into intermediate document structures and import into the R/3 system via a remote function call (RFC) in the ALE interface.

Conclusion

As organizations continue to realize the benefi ts of driving their day-to-day business with SAP R/3 systems, the need to merge that productive operational environment with the analytical applications throughout their enterprise grows. In the era of e-enabled business, it is those organizations that effectively integrate these two IT worlds that will reap the lion's share of the tremendous opportunity posed by e-business.

In conjunction with Hummingbird Genio Suite, Genio MetaLink for SAP R/3 enables organizations to exchange SAP R/3 data effi ciently and effectively with external data stores and analytical applications on an enterprise-wide basis. Genio Suite provides organizations with the ability to integrate SAP R/3 data at the application layer, directly from physical and logical tables at the data level, and by allowing for the staging of non-SAP data for loading and replenishing the SAP Business Information Warehouse. Because of this, it is the complete solution for e-enabling the enterprise through SAP R/3 integration with analytical environments and capitalizing on the opportunities that it presents.

Storage Area Networks: Smart Storage, Fat Pipes and Industrial Grade Data Warehousing

Title:	*Storage Area Networks: Smart Storage, Fat Pipes and Industrial Grade Data Warehousing*
Author:	*Ken Orr, The Ken Orr Institute*
Abstract:	*This white paper describes how Storage Area Networks (SANs) can help organizations improve the delivery of their critical decision support information via data warehouses. This is not an accidental connection. The need for data from data warehouses is growing at an enormous rate: one that puts increasing pressures on our information delivery infrastructure. SANs can help relieve many of these pressures.*

Biography: Ken Orr is the founder and Principal Researcher of the Ken Orr Institute. Mr. Orr has been involved in emerging information technologies for over 30 years. He is the author of three books on systems development and management and the author of dozens of papers on systems development, systems architecture, data warehousing and data quality. The Ken Orr Institute is located in Topeka, KS. Mr. Orr can be reached at KenOrr@KenOrrInst.Com

1. Data Warehousing

The concept of data warehousing first emerged on the IT scene in the late 1980s. At the time, it was seen as a way of both integrating information from a variety of sources and providing end users with easy access to that information through a new generation of multidimensional analysis tools. It seemed to be an incremental, but important, improvement of the existing decision support systems (DSS) "en vogue" at the time.

Tens of thousands of these early DSS systems had been developed over the years to answer specific management needs (e.g., new marketing campaigns and new product introductions). And many of these DSS applications had grown into significant systems that were used to support critical day-to-day business activities. But major enterprises were finding that these ad hoc systems were becoming increasingly unable to support either their current or future business requirements. The 21st Century was beginning to look much different and organizations found they needed a new technology to cope with their new problems and business needs.

2. Business and technology are changing data warehousing

Although the access of high quality information has always been important for management and analytical purposes, the demands for rapid access to critical information has been increasing exponentially in recent years. Rapid changes in both businesses and the technologies that serve them have made quality information an absolute necessity. A number of key trends have been driving enterprises everywhere:

- Globalization
- Mergers and Acquisitions
- Deregulation
- Business Process Reengineering
- Technology, especially the Internet
- Mass Customization
- One-to-one Marketing

These drivers, in turn, have changed the way that enterprises do business. Each requires better, more timely, and more accurate information about all aspects of the business, especially about its customers and products. And whereas products and markets used to change slowly, technology and globalization have altered the rules, so that today, business trends and hot products burst on the scene almost instantaneously. Businesses have to react just as quickly. Those organizations that can react rapidly and still maintain control over their costs and their customer service will be the big winners. The key strategies today involve Customer Relationship Management (CRM) because organizations worldwide have learned that retaining current customers and encouraging them to buy more is much more profitable than prospecting for new ones. Programs for customer acquisition, customer development, and customer retention are at the top of everyone's agenda for the 21st century.

At the bottom everyone is running scared. Even Andy Grove, the former CEO of Intel, entitled his latest book "Only the Paranoid Survive!" The most successful enterprises constantly have to look over their shoulders because someone - some Amazon.com - may be perfecting a new way to sell things over the Internet that doesn't require stores, doesn't require salesmen, and doesn't even require inventory.

Several sales, marketing, and customer service tools are needed to stay on top of this warp-speed, CRM-oriented marketplace:

- Customer Profitability Analysis
- Data Mining
- Database Marketing
- Mass Customization/Mass Personalization
- Niche Marketing Analysis

But none of these tools works without accurate and timely data - data about customers, data about sales, data about costs, and data about competitors. In today's business environment, information is a competitive/strategic weapon. After promising management better information for decades, IT can finally deliver - given the right tools and technology. But the demands for more and more data place enormous stress on the underlying data infrastructure (Figure 1).

Figure 1: The Growing Demand for Data

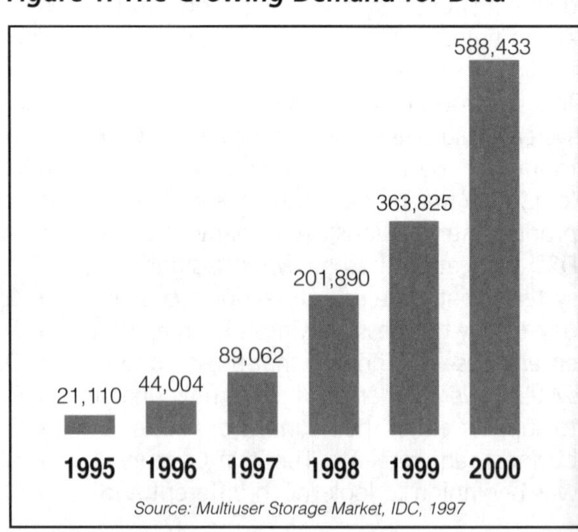

3. How is the role of data warehousing changing?

Data warehousing began by expanding on things we knew how to do. Consider the following definition of data warehousing:

"A data warehouse is a nonvolatile source of time-series, subject-oriented, data copies for end user computing." 1

That was in the early days of data warehousing, but CRM and similar programs have driven organizations to spend more of their corporate budgets on customer-related IT initiatives like database marketing and data warehousing. As a result, managers and knowledge workers have come to depend upon their data warehouses for more and more critical information. As a result, they have to rethink the role the data warehouse should play in the organization's strategic plans.

Data warehousing's scope has expanded far beyond its initial role of just providing management reporting for end-user decision support to a point where it is now seen as supplying critical information to all areas of the business and to key business partners as well.

Instead of "nonvolatile" updating, data warehouses today are moving to "near real-time" updating and access. Instead of "time series" data, organizations are loading their data warehouses with detail "event/transaction data". Instead of focusing on "subject-oriented" data warehouses, organizations are building "process-oriented" ones. And instead of focusing just on supplying information to end-users and management, data warehouses are increasingly being built to support everyone in the enterprise who needs information (e.g., customer service representatives) as well as many of the enterprise's customers and business partners.2 Like the ripples caused by dropping a large rock in the middle of a pond, the waves of the data warehousing revolution are moving constantly outward.

But providing all (or most) of the critical information that the primary users need is a difficult undertaking. Early data warehouse designers could focus their attention on developing data warehouses and data marts that could be installed rapidly and that would insure fast retrieval. Today, users are asking for more extensive data analysis based on more expanded data. This has created pressure for "detail data warehouses" and "near real-time updating" that, in turn, has put much more pressure on already shaky data warehousing infrastructures.

Not surprisingly, data warehouse designers and managers are becoming much more concerned with the process of pulling transaction data in from operational systems as the data is captured, transforming that data, and making it available in the data warehouse around the clock. They are also becoming interested in the managing the storage, retrieval, and archiving of truly enormous amounts of data.

1: Inmon, W.E., Building the Data Warehouse, QED Publications, 1993
2: A more detailed discussion is found in Appendix B.

4. What are the major operational problems with mature data warehouses?

As their data warehouses have matured, large organizations around the world have encountered some significant problems in meeting their CRM goals. There are problems with:

- Management Costs
- Integration
- No Single Point of Control
- Network Bandwidth
- Backup, Recovery, and Archiving

Management Costs

Managing complex, heterogeneous data warehouse environments is a difficult undertaking on a good day. Because each component is nearly unique in these environments, it is almost impossible to leverage standard management practices in any meaningful way. And because data warehousing usage is mushrooming across the enterprise, controlling the associated costs is a major problem for many organizations. Data warehouse managers need better tools to manage their environments.

Integration

Integrating systems from multiple vendors is also always a difficult task, but data warehousing tends to compound the problem by introducing more sources and more users of data, many with hard-to-integrate hardware and software interfaces of their own. Data warehousing developers need new tools and technology to be able to better manage the needed integration.

No Single Point of Control

The management of a major data warehouse is every bit as critical as the management of a major OLTP application. Data must be uploaded from legacy databases to the data warehouse and downloaded to individual users and data marts, often overnight or in a very narrow time window. It is especially critical that all these functions be carefully choreographed, otherwise large numbers of users get the wrong answers. Systems management is particularly difficult in data warehouse environments because there is no single point of control over all the systems involved. There is no one place, for example, where all the meta-data or all the systems management information resides. Tools and technology are needed here as well to help data warehouse operations.

Network Bandwidth

Because data warehouses often involve very large batch updates, network bandwidth is becoming a serious problem. When updates only occurred weekly or monthly, getting this done wasn't particularly a problem. But as the data warehousing cycle moved to daily, or hourly, the problem has become pressing. Increasingly, data warehousing update data flows over the same backbone LAN/WAN networks that are being used by thousands of users and hundreds of other systems.

In most organizations, the pipes simply are not big enough. Transporting tens or hundreds of gigabytes of data is putting a major load on the communications infrastructure of most large organizations.

Backup, Recovery, and Archiving
As data warehousing becomes more important to decision-makers across the enterprise, the requirements for availability, backup, and recoverability increase as well. And since the need for real-time data is growing at the same pace, traditional methods for backup and recoverability are not adequate.

Future data warehouses need an integrated archiving strategy that integrates with their day-to-day back up and recovery activities. Most operational systems archive their data if it is needed. But data warehousing environments archive so the data can be easily retrieved when it is needed. There is a major difference in philosophy. Increasingly, organizations need to be able to recover data that goes back years, if not decades, for a variety of uses. All these problems create demands for new, industrial grade, data warehousing technology.

5. An architecture for enterprise data warehousing

In the past decade data warehousing has been evolving to meet its rapidly changing needs. A majority of large enterprises around the world have already installed, or are in the process of installing, large-scale data warehouses. Early warehouse pilots have led to even larger data warehouses. Organizations have learned that data warehousing, where successful, is extremely valuable to the enterprise. But with all of the successes of early data warehousing activities, organizations are also learning that developing and managing large-scale data warehouses is a difficult undertaking.

Figure 2 – An Enterprise Data Architecture 4

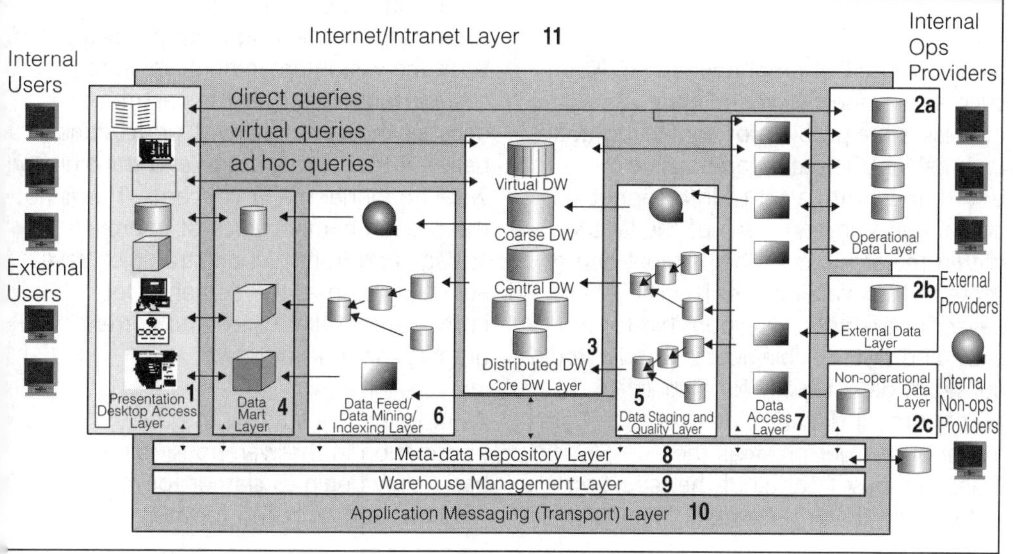

A data warehouse framework must simultaneously meet a number of conflicting goals: performance, flexibility, scalability, ease of use, audibility, and management.3

Meeting all of these factors at the same time puts a serious burden on those developing and maintaining enterprise data warehouses. Data warehouse developers must not only make their data easy to use by their initial set of users, they must also plan so that their data warehouse environments can grow and expand. Data warehouse managers must be able to provide the same levels of service, security, and reliability as are available for operational systems. As a result, the data warehouse environment must be designed and implemented as an expandable backbone systems framework for the organization to build on.

3: For further discussion of data warehousing goals, see Appendix A
4: Orr, K.T., Data Warehousing Technology, copyright 1999, The Ken Orr Institute, Topeka, KS.

An Enterprise Data Architecture (EDA), such as the one shown in Figure 2, addresses the problem of conflicting goals by breaking the data warehousing environment into a set of interconnected components (layers). Each of the layers within the architecture helps meet one or more of the overall goals. The Data Mart Layer, for example, is responsible for providing fast, flexible access to a limited subset of data, usually for a specific workgroup or department. The Core Data Warehouse Layer provides the "clearinghouse" for all of the reporting data within the organization. The Core Data Warehouse is intended to support the goals of flexibility and audibility. The Data Access, Data Staging and Quality, and Application Messaging Layers provide the architecture with the efficient transfer and transformation of operational data from the Operational Data Layer to the Core Data Warehouse Layer.

By using an architecture such as this, experience has shown that it is easier for data warehouse developers and managers to construct and test new requirements (business needs) incrementally as the role of the data warehouse evolves and expands. The architecture can also make it easier for everyone to understand where some of underlying problems with mature systems are likely to occur and to see, at the same time, how various new tools and technologies could solve these problems.

6. Storage Area Networks (SANs)

Data storage, data access, and data transmission have long been problems in IT. With the vast improvements in storage cost/performance over the past three decades, however, many IT professionals believed that data storage and transmission were no longer major concerns. This is not the case. The importance of improved storage and transmission strategies have actually grown as the demands for immediate (on-line) access to current business data have grown.

As more people start to use the information in the warehouse on a regular basis, they begin to clamor for more frequent updating and for more detail information. As a result, there is pressure to accelerate updating from a weekly cycle, let's say, to a daily cycle, or near real-time. At the same time, the users also begin to ask for reports and queries that can only be answered by a data warehouse with all the detail transactions in it. Soon, the batch windows for updating the data warehouse come crashing closed. More data is needed more frequently from the already overworked operational databases. Without better technical solutions both the operational and data warehousing environments become highly stressed (i.e., really slow). This is where the idea of using new technologies such as Storage Area Networks (SANs) has become increasingly attractive to users and managers alike.

What are SANs? Well, let's begin with an overview of data networking strategies. Over the last two decades data storage architectures have evolved from a systems model that is built around a central storage control model (Figure 3a) to one built around LANs (Figure 3b). And, more recently, a number of major organizations such as IBM have introduced a third model- - Storage Area Networks (SANs) (Figure 3c).

The central host (mainframe) model took advantage of fast central processors that could access a variety of storage devices via "channels." The central computer managed the processing load while the channel computer sent and received data to and from storage devices asynchronously. This was the first stage of introducing intelligence into the data transfer process.

Local Area Networks (LANs) came into being to help share data files (and printers) among groups of desktop microcomputers. Soon, it was clear that LANs would be a significant step toward distributed, client-server systems. Large-scale client-server systems were then constructed tying sizable numbers of LANs together via Wide Area Networks (WANs). The idea was to leverage cheap microcomputers and cheap disk storage to replace expensive (but reliable) central computers. Somewhat overlooked in this design strategy was the fact that the bandwidth of the WAN is typically an order of magnitude smaller than that of the LANs it connected. LANs can be seen then as a second step toward separating access from physical control.

Figure 3: Storage Architectures

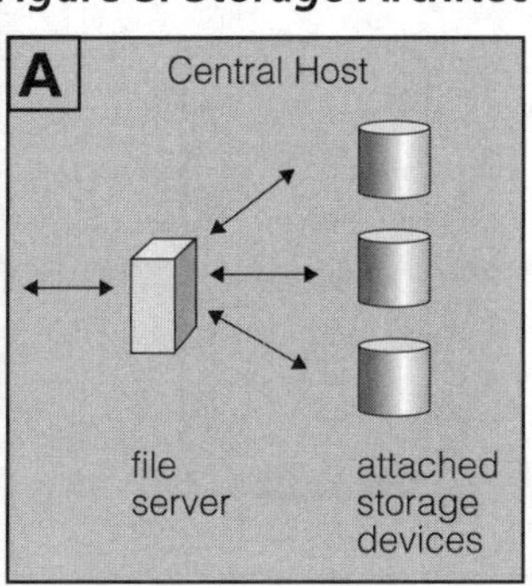

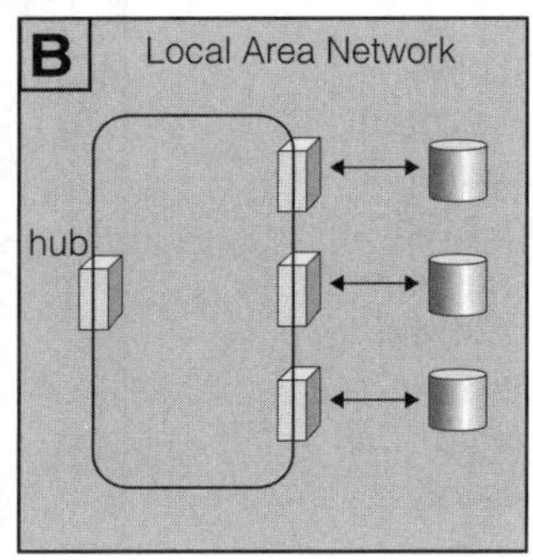

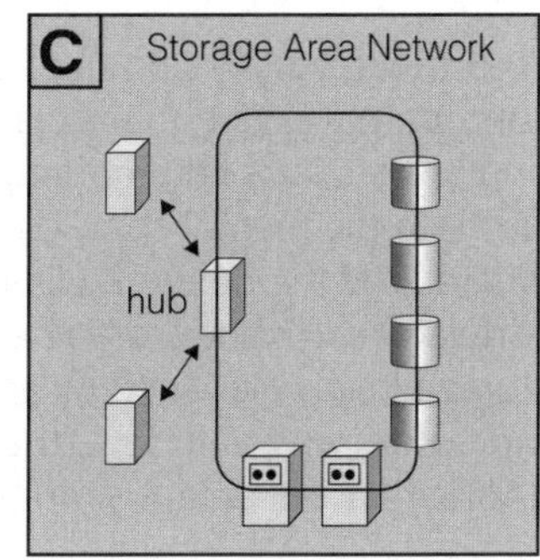

Figure 4: A Wide Area Network Configuration

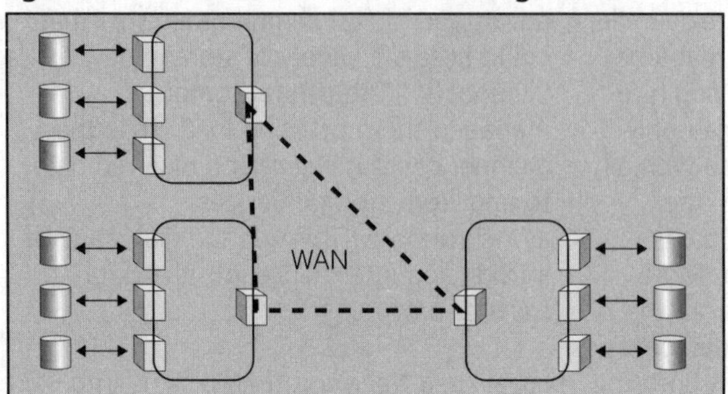

After a fashion, SAN technology can be viewed simply as a natural result of designers working to free up bottlenecks in the access and delivery of large amounts of data. SANs take advantage of fibre channel connections to move the data at very high over extended distances using smart data hubs to manage the connections.

High-speed fiber-optic cables have been used for some time within large, multiprocessor architectures to provide rapid access to huge on-line databases. As computer, transmission, and direct access costs have all come down, it has made sense to create computer/network/storage complexes where large numbers of very fast processors could access large numbers of data storage devices directly.

Even though SAN is not a totally new concept, data warehouse planners often find SANs take a little getting used to. To illustrate the mental shift, consider that with a SAN the network (via management software) owns the storage as opposed to storage being managed by a specific processor (server). In fact, the idea of the SAN is that the data is simultaneously accessible by a number of heterogeneous servers. It is as if each server had independent, transparent access to all of the devices on the SAN simultaneously.

Imagine for a moment an environment in which all (or most) of the major servers in an IT complex can access all (or most) of the data storage devices. Imagine further that data storage devices can be added incrementally, as needs change. Finally, imagine that storage devices can send and receive large amounts of data from other SAN devices at high speeds with minimal involvement by any server. Computer architects are just now figuring out how to use this technology to address many of the day-to-day problems of data warehousing management.

Figure 5: Storage Area Network using a fibre channel

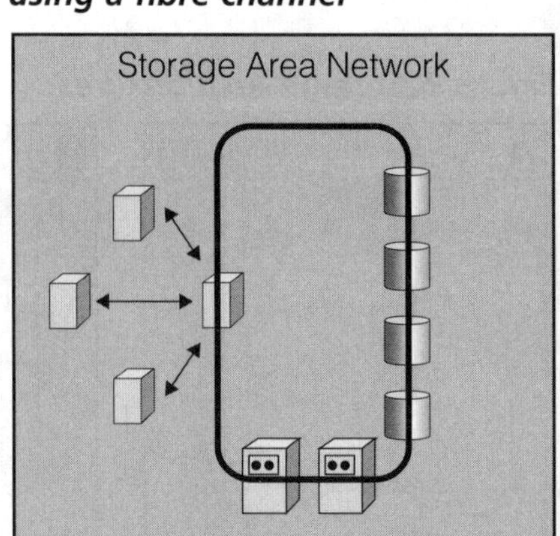

7. How can a Storage Area Network help solve real data warehousing problems?

Example 1: Improving the data warehouse update cycle

As organizations build bigger and better data warehouses, their data storage, data processing, and data transmission infrastructures become severely taxed. And because most significant problems occur deep in the IT organization in the linkage between the existing OLTP systems and the data warehouses, most users and managers are only aware of their wait time growing longer and longer. Most can't visualize the "information plumbing" it takes to get the data from the operational systems and move that data to their data warehouse or data marts. Figure 6 is a graphic representation of the process involved. (The boxes below the diagram show the earliest start time that the system could begin using the given data sets with updated data.)

One of the underlying problems is that in most organizations this activity is not so much a continuous process as it is a serial one. Most organizations still use tools and technology that require the data extract process to be completed before the transmission process can occur. As you can see by the start times at the bottom of Figure 6, the elapsed times involved can be considerable. In many cases, this means that the Operational DB is out of service for a considerable period of time_a significant problem if you are required to support a 24 x 7, worldwide operation. Organizations also find that the problems associated with this configuration only get worst with time. Increased demand for additional, timelier data makes the extract process more frequent.

But with a SAN combined with support software, it is possible to create a very different infrastructure, one that not only improves the process with bigger pipes (faster transfer), but also reduces the processing loads on the servers.

Figure 7 shows how the SAN solution to the same problem might look. Notice that, not only are the pipes bigger, 100 MB/sec vs. 8-25 MB/sec, but there are no servers involved. You might imagine, for example, that the SAN network would include connectors (attachments) to connect the different data storage devices to the

Figure 6: Data Warehouse update process

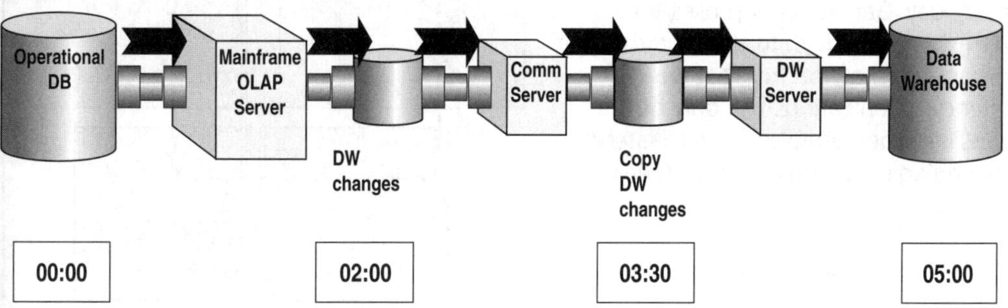

Figure 7: Bigger pipes, Smarter Storage

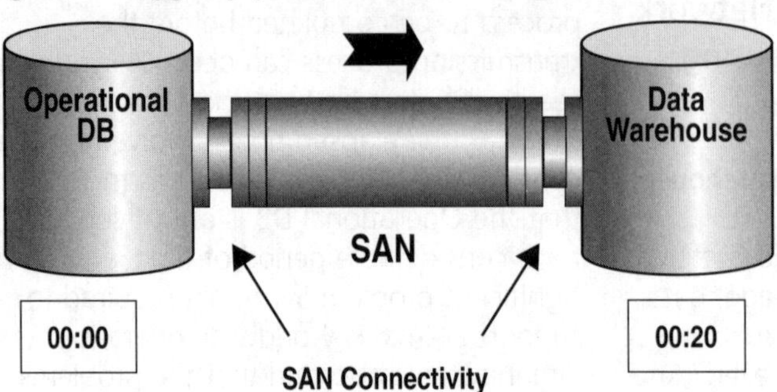

network (SAN Connectivity), a set of SAN internal data management functions, e.g., snapshot, transmit, and update (SAN Exploitation), and a set of functions that resolves any conflicts, backup, or recovery processes (SAN Management). Although they might appear exaggerated, the times associated are taken from real examples.

Data warehouses are becoming the core for what might be called On-line Enterprise Reporting (OLER). By using a SAN combined with new techniques to "snapshot" existing database transactions, it is possible to create a totally new environment that marries OLTP and OLER (detail data warehouse). The need to integrate the OLTP and the data warehousing environments grows more important every day. Gartner Group uses the term "zero-latency" to describe the organization of the future. Zero-latency organizations will only be possible when enabled by zero-latency technologies such as Storage Area Networks.

Example 2 - Integrating Operational, Data Warehouse, and Archiving DBs

For this example, imagine a situation in which a large 24 x 7 organization wishes to improve its physical environment by using a SAN to facilitate linking the following components:

1. The data storage for an OLTP Facility where the Order Processing and Customer Care transactions are processed
2. A Data Warehouse Facility where the Core Data Warehouse is located
3. A Data Archive Facility where the backup facility for both the OLTP and Data Warehouse is located (Figure 8)

In this case, it would be possible to configure a SAN that could capture data (in

Figure 8: Using a SAN in an Industrial-grade Data Warehouse Environment

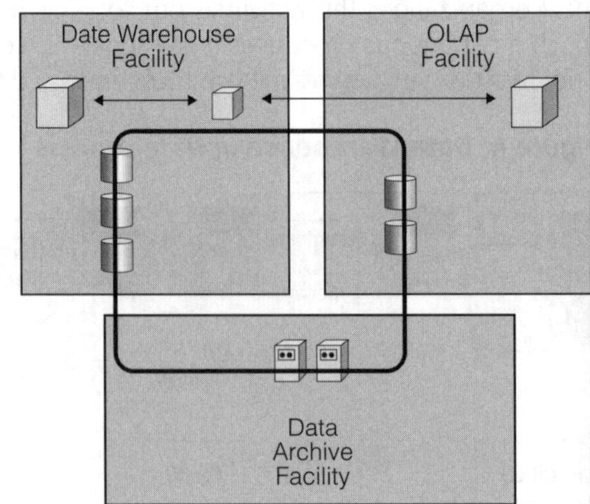

the background) from the OLTP database, do the processing outlined in Example 1, and automatically do backup and archiving functions of both the OLTP and Data Warehouse databases to a separate facility at the same time. These are only a couple of examples of the power of SAN technology, but they give some idea of how the technology can help organizations solve real problems.

8. Why IBM is a major player in SAN technology

IBM has long been a pioneer in the technologies required to support very large databases (VLDBs). For example, IBM has been marketing and supporting ESCON fibre-channel technology, a precursor to SANs, since the early '90s. They have also been doing research in OLTP, database, and data warehousing for decades. Indeed, IBM's experience dealing with very large databases with very large transaction volumes has generated many of the key technologies that are now coming on-stream as part of SANs.

IBM's great strength has always been the engineering and management of "bullet-proof" large-scale solutions. For some time now, IBM has been developing a strong program to support SAN technology that leverages its strengths. The program includes four main initiatives that were touched on in the examples above:

- SAN Connectivity,
- SAN Management,
- SAN Exploitation and
- SAN Services and Support.

SAN Connectivity
SAN Connectivity has to do with providing "open" connectivity (wiring) to both new and existing devices. Since most organizations can't replace their existing storage/transmission framework all at once, IBM's goal is to provide its customers with a straightforward transition strategy into the SAN any-to-any world. SAN Connectivity is provided by two basic connection (wiring) approaches: fibre channel and SCSI, each of which has distance limitations.

Figure 9: IBM SAN Initiatives

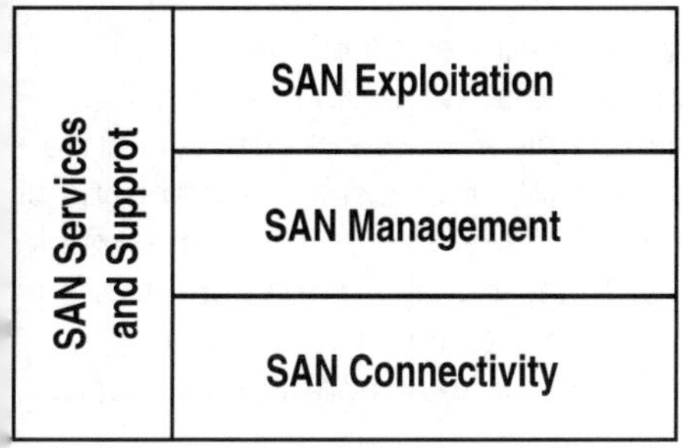

SAN Services and Supprot	SAN Exploitation
	SAN Management
	SAN Connectivity

Figure 10: IBM SAN Connectivity Alternatives

Wiring	MB/sec	Maximum Distance
SCSI	1-10	25 m
SCSI	80	7-8 m
Fibre channel (62.5 micron)	100	300 m
Fibre channel (50 micron)	100	500 m
Fibre channel (9 micron)	100	10 km

SAN Management (Software)
Although SAN technology offers enormous advantages, it also opens the door for a wide range of additional complexity. Device contention, a serious problem with a single multiprogramming processor, becomes significantly more difficult in a SAN environment where, theoretically at least, any server can get at any storage device and every storage device can communicate directly with any other device.

Using the experience gained through two decades of device sharing in multiprocessor environments, IBM is developing a closed loop, zero-administration SAN Management infrastructure designed to support both traditional server-centric storage models and new storage-centric ones_an approach that will support both IBM and non-IBM products. Obviously, such an environment provides significant systems management advantages.

SAN Exploitation (functionality):
Ultimately, connectivity and management only provide the basic structure of SAN technology. To leverage (exploit) SAN technology so that its customers can readily utilize it, IBM is developing a full range of functionality. In IBM terms, exploitation, then, means the ability to provide the following:

- Disk pooling by policy
- Tape pooling by policy
- Storage copy services
- High-availability clustering
- Global SAN file system

SAN Service and Support
More than most storage technologies, implementing SAN technology requires an understanding of how to put this emerging technology in place. SAN's any-to-any increased capacity and complexity highlights the critical nature of systems integration and service in any SAN strategy. As a result, IBM is gearing up its Global Services Division to provide the support, services, and education required supporting end-to-end SAN solutions. In doing this, IBM is leveraging the experience it gained supporting its clients in moving from bus and tag to 1st generation SAN (ESCON) architecture. The service and support strategy is for IBM Global Services to deliver a comprehensive set of support offerings– from early consulting, planning, and design, through integration, testing, and certification – that will both minimize the risk of SAN deployment and maximize the benefits of information sharing across the enterprise.

9. Conclusion - Storage Area Networks and "Industrial-Grade" Data Warehousing

"Any technology sufficiently advanced is indistinguishable from magic."
Arthur C. Clarke –"Clarke's Third Law"

Every day, we take advantage of technology that we could not have imagined only a few years ago. When we flip a light switch or pick up a telephone or log on to the Internet, technological magic occurs. Today, it may seem natural to wait days or weeks to find out how our organization did last month or last quarter, but soon, as a result of near real-time updating, everyone inside and outside the enterprise will expect, and then demand, near real-time responses. In the same way that organizations around the world are rebuilding their telecommunications infrastructure to support the millions of new uses and new users of the Internet, organizations desiring to operate in the 21st century will have to upgrade their decision support infrastructure as well.

Data warehousing has come a very long way in the last decade. Enterprises around the world are using data warehouses daily to help cope with the needs of "managing in real-time." Because there is no hope that the business world will become less complex or less competitive in the foreseeable future, managers, professionals, and workers at all levels in the organization need better, faster, higher-quality information to make critical decisions.

Just as the computer industry learned how to provide highly-reliable, scalable OLTP systems to support the operational side of our businesses, the industry is now attacking the problems of providing highly-reliable, scaleable data warehouses that can store and retrieve the enormous multimedia databases of the future. Storage Area Networks represent a major component for implementing these advanced 21st century data warehouses.

Such a configuration will allow each functional component to be directly connected over high-speed SANs, yet housed for operational, security, and backup purposes in different physical locations miles (kilometers) apart with dramatically increased performance. Given the flexibility and scalability of SAN technology, additional storage and servers will be able to be added to this complex at any time, with a minimum of disruption or downtime to any of the 24 x 7 systems. This approach will go a long way to help data warehousing developers and managers meet their performance, flexibility, scalability and manageability goals.

Appendix A - Data Warehousing Goals

1. Performance - Data warehouses must be able to provide fast access to standard, formatted data for multidimensional analysis, for canned reports and for an enormous variety of ad hoc queries.

2. Flexibility - A data warehouse environment must be able to change both the way data is made available and the kind of data that is available to managers and analysts. A data warehouse must also be able to access any and all data that the organization currently has and must be able to bring new data elements and new data types into the data warehouse environment in short order. Ultimately, data warehousing is about questions, not answers.

3. Scalability - If a data warehouse is successful, its use will skyrocket. Data warehouse developers must be ready from the outset to support more data, more users, and much more frequent use by each user. With the Internet, enterprises are moving from hundreds of data warehouse users to thousands of users.

4. Ease of Use - Historically, IT has been concerned about supporting operational computer users. Wherever the tradeoff has been between ease of use and performance, performance has won out. But in the 21st century, data warehouses will have to be orders of magnitude easier to use.

5. Quality - Data quality is one of the most important factors in any data warehousing activity. It matters little how fast or how flexible a data warehouse is if the data that it produces is inaccurate or dated.

6. Audibility - Data on data warehouse screens or reports must also tie back to the other sources of information within the enterprise. Accounting and marketing must be able to reconcile their data, otherwise users will become suspicious of the quality and integrity of the data warehouse's data and cease to use it.

7. Manageability Since data warehouse requirements and demands are constantly changing, it is critical that the IT organization be able to provide highly reliable, updateable environments that manage the flow of data from source entry all the way to end-user presentation.

Appendix B - Changing Data Warehousing Needs

Original Data Warehouse Concepts (early 90s)	Current Data Warehouse Thinking (late 90s)	Reasoning
Non-volatile	Near real-time	The time frame for doing business has reduced dramatically. Where many data warehouses were initially designed with idea of weekly or monthly updating, more and more organizations are moving to near real-time so that they can report the current status of the business everywhere.
Time-series	Event data	Traditionally, decision support systems were assumed to be based on summary information. As data warehouses have become more important, managers are demanding access to detail business transactions.
Subject-oriented	Business process oriented	The early idea that it was possible to build data warehouses that only included Customer data are rapidly being replaced by data warehouses that include, for example, that support the entire "order process" -data on all the customers, products and transactions with the customers.
Data copies	Source data	With the idea that the data warehouse should contain all the source transactions for ad hoc reporting and audibility has come the idea that the data warehouse is the ideal place to store and archive the basic enterprise source data.
End user computing	Everyone in the enterprise, customers, vendors, etc.	Initially, data warehousing was considered an extension of the idea of "end user computing". Now, organizations are looking to the data warehouse environment to provide information not just to internal managers, but to everyone in the organization and to key business partners (customers, vendors, banks, etc.) as well.

Chapter 3: Strategical Considerations

The 7 Steps to Calculating Data Warehousing ROI

Title: *The 7 Steps to Calculating Data Warehousing ROI*
Author: *Informatica*
Abstract: *Informatica is bringing its experience to bear on an industry quest: ROI modeling. To produce this white paper, Informatica researched past efforts at defining and calculating data warehousing ROI, then added new insights gleaned from its work in the lab and in the field, helping some of the world's greatest organizations improve their decision support infrastructures. Informatica hopes that, through this work, new firms in virtually all industries will benefit from a fresh look, and a fresh approach, to data warehousing ROI.*

Data mart/data warehousing projects have become critically important staples of decision-support architectures for many organizations. For some, the benefits are immediate and distinct, with users obtaining analytical reports that were never before accessible. For others, benefits are less distinct, but at least as valuable: management information is more robust; executive decisions better informed.

Data warehouse/data mart implementations can make sense out of the volumes of data that populate operational databases. They can cut through to meanings and implications behind the raw statistics gathered every day. They can give knowledge workers at all organizational levels powerful tools for testing theories and contrasting research results. They can help one organization win out over another by supplying strategic competitive advantage via effective information analysis.

But data warehouses and data marts do not represent blanket solutions to the general decision-support needs of all organizations. Neither are they simple answers to what are typically highly complex questions. Each data warehouse and data mart must be planned and constructed according to each organization's specific objectives, resources and limitations.

And, increasingly, each data warehouse or data mart must play a role within a larger, enterprise-wide decision support framework. No longer are data warehouses and data marts the exclusive property of far-flung line-of-business users; more and more, they are brought to the attention — and within the responsibility — of CIOs, CFOs, and even CEOs. Companies are committing more capital for data warehouse/data mart development; they are escalating planning to a more strategic level. Rather than let each LOB define its own data mart requirements, for instance, central planners are more likely to advocate an architectural approach for the LOB efforts; and they are necessarily asking for more formal evaluations of data warehouse/data mart justification. Increasingly, they look to ROI (Return On Investment) modeling as a means of evaluating data warehouse/data mart projects.

As a pioneer in the burgeoning distributed data warehousing market, Informatica has led partners and customers through important industry milestones: Informatica developed the first integrated tool suite for designing off-the-shelf data marts, and the company introduced the first fully metadata-enabled distributed data warehouse architecture.

Now Informatica is bringing its experience to bear on another important industry quest: ROI modeling. To produce this white paper, Informatica researched past efforts at defining and calculating data warehousing ROI, then added new insights gleaned from its work in the lab and in the field, helping some of the world's greatest organizations improve their decision support infrastructures. Informatica hopes that, through this work, new firms in virtually all industries will benefit from a fresh look, and a fresh approach, to data warehousing ROI.

ROI: Benefits and Limitations

ROI modeling is valuable for several reasons. First, it supplies a fundamental cost-justification framework for evaluating data warehouse/data mart performance. Second, it encourages (actually, mandates) advance planning among all appropriate parties, from IS to users and executive management. Third, it helps organizations clarify and agree on the benefits they expect, and in that process helps them set realistic expectations for data warehouse/data mart performance.

But ROI modeling does have limitations. It can predict measurements for only those benefits that are tactical and therefore tangible, such as dollars saved, hours reduced, or reports generated. It can't convey the value of what might be more far-reaching, strategic benefits: gaining better, faster access to customer information, or making better informed business decisions.
For many, however, the value of ROI modeling will overcome these limitations. Moreover, once ROI modeling is underway, companies can use their experience to fine tune models regularly, replacing assumptions with actual statistics. Over time, ROI modeling can thus become increasingly accurate and effective.

Defining ROI

ROI, or Return On Investment, is a traditional measure of corporate-resource value. Although variations exist, ROI is essentially employed as a tool for weighing expected benefits against the costs of a specific project. The resulting ROI calculation measures the return on investment for the project.

The models discussed in this white paper will employ the four most common formulas. They are:

- Cash flow analysis — A method for projecting positive and negative cash flows for the anticipated life of the project. Typically, ROI measurements use the cash flow formula to depict results.
- Net present value — A method for evaluating cash flow according to the long-term value of current investment. Net present value shows how much capital would have to be invested currently, at an assumed interest rate, in order to create a stream of payments over time. For instance, to generate an income stream of $500 per month over six months at an interest rate of eight percent would require an investment — a net present value — of $2,311.44.
- Return on investment — This calculates net present value of total incremental cost savings and revenue divided by the net present value of total costs multiplied by 100. This type of ROI calculation is also frequently referred to as return of equity or return on capital employed.
- Payback — A calculation for determining how much time will pass before an initial capital investment is recovered.

Recommended: A Seven-Step Approach to ROI

Informatica has constructed a seven-step approach to modeling data warehouse/ data mart ROI. This approach draws from — and builds on — work conducted by expert consultants and executives.

These include:

- International Data Corporation (Canada) Ltd., in a report by Stephen Graham entitled The Foundations of Wisdom: A Study of the Financial Impact of Data Warehousing;
- KPMG Peat Marwick LLP; in a presentation by Kelvin Womack entitled Practical Techniques for Measuring Return on Investment;
- NationsBanc Services, Inc.; in a presentation by Duncan M. Witte entitled Data Warehousing Project Economics;
- Patricia Seybold Group; in a report by Pieter R. Mimno entitled Cost-Justifying a Data Ware-house.

The Informatica approach reflects some key assumptions. First, organizations should look well beyond the 90-to 120-day project scope to take a long-term view toward ROI, and should invest initial resources in developing a multi-year deployment map that articulates certain agreed-upon attributes. Time spent in enterprise deployment planning will pay substantial rewards later, both in ROI accuracy and in project success.

Second, risks as well as costs and benefits should be entered into the ROI equation, and quantified as precisely as possible. Only by managing the interplay among benefits, cost and risk can organizations gain a realistic perspective of data warehouse/data mart ROI.

Third, even the best ROI model will convey only quantifiable results. It is up to each organization to realize which strategic (and typically immeasurable) benefits are important as well, and if possible to assign values to them.

Step One: Build an Enterprise Deployment Map

Through tactics that range from formal surveys to offsite meetings and enterprise modeling, organizations should begin the ROI model by creating a map showing likely enterprise-wide data warehouse/data mart deployments over a reasonable period of time.

The accompanying chart (Figure One) shows enterprise deployment for an international bank. Key attributes include numbers, types, and other details about the data warehouses/data marts that might be developed over a five-year timeframe, as well as expected user numbers and types of analytical tools.

As difficult as long-term planning can be — especially in large, decentralized organizations — this process aids substantially because it creates a dialog among constituencies that will be instrumental in the long-term success of the data warehouse/data mart.

This dialog should be maintained throughout, with updated information entered regularly into the enterprise deployment map, and hence into the ROI model. For instance, in year two of the figure, the bank's retail group may decide it wants to accelerate the schedule for the Australian data mart, initially proposed for year five. Thanks to the enterprise deployment map and the organization's ongoing dialog, this information can help to update the ROI model — and to alert appropriate individuals and departments.

Step Two: Analyze Potential Benefits

Analyzing expected benefits would seem to be a simple task, but it can be extremely challenging — and rewarding.

For some organizations, determining benefits is straightforward: a baseline is

Figure 1: International Bank enterprise deployment map

BASE ATTRIBUTES	YEAR 1	YEAR 2	YEAR 3	YEAR 4	YEAR 5
# of Data Marts	1	2	4	6	6
No. of Sources	3	6	3	3	3
Type of Sources	DDA	Loans	Mortgages	Credit Cards	Trust
Physical Location	CORP	CORP	EUROPE	ASIA	AUSTRALIA
LOB Organization	Retail	Retail	Comm	Comm	Retail
Subject Area	MKTG.	Service	FINANCE	SALES	SALES
Size of Data Base	100	200	500	800	1000
#USERS					
Corporate	50	100	200	300	400
Europe	10	20	30	30	30
Asia/Pasific	10	20	40	80	160
Total Users	70	140	270	410	590

both simple and clear cut ("The average analytical report takes two weeks to process and deliver to the user. We want to cut that time to one day.")

But for most, benefits are not so clear. One group may feel that the most important benefit involves obtaining faster access to customer records for the purpose of cross-selling services. But another group might say that the most important benefit is the increased market share that would result from this cross-selling. Yet another group may argue that the more strategic (and less tangible) benefit — that of being able to better serve customers — outweighs the other two.

To aid the benefits analysis process, it is valuable to first differentiate between tangible and intangible benefits, then to prioritize both groups relative to their impact on actual business goals. Figure Two shows examples of tangible and intangible benefits. In order to predict and measure tangible benefits, a baseline analysis should be conducted to serve as a "before" snapshot. If improving report response time is a high priority, the actual pre-data warehouse response time should be measured by a standard set of rules, and then documented; that way, post-data warehouse improvements will be both measurable and credible, since they will be determined using the same measurement rules.

Applying numerical measures to strategic, intangible benefits is, of course difficult or, for most, impossible. This is unfortunate because strategic value is really the primary driving force behind data warehouse/data mart implementations. As Stephen Graham said in the IDC report, "...the true benefits of the warehouse lie in the decisions that it enables." Graham goes on to list other important strategic benefits. These include managing the total customer relationship/opportunity; creating value-add for the customer; building organizational empathy; reacting quickly to volatile controls and opportunities; managing both

Figure 2

Tangible Benefits

- Reduced inventory days from 90 to 30 days
- Increased sales by 30%
- Eliminated 240 weekly reports
- Lowered development costs by 6 person years
- Reduced response time for report requests from three weeks to three days
- Reduced the number of data extract programs maintained
- Increased market share by 1%

Intangible Benefits

- Faster more informed decision making
- Improved data accuracy, quality, consistency
- Improved customer service
- Faster delivery of products to market
- Migration from product focus to customer focus
- More efficient management of suppliers
- Improved quality of products and services

the macro and micro perspective; and improving managerial ability.

Once the expected benefits are grouped into tangible and intangible (tactical and strategic) sets, the organization should then prioritize them according to their impact on real business goals. For instance, reducing the number of paper reports might be important as an aid to saving administrative time and costs, but it's not nearly as meaningful from a business-goal perspective as, say, generating a 50 percent increase in sales.

Step Three: Calculate Net Present Value for all Benefits

An effective ROI model should put all findings in terms of current dollars. This means it must employ a formula for expressing future dollar benefits in meaningful, current-value terms.

To do this, the organization must allocate benefits defined and quantified in Step Two over a period of time (preferably five years). Here, the enterprise deployment map is valuable in helping managers and users project their hoped-for benefits over time. Figure Three shows an example where costs remain stable while incremental revenue rises substantially, as the organization feels the effects of anticipated gains in market share.

Step Four: Define Overall Costs

For the cost part of the ROI model, the organization should assess the dollar impact of 10 fundamental cost components:

- Hardware — Includes target database servers, desktop PC upgrades and related hardware. As Pieter R. Mimno points out in the Patricia Seybold Group report, "During the pilot phase, companies may be able to reduce costs by running the warehouse on an existing in-house server. However, most companies run their production data warehouses on dedicated servers, with the exception of companies that have excess capacity on their DB2/MVS mainframes."
- Networks — Although unusually complex network connections might call for inclusion in an ROI model, networking equipment costs typically fall within the realm of organizations' IT infrastructures. Because of this, we have

Figure 3

BENEFIT SIDE						
Incremental Revenue	1000000	4000000	12000000	20000000	25000000	62000000
Net Present Value of Incremental Revenue	$48,244,161					
Cost Savings	0	100000	100000	100000	100000	400000
Net Present Value of Cost Savings	$331,213					
Total Benefits		4100000	12100000	20100000	25100000	62400000
Net Present Value of Total Benefits	$48,575,373					

not included network costs in the ROI model examples shown in this white paper.

- RDBMS software — Licensing costs for the database products that will be used as the data warehouse/data mart storage facility. If the organization maintains an enterprise-wide licensing program, this cost may be minimal.
- Back-end tools — Data-modeling and data cleansing tools fall into this category. Tool costs may rise substantially in companies with complex organizational structures and/or diverse modeling requirements.
- Query/reporting tools — Include data access and analysis software such as OLAP/ROLAP/MOLAP, data-mining and other tools. In the Patricia Seybold report, Pieter R. Mimno points out that "Most companies buy three or four different types of tools to support various groups of users. Distinct user groups are: (1) programmers, (2) business analysts, (3) executives, and (4) line-of-business and product managers."
- Metadata repository — Although the metadata repository may be implemented as an inexpensive, tightly confined set of tables or document that shares space on an existing server, in most cases the repository will require a dedicated database. Because of this, repository hardware and software should be included as a distinct cost component.
- Internal labor — Includes database administrators, project managers, programmers, and other employees associated with the project.
- External labor — Includes outside consultants, systems integrators, contract programmers and other non-employee help.
- Ongoing support — Includes Help Desk and other forms of support, often difficult to assess accurately because of the formal/informal nature of most company support structures.
- Training — Training is a critical function, necessary for ensuring that end users and programmers gain easy familiarity with data warehouse/data mart query tools, administrative tools and programming languages. The importance of training cannot be overlooked, since ultimate success will depend on the willing participation of users and programmers.

Step Five: Calculate Net Present Value for all Costs

Once these components are quantified, the organization can then calculate net present value for costs, as a means of filling in the cost side of the ROI model. This can be accomplished by either of two methods, actual cost and percentage. Each has advantages and disadvantages that must be weighed by the organization.

The actual cost method requires detailed estimates for all cost components, projected over the enterprise deployment map timeframe. Once in place, these costs can be entered into the net present value formula, as shown in Figure Four. Although the actual cost estimates can be tedious and time-consuming to generate, they do reflect a relatively accurate assessment of projected costs.

Figure 4

ENTERPRISE DM STRATEGY	Five-Year Data Warehousing Cost of Ownership Model- Base Economic Cost Justification				
	YEAR 1	YEAR 2	YEAR 3	YEAR 4	YEAR 5
Informatica Power Center 1.0					
Base License (Class II UNIX)	300,000				
Add'n Source & Target	N/A				
Lab Lincense (Class II UNIX)	$100,000				
Power Mart 4.0 Network Edition (Unlimited S & T)					
Base Enterprise License (UNIX), Unlimited Targets		&60,000	$120,000	$60,000	$60,000
Enterprise Lab License	$20,000		$20,000	$20,000	$40,000
Total Licensing Fees	$420,000	$60,000	$140,000	$80,000	$100,000
Implementation Services (10 days/org)	$11,145	$22,290	$11,145	$11,145	$11,145
Training (3 days per org and geo)	$5,400	$10,800	$5,400	$5,400	$5,400
Total expenses	$6,000	$12,000	$6,000	$6,000	$6,000
Total cost	$442,545	$105,090	$162,545	$102,545	$122,545
Applicable Volume Discount (15%)	$44,255	$0	$0	$0	$0
Net Cost	$398,291	$105,090	$162,545	$102,545	$122,545
Net Present Value of Net Cost	$806,430				

Alternatively, the organization can employ a type of shorthand by assigning percentage-of-cost values to these components, then projecting them into more broadly estimated costs. This requires use of basic assumptions for cost breakdowns — shown in Figure Five are percentages developed by Informatica, based on research and field experience.

With the percentage cost method, an organization can roughly estimate project costs quickly, by calculating a single cost component via the actual cost method, and then projecting relative costs of other components according to their percentage values. The advantage is time saved over the more laborious actual cost method; the disadvantage is reduced accuracy. Depending on the circumstances, however, percentage-based costing may ideal for creating initial ROI snapshots.

Step Six: Assess Risk, Adjust Costs and Benefits

A key element in the Informatica ROI approach is risk assessment; by identifying and evaluating potential project threats — those that may cause serious budget or time overruns — organizations can take proactive preparatory or avoidance actions. Types and areas of project risks can be difficult to identify and evaluate, but each organization should strive to generate a

Figure 5

ENTERPRISE DM STRATEGY	Five-Year Data Warehousing Cost of Ownership Model-Base Economic Cost Justification				
	YEAR 1	YEAR 2	YEAR 3	YEAR 4	YEAR 5
Power Mart 4.0 Standalone Edition					
Base License (Class II UNIX)	$100,000		$135,000	$100,000	$100,000
Additonal Source Types	$545,000	$45,000	$110,000	$55,000	$55,000
Additional Target Instances (UNIX)	$0	$60,000	$300,000	$150,000	$150,000
Lab License (Class II UNIX)	$40,000		$40,000	$40,000	$40,000
PowerPlugs	$10,000		$10,000	$10,000	$20,000
Total Licensing Fee	$195,000	$105,000	$595,000	$355,000	$365,000
Implementation Services (10 days/org)	$16,500	$33,000	$16,500	$16,500	$16,500
Training (3 days per org and geo)	$5,400	$10,800		$5,400	$10,800
Total Expenses	$6,000	$12,000		$6,000	$12,000
Total Costs	$222,900	$160,800	$611,500	$382,900	$404,300
Applicable Discount	$11,145	$8,040	$91,725	$38,290	$40,430
Net Cost	$211,755	$152,760	$519,775	$344,610	$363,870
Net Present Value of Costs	$1,339,841				
Maintenace (20%)	$39,000	$60,000	$90,552	$212,862	$281,774
Net Present Value of Maintenance	$548,270				

realistic assessment of risks that are potentially most harmful. Some of the major risks are:

- Scope creep — Frequently, data warehouse/data mart projects tend to grow in scope — user numbers, storage size, report numbers and so on — with accelerating pace as users gain familiarity with their capabilities. Users may start out requesting simple analytical reports, for instance, then progress to more complex requests once they see the analytical potential. Also, new, unanticipated users may be encouraged to try out the new data warehouse/data mart when they see their peers' analytical efforts. Scope creep causes performance to suffer as the data warehouse/data mart is asked to go beyond the bounds of its original definition.

Solution: Thorough planning and tightly defined project parameters can guard against scope creep.

- Integration complexity — It is difficult to assess the time and cost required for integrating complex sets of data warehouse/data mart tools and other components, since complex systems integration projects frequently run over time and over budget.

Solution: Addressing the "build vs. buy" decision early in the project life, and standardizing on vendors with integrated product sets, can reduce the threats associated with integration overruns.

- Architectural strategy — An inappropriate architectural strategy can prove disastrous, since architecture is the foundation upon which the decision-support systems will be built.

Solution: Investigating the advantages and disadvantages of various architectural approaches — and overlaying these with the enterprise deployment map — will help organizations with accurate architectural planning. For instance, if the enterprise deployment map calls for multiple data marts to be built over time, the best architectural strategy is to begin with a distributed, dependent data mart framework such as Informatica's PowerCenter. That way, adding incremental data marts will be both simple and economical, since metadata synchronization and other elements of distributed architecture will be in place.

Other risks come from management or end users who may withhold project support; from the entanglements of internal politics; and from technologies that don't function as promised.

To deal with the human aspects of risk — reluctant managers and users, "political" problems — the best solutions involve thorough up-front planning, realistic expectations-setting, and establishment of processes for keeping managers engaged and users informed. These are typically accomplished by honest effective communications, by maintaining regular "dialog" with management and end users. This way, managers won't harbor unrealistic expectations for their newly constructed data warehouse/data mart, and users, regularly solicited for input into the design process, won't feel neglected as query tools are configured and prepared for use. Also, particular care should be taken with data element definitions and data cleansing efforts in general, in order to avoid "Garbage In/Garbage Out" problems.

As for technology risks, organizations should carefully assess the performance of their prospective vendors' products. And in some cases they should apply best case/worst case metrics to critical technology resources.

Step Seven: Determine Overall ROI

With the preparatory calculations discussed in Steps One through Seven now in place, the final step, calculating ROI, is largely a matter of activating the ROI formula: subtract net present value of total costs from net present value of (total incremental revenue plus cost savings). As shown in Figure Six, this delivers a total return on investment of 397 percent, with a payback of just over two and a half years.

This result matches closely the findings of the 1996 IDC report, The Foundations of Wisdom: A Study of the Financial Impact of Data Warehousing. Among approximately 50 companies in industries ranging from financial and manufacturing to retail

Figure 5

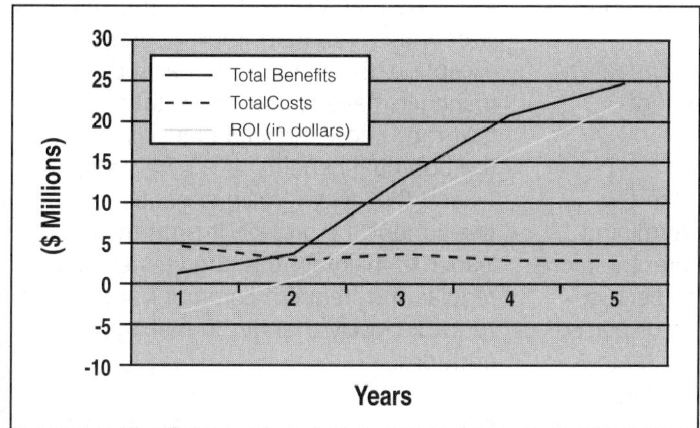

ROI is most effectively employed to compare and evaluate four fundamental business and architectural approaches to data warehouses/data marts.

These include:

- Build vs. Buy — Here ROI modeling can help to uncover long term maintenance costs incurred for custom-coded or generator-produced systems that are sometimes hidden by conventional product evaluations;
- Standalone proof of concept — ROI modeling can give line-of-business users a snapshot of how a dedicated data mart might help them achieve decision support benefits;
- Independent vs. dependent data mart growth analysis — ROI can help guard against a shortsighted approach to building multiple data marts. For organizations planning for multiple data marts over time, it is far less costly to put the elements of an enterprise architecture — data cleansing and definition standardization, metadata synchronization, and network interfaces for distributed data marts — in place during implementation of the initial system. Many organizations today employ ROI modeling to contrast the differences between this approach and

transportation and government, this study found an average three-year ROI of 401 percent. Average payback for data warehouse applications was 2.3 years; average data warehouse cost was $2.2 million.

ROI Insights from Informatica

But the IDC study also found that ROI can vary widely, so it does little good to over-value industry averages. Each organization must find its own best ROI, and each must carefully consider its own organizational makeup, personality and culture in determining what defines a successful data warehouse/data mart ROI.

Based on our own experience serving data warehouse/data mart applications for large and small organizations across a range of industries, Informatica can offer valuable insights into using ROI modeling to evaluate data warehouse/data mart feasibility.

the more costly approach of creating after-the-fact data mart distribution.

Organizational size, structure, complexity play significant roles in ROI level of difficulty.

A number of factors can increase the complexities involved with determining ROI. Organizational scope is one: the more decentralized an organization's decision-making structure and the more dispersed its offices, the greater the difficulty in generating accurate multi-year plans. Another factor involves equipment and topological complexity: numerous legacy database systems and complex, multi-tier client-server networks can confound data warehouse/data mart planning substantially, and adversely affect ROI.

For these reasons, the more care taken with the enterprise deployment map, the better. The enterprise deployment map is an opportunity to bring together dispersed resources and points of view, and to achieve agreement on fundamental business goals and other issues. Every hour spent on the enterprise deployment map may save hundreds of hours subsequently, when errors must be corrected in the heat of hardware and software implementation.

The importance of "human" issues in determining success or failure must not be overlooked.

The vision and commitment of management and the willingness and enthusiasm of end users play vital roles in accurate ROI modeling and in determining overall project success.

Any major project needs at least one executive-management advocate, and data warehouse/data mart implementation is no exception. But it is critical that such managers have realistic expectations — that they know the limitations as well as the potential benefits of the new systems — and that they remain engaged throughout the project. It is up the project leader to maintain this engagement via regular and frequent communications, and to track closely changes in management attitudes.

Key end users must also be engaged to understand and work with the new system. Particular care must be taken with data cleansing and with implementation of query tools so users don't become disillusioned by "bad" data or difficult-to-use analytical tools. For this reason, user input should be included at every step of ROI planning and system implementation, and users should be guided carefully through report-building and subsequent processes. Needless to say, comprehensive support and training are vital elements, not to be overlooked in ROI modeling.

Strategic benefits, while not immediately quantifiable, must be considered and valued.

As mentioned earlier, one of the greatest difficulties in constructing an ROI model involves how (or whether) to value intangible, strategic benefits. Industry experts recommend at a minimum that strategic benefits be considered, and at a maximum that they be factored in as distinct elements of management-productivity analysis.

Yet another point of view comes from former Kmart CIO Dave Carlson, who was quoted in Computerworld (November 1, 1996): "I have always believed that in fact the most important systems are often those which are strategic and by definition have benefits which are not well understood. I suspect that American Airlines' Sabre system was not cost-justified but still changed the airline business forever."

Another sentiment in favor of strategic benefit comes from Howard Edels, senior vice president/CIO for CVS, quoted in the same Computerworld article. He said "Executives make key strategic decisions based on insight or gut. Then they use financial numbers to get a sense of cost benefit. But the cost will only guide how they will proceed, not if they will stop."

The Benefits of Data Warehouse/Data Mart ROI

With ROI modelling, organizations can build strong internal support for data warehouse/data mart projects, and can put in place a credible yardstick for measuring the value of such endeavors.

Recent results from some Informatica customers bear this out. These customers, in industries ranging from banking and utility to education, defined ROI according to their unique objectives. Each went into production within six months of project start, and each determined that an architected approach to data mart distribution would produce the greatest return on investment.

For these companies, and for others now embarking on data warehouse/data mart projects, ROI modeling can bring substantial benefits. It may serve as a key to helping define data warehouse/data mart projects in ways that are most appropriate and valuable for the organization. And it may be the best means of satisfying even the most risk-averse CEO that the IS group is using scarce corporate resources as effectively as possible.

Sidebar:

Assuring Success Through Proactive Risk Avoidance

During ROI modeling and project implementation, the data warehouse/data mart sponsor(s) should take any steps possible to minimize project risks proactively. Such risk-avoidance actions include:

- Assess closely the timing of various costs, since these have direct impact on payback ratios.
- Define baseline measurements as precisely as possible.
- Evaluate and monitor regularly executive involvement and end-user participation.
- Track corporate commitment/funding — does executive management consider this a "skunkworks" project or a strategic venture?
- Document assumptions, check and re-check expectations of appropriate individuals.
- Put processes in place to guard against and manage "scope creep."

- Regularly assess skill levels among the data warehouse/data mart project team.
- Calculate accurately the degree of data cleansing necessary to ensure consistent, meaningful reports.
- Determine quality and appropriateness of reporting tools for each end-user segment.
- Maintain effective internal data warehouse/data mart marketing via end-user training and Help Desk support.

Data Mining: Statistical Analysis

Title: *Data Mining: Statistical Analysis*
Author: *Rob Mattison*
Abstract: *This white paper is an excerpt of Rob Mattison's Data Warehousing: Strategies, Technologies and Techniques: Statistical Analysis report. Today, as we are confronted with increasingly large volumes of data, statistics are, more than ever, a critical component of the data mining and refining toolkit that facilitates making effective business decisions.*

Data mining is uncovering the hidden meaning and relationships in the massive amounts of data stored in the data warehouse. In short, the value of the data warehouse lies in the information that can be derived from its data through the mining process. Successful mining of data relies on refining tools and techniques capable of rendering large quantities of data understandable and meaningful. Since its creation in the 18th century, statistics have served this purpose, providing the mathematical tools and analytic techniques for dealing with large amounts of data.

What are statistics and why use them?

Way of thinking

Statistics is a general method of reasoning from data. It is a basic approach shared by people in today's society to draw conclusions and make decisions in business and in life. It lets us communicate effectively about a wide range of topics from sales performance to product quality to operational efficiency. Statistics is the way that we "reason effectively about data and chance in everyday life." The goal of statistical analysis is to gain insight through numbers. We will consider four important aspects of statistics: developing good data, strategies for exploring data, and drawing conclusions from the data, and presenting your results.

Because data from different sources can vary, the conclusions we can draw from them are uncertain. For example, as we measure sales, attitudes, and characteristics, we will get different measures because people and things vary--or sometimes the measurement system itself introduces variation into the measures. Since we are making inferences from variable data, our conclusions have some uncertainty. David Moore, in his book Statistics: Concepts and Controversies says:

"Statistics faces the variability and uncertainty of the world directly. Statistical reasoning can produce data whose usefulness is not destroyed by variation and uncertainty. It can analyze data to separate systematic patterns from the ever-present variation. It can form conclusions that, while not certain--nothing in the real world is certain--have only a little uncertainty. More important, statistical reasoning allows us to say just how uncertain our conclusions are."

Producing data

You will have a wealth of data in the warehouse and available from outside sources. There are important concepts to consider in selecting the data you actually use in your analysis. These concepts are: sampling, experimentation, and measurement. They are important because the efficiency and accuracy of your analysis-- and therefore your ability to draw useful conclusions in a timely manner--are dependent on the quality of the data reflecting the business situation.

Sampling is based upon the idea that we can draw conclusions about an entire group of people or objects by examining part of the group. It is used to gain information about the group. With proper sampling, we do not need to look at every piece of information to draw reasonable conclusions. In regards to the data in a data warehouse, you will find that with certain types of analysis, you will prefer to obtain sample data rather than including every case in storage. You can get an accurate picture of your order-to-shipment turnaround by randomly selecting a subset of orders to analyze rather than pulling every order over the time period from the warehouse. Similarly, we can conduct a quarterly survey of employee satisfaction using sampling techniques and get good information with less time and expense (and annoyance to the employees) than polling each person each quarter.

Experimentation is used to produce data when you are interested in cause and effect relationships rather than just collecting information. Experiments require that we impose change on the subject of the study, to see the impact of the change. We look at explanatory and response variables (or fields) and try to isolate and understand the impact of a change in an explanatory variable on a response variable. You might, for example, try altering the machining speed used in manufacturing parts to see if there is an impact on the number of defective parts or experiment with decreasing the time to preventive maintenance to see if machine failures also decrease. With designed experiments, we can test a variety of explanatory factors in a group of experiments to see which will have the greatest impact on reaching the desired state of the response variables. For example, two materials are not bonding properly in the assembly process. Is the answer a change in one or both materials, the bonding agent, the bonding temperature or pressure, or the speed of the cool-down process. Since you need multiple measures to distinguish variability in measurement vs. true change, testing one factor at a time could result in a very lengthy and expensive experimentation process. Statistical design of experiments lets you test multiple factors simultaneously and get the most informative results with the least number of experiments.

Understanding measurement is important for data analysis. You cannot draw valid conclusions if the data does not accurately represent what you assumed. Sometimes we use something we cannot measure as a proxy for what we are really interested in measuring such as number of returns are equated to unhappy customers. It is possible that returns are caused by multiple factors and not all of them indicate problems. Understanding the measurement will improve your analysis. For example are monthly sales numbers in the data warehouse gross shipments or net of returns? Does the organization measure and store both numbers or only the net numbers? Are they coded in one field or two different places?

Measurement is how we produce data in either observation or experimentation. Statistics deal with cases, variables and values which are the individual objects being measured, the specific properties being measured, and the assigned number measuring the property in that object. We define a sales representative's performance in terms of sales, returns, pipeline value, and number of calls made. Each variable has a different measure. All measurement varies, however, and one goal of analysis is to understand if the measurement variation is random or biased in a specific direction. Since much of this book is related to producing and storing data, we will note that understanding the data is essential to effective data mining. That means understanding the source of the data whether observation or experimentation as well as the meaning of the variable and its measuring system. To draw meaningful conclusions from the data, it must actually measure the characteristic that you are interested in understanding.

Exploring Data

Exploring data is important for understanding the quality of the data in the warehouse and to begin looking for areas to mine for information. Exploring data will tell you if most of the observations are missing or will indicate if the measurements are suspect because of extreme variability. In effect, exploratory data analysis gives you a "feel" for the data and will help uncover possible directions the analysis can go. Just as the mining company explores the terrain looking for the place to put a mine with the highest likelihood of success, so too does the data miner need to gain a sense of where the key relationships are in the data. Probably equally important, exploring data will serve to highlight any problems inherent in the database in terms of inaccurate or missing data.

The first step in data analysis must be exploring it to see overall patterns and extreme exceptions to the patterns. This is best done by graphing the data and visually identifying the patterns and the number of exceptions. In exploring data we typically look at each variable separately starting with basic counts and percentages which tell us the number and proportion of measures at each level. Then we look at the distributions of the data using charts like histograms, dot plots, boxplots, line charts, and others. We also look at some measure of the data that describe various characteristics of the data in terms of average, variability, and distribution.

- Descriptive statistics include the following measures:
  - -mean arithmetic average of the values
  - -median the midpoint of values
  - -mode the most frequent value
  - -percentiles breaking the numbers in to groups by percentage of values above and below
  - -variance average deviation of observations from the mean
  - -standard deviation the spread of values around the mean

Data exploration will also show you if there are a few extreme measures that are wildly inflating or deflating the measures of the variable. In cases like this, you will get more accurate information from your data by eliminating these extreme outliers before continuing with the analysis. They are typically reflective of data entry errors or odd circumstances and will not reflect the true situation that you are trying to understand. You may want to investigate the source of the oddity, but for statistical analysis, you can eliminate the cases from the sample without jeopardizing the quality of your analysis.

In data mining applications, there is often a problem related to the sheer size of the data set being used. In addition to computer resource limitations, you may find that the vast number of inter-relationships between data items can obscure the relationships we are truly interested in. Statistical tools can also sample or summarize data to make it easier to work with. Random sampling allows us to create a smaller, more manageable, working subset of the data from which statistically valid conclusions can still be drawn. Techniques like principal components or factor analysis allow us to reduce a data set to its underlying dimensions by grouping together fields that are very closely related into a single measure.

Exploring your data first will keep you from spending time and effort on unsupported analyses and will help prevent drawing conclusions which are not supported by your data. The goal of data exploration is to start you on a successful path towards full data mining and refining--drawing actionable conclusions from your data.

Drawing Conclusions from data

Statistics are concerned with finding relationships between variables. Once one has mined to an area with an interesting relationship, statistics provide the additional tools to "refine" the data into an understanding of the strength of the relationship and the factors that cause the relationship. For example, order values and sales lead sources are interesting characteristics to measure and summarize. But order value and sales lead source for the same order give us significantly more information than either measure alone. When we have the source and the value of orders linked, we can look for associations between the source and value which will lead us to evaluating higher promotion spending on the sources which bring the most high value orders or possibly on the sources which bring the highest total revenue even if it is booked as smaller transactions in higher volume.

We begin by describing the association of two variables, usually with a table or chart. We can also indicate the strength of a straight-line relationship using a correlation coefficient. Then we begin to look for an explanation of the relationship. Does one characteristic cause the other--does lead source cause order size? Or does one measure predict another --can we predict the average order size from the lead source? In some cases, a variable can predict another even though there is no cause-and-effect relationship between them. Typical explanations for association between variables are causation, common response, or confounding. Causation means that changes in variable A cause changes in variable B such as increased employment of temporary workers causes a change in salary expenses. Common response means that changes in both A and B are caused by changes in a third variable, C. For example, sales revenue generated and hours of customer contact are both influenced by length of tenure as a sales rep. Confounding describes the association when changes in B are caused both by changes in A and by changes in the third variable, C. Sales revenue fluctuates from both changes in promotional spending and changes in the number of sales representatives available to follow up on leads and take orders.

It is not a simple leap to go from association of variables to causation. Causation can only be concluded with significant evidence. Without conducting properly designed experiments to demonstrate the causal link and eliminating any other possible explanations, statistics do not support concluding that associations are due to causation. But statistics can help determine the likelihood that the relationship is coincidental. This is particularly useful when we want to explain an unusual occurrence such as if we discovered that the sales for a product were generated by one salesperson. Are we missing the data on other sales? Or does only one salesperson understand the product well enough to close orders? Or is the market so small that the only customers are in one territory?

Strong relationships between variables are useful when we want to predict the value of variable from others. If we can describe the relationship as a line or curve, then we have a formula for predicting certain values when the data exist for the other predictive variables. The basic technique used is regression which fits a line between the data points in such a way that it minimizes the distance from the known data points to the line. Prediction does not depend on having causal relationships between variables. A high college grade point average does not cause high quality job performance in a new employee. But an employer might predict that the study skills, work ethic, and intelligence which resulted in high grades will also be reflected in the applicant's performance on the job once hired.

A special case of prediction is time series analysis where the same characteristics are measured over time intervals. For instance, daily or monthly sales revenue could be predicted from past measures of revenue along with corresponding measures of inventory status, promotional dollars spent, sales reps available, etc. Similarly, past history of absenteeism does not cause an employee to miss work but an employer interested in projecting a worker's available days can reasonably start from the worker's prior years' days worked. Another special case of prediction is called classification. This technique is used when we want to predict membership in a group or category, rather than a specific number. In our database marketing example which follows, the company was predicting whether the account would respond or not respond to the new product offering based on attributes of the company and its previous purchases.

There are more advanced statistical techniques available to draw stronger conclusions or to tease out relationships which are not described by a straight-line. The fundamental principles are the same. Statistics are the method by which we describe relationships, draw conclusions, and state the level of uncertainty associated with our conclusions.

Some practical applications of statistics in business

Applications of statistics in data mining
Statistical analysis is the secret weapon of many successful businesses today. It is the essential tool for mining the data you have, refining the data into useful information, and for leading you to other data you might want to acquire. Businesses who effectively employ statistical analysis can increase revenues, cut costs, improve operating efficiency, and improve customer satisfaction. They can more accurately identify problems and opportunities and understand their causes so that they can more quickly act to eliminate threats or capitalize on opportunities.

One particularly rich and easily accessible solution for statistics in the data mining area is represented by the products of SPSS Inc. They have focused their business on developing statistical product and service solutions to bring the power of statistics to bear on the analytic problems emerging in today's marketplace.

Variety of examples in all fields
SPSS's products have helped their clients solve problems in a variety of fields from customer satisfaction and database marketing to credit risk analysis and sales force productivity. In the remainder of this section, we will highlight cases in each of these areas. But first, let's look at additional applications of data mining using statistics:

- sales forecasting resulting in more efficient manufacturing planning
- sales territory evaluation resulting in better coverage of sales opportunities
- payable analysis resulting in more effective cash management
- product line performance resulting in rationalizing or expanding product offerings
- employee success analysis resulting in more effective recruiting of personnel
- employee satisfaction assessment resulting in reduced staff turnover
- benefits analysis resulting in the most attractive and cost effective plan offerings

- promotions analysis resulting in more effective spending to generate business
- customer service analysis resulting in elimination of sources of errors and complaints
- customer support analysis resulting in most effective staffing levels to meet demand
- customer attrition analysis resulting in more effective revenue planning<
- customer value analysis resulting in increased repeat business at lower cost

Customer satisfaction

IBM was experiencing a steady three year decline in customer satisfaction. The company's management decided to focus on improving customer satisfaction and designated certain people as "Customer Satisfaction Advocates." Their job was to figure out what was wrong and how to fix it. One of the advocates used statistical tools to refine data to identify the key areas of opportunity and to measure improvement in customer satisfaction levels.

The advocate used two surveys to collect his data. One was a national blind survey while the other was specific to his region and was developed in conjunction with other members of the IBM team. The advocate used statistics to identify patterns in the data--or to refine the data into nuggets of useful information. Using correlations, F-tests, regression, and other statistical techniques, he identified five specific traits of Technical Service that IBM customers in his region really cared about:

- Continuity of their relationship with IBM -- customers wanted to be able to count on their IBM team
- Value of their investment -- customers wanted to know they were getting the most value out of their hardware, software, manuals, training, support lines, etc.
- Technical support -- customers wanted reliable technical support that was there when needed and that provided useful, accurate information.
- Hardware service -- customers wanted to know that there hardware was the best, guaranteed, and with a warranty. And, if it needed to be fixed, IBM would fix it properly.
- Good company to do business with -- customers wanted to feel like IBM was taking care of them

Based on this understanding of what was important to their customers, IBM was able to "manage by fact" and develop specific programs and initiatives that enhanced the five key areas of interest. They developed a custom application which was effectively a specialized customer database. The system, called QUEST, was installed in each IBM store or office in the region. Using the QUEST system, IBM managers could more easily tailor their service to key customer issues. They can look up a specific customer's service records or they can look at how other reps in similar situations in other regions are solving customer problems. The system gives each business segment owner a unique customer satisfaction model. Each model provides:

- Unique predictors of customer satisfaction for the business segment
- Expected improvement
- Focused actions, and
- Forecasting methodology

In other words, it lets the business unit manager identify factors which indicate whether a customer will be satisfied. Then it lets her identify what improvement is expected by the customers, set plans to focus on solving that problem, and finally measuring results of the program and forecasting the satisfaction of the customers based on their experiences with the company.
For example, "Red" customers in the territory with a "stripes" installed less than 12 months, showed a statistically significantly lower customer satisfaction index when compared to other "Red" customers. The IBM business unit responsible for "red"customers decided to focus on the delivery of technical support as the best, most targeted, most impact-potential opportunity. The result of the QUEST system and its ability to identify and focus attention on specific problems, is that customer satisfaction has increased over three consecutive quarters. This was based on a logical, structured process using statistical analysis to highlight requirements for a highly targeted program.

Database marketing
Industrial components supplier RS Components of Corby England planned to attack a new sector of its target market but needed to ensure that telesales effort was not wasted on no-hope prospects. RS Components main business is the supply of electrical components. An opportunity was identified in mechanical parts and tools, for which it was expected many potential customers would be found within the existing user base.

In order to determine where the best prospects lay, the business development manager, Nigel Thompson set the sales force a four month task to approach the top 75% of their customer base. This exercise yielded a success rate of 11%--one solid prospect for each nine sites approached.

The remaining 25% of their customers were to be addressed with a telemarketing campaign. Since it was known that the previous exercise had probably creamed off the best prospects, some way had to be found to ensure that the telemarketing campaign targeted those remaining sites offering the best chance of live prospects.

During the initial exercise the sales force had recorded a lot of information about those sites that had, and had not, yielded prospects and these attributes were added to the customer database. Thompson decided to review this information to see if the characteristics of those sites which yielded prospects differed from those sites which did not. If they did then the groups could be meaningfully segmented.
The attributes added to the customer database were:

- Industrial classification
  - -Size of company
  - -Geographical location
  - -Status of sales force assessment
  - -Transaction history
  - -Recency of last order

-Order value
-Product(s) purchased.

The database was queried using SPSS statistical analysis software. The first step was to run some simple summary statistics to determine measures such as averages and ranges for each attribute. The process itself revealed some interesting facts about the customers that had not previously been measured. Of more interest, however, was determining which attributes were related to prospect yield. Did companies of a particular size yield more prospects than others, for example. Identifying such relationships would enable RS Components to predict which companies in the remaining 25% were likely to yield prospects. They began exporting the data with crosstabulations (crosstabulations are counts of one variable against another) to get a feel for how different attributes interacted. However, it quickly became clear that while this approach was useful in identifying the most significant attributes, that they would miss something because there were potentially five million crosstabulations cells to examine.

Crosstabulations were limiting for two reasons. First, if there are numerous attributes, the number of crosstabulations required to investigate every possible relationship can be unmanageable. Secondly, crosstabulations do not take into account how attributes may interact. For example, it may be that geographical location is a significant predictor--sites in the South East yield more prospects than sites in other locations. It could also be that size of company is an important predictor--companies with over 100 employees yield more prospects than other sites. But what about sites with 100+ employees in the North West? Which is the most important predictor--geographic location or size of company? Or is it the combination of the two that is important? SPSS CHAID analysis solves these problems by analyzing and ordering every possible combination of attributes. It then identifies which attribute is the most important predictor, which attributes have no predictive value and how attributes combine or interact together to help in prediction.

SPSS CHAID segments a database into groups according to their prospect yield, or whatever attribute you are trying to predict. Each group can be identified by a combination of attributes and ranked from best (e.g. the best group yielded 50% prospects and was made up of companies with the following characteristics...) to worst (0% prospect yield in companies with these characteristics...).

By applying this information back into the remaining 25% of the database, half the sites were identified as not being worth a telemarketing call. This in itself produced a cost saving of $80,000. Those that were called produced a success rate very close to the anticipated 15%--a better rate than had been achieved by the blanket approach to calling the top 75% of accounts who were supposedly the best targets. The company was highly encouraged by the results. They continue to use these techniques for further profiling and segmentation of the customer base, and with similar success. SPSS and SPSS CHAID are now vital elements of RS Components' database marketing analysis.

Credit risk analysis

Our example of the application of data mining techniques to credit risk analysis comes from the UK. The banking industry has used statistical models widely for many years. Banks would like to make consistent, accurate and efficient decisions about whether or not to extend credit to customers. Initially, the data were quite limited. But since the industry practice is to justify and document credit decisions, there has grown a vast wealth of data and the problem has been how to store and harness it effectively for use in modeling and decision-making. Estimates are that a bank may have roughly 1500 pieces of information per month for each customer. Since in the UK they are required to keep information for six years they could reasonably have 108,000 pieces of information per customer. If a large bank has 9 million customers, they will have roughly 1 billion pieces of customer information. Unfortunately, in most banks there are no links between different accounts such as credit card vs. checking vs. savings accounts for the same customer. Banks are beginning to assemble customer information in data warehouse form because they are recognizing the importance of understanding and managing the complete relationship with the customer as a whole.

One bank has worked extensively with a statistical modeling firm using SPSS to pull together the relevant information and develop a model for making credit decisions--consistently, accurately, and efficiently. A collections model was developed with a goal of understanding which customers are likely to go into default and when an effort should be made to collect against them.

Initially the collections model looked at all accounts that had reached a trigger point, usually the due date of an installment payment. The accounts were divided into good and bad and a cutoff score was established, similar to the approach banks use in scoring credit applications in the first place. This approach is probably the most widely used in the banking industry today. But if we reflect on the situation further, we may begin to believe that this simple categorization of customers into "good" and "bad" is not accurate, or useful enough, particularly when the measure of good and bad is a given level of delinquency.

There are many different patterns of behavior which can be expressed as levels of delinquency or movements between levels. Some customers will consistently fail to pay the credit card outstanding balance if the amount is small, so they may miss one or two months payments and then pay off the entire debt. An examination of past payment patterns revealed that there was no significant risk attached to customers in this group. Other customers may be consistently 30 days past due on their accounts. In this group are often customers using their card for business purposes and facing a built-in administrative delay in payment as a result of claiming the expense for reimbursement before paying off the card debt. Use of cluster analysis led to the identification of different customer groups based on their behavior patterns. Once the behavioral groups are defined, then the decision models were built to effectively separate the groups. This analysis was based on the data set which described the customer's behavior only in terms of the amount owed at each time of billing. The question then arises whether we can identify when a customer will leave the group, i.e. change behavior. The state of the bank's data made it infeasible to analyze delinquent balances but it was possible to construct a model for payment patterns. When the data on payment dates and amounts was incorporated into the data set, analysis showed a very strong and consistent pattern of payment behavior for customers. Once the pattern was breached, it appeared that the customer was much more likely to default. This was true whether or not the account was overdue before the behavior change.

The models used have evolved over a five year period. The issues were a combination of data assembly and analysis. Data comes into play when better decision-making is required. And often, useful and powerful pieces of information are already available to be retrieved from storage and used to understand the underlying situation. In this case a huge amount of data on each customer, probably 95% was of no interest. Creating an all-encompassing historical database from which to develop perfect decision models for customer management is unrealistic and unnecessary. Applying the techniques of exploration, mining, and refining with statistical tools allows good conclusions with known levels of uncertainty from a much smaller, simpler data solution.

Sales and marketing productivity

A software company uses statistical analysis for data mining in sales force productivity analysis. They combine data from their customer database, order entry system, and telephone system to measure their effectiveness in generating prospects and closing orders. This approach grew out of a basic exploration of their customer database system and analysis of leads generated through promotional activities such as advertising, direct mail, and public relations programs. They quickly realized that they could generate leads much more easily than they could close them--leads piling up waiting for sales reps seemed to indicate a capacity problem in the sales group.

Further analysis found that there were two distinct patterns in the time to close an order. For a large number of orders, the time between the initial inquiry call and the order was one week or less and the number of contacts with the prospect was small. For another group, the duration was substantially longer--three to six months in many cases--and there were many contacts with the prospect over time. This led them to conclude that the first group of prospects required little "selling" by sales reps; they basically called to order or for some specific information required before placing an order. Their calls could be handled through a group of more junior sales representatives who had access to price sheets, product specifications, and delivery information. Thus the data mining led to establishment of an "order taking" group within the sales department which provided excellent customer service at lower cost to the company than processing simple orders through experienced sales representatives.

Regular analysis of measures across sales groups has led to more effective allocation of sales resources and identification of personnel development opportunities. Call volumes were tracked by sales representatives. Measuring the hours each rep spent on the phone indicated two opportunities for improvement. The sales systems required significant time by the rep to record information on their sales calls and even longer to actually enter an order in the system. Since reps were required to spend so much time off the phone on paperwork, it was difficult to evaluate when they were on essential but non-selling tasks and when they were not. Improvements in the sales information and order taking processes and regular measurement--with known standards--of phone time at the individual rep level, led to a significant increase in actual selling time available. Patterns became identified in the ramp-up for a new sales representative to reach average phone time levels and representatives who have difficulty achieving expected call volumes can be identified easily without waiting for them to miss their sales quota further down the road. The early intervention with additional coaching and skills training has resulted in decreased sales rep turnover and in new reps reaching full productivity sooner and more consistently.

In addition, business units within the sales organization can now be compared on a quarterly basis. Each unit reports standard statistics on rep call volume and phone time, pipelines in expected revenue and number of active sales opportunities, and sources of leads. Sales management can quickly see if certain business units are still severely capacity-constrained and are losing business because of their inability to contact prospects quickly. Business units with lower lead to rep ratios and close rates could shift resources either temporarily or permanently to units where the incremental revenue of an additional sales rep is significantly higher. Similarly, promotion dollars can be shifted to markets where the incremental return is highest and out of markets which are producing revenue for the company at a slower rate. This ability to capture opportunities by shifting resources to the highest performing areas is a significant advantage in today's competitive business environment.

Who does the data mining and when?

End users are the best data miners

With flexible, easy-to-use statistical tools, the subject matter experts become the best data miners and refiners. In effect, who is better to explore customer characteristics than the marketing and sales personnel in the company. Who will spot trends appearing across the industry in the employee satisfaction levels of the company, if not the human resources professionals? The best data miners are those who have an understanding of interesting places to look for problems and opportunities, typically those people who love their professional area and have a vision of making the company more profitable, more nimble, more competitive.

SPSS software takes statistics beyond the realm of the statisticians and puts them in the hands of people who are interested in exploring, refining, understanding, and drawing conclusions. The result is that these professionals are no longer locked into turning spreadsheets inside out and upside down to subset and analyze data. They can pursue interesting ideas immediately. As long as they have access to the data--and to an accurate description of the source and measurement system used to collect or generate the data--they can mine for the new and interesting information that will change the organization.

Application developers deploy statistical tools in the organization

Application developers have an opportunity to build statistics into their programs in order to capitalize on the full potential of the stored data. SPSS provides a developer's kit which enables IT professionals or others to quickly link the SPSS data management, statistics, and graphing routines into their custom application. This means that when the organization wants to look at the same relationships regularly and in consistent form, that the most effective approach is building the application. The SPSS Developer's Kit provides the option of including SPSS functionality in three ways: completely hidden to the end user but performing statistical analysis in the background; partially exposed where the user sees the SPSS dialog boxes, probably with the language of the organization or application substituted in for the standard statistical terms but allowing the user to make selections which define exactly how the data is analyzed and presented, or fully exposed where the application provides SPSS access for ad hoc analysis or more sophisticated users. The advantage of incorporating SPSS into your data mining applications is that you save massive programming and testing time by plugging in known routines rather than coding your own from scratch. You have the proven algorithms and usability of the leading end-user statistical tool right at your end users' fingertips. And you have a powerful tool for prototyping reports, analyzing data, assessing the status of the data warehouse, etc.

Start mining immediately for your best payback

Your statistical tool should be one of the first things you acquire when you begin your data warehouse. If you begin to work with the data immediately, and have users mining for gold right from the start, you are likely to avoid some overbuilding and to substitute in data that has more value. You cannot predict what you will find to explore once you start delving into the data. The techniques described are designed to look for interesting patterns and associations and then dig down into them to draw conclusions or make predictions. As in the case of the bank developing the credit scoring application, there was a lot of data available, but the cost of bringing it all together was exorbitant and not justified. Instead, they began by building a simple model for predicting defaults and then making it more sophisticated over time. They could use it from the beginning and they could identify areas of potential gold to dig into before making the investment in bringing together disparate data. Often the data which is easily available can approximate another measure of the same characteristic which is more costly to acquire or integrate. Keeping an eye on the payback is not completely at odds with developing good analyses and drawing actionable conclusions.

Ad hoc and periodic analysis are both important

You have seen examples of both ad hoc and periodic analysis in our data mining applications. In many cases, ad hoc analysis leads to periodic reporting as it did with SPSS's investigation of sales rep productivity or the automotive company's customer satisfaction, loyalty, and profitability measures. Both approaches have value in the data mining context. You cannot find the new exciting nuggets of information without some data exploration, asking questions, examining relationships, and so forth. But to continuously improve the profitability and operations of the organization, the maxim "you get what you measure" always holds. If you don't put systems in place to measure and evaluate the associations that are important to your success, how will you know if you are succeeding? SPSS tools give you the flexibility and flow-of-consciousness operation to make ad hoc analysis both fun and productive. And they provide the features required to repeat the analysis every year, quarter, month, day, or hour--and to compare the results over time. Once you know what you are looking for SPSS tools let you easily measure that the relationship still holds and/or how it is changing as a result of changes in other factors.

Statistics are essential for effective use of a data warehouse

Powerful, flexible, usable statistical tools are must-haves in a data warehousing environment. There is no purpose to saving and storing data beyond using it to make more informed business decisions. Statistics let you begin to explore the data and discover interesting hypotheses to test further. They let you test whether the data is truly reflecting what you think it measures or not. And most importantly, good statistical tools make it easy to add new data to the analysis with facilities for aggregating data from multiple sources, adding new data (either new variables or additional cases in the same fields), and determining which piece of data provides the most useful information. Statistical analysis fits comfortably with the approach of getting started with your warehouse rather than spending years specifying the ever-changing data requirements before you begin bringing data elements together.

DataMines for DataWarehouses

Title: *DataMines for DataWarehouses*

Author: *Information Discovery, Inc.*

Abstract: *In this article discussed is how the data to be mined is placed within "The DataMine", a repository which can either co-exist with, or be distinct from the data warehouse. The Sandwich Paradigm then acts as a design approach which ensures that the Warehouse and the Mine work in unison.*

Introduction

In the early days of data warehousing, data mining was viewed as a "subset" of the activities associated with the warehouse. But today the paths of warehousing and mining are diverging. While a warehouse may be a good source for the data to be mined, data mining has been recognized as a bonafide task in its own right, and is no longer regarded as a colony of the warehouse.

In fact, not only has data mining gained independence, but it is directly and significantly influencing the design and implementation of large data warehouses. In the early days, the "build a warehouse first, mine later" paradigm seemed simple and intuitive, and in many cases was followed by default. As I showed in the Sandwich Paradigm (Database Programming and Design, April 1995), this "build first, think later" approach was really a "data dump paradigm" since in many cases it led to the construction of a toxic data dump whose contents were not easily salvageable. A much better way is to "sandwich" the warehousing effort between two layers of mining -- thus understanding the data before warehousing it, as shown in Figure 1.

Although warehousing and mining are undoubtedly related activities and can reinforce each other, data mining requires

Figure 1

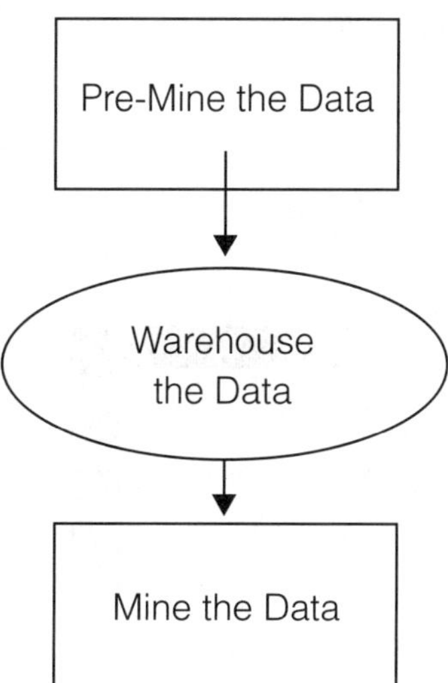

different data structures, computational processes and caters to a different group of users than the typical warehouse. We need to carefully separate these processes and understand how they differ in order to use them effectively.

Storing Data, Analyzing Information

The purpose of most warehouses is to bring together large amounts of historical data from several sources and to use them for decision support. The overall, top level, structure of a decision support system is shown in Figure 2.

Note that I have used the term repository rather than warehouse in Figure 2, since later we will see that the repository may have distinct components such as the warehouse and the data mine. The activities performed on a large corporate data repository are usually diverse, but often include the distinct tasks such as query and reporting, multi-dimensional analysis and data mining. These tasks naturally break into separate user groups, as well as distinct computational processes.

As I showed in New Realms of Analysis (Database Programming and Design, April 1996), access and analysis work on different computational spaces -- the more informational spaces being "derived spaces". Data access operations such as query and reporting deal with the data space, OLAP uses the multi-dimensional space and data mining takes place on the Influence Space. The four spaces which form the basis of decision support are shown in Figure 3. They are the spaces for data, aggregation, influence and variation. A fifth space based on geographic relationships may also be used for some analyses.

A data warehouse is thus the natural place for storing the "data space". It is where we store base level data elements that are later analyzed to deliver information. And, just as OLAP is no longer viewed as a pure warehousing effort, a datamine is where we perform analyses to deal with the "influence space".

Figure 2

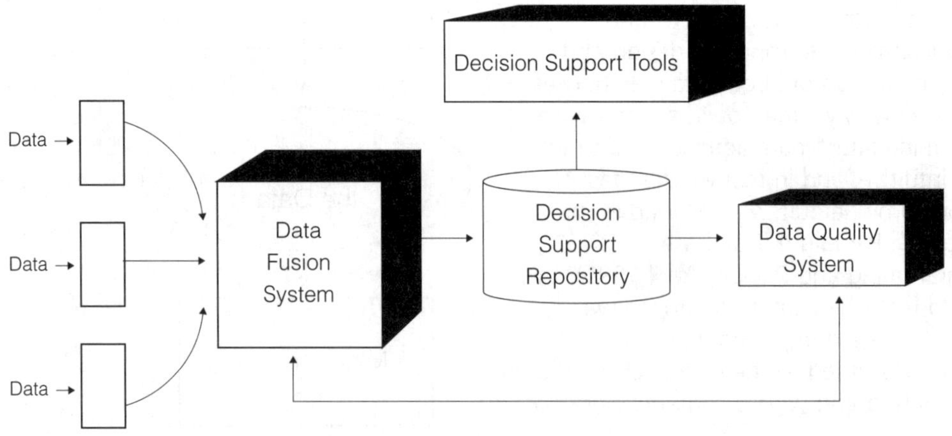

Figure 3

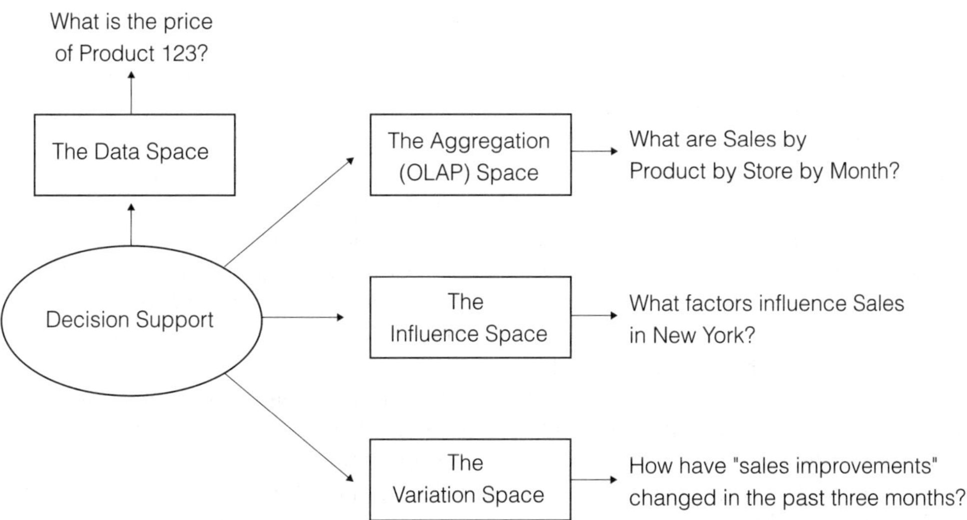

The questions posed to these spaces are inherently different. Some questions such as "what influences sales?" are almost impossible to answer "directly" from the data space. Moreover, the derived spaces are often so large that they can not be fully pre-computed and stored like the data space, e.g. we can not easily pre-compute all influence factors within a large database beforehand. Hence, we often have to rely on a partial pre-computation of these spaces, with further dynamic computations performed for providing actual answers. The data space includes all the information contained in the other spaces, but in less refined form. It forms the basis for the derivation of the other spaces. However, once computed these become real spaces in their own right. Hence we start with the data space and derive the other spaces from it. We can go further and derive hybrid spaces, e.g. influence analysis on aggregations and/or variations. These hybrid spaces deliver highly refined and usable information from the raw data stored within the warehouse.

In the process of analysis, the data space often needs to be enriched with additional semantics by adding information about hierarchies and periodic behavior. This additional semantics goes a little beyond the simple relational model, but often helps the user. For instance, {month, quarter, year} and {city, state, country} form natural hierarchies which the simple relational model ignores. By adding such semantics to the OLAP space we provide a good deal of additional benefit to the user.

While the OLAP space mostly deals with the computation of numeric values, the influence space has a "logical nature". It deals with the influence of specific groups of items on the others. What makes this space most interesting is that the information it provides is potentially much more useful than the other spaces -- because such information is typically very general and may be referred to as "knowledge". Since information is now one of the most valuable commodities in the world, and with the increasing complexity of today's society, the information obtained by data mining can be exponentially more valuable than any other asset.

It should, however, be noted that the size of the influence space and the number of logical combinations of influence factors can be extremely large, making it very hard to pre-compute this space. Restricting this to a smaller space does not help since the goal is to find unexpected patterns and the four fields that are excluded may just hold the key to the problem! Hence discovery is inherently a very dynamic process. Moreover, discovery often needs to be performed dynamically since once some unexpected item has been discovered, the user will soon begin to think of other items of interest for the program to pursue.

Exploratory and Confirmatory Analyses

I define data mining as a "decision support process in which we search for patterns of information in data". This search may be done by the user, e.g. just by performing queries, (in which case it is quite hard) or may be assisted by a smart program that automatically searches the database by itself and finds significant patterns. This process is called "discovery".

Discovery is the process of looking in a database to find hidden patterns without a predetermined idea or hypothesis about what the patterns may be. In other words, the program takes the initiative in finding what the interesting patterns are, without the user thinking of the relevant questions first. In large databases, there are so many patterns that the user can never practically think of the right questions to ask. This aspect distinguishes the space from the others.

In fact, from a statistical point of view, there are two types of analyses: Confirmatory Analysis and Exploratory Analysis. In confirmatory analysis, one has a hypothesis and either confirms or refutes it through a line of inferential statistical reasoning. However, the bottleneck for confirmatory analysis is the shortage of hypotheses on the part of the analyst.

In Exploratory Analysis, as pioneered by John Tukey [Tukey 1973], one aims to find suitable hypotheses to confirm or refute. Automatic discovery automates the process of exploratory data analysis, allowing unskilled analysts to explore very large datasets much more effectively.

The data warehouse may be a suitable place for performing confirmatory analysis and looking at the data space. However, it is certainly no place for performing exploratory analysis due to the unexpected nature of the queries posed to the data. The natural place for exploratory analysis is a datamine, and not a data warehouse.

The Paradox of Warehouse Patterns

The concepts of "large warehouse" and "useful pattern" often interact in a seemingly paradoxical way. On one hand, the larger a warehouse, the richer its pattern content, i.e. as the warehouse grows the more patterns it includes. On the other hand, after a point, if we analyze "too large" a portion of a warehouse, patterns from different data segments begin to dilute each other and the number of useful patterns begins to decrease! So the paradox may be stated as follows: "The more data in the warehouse, the more patterns there are, and the more data we analyze the fewer patterns we find!"

The basic idea is shown in Figure 4, but a few simple examples easily clarify this further. First, consider a large data warehouse that includes details of bank's customer accounts, marketing promotions, etc. There can be several business objectives for mining this data, including campaign analysis, customer retention, profitability, risk assessment, etc. To begin

Figure 4

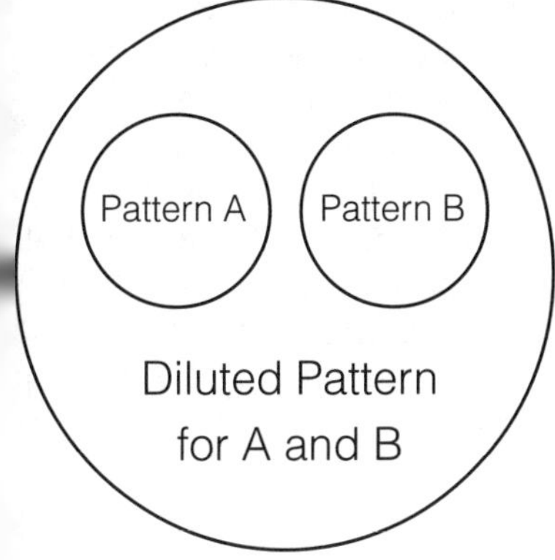

with, these are distinct business tasks and it does not make sense to mix the analyses -- hence each of the data mining exercises needs to be performed separately, and will require different data structures as well, because some are association analyses, some are clusterings, etc.

However, even the campaign analysis task itself should often not be performed on the entire warehouse. The bank may have undertaken 30 different marketing campaigns over the years, and these campaigns will have usually involved different products and gone to different customer segments -- some of the products are even discontinued now. To understand who responds best to marketing promotions, we need to analyze each campaign (or group of campaigns) separately because each case will involve patterns with distinct signatures. Mixing the analyses into one data mining exercise will simply dilute the differences between these signatures. And the campaigns are often different enough that mixing them simply may not make sense. So we need to have a separate "Analysis Session" for each group of campaigns.

To demonstrate this with a simple example, let us assume that those customers who are over 40 years old and have more than 2 children have a high response rates to credit card promotions. Now, let us also assume that customers who are less than 40 years old and have only 1 child are good prospects for new checking accounts. If we combine these campaigns within the same data mining study and simply look for customers who have a high response rate, these two patterns will dilute each other.

Of course, we can get a rule that separates these campaigns and still display the patterns, but in a large warehouse so many of these rules will appear that they will overwhelm the user. Thus, the smaller patterns may be found in the warehouse if we are prepared to accept large amounts of conditional segment information, e.g. "If Campaign = C12 and ... Then ...". However, in a large warehouse, there are so many of these that the user will be overloaded with them. The best way is to analyze each group of campaigns separately.

The need for segmentation is even more clear when we consider predictive modeling. When trying to predict the response to a new campaign, it simply does not make sense to base the predictions on all previous campaigns that have ever taken place, but on those campaigns which are most similar to the one being considered. For instance, responses to campaigns for a new checking account may have little bearing on responses to campaigns for a new credit card or a refinancing a home. In this case, the paradox of the warehouse patterns comes into play in that by considering more data, we lose accuracy. This is, of course, because some of the data will not be relevant to the task we are considering.

But what happens if there are one or two key indicator that are common to all of the campaigns? Will they be lost if we just analyze the campaigns a few at a time? Of course not. If a pattern holds strongly enough in the entire database, it will also hold in the segments. For instance, if the people with more than 5 children never respond to campaigns, this fact will also be true in each individual campaign.

As another example, consider a vehicle warranty database. In order to find patterns for customer claims it is essential to store details of each claim in a large data warehouse. But does it make sense to analyze all of the warehouse at the same time? No. In practice, cars are built at different plants and different models of cars use different parts -- and some parts are now discontinued. Moreover, over the course of years the parts used in cars change, so analyzing the entire warehouse may tell us less than analyzing part of it. What works best in practice is to analyze the claims for a given model year for cars built at a given plant -- again a segmentation task. Once again, the paradox of the warehouse comes into play here in that by analyzing all of the warehouse at once we reduce the number of useful patterns we are likely to get!

Hence, most of the time it does not make sense to analyze all of a large warehouse because patterns are lost through dilution. To find useful patterns in a large warehouse, we usually have to select a segment (and not a sample) of data that fits a business objective, prepare it for analysis and then perform data mining. Looking at all of the data at once often hides the patterns, because the factors that apply to distinct business objectives often dilute each other. Hence, the thirst for information can go unquenched by looking at too much data.

The Pitfalls of Sampling and Summarization

Although I have emphatically used the term "segment" rather than sample several times in this article, it is still worthwhile to explicitly point out the shortcomings of sampling and summarization as potential candidates for anything. While sampling may seem to offer a short-cut to faster data analysis, the end results are often less than desirable.

And, let us remember where sampling came from. Sampling was used within statistics because it was so difficult to have access to an entire population, e.g. one could not interview a million people, or one could not have access to a million manufactured components. Hence, sampling methods were developed to allow us to make some "rough calculations" about some of the characteristics of the population without access to the entire population. But does this not fly in the face of having a large database altogether? Of course it does. We build databases of one million customer behavior exactly in order to have access to the entire population. Else, we could just keep track of a small group of customers.

Segmentation is an inherently different task from sampling. As we segment, we deliberately focus into a subset of the data (e.g. one model year for a car, or one campaign), sharpening the focus of the analysis. But when we sample data, we lose information, because we throw away data not knowing what we keep and what we ignore.

The hardware technology for storing and analyzing large datasets provide an unprecedented opportunity for looking at historical patterns by making more data than ever before accessible for analysis. Sometimes it may seem daunting to look a really large dataset straight in the eyes and try to analyze so much data. It is tempting to try and obtain a smaller "sample" of the data to build a predictive model. This shyness to look at the whole data is often very expensive, and in most cases the temptation to sample must be resisted.

At times, when we have a 100,000,000 record retail database, it may be suggested that a 100,000 record sample may be good enough. This is not so. Sampling will almost always result in a loss of information, in particular with respect to data fields with a large number of non-numeric values.

It is easy to see why this is the case. Consider a warehouse of 1,000 products and 500 stores. There are half a million combinations of how a product sells in each store. However, how one product sells in a store is of little interest compared to how products "sell together" in each store -- a problem known as Market Basket Analysis, e.g. how often do potato-chips and beer sell together. There are 500 million possible combinations here, and a 100,000 record sample can barely manage to scratch the surface. Hence the sample will be a really "rough" representation of the data, and will ignore key pieces of information. In using a small sample, one may as well ignore the product column! Hence we no longer have a large database, since in effect we have reduced it by removing fields from it. Hence sampling a large warehouse for analysis almost defeats the purpose of having all the data there in the first place!

Apart from sampling, summarization may be used to reduce data sizes. But summarization can cause problems too. In fact, as shown in Figure 5, the summarization of the same dataset with two sampling or summarization methods may result in the same result, and the summarization of the same data set with two methods may produce two different results.

As another intuitive example of how "information loss" and "information distortion" can take place through summarization, consider a retail warehouse where Monday to Friday sales are exceptionally low for some stores, while weekend sales are exceptionally high for others. The summarization of daily sales data to weekly amounts will totally hide the fact that weekdays are "money losers", while weekends are "money makers" for some stores. In other words, key pieces of information are often lost through summarization, and there is no way to recover them by further analysis.

Figure 5

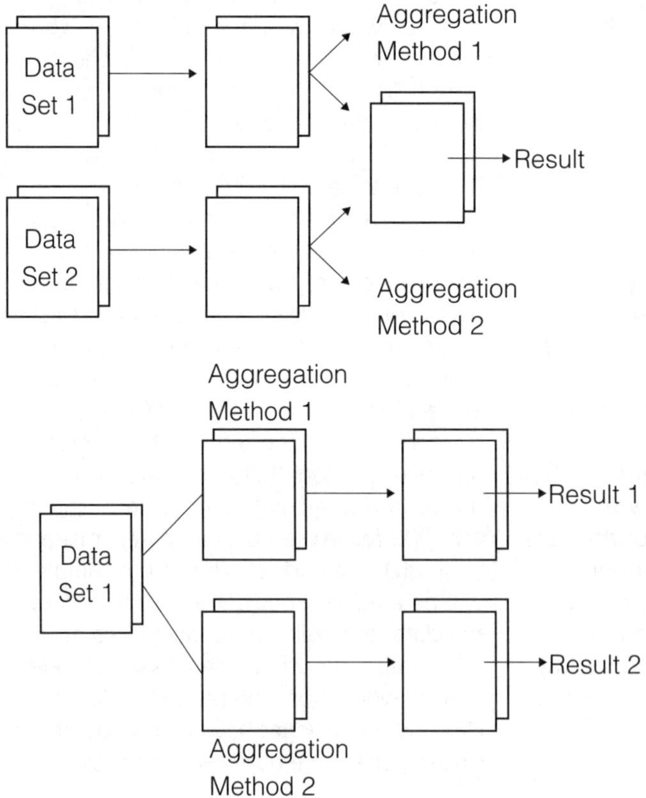

Exceptions to the Rule

Having established general criteria for where analysis takes place, let me also note that (as expected) there are exception to these rules. In other words, the answer to the question: "Do we ever sample the warehouse for analysis?" is "In some cases, yes." And the answer to the question, do we ever perform analysis on the entire warehouse rather than within a datamine is "In a good number of cases, yes."

Sampling is sometimes recommended to get a general feeling for the data, and in such cases, one would recommend to have several samples and compare them. Sampling is only done when the computing power is not sufficient to manage the task at hand within a given time-frame.

The question of analysis on the entire database is a slightly different, yet related, matter. In some cases, segmentation alone will not give us all the answers, and we may need to look at some of the overall characteristics of the database. But even in these cases we need not perform full exploratory analysis, and can simply compare some of the distributions within the warehouse with those within the datamine.

For instance, as we perform affinity or market basket analysis, we may wish to compare how two products sell together in all stores, compared to how they sell together within specific clusters of stores analyzed within a datamine. However, some of these computations may be routinely performed when data is refreshed within the warehouse, and the overall distributions may be kept for such comparisons. In some cases we nay have to perform these computations in a "live" setting on the warehouse.

And, in some cases we may wish to perform "segmented affinity analysis" on the entire warehouse in order to find out how to segment the data. Thus specific operations on the entire warehouse are performed first in order to guide the segmentation process. Hence, we do sometimes need to look at the warehouse as a whole -- but we need to do so selectively and with proper planning.

The Concept of an Analysis Session

When using a datamine, we bring a segment (and not a sample) of data from a warehouse (or other sources) to the datamine and perform discovery or prediction. The process of mining this data segment is called an Analysis Session. For example, we may want to predict the response to a proposed direct mail campaign by analyzing previous campaigns for similar products, or we may want to know how customer retention has varied over various geographic regions, etc.

An analysis session may be either "structured" or "unstructured". A structured session is a more formal activity in which we set out with a specific task, e.g. analyzing profitability by customer segments and/or products. In fact, structured sessions are often performed in a routine manner, e.g. we may analyze costs, revenues or expenses every quarter, and understand the reasons for the trends. Or we may routinely perform forecasting for various items such as product demand in various markets. Or, we may look for unusual transactions that have taken place in the past 30 days. In fact, a structured analysis session usually is of three forms: a discovery, prediction or forensic analysis activity where we perform a specific task.

An unstructured session is a "wild-ride" through the database, where the user wanders around without a goal, hoping to uncover something of interest by serendipity -- or by help from a "exploration-agent". This type of abstract wild-ride usually uncovers some very wild facts hidden in the data. And the mine is a natural place for this activity because the unexpected nature of queries may interfere with the more routine tasks for which the warehouse was designed, e.g. looking up the history of a specific claim.

The data in the datamine often needs to be enriched with aggregations. Again, let me emphasize that these are not just summaries, but additional elements added to the data. How these aggregations are built is partly decided by a business analysis. For instance, we may need to look at the number of credit cards a customer has as an item. And we may want to look at the "volume" of transactions the customer has had. We may also want to look at the number of claims a customer has had in an insurance setting, etc. These aggregations enrich the data and co-exist with the atomic level data in the mine.

The Warehouse, the Mart and the Mine

There are three separate components to an enterprise-wide decisions support system:

- The Data Warehouse, where the mountain of corporate data is stored all in one place. Here data volumes are very high as multi-terabyte data warehouses are beginning to appear more frequently. These designs are usually either star-schemas (or snow-flakes, etc.) or highly normalized data structures.
- The Data Mart where departmental data is stored, and often various external data items are added. The data volumes are usually 15% to 30% of warehouse sizes, and the envelope is being pushed towards the terabyte limit. These databases are also usually either based on star-schemas or are in a normalized form. They mostly deal with the data space, but at times some multi-dimensional analysis is performed.
- The Data Mine, where the data is re-organized for analysis and information is extracted from the data. The data volumes here are the same as the Data Mart, but the data is much more richly structured and is no longer just depart-mental. The data here refers to a specific business objective and is analyzed for the purpose of information extraction.

While the data structures used within the warehouse and the mart may be similar, the data structures used within the datamine are significantly different. The data mine differs from the data warehouse not just in the size of data it manages, but in the structure of the data. The content of the data in the mine is also often different from the data in the warehouse, because it is often enriched by additional external data not found within the warehouse. However, content aside, the key issue about data mining architecture is that the existing theories of data structuring do not apply to it.

The two key approaches to data structuring within warehouses are "normalization" and "star-schema families", which include snow-flake schemas. Once we think of the origins of these approaches, and the four spaces of decision support, it is not surprising that these two design methodologies do not easily lend themselves to successful use within a datamine.

Normalization theory was invented by Ted Cod in the 1970's as a theory and methodology for data structuring for OLTP applications -- and it produced extremely good results in the 1980's, during the rush towards the deployment of relational databases for operational purposes. In fact, without normalization theory many of the successful large-scale database projects of the 1980's and early 1990's would have failed altogether.

However, the limitations of normalization theory became evident when it was applied to dimensional analysis for decision support. The observations made by Ralph Kimball and others about the dimensional data needs of large retailers, gave rise to the introduction of star schemas and databases engines such as Redbrick successfully took advantage of these ideas in the late 1980's. While normalization theory deals with the data space, star schemas deal with the aggregation space. By the same token, while star schemas may be suitable for dimensional analysis in the aggregation space, they are not ideal for datamining within the influence space -- because the structure of this space is logical, and not arithmetic or polynomial.

The data structures in the datamine need to be both denormalized and super-dimensional. The details of a new theory of structuring for datamines based on "Rotational Schemas" is beyond the scope of this paper, and will be presented elsewhere [reference 7]. However, let us note that within the datamine we sometimes need to look at super-dimensions which exist above the dimensions used in the OLAP space, i.e. the data mining dimensions subsume the OLAP dimensions.

Data Mining Above, Beside and Within the Warehouse

Once we accept the fact that the data mine is distinct from the data warehouse, the next logical question is: "Where does the datamine actually exist? Is it a separate repository next to the warehouse, a set of views above the warehouse, or just part of the warehouse?" We can answer this question in each of these three ways and get a different architecture for the datamine.

The datamine can exist in three basic forms:

- Above the warehouse, as a set of conceptual views.
- Beside the warehouse, as a separate repository.
- Within the warehouse, as a distinct set of resources.

Datamining "above the warehouse" provides a minimal architecture for the discovery and analysis. It is suitable only in cases where data mining is not a key objective for the warehouse. In this approach, as shown in Figure 6, SQL statements are used to build a set of conceptual views above the warehouse tables. And, additional external data from other tables may be merged as part of the views.

The views built above the warehouse may either be materialized (i.e. saved to disk as new tables), or not. Therein lies the

Figure 6: DataMining Above the Warehouse

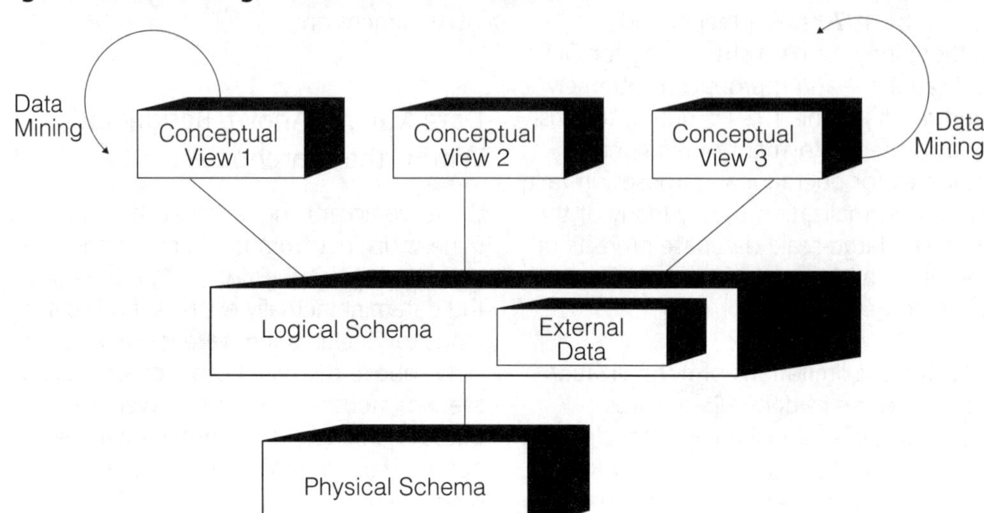

fundamental problem (if not contradiction) built into this approach. If the views are not of significant size, then serious data mining can not take place. However, if the views are of a significant size, then without materialization the effort in computing them again and again will require very large amounts of processing power -- in some cases significantly affecting the availability of the warehouse resources and interfering with other applications performing indexed retrievals.

On the other hand, if the views are of significant size and they are materialized, we are no longer datamining "above" the warehouse and will be using a disorganized form of the third approach, i.e. data mining within the warehouse. If the views are materialized, the third approach will almost always work better, because it can utilize a suitable data distribution approach and a specific processor allocation strategy, as well as using different data structures for data mining. Without these precautions, the number of potential pitfalls increase rapidly, sacrificing both performance and functionality.

Hence data mining above the warehouse should be restricted to applications in which data mining is only of peripheral business interest, and not a key objective. However, holding this view is often a big a business mistake in itself -- i.e. why have so much data in a warehouse and not understand it?

In most cases, data mining is effectively performed beside the warehouse, with data structures that lend themselves to detailed analyses. And, in most cases additional data suitable for the analyses is merged with the warehoused data in order to perform specific analyses for focused business needs.

The concept of data mining beside the warehouse fits well within the context of "three-level computing", which resembles a three-tiered client server architecture. Within a three-tiered client-server architecture, a first tier client interacts with a middle-tier server which also interacts with a third tier large system. While in three-tiered client-server systems the interaction between layers 2 and 3 is on-going, in a three-level computing system, most of the interaction is between the client and a "specialized server" which occasionally accesses a "huge server". In other words, the "huge server" holds very large amounts of data, and is surrounded by a number of specialized servers that interact with the clients.

The overall architecture for data mining beside the warehouse is shown in Figure 7. Here, the process of data migration and fusion populates a data warehouse with large amounts of historical data. The data structures used within the warehouse may be either normalized or members of the star schema family. However, the data schemas for the datamine will be different.

Query and reporting tools, as well as other applications utilizing traditional database index structures may directly access the warehouse with very good results, i.e. the warehouse will support access to the data space. However, detailed analyses such as discovery and prediction, are not performed within the warehouse because they do not relate to the data space. Instead these activities are performed in the datamine, with data structures suitable for data mining.

Data mining beside the warehouse both overcomes and sidesteps several problems

Figure 7: The DataMine Beside the Warehouse

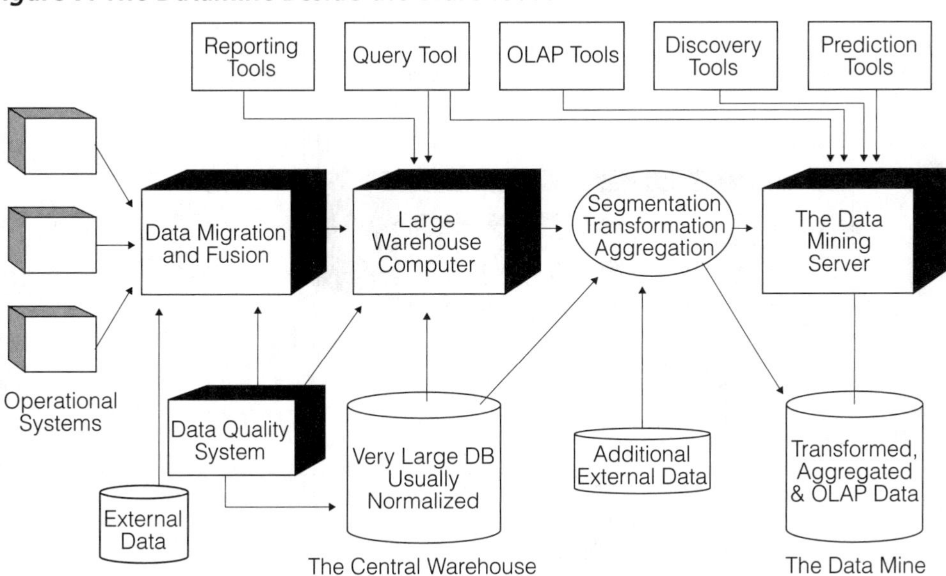

at once. To begin with, it allows data mining to be done with the right data structures, avoiding the problems associated with the structures of the data space. Moreover, the paradox of warehouse patterns can be avoided by selecting specific data segments, corresponding to specific business objectives. And, the interactive exploratory analyses that are often performed in the datamine with "wild rides" through the data no longer interfere with the warehouse resources that are responsible for routine processes such as query and reporting.

In fact, different business departments can use their own datamines that address their specific needs, e.g. direct marketing vs. claim analysis. The data is then moved from the large warehouse to the mine, is restructured during the transformation and is analyzed. It is, however, important to design the transfer and transformation methods carefully, in order to allow for optimal "refresh methods" that require minimal computing. For instance, as we bring new data into the datamine every day or every week, the over-head for re-aggregation should be minimized.

In some cases, where the warehouse is a very large, massively parallel processing (MPP) computer, the data mine may actually reside as a separate repository within the large warehouse. As shown in Figure 8, this is very similar to a data mine beside the warehouse, where the mine uses a portion of the physical warehouse, but is independent of the warehouse structures, in effect being a "republic within a republic".

In this scenario, the disk apace and the processors for the datamine are specifically allocated and separately managed. For

Figure 8: The DataMine Within the Warehouse

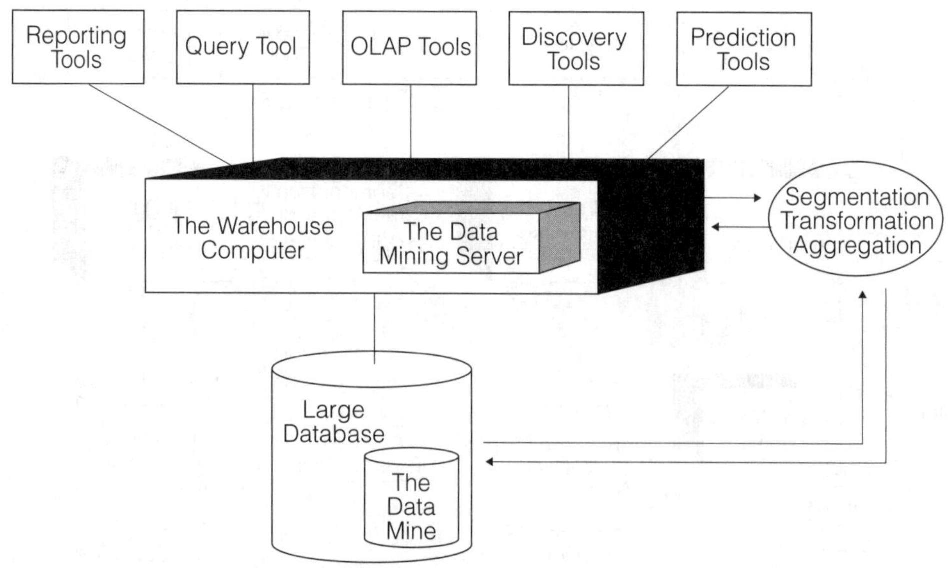

instance, on a "shared nothing" MPP machine with 32 processor, the disk space for the data mine is separately allocated on 8 of the 32 nodes and 8 processors are dedicated to data mining, while the other 24 processors manage the rest of the warehouse. And, when needed, additional processing capability may be directed towards the needs of data mining.

Although this idea may sound attractive based on arguments for centralization and scalability, in practice it usually leads to loss of flexibility, without providing any significant benefits for data mining. In most cases, when we consider at the technical, marketing and business issues, the problems with mining within the warehouse multiply quite rapidly, and the datamines planned for use within the warehouse will eventually find themselves beside it.

The key point is that the likelihood of serving the needs of many people within the data space is much higher that the likelihood of serving their needs within the multi-dimensional and influence spaces. While the data elements may be almost the same for several departments, the dimensions, the influence relationships and the predictive models they all need will vary far more than their simple data needs. Hence, the datamine within the warehouse will soon become the lowest common denominator of all designs.

Therefore, while the design of the data space may be subject to compromises to please the various user groups, there should be no compromises in design of the data mine where serious and detailed analyses take place. The data mine should be optimized to deliver effective results by focusing on specific business needs, because influence analysis is so much harder than data access.

Stand-alone DataMines

Can a data mine exist without a warehouse? In some cases, yes. This usually happens when a business unit within an organization needs to get results "next quarter", not "next year". When it takes too long to build the very large corporate warehouse, some business units have no choice but to take things into their own hands -- often with excellent results!

And, coupled with the Sandwich Paradigm, a stand-alone data mine is the best way to guide the data warehouse design process. Often, a significant portion of the business benefits from the system are to be obtained from the data mine, and the horizontal and vertical prototypes built with the Sandwich Paradigm will make sure that the eventual system will conform to the implicit needs of the user.

The key issue of concern for managing a stand-alone data mine is data fusion and quality management. But these are problems that a large warehouse faces anyway, and dealing with them in the context of a data mine is not much more difficult, although they still do need to be handled with a great deal of care and attention.

The need for stand-alone datamines usually arises when large warehousing projects have to deal with so much data and need to please so many different departments with distinct requirements that they are inevitably forced into becoming a "QE2 Sized Solution", i.e. they attempt to build the largest ship possible, hoping to carry all passengers " any" port. Yet it often takes too long to deliver the QE2 and it is later discovered that a ship that size can not sail to "every" port for data analysis. In such cases, stand-alone data mines become a very attractive option, delivering rapid and focused benefits.

Stand-alone OLAP engines have already followed this very path to success. Many a departmental system for multi-dimensional analysis has been effectively deployed while the meeting dates for the design of the corporate data warehouse were being discussed. Thus stand-alone data mines deployed prior to the warehouse not only provide a Sandwich Paradigm effect by clarifying the needs of user groups, but deliver significant business benefits during the two years it takes to deliver a QE2 sized data warehouse.

Data Warehouse Scorecard: Cost of Ownership and Successes in Application of Data Warehouse Technology

Title: *Data Warehouse Scorecard: Cost of Ownership and Successes in Application of Data Warehouse Technology*

Author: *META Group*

Abstract: *This report will augment but not necessarily match trend reports that are focused on acquisition and expansion plans. This report focuses more on what is in place and working today. For example, where a respondent reports a data mart in production and a centralized DW under development, only the production data mart is considered in the data. DW project sponsors, managers, and architects should use this report as a set of data warehouse technology and approach benchmarks. The report offers mature project teams DW characteristic reference points to rationalize their own levels of success, and it offers all teams implicit suggestions to improve their odds of success.*

Data warehouse (DW) technology has become the preferred approach to address information delivery and analytical needs for the overwhelming majority of Global 3000 organizations. Those few organizations that are not maintaining an active data warehouse are in the throes of developing or planning one. The surge in data warehousing has been spurred by several factors:

- Tacit benefits and the compounding effect from reported DW successes and perceived accomplishments
- Explosive growth in enterprise resource planning/management (ERP/ERM) package implementations and the opportunities presented by these storehouses of raw data, along with their native deficiencies in reporting and data output
- Broadening spectrum of DW tools, as well as improvements in technology capabilities and ease of use
- Continuing desperate need for information and analysis
- Growing sense that competent information management is the prerequisite to knowledge management

The traditional DW concept has evolved a broad set of architectural variations. Data marts (standalone and federated), operational data stores, exploration warehouses, and application data stores, in addition to the conventional hub-and-spoke DW, have enabled sophisticated information management solutions to meet exacting business requirements. Along with leveraging the volume of data generated by ERM applications (e.g., SAP, PeopleSoft, Baan), there is a burgeoning need for the DW to sustain customer relationship management (CRM), supply chain management (SCM), and electronic commerce initiatives. The increase in business velocity and level of integration afforded by these business systems roughly translates into shrinking cycle times for collecting and examining data, along with a need for holistic information supply chains beyond mere decision support applications.

Data Warehouse Scorecard: Cost of Ownership and Successes in Application of Data Warehouse Technology

Maturing technologies present a unique set of opportunities, risks, and unknowns, as do new technologies. Therefore, organizations become interested in benchmarks for costs, usage, and ongoing benefits. Data warehousing, like other IT-related initiatives, introduces multiple challenges. Prevailing DW challenges revolve around the difficulties of administering and managing large data stores accessible by a broad spectrum of constituents.

This study addresses the aspects of a maturing technology from the subjective perspectives of those deploying it. Correspondingly, resource levels for development and ongoing support were captured. Finally, to allow survey readers to contrast themselves with organizations in similar circumstances, "report card" style strata were formulated and applied throughout the report.

KEY FINDINGS

DATA WAREHOUSE TRENDS

Most of the data in this study is presented in a scorecard format; responses are ranked by reported levels of actual and perceived success on DW-type projects. Successful projects were scored A (outright success) or B (moderate success). The delineation between the A and B scores is the calculation and reporting of financial ROI. C and D rankings represent less than successful projects and reported failures, respectively.

DW-type solutions continue to pervade industries. While growth in large-scale enterprise DW projects may not be as robust, we continue to find companies striving to implement organic DW architectures comprising hub-type data stores and distributed data marts. Whether the approach is iterative or "big-bang,"

Figure 1: Responses by industry

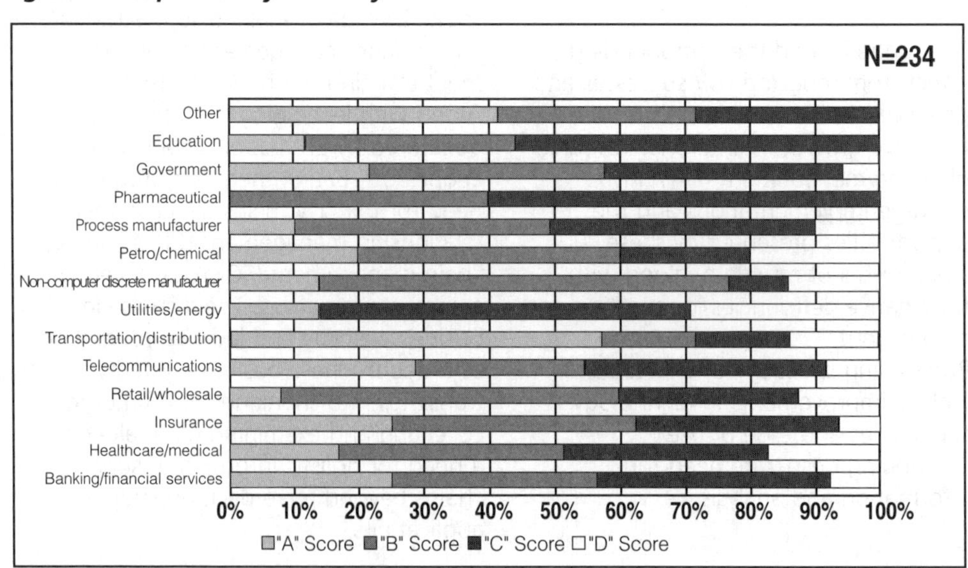

experienced personnel and solid architectures are the keys to successful DW initiatives.

DW project success is not strongly correlated with industry, though varying adoption rates by industry yielded a range of overall scoring results. Of note, retail and education organizations (overall DW laggards) are experiencing slightly lower rates of success, while transportation and the historical technology leader, telecommunications, achieve success more often. Overall, however, success rates are relatively consistent across industry (see Figure 1).

ARCHITECTURE

We classify data warehouse architectures in three general classes: centralized, more data mart intensive (employing primarily data marts), and operational data store (ODS) oriented (employing more near-real-time data feeds from source applications). While little preference exists for one approach over another in the aggregate, the profiles of organizations adopting one architecture over another tell a different story (see Figure 2).

When we consider success rates, higher scores result from centralized enterprise approaches (including hub and spoke), while data mart-oriented environments score lower (see Figure 3). This is significant, especially given the recent promotion of data mart-centric approaches. This also validates the archetypal enterprise DW approach as an enduring solution, while at the same time highlighting the value of solutions that enable users to access the central DW directly (as in data mining applications, low-volume/low-user DWs, and most Teradata-based implementations).

APPROACH

Not surprisingly, companies that have been engaging in DW efforts for more than 24 months are more likely to be successful than short-term efforts (see Figure 4). Successful shorter-term efforts are characterized by a high degree of reliance on technology and larger team sizes. We believe the high number of failed efforts lasting three years or longer results from politically mired projects, overscoped (noniterative) efforts, sponsor turnover, and DW revisions.

Figure 2: DW environment classification: all responses

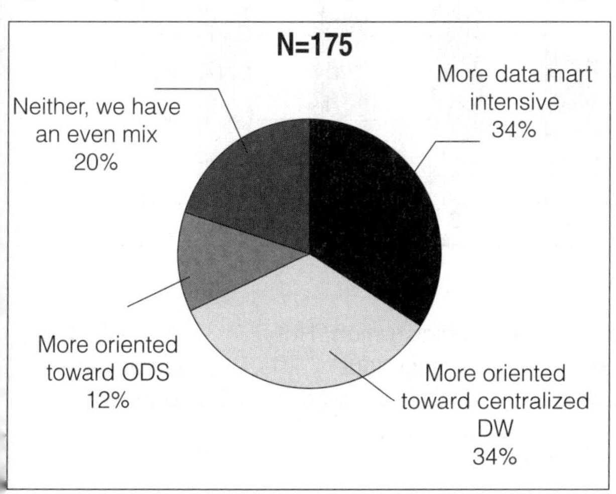

Figure 3: DW environment classification: all responses

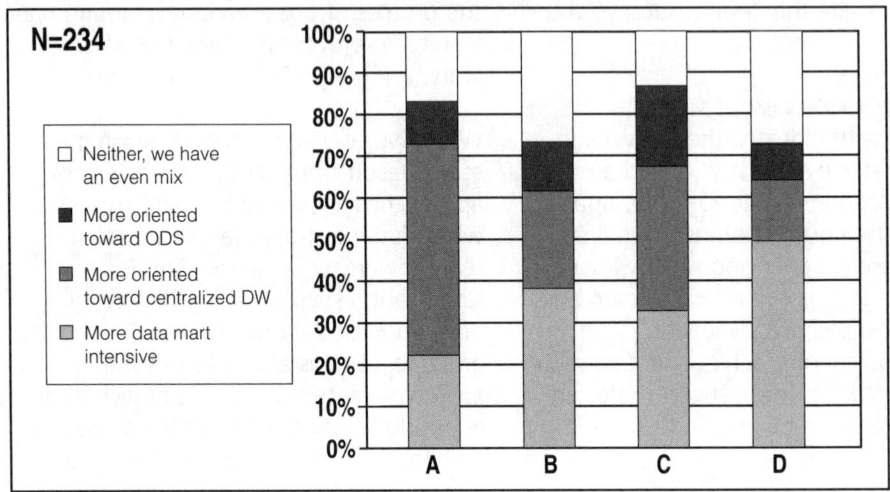

Figure 4: Project duration distribution, by success profile

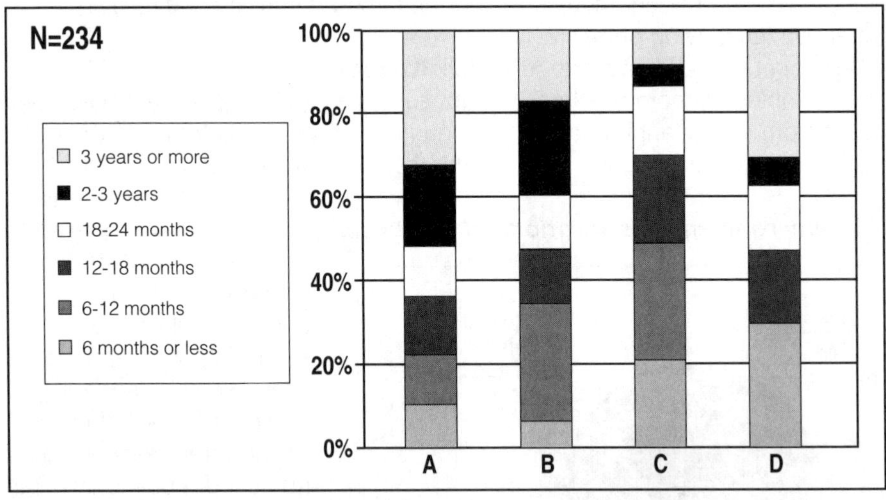

Maturing technology creates a need for maintenance and administration. The survey yielded limited data on DW process automation and scheduling, usage tracking, chargeback, and DW environment administration. However, the issue is high on practitioners' lists, which indicates a pending demand for commercial approaches.

The use of outside services continues to be strong, but not among the premium-priced, global systems integrators. In fact, the use of external resources is spread evenly across boutiques, vendors, and global system integrators (see Figures 5 and 6).

This "nonfinding" is actually significant in that, unlike many other technology pursuits, systems integrators have not managed to corner the DW consulting market. Our research indicates DW vendors, DW-specific consulting firms, and others maintain the lion's share of consulting engagements.

Figure 5: Use of consultants, overall

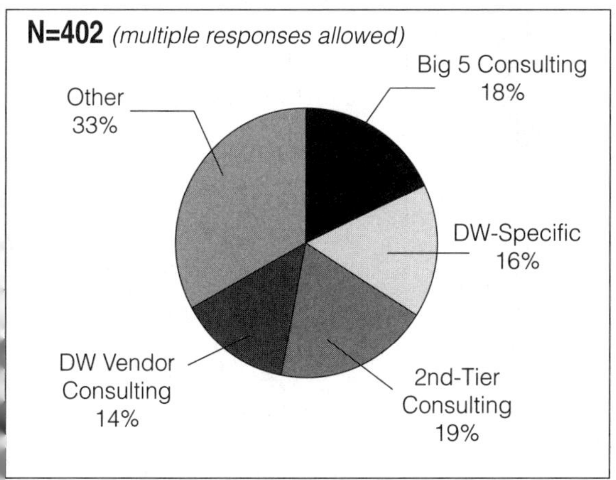

Figure 6: Use of consultants: A and B profiles

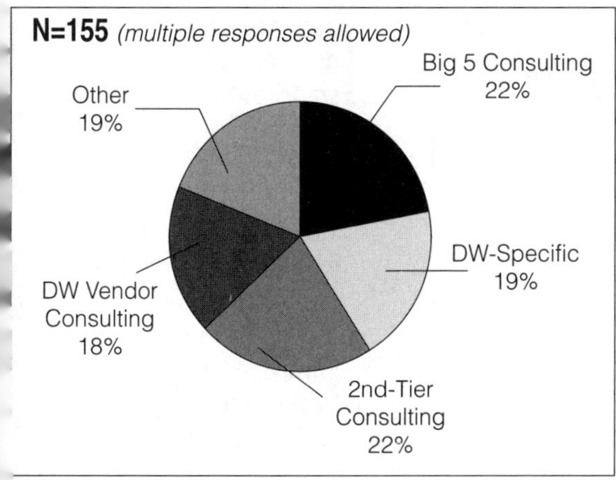

DATA WAREHOUSE ADOPTION

DW continues to be adopted widely (see Figure 7). All sectors are reporting a large number of installed applications and many years of DW activity. The more experience an organization has with DW, the more likely success will result. The earliest adopters tend to score significantly higher (2 to 1 A profiles over all others), representing not only brute-force success over time, but also a cultural propensity toward innovation and acceptance.

DATA WAREHOUSE SUCCESS RATE

More than half the survey respondents report moderate success or better, though outright documented ROI is reported by only one-third of respondents. With the emerging knowledgebase of DW best practices and growing skill base of DW practitioners, fewer than 10% of DW attempts are regarded as utter disasters (see Figure 8).

Scrutiny of the survey data substantiates META Group's position on vital DW success characteristics. Organizations reporting failed DW implementation are two to three times more likely to have employed a data mart-oriented approach, while classic DW architectures, revolving around a centralized data store, enjoy a strong lead among acknowledged successful implementations.

Figure 7: Adoption profile, by success profile

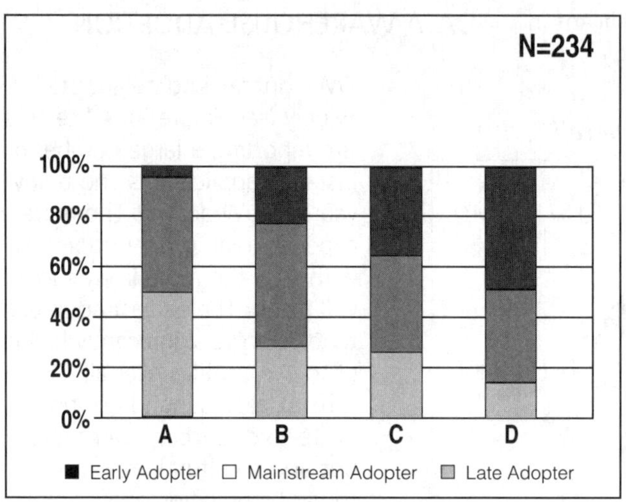

Figure 8: Data warehouse success rates

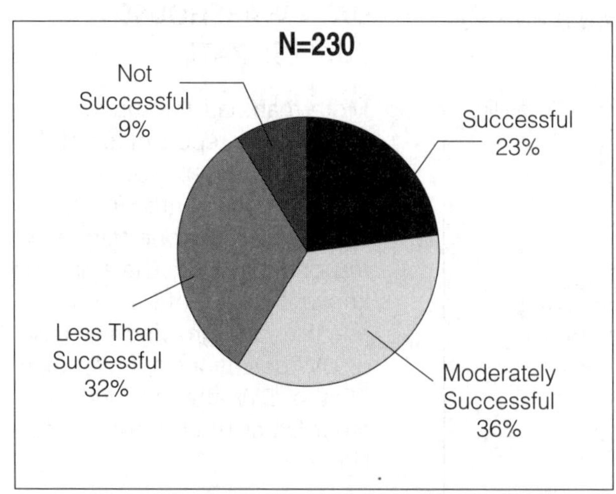

SUBJECT AREAS

A breakdown of scores by subject area (see Figure 9) reveals:

- The most popular subject areas
- The subject areas easiest to implement successfully

The large relative percentage of customer relationship-oriented DW solutions (e.g., sales, marketing, customer service) illustrates just how feverishly organizations are implementing horizontal CRM solutions. Vertically, healthcare-related DW solutions (e.g., claims, patient, provider, clinical, drug analysis) appear to stand out among other verticals and yield high relative returns.

The limited number of insurance-oriented subject areas is conspicuous. Many are mired in DW "analysis paralysis," resulting in heavily scoped projects with severe data quality

Figure 9: Data warehouse subject areas

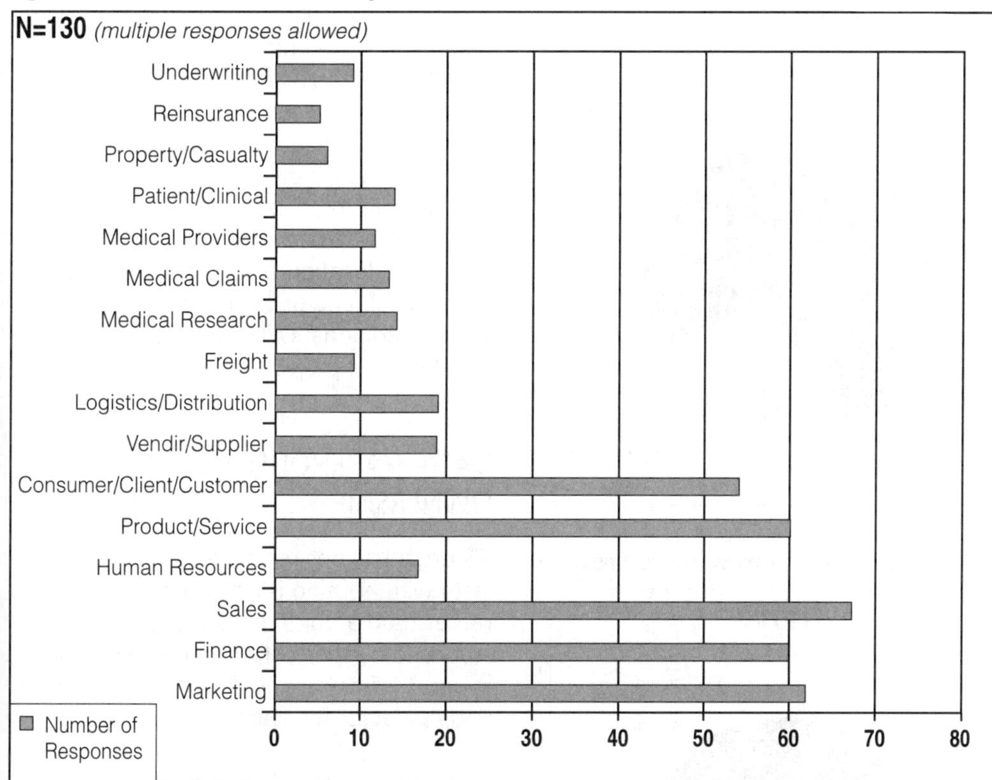

challenges. Reinsurance DWs, though, do show strong success rates. With respect to general success rates, implementing DW subject areas for customer, supplier, sales, and financial analysis leads more often to triumphs. Product/service subject areas are DW themes that should be justified more diligently or avoided altogether.

RETURN ON INVESTMENT (ROI)

The survey shows that few organizations are measuring tangible or quantifiable returns from their DW (see Figure 10). Of those that are, reported returns have been modest. While more than half report levels of ROI satisfaction, only 6 % report that ROI levels met or exceeded expectations (see Figure 11).

Figure 10: Organizations measuring return on DW investment

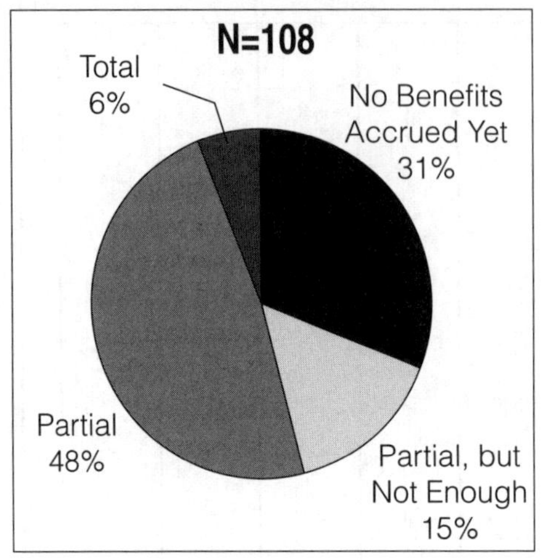

Figure 11: Satisfaction with ROI results

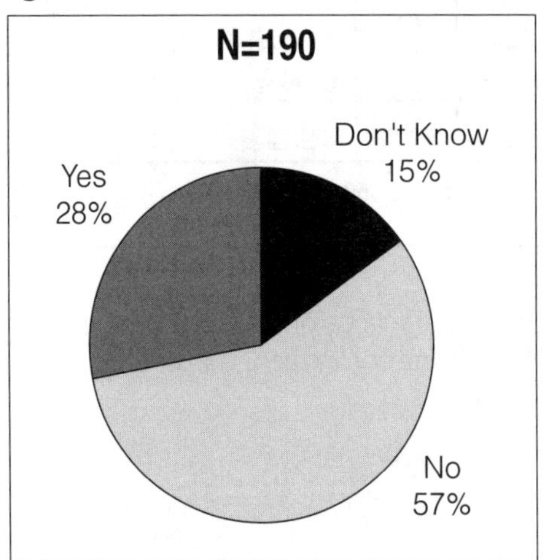

BARRIERS TO SUCCESS

Survey respondents were asked to name the top three barriers to the success of their DW projects (see Figure 12). Data quality and expectation management continue to be the foremost barriers to success across all organizations. However, managing expectations was a problem of slightly greater significance in A and B organizations; C and D organizations were more often stymied by a lack of suitable access/analysis tools or the requisite IT skill sets. Within the IT ranks themselves, we find positive expectation management includes education on the architectural, managerial, and usage distinctions of DW versus traditional OLTP systems development projects.

DATA WAREHOUSE COST OF OWNERSHIP

As organizations realize that successful data warehousing is an enduring initiative rather than a one-time project, many are surprised by the cost of maintaining a DW support infrastructure. DW cost is a critical success factor for ongoing DW viability.

In this study, cost of ownership is a function of reported budgets, full-time-equivalents (FTEs), database sizes, and number of users. Projected usage increases and additional data sources also are factored into the cost-of-ownership figure. The cost-of-ownership results include only organizations with a DW in production, and not development costs.

Budget amounts do not seem to differentiate for success. While more IT money tends to be spent on more successful projects (i.e., A plus B); A-level project spending is not highest. Budgets did not trend along with revenue or company size for DW projects; larger

Figure 12: Barriers to success

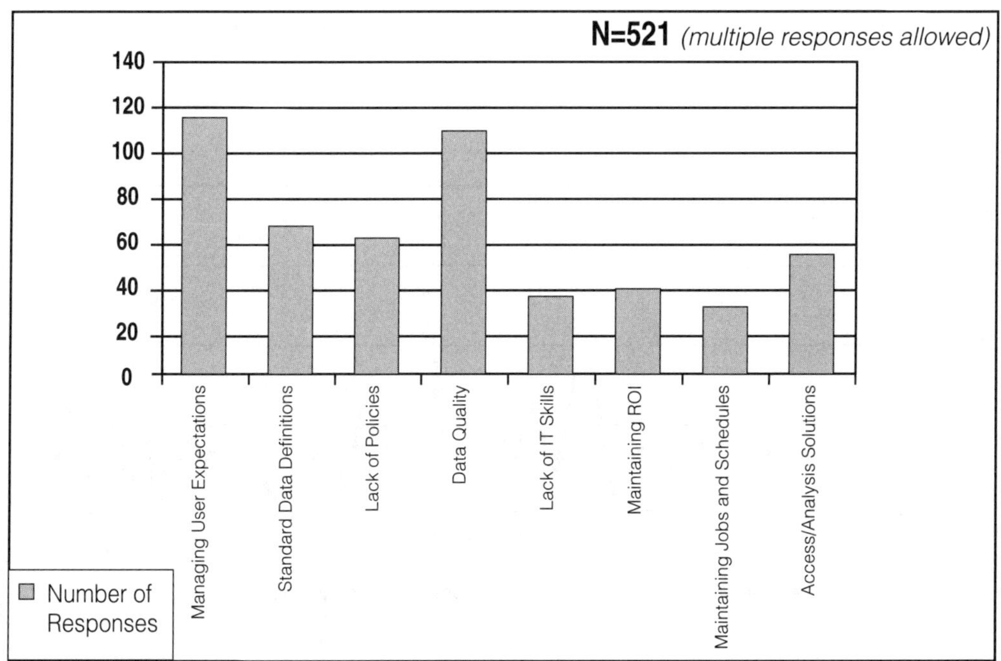

companies are no more likely to be successful than smaller ones.

Content appears to influence costs. For central DW environments, subject area count nearly always is associated with budget size. The incremental cost of each additional subject area remains constant. Also, the historical price tag of $500,000 per subject area seems to be holding up over time, regardless of industry. However, in data mart-oriented environments, the incremental cost of each mart is increasing. META Group's qualitative analysis suggests this stems from the exponential administrative overhead of decoupled data marts and the technical burden to ensure the consistency and synchronization of federated data mart environments. For data warehouses, the number of subject areas tracks closely to DW budgets for each respondent (see Figure 13).

(In Figure 13, budget totals are developed by using the midpoints from a series of budget data.)

OTHER SURVEY HIGHLIGHTS

Consulting

Of great interest is the lack of differentiation between shops employing global systems integrators (like the Big 5) and second-tier (boutique) integrators. This is as much a reflection of global integrators' inability (or lack of desire) to capture, package, and share DW best practices as it

Figure 13: DW budget to DW subject area correlation

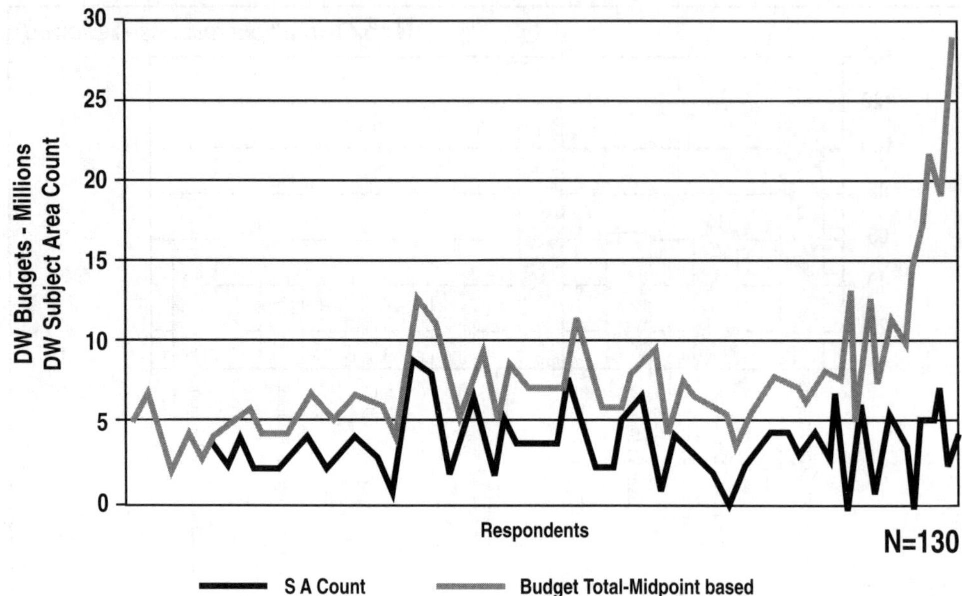

is a reflection of the prevalence of targeted competencies throughout the smaller/boutique firms. We conclude that it is not the firm, but rather the individuals, who make the difference in DW. For example, global integrators typically hire newly minted graduates having little or no familiarity with complex batch architectures — a requisite DW skill.

Spending Levels

The majority of respondents report modest use of outside help following the initial project rollout (less than $250,000 annually). Success rates appear to be unaffected when organizations spend large dollar amounts (see Figure 14) on consultants during postimplementation efforts (i.e., next-iteration subject areas or maintenance).

Team Size

While it is not evident that larger teams are more successful, undersized teams can hurt a project (see Figure 15). Teams ranging around 7-10 FTEs seem to be the optimum size for delivering successful implementations. The survey shows that, because more single-subject data marts fail than formal multisubject DWs, the insulated data mart project is not a guarantee of success.

Clearly, DW teams, even for data marts, must be adequately staffed with experienced personnel to reduce the chance of failure. While this may seem like an obvious message, META Group's anecdotal experience with smaller efforts shows that IT staff associated with such projects face a continual struggle to obtain the requisite resources. The common belief

Figure 14: Consultant expenditures, by profile

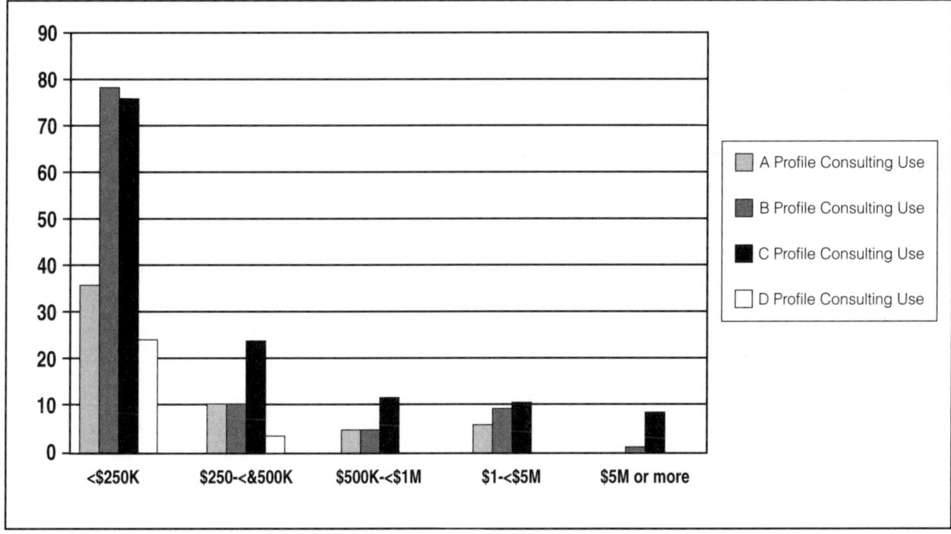

Figure 15: Average team size, by success profile

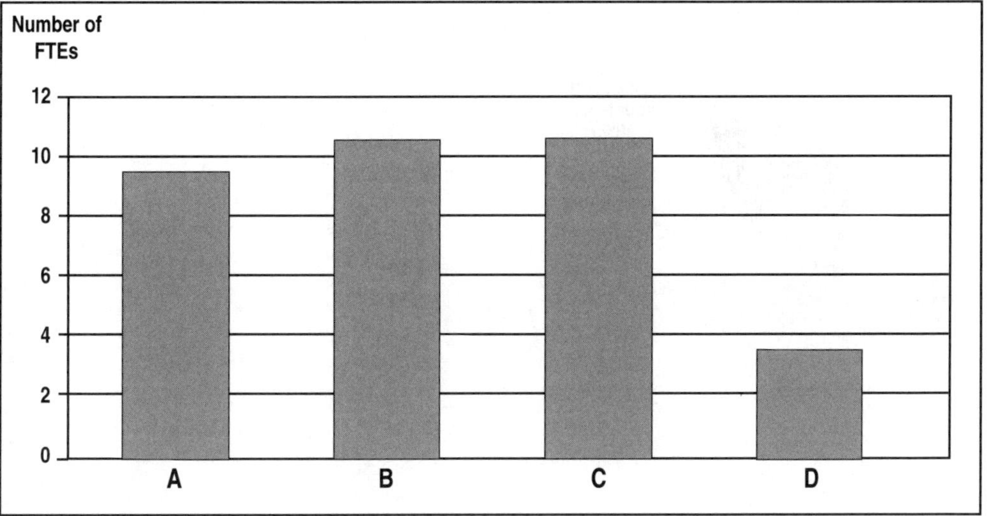

that a small data mart project can be supported by one or two FTEs simply does not hold true.

Overall Vendor Expectations

In general, vendors meet or exceed expectations of their customers nearly 60% of the time (Figure 16). According to the respondents, only 15% did not meet some or all expectations. Within certain tool categories, there are some differences. Extract, transform, load, and manage (ETLM) tools, for example, tend to be a bit more challenging to implement satisfactorily than more established technologies like DBMSs or hardware — thus leading to lower scores

Figure 16: Overall user satisfaction with vendors

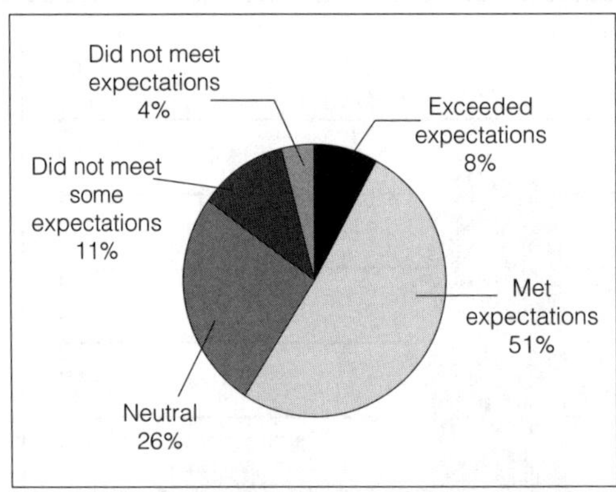

Driving Customer Retention, Development And Acquisition For Profit In The Insurance Business

Title: *Driving Customer Retention, Development And Acquisition For Profit In The Insurance Business*

Authors: *Chris Saunders and Michael Meltzer*

Abstract: *In the Age of the Consumer, the marketing dilemma that many financial institutions face is whether to focus on increasing market share, customer share, or both. Which is more profitable? Which has the greater long-term payoff?*

This paper explores how data warehouse technology and clear marketing strategies can be applied to building customer loyalty and retention, cross-selling opportunities, improved direct marketing campaigns, and marketing to "a segment of one."

Driving Customer Retention, Development, and Profit

For traditional insurance providers and for bancassurers it is becoming increasingly difficult to win new customers. This is especially true now as competitors are becoming larger and because more non-insurers are offering financial services and products. This is in an environment where both costs and competitive pressures have risen - to such an extent that many insurers face real issues of survival.

A steady flow of new, innovative services and delivery channels is usually necessary to build market share. Of course, these are costly to develop and execute, taking the business further round the vicious circle of increasing cost, reducing profit and decreasing retention.

However, with a greater customer focus, greater emphasis on relationship marke-ting, and effective customer retention plans, you may discover greater profitability within your existing customer base.

In the past, it was always easier to attempt to "poach" your competitors' customers. However, studies have shown that companies spend five times more money on acquiring new customers as they do on retaining those they already have. Further studies demonstrated that: "As a customer relationship with a company lengthens, profits rise. " And not just a little. Companies can boost profits by 100% by retaining just 5% more of their customers for one year longer. Pareto's Law, of course, still seems to apply very widely: one insurer found that the top 20% of its customers made all the profit, while the other 80% cost it money. The question is, have you considered the lifetime value of each of your customers? And, who makes up the 20% that accounts for the majority of your current and potential future profits?

Companies can boost profits by 100% by retaining just 5% more of their customers

Who asks the right questions?
The key to marketing success is the ability to ask the right questions that relate to a well-thought-out and actionable strategy. These are usually fundamental questions and should be answerable with available data. Unfortunately, finding that data and getting the answers you need is typically impossible with the way information systems are structured.

The problem is so deep-seated in most insurers that it is not even as if marketers are frustrated by not being able to get answers to their questions: they have never even bothered working out what the questions are!

The key to marketing success is the ability to ask the right questions that relate to a well-thought-out and actionable strategy

Refine your strategy
The key to profitable growth is the ability to refine the marketing strategy by concentrating on the most profitable opportunities: not just by promoting the most profitable products on average, but by understanding the most profitable combination of product offering, market segment, and channel. In other words, which products or services should I be offering to which group(s) of customers through which channel, in order to maximize my profits? Few insurers are in a position even to ask a question like this! Those who are will have a head start in the survival stakes and, more than this, will be on the way to achieving sustainable, competitive advantage.

A data warehouse provides an opportunity to ask these questions, with a good chance that most of them will be answered. For example:

- with better information about just who are the insurer's customers, you are better able to serve and keep them
- with better information about where profits arise in the business, you are better able to do this and maximize profits at the same time.

One financial institution in the United Kingdom attempted to find out just how many customers it had. They derived a number from a range of disparate computer systems that provided different financial products and services. That number was 25 million. When they finally cleaned up the data and used matching software to eliminate duplicates, they actually found they had seven million distinct customers. There were customers in different databases that were not stored by name, but by account number. In addition, incomplete records existed in many systems that focused on products. Some customers only had paid-up products; some had a combination of active and paid-up. They were even able to go a long way towards identifying products which these customers used to hold, but which had matured or been surrendered.

Understanding where profits arise is the secret to sustainable competitive advantage

To make specific offers to your customer base, you have to know who they are and what the status of the products they hold (and used to hold) with you is. Without a clear picture of who your own customers are, it is just as easy to pursue your competitor's customers - or to offer your existing customers products they already have.

But, who are your customers?

To be able to do even rudimentary segmentation, you need to know at least your customers' names, addresses, ages and genders. You also need to know the channels through which they have dealt in the past, and you need to be able to identify orphan clients. The traditional marketing segmentation methods which can add to this information - demographics, psychographics, geo-demographics, behavioral, and clusters - are only just coming into play in many insurance companies; unfortunately, however, they are not enough.

In many cases, the data does not reflect household-by-household information. Profiles taken of particular types of households don't represent the individuals and their likely propensities to act in particular ways.

Zurich Kemper Life
The data warehouse has delivered some insurance companies into the twentieth century. At Zurich Kemper Life executives can now rely on the data warehouse for information that was previously delivered in stand-alone, hardcopy reports. According to David Little, CIO for Zurich Kemper Life, the data warehouse has been well received as users move across to this electronic-based system. The data warehouse creates a level of reliability and consistency in our enterprise information that was previously unattainable. We now have the ability to cut, slice and dice the data so that we have a clear, in-depth understanding of our business". In addition to providing Zurich Kemper Life a "single version of the truth," the data warehouse has helped shorten its forecasting cycle. Rather than having to wait several days after the books have closed, executives have the ability to analyze information in almost real time. The data warehouse maintains historical information on 1.5 million life insurance policies and pulls information nightly from 20 different sources, averaging 50,000 nightly updates. One of the key messages about data warehousing is that it is an integrative force that enables disparate pieces of information and disparate systems to be welded together to create a means of building a customer centric view

A reliable predictor of future behavior is past behavior

The future from the past
It has been shown that one of the most reliable predictors of future behavior in humans is actual past behavior; this is why transactional information is key. The future success of your company depends on knowing as much as you can about each individual customer, rather than what you know about all of your customers. A culture must be fostered that continuously gathers customer-specific information that enhances your customer information repository. Every encounter - whether with the customer services department, through an intermediary, or via a completed or updated fact-find - must be seen as

another opportunity to collect additional information. This information forms the basis of a insurer's real assets: its relationships with its customers.

Until now, few insurers have had this depth of information to mine. And even if they did, there was little they could do with it. The sheer amount of data they had could not be turned into answers because of duplications of inaccurate information, the lack of focused base data, and the weakness of their existing technology.

To overcome this, some insurers now use data warehouses with a customer focus that is set apart from their traditional operational databases. Operational and often organizationally disparate databases, by the very nature of their data structures, mitigate against easy customer-focused analysis. The data warehouse has become the basis upon which specific business aims can be achieved and predictive models can be built - far more, in other words, than something that just stores data.

Information forms the basis of a insurer's real assets; its relationships with its customers

One version of the "TRUTH"
These companies are now able to consolidate names and addresses using matching software to clean their data. With this "one version of the truth," they are now able to identify customers as individuals; to identify all the products they hold with the company; and to recognize separate members of a single household.

How long has that customer been with the insurer? Are there any other accounts in the same family? Are they a one, two, or many product family? Have they dealt through more than one intermediary? Do they use different distribution channels for different products? The questions keep coming.

The data warehouse has become the basis upon which specific business aims can be achieved with this "one version of the truth. " Customers can now be identified as individuals

The difference is that these questions can now be given answers. Through data mining, predictive models can be built for database marketing, as well as for decision support. At the same time, different parts of the organization find profitable use for the same information. For example:

- Actuarial can start looking at the characteristics of the people who buy the products, not just at terms, ages, premiums and persistency
- Finance can start to model various scenarios of activity-based costing without affecting the ongoing business, and can use sensitivity analysis to test the robustness of various cost allocation models
- Customer Services can use image and workflow technology to analyze costs down to the lowest, granular level, and use the results to improve business efficiency

When you can see who the customers actually are and what interaction they have with the provider, the opportunity arises to market to them more effectively. When you can also identify where profit arises within the business - by customer group, by product and by channel - you can have a direct effect on profits, not just business volumes.

Cross-functional use of corporate data is where the bottom-line benefit really arises

This approach is just as valid for the Independent Financial Adviser (IFA) - based insurers as for those with direct operations: indeed, "customer focus" applies at two levels, both to the end customer (you can add value to the IFA by helping him understand his own market better) and directly to the IFA (by targeting the right services at the right IFA at the right time, based on present and potential IFA profitability).

The move to a greater customer focus is an attempt to see things from a customer perspective. Always keep in mind that the purpose of marketing is to generate customer-perceived value. When looking at retention programs, you must appreciate who you want to retain and why. What would you plan for the marginal customer and those on which you make a loss? Customer retention planning is where the solution begins, and its implementation is where you add to bottom-line profitability.

When looking at retention programs you must appreciate who you want to retain and why

Metadata for Data Warehouse

Title: *Metadata for Data Warehouse*

Author: *Satya Sachdeva, Principal Consultant Data Warehouse Practice Sybase Professional Services*

Abstract: *Metadata is the foundation for success of Data warehouse. Metadata is central piece of the whole Data Warehousing Concepts. Metadata allows the end user to be pro-active in the use of the warehouse. It is the Information Directory containing Yellow Pages, Road Map and ' Places Of Interest' for navigating the warehouse.*

Biography: Sybase, Inc is one of the largest global independent software companies. Sybase helps businesses integrate, manage and deliver applications, content and data anywhere they are needed. With a commitment to distributed, open, and end-to-end computing, Sybase Inc. is helping companies build advanced data warehouse solutions. The company is also leveraging core enterprise product strengths to capitalize on the emerging enterprise information portal market to provide dependable solutions that deliver on the promise of e-Business. http://www.sybase.com/bi.

According to a recent survey by International Data Corporation(IDC) a Framingham, Mass. based market researcher, Worldwide Sales of Data Warehouse related software are expected to grow at an annual rate of 24% to reach a staggering $2.2 billion by 1998. This projection includes Software related to Data Access, Data Management and Data Extraction and Transformation. In another study, META Group, a Connecticut based consulting firm found that the number of CIOs who indicated that they were interested in planning for or implementing a data warehouse grew from only 5 percent in 1993 to 90 percent a year later.

Data warehousing provides a means for implementing effective Decision Support Environment by utilizing existing data scattered all over the organization in disparate sources of data.

Information Warehouse - Metadata = Raw Data Warehouse

Without Metadata, information is reduced to meaningless repository of data. However before diving deep into the World of Metadata, let us look at its definition. In simple words, Metadata is data about data. While a simple number 5.32 does not mean anything, 5.32 % means a little better while 5.32 % hit rate from a mailing campaign. '% hit rate from a mailing campaign' tells us about the data and is Metadata about data '5.32'. However this is very simplistic definition of the Metadata and to understand its importance, we'll look at various views of the Metadata. Even though Metadata is of strategic nature to the organization as a whole, the onslaught of data warehousing as a tool for slicing and dicing of information for informed decision-making, has raised Metadata to new heights in terms of its importance.

"Effective Metadata determines the success or failure of many a data warehouse projects" says Siva Prakasm Velu, a Business Unit manager at, Complete Business Solutions Inc., a consulting company based in Farmington Hills, MI.

The company has undertaken many Data Warehousing projects in Banking, Retail, and Pharmaceutical industries. The company attributes the success of Data Warehousing to the key role played by Metadata toolsets.

For the business end user, metadata acts as an information directory, showing the location of data so it can be easily accessed in the data warehouse

Different Views of Metadata:

To further understand Metadata and its relationship to data warehousing, we shall look at what Metadata means to the Business Users, Data Warehouse Administrators and DSS Developers.

Business User' View

As mentioned earlier, for business users, Metadata is an Information Directory showing where they can find what Information. The End user' View of Metadata data can be best understood by considering a situation in which there is no Metadata. When a manager requests for an analytical query and he does not know how to proceed, he would be like a tourist in a new city without any road map. Metadata will be like a tourist information center, which will give home complete information about how to proceed about seeing various places of interest.

Metadata precisely acts like a tourist information center to the user who then is in a commanding position to plan his itinerary without wandering around aimlessly. With Metadata user knows how to get what.

From an end user's perspective, Metadata should contain the following:

- Table of Contents: Which should start with the subject areas about which information is available. What are the major dimensions where he can start and the slicing and dicing he can do. What are the various data elements which he can look at? What levels of summarization are available and to what level of detail can he go? This table of contents should also include different aliases used by different people in the company. These aliases should be meaningful names and should avoid all abbreviations unless abbreviations themselves are de-facto standards, e.g. 'Zone Improvement Plan' be better called as ZIP.
- The Origin of Data for the warehouse: Data warehouse users would like to know from which systems (legacy or other client server world) did the data come so that the user knows exactly what he is looking at. For example in case of a distribution company it will be important to know what is the origin of he movement information, did it come from the ordering system, or the warehouse system or the actual consumption from POS (Point-Of-Sales)

data. Over time, the source of data may change. So this part of the metadata should maintain a complete history of origin of data.

- Transformation Sequence: Its is very important for the user to know what formulae, calculations or decoding/ encodings have been applied to the original data on its journey from Operational Environment to the Warehouse environment.
- Access Levels: Metadata should also contain information about the access permissions available to the user and how can he obtain access to the information which may not be currently available.
- Timeline of the journey: The date and time of the latest data contained in the data warehouse. It does not mean that each line of data needs to have the timestamp. Usually the data warehoused do not have the current data. They lag behind the Operational Data by a time period ranging from a few hours to in some cases a month. The users want to know the lag and the Timeline of the journey of the data from operational world to the data warehouse world.
- Access Estimates: One of the most important reasons of failure for data warehouse projects is the frustration users face when queries take much longer than they can wait. As per studies conducted, it has been established that users will be more tolerant of such delays if they are fore-warned about how much time a particular type of query may take. For success of the Data warehouse, it is much better if the warehouse manager includes important statistics about how much time and resources queries may take.

Data Warehouse Administrator's view

Data warehouse administrator, responsible for Populating, Maintaining and Ensuring availability of Data warehouse, can make his tedious tasks simpler through his own special view of metadata data. Upkeep of metadata is as important as the metadata itself. Without effective management and use of appropriate tools, it may soon be out of sync with the actual data warehouse, thus rendering it completely ineffective. The Data Warehouse Administrator has to ensure that metadata is up to date and accurate. His/her view of the Metadata will include the following besides other things discussed above.

- Version Control: The Data warehouse should not only contain the current metadata but also the history of metadata which will let the administrator manage the Data Warehouse over a period of time by understanding impact of Changes on the availability and effectiveness of the data warehouse as Version control information will let him keep track of the changes in the data warehouse.
- Profile and Growth metrics: Spiral growth of databases may throw surprises in terms of performance as well as the Loading time, which may increase to an extent that it results in out-of-date information in the Data Marts.

One Data Warehousing project in a banking Environment failed because daily data uploads were taking more than 24 hours. Pro-active monitoring and predicting growth patterns of data accompanied with appropriate actions, will go a long way in preventing failure of data warehousing projects. Profile information also contains Purging and archiving requirements of various categories of data. Performance metrics should also be an integral part of he administrator's view of the metadata. It will also let the administrator procure the right system resources at the right time.

DSS Developer's View:
Metadata of an organization can become the starting point for the person responsible for Analyzing the requirement and designing or enhancing the Data Warehousing Systems for the DSS users. The analyst may start by interviewing the users to understand their requirements.

These requirement may be asking for the blue sky unless they are analyzed using Metadata which will show the analyst how and from where can those requirements be fulfilled. Metadata will show him:

- The table of contents of data in the current data warehouse if any
- Transformation and Business rules
- Data models
- Operational data Available

Corporate View
Now that we better understand Metadata and its different views, let us look at components from corporate perspective. Metadata is a logical collection of metadata from various sources described below.

Sources of Metadata
Legacy Systems: Metadata should ideally consist of a data dictionary containing information about Program Libraries, Database Catalogs and File Layouts. Program libraries in turn consist of Data Definitions up to field levels and various modules. Database Catalogs should contain definitions of all tables, relationships, columns and indexes. All this information should be in a repository accessible by different levels of users. However most organizations have this information scattered all over and are not in a position to use Legacy Metadata in an effective manner. Manager Software Products, Inc. (MSP) a company based in Mass. provides a whole suite of solutions to manage Metadata for Legacy environments even though the company also offers products for the Client Server environments.

Operational Client/Server: Client/Server era brought in never ending Multiple Layers of Software components bought from a variety of vendors and distributed all over the enterprise. Use of Repositories to track, all these components, to harness the power of Information, presents a major challenge to IS organizations. However the onset of New repository Technology and associated tools has provided avenues for managing metadata through a flexible architecture provided by Repositories today. This architecture gives the capability to create user defined meta-models and extensions and thus support ever changing environments.

Enterprise Data Architecture is playing a major role in today's' client server world. In today's organizations data is to be found in: PC based Local Databases, Work-group Environments including Lotus Notes and UNIX Mega servers/ mainframes. To keep track of all the data, metadata repository should be able to track what physical data resides where so that Corporate management should be able use the wealth of information hidden across the organization.

Metadata from Legacy data Mining: This constitutes a very important component of Metadata most often neglected Essential metadata often remains buried in the legacy data. Legacy Data is rich in critical business information but nowhere is this information documented. It might be in the minds of the programmers who had over the years built intelligence into the data and are no more with the company. Data re-engineering tools can be of great help for metadata mining from heaps of Legacy Data. This metadata can be used not only during the process of migration to client server but also to build data warehouses. Integrity Toolset from Vality technology Inc., a company based in Boston, Massachusetts, is one such tool which can perform the actual data investigation, identify information types and tag them for movement to the Metadata Tool. According to Ken Orr of the Ken Orr Institute:
"metadata mining will help prevent the building of overly simplistic data models by ensuring that organizations take into account the real world experiences and complexities of their business"

Data warehouse: At every stage of building a data warehouse: form conceptualization to Implementation, associated Metadata should be created and updated to make Data Marts effective for use. Since most organizations are either in the process of migrating or are actively planning to build, this component of metadata can most easily be constructed and maintained.

Moreover there are tools in this area which help automate the process. The component of Data Warehouse Metadata will be used not only by the end users for Information Surfing but also by the Data warehouse administrators and DSS/EIS analysts. Most DSS toolsets have some degree of metadata support.

Enterprise Models: These models are a very important component of any organizations Metadata. In fact Data Models are the first stage in the ultimate goal of Building a Corporate Metadata. The Repository or Metadata tool should have a bridge with CASE tool which is used build and store the data models. Transtar Software Inc., and Brown Stone Solutions Inc. both offer repository products to integrate with popular CASE tools like IEF, ADW, Bachman's DBA and Analyst, LBMS's System Engineer.

Metadata Tools:

There are two major categories of tools available in the market for metadata handling and management. Essentially organization may need more than one tool to manage their enterprise wide Metadata requirements. However they must take care to ensure that the multiple tools do not live in isolation and can actively interact with one another.

Generic Repositories:
Tools in this category allow managing of Metadata for the enterprise as a whole. Data Shopper from Reltech Products, Arlington, VA is one such tool for the end user. It provides a windows based interface that allows the retrieval of descriptions and corporate data structures and shows rules of access associated with the data. Data Dictionary from Brown Stone Solutions, and Manager link from Manager Software Products, Inc., MA are the other companies providing solutions in this area.

Tools specific to Data warehousing:
Tools in this category are generally available from the Vendors supplying various components of Data Warehousing infrastructure.

The Prism Directory Manager from Prism Solutions Inc., is a client server suite of products for building storing and navigating an Information Directory of the metadata in Data Warehouse.
It consists of three components:

1. Directory Builder, which gathers and integrates Metadata into the directory from a variety of sources and enables Data Warehouse administrator to build different views of Metadata Data for the business users, administrator and developer.
2. Information Directory contains integrated storage of metadata models describing contents and meaning of the information in a data warehouse.
3. Directory navigator provides a point and click navigation of the metadata data stored in the Information Warehouse.

Carleton Corp., Mass., has strategic alliance with Software AG to offer Passport, a metadata management tool as part of their overall Data Warehousing Solutions. Passport's Relation architecture supports end-user browsing and data warehouse administration for extraction, conversion and metadata data support.

The Virtual warehouse Metadata Intersolv Inc., MD is delivering second-generation technology through its SmartData Warehouse, which contains several layers of metadata: The SmartData Warehouse, Warehouse Databases and Databases SmartSets. Within the warehouse, "virtual" databases are created for each data source to be encapsulated. For example, a warehouse that encapsulates information from an Informix System and a Sybase system would have at least two virtual databases, one for each system. SmartSets are dynamic in nature and thus keep the metadata synchronized with Physical databases.

The Future

Most of the current repository or metadata tools rely on relational architecture, which is insufficient to handle complexities of the different views of Metadata integrated with disparate sources. Objectification of this architecture will offer much more flexible environment both for Data warehousing and other needs for a true corporate Metadata Model.

Meta-Data Management for Business Intelligence Solutions - IBM's Solutions

Title: *Meta-Data Management for Business Intelligence Solutions*
Author: *IBM*
Abstract: *This paper presents IBM's strategy for managing meta-data for Business Intelligence solutions. The paper covers meta-data concepts and reviews IBM's strategy. Also covered is an overview of how IBM's Visual Warehouse solution manages meta-data.*

This version adds in information about the Common Warehouse Meta-data Interchange proposed standard.

Introduction

What is Meta-data?

Being able to consolidate and analyze your data for better business decisions can often lead to competitive advantage, and learning to uncover and leverage these advantages is what business intelligence is all about. All of this is possible if you have the right applications and tools to analyze data, and more importantly, if the data is prepared in a format suitable for analysis. Setting up this infrastructure for business intelligence solutions requires integrating a variety of tools -- tools to build and manage the infrastructure, databases to store the data, and tools for analysis. Integration can be facilitated by sharing certain types of information (meta-data) across the components of the business intelligence environment.

Meta-data, or information about data, provides administrators and business users with descriptions of the data or informational objects that they can access. There are two types of meta-data: technical meta-data and business meta-data. Both types of meta-data are important in building, maintaining, and using a datamart or data warehouse.

Technical meta-data is used by administrators and software tools and provides the technical descriptions of data and operations. Technical meta-data includes information about source data, target data, and the rules that are used to extract, filter, enhance, cleanse, and transform source data to target data. Technical meta-data could be created by a relational database management system (e.g. database statistics), by warehouse and transformation tools (e.g. descriptions of transformations), by the warehouse manager (e.g. schedules), etc.

Business meta-data is used by business analysts and end users and provides a business description of informational objects. It assists end users in locating, understanding, and accessing information in the datamart, data warehouse, or other informational sources. Business meta-data might include the calculation used to create a particular value, the date and time that a report was created, or a description of the approval state of the company forecast.

Business meta-data not only applies to the data in the warehouse but equally to information about a broader class of informational objects such as a graph or chart viewed through a presentation tool, a query or report returned from a decision-support or OLAP tool, or a Web page retrieved from the Internet. For example, a business information directory could contain meta-data about all the reports having to do with sales in the southeast region.

Why is Meta-data Important?
Meta-data helps to achieve two major objectives:

1. It provides a means to improve the productivity of administrators and the reliability of solutions

   Many components are used when building a system supporting Business Intelligence. They include database management systems, modeling tools, transformation tools, process managers, data mining and decision support tools, etc. These tools leverage many different platforms, data formats, and vendor suppliers. And each tool typically has its own meta-data store and administrative interface. Making a mix of tools work together, as part of a data warehouse process, requires passing data and meta-data between them. Administrators must create and maintain such data bridges. Often, identical information (i.e., meta-data) must be fed to multiple tools, creating meta-data consistency problems. Thus, meta-data interoperability between tools simplifies integration tasks for administrators and reduces maintenance requirements.

2. It provides a means to assist business analysts end users in locating and understanding data.

   Users need to understand where a given piece of information comes from -- its lineage or genealogy -- and how current the information is. For example, how current is sales data? Or, what calculations were used to derive profit? Making users self-sufficient is critical given the growth in the number of users accessing datamarts or data warehouses. Otherwise, deployment will become gated by the bandwidth of the help desk staff to answer user's questions about finding or understanding information available to them.

Integrating Meta-data - Centralized vs. Decentralized Approaches
If administrative efficiency is the objective, then a means must be found for tools from different vendors to share common information. However, this can be a very difficult task. Each tool defines the same object in a different manner (the tool's information models are different) and therefore the objects are not easily shareable. Furthermore, the same meta-data is redundantly defined and stored in many meta-data stores - data dictionaries, repositories, encyclopedias, database catalogs, copy libraries, etc., each with a

different Application Programming Interface (API). Typically, the tools cannot exchange meta-data among themselves because the meta-data is stored in a proprietary format understood only by a specific tool. As a result, changes to meta-data in one meta-data store are not easily changed in the others.

There are two primary approaches to meta-data integration: centralized and decentralized. In a centralized approach, each tool stores and accesses meta-data using a central repository. This is an appealing approach for most customers as it can simplify tool integration and operations. However, it is generally problematic because:

- Each tool has different private meta-data that must be stored to support unique product features. Replacing a tool's proprietary meta-data store is a costly undertaking with little added competitive differentiation to warrant the investment.
- Tool meta-data is continually evolving so a complete centralized information model of all relevant meta-data is difficult to achieve.

This approach has only been successful where a set of products or components from a single vendor have been designed to work together from the beginning.

With a decentralized approach, individual tools use portions of a common model definition and then exchange this meta-data using an agreed-to interchange language. In this approach, a central repository can still fulfill the role of an information source but the repository is not a component upon which other tools rely during execution mode.

- This approach provides the widest range of tool interoperability, allowing each tool to be autonomous with its own proprietary meta-data store while still sharing common meta-data.
- This approach can be used between two or more tools, allowing for simple to complex scenarios as to the number of tools involved.
- Each tool can be used "as is" without any need to replace a tool's existing meta-data store.
- Because the tool is not changed, execution and performance should not be affected.

The decentralized approach facilitates the integration of tools from multiple vendors with lower cost and more flexibility ... and therefore, with greater likelihood of success. This approach creates the need for meta-data synchronization.

The business need for meta-data standards
Today, companies and organizations in various stages of data warehouse implementations are working to meet the demands of business users for the delivery of useful, reliable, and timely information. Many components (or tools) are used when building a business intelligence system. These tools are heterogeneous in their platforms, data formats, and the vendors that supply them.
The value of meta-data integration is in the reduction of the time it takes to implement a business intelligence system, making the maintenance and management more

productive, as well as improving productivity reducing errors for business users.

Meta-data management and meta-data standards has become a critical issue for data warehousing customers. According to the Giga Report, "Standards for Data Warehousing," published October 15, 1998, a fundamental strategic shift in data warehousing will be facilitated through meta-data standards, which will play an important role in increasing the value proposition for data warehouses. Meta-data standards will allow companies to start data warehousing projects on a small scale and then have the confidence to deploy them on a larger scale; this means that the initial annual average expenditure for the data warehouse can drop from millions of dollars to less than $250,000 and implies that the inhibitors of budget and sponsorship for initial projects can be removed. In addition, companies that take advantage of meta-data standards to incrementally scale their data warehouse over time will have a major competitive advantage for project initiation over other organizations that either insist on obtaining support and budget in spite of stringent business justification guidelines, or select low-cost architectures that don't scale.

IBM's Business Intelligence Meta-data Interchange Strategy

Following are the key elements of IBM's Business Intelligence meta-data interchange strategy:

Decentralized Approach to Meta-data Integration

Since it is unlikely that a totally new set of tools can be developed which would satisfy all the flavors of Business Intelligence one must assume that specific customer solutions will require different tools, some from different vendors. Therefore, for Business Intelligence, IBM has chosen the decentralized approach to meta-data integration. Here, each tool can be autonomous with its own proprietary meta-data store, however, it shares common meta-data, that is, it is part of a federation of meta-data stores. In essence, the approach consists of a meta-data interchange facility as well as a meta-data integration hub used to validate the objects being interchanged and provide specialized services in a Business Intelligence environment.

Support for Both Technical and End-user Meta-data Using the Visual Warehouse Information Catalog

The Visual Warehouse Information Catalog contains meta-data for both technical and business users.

- Administrators are able to use the meta-data to help manage the data warehouse or datamart.
- Business analysts and end users are able to use the meta-data to identify available information in a business context.

Typically, data warehouse products collect meta-data for the use of the warehouse administrator. This meta-data is neither available nor oriented to the business user. The Visual Warehouse Information Catalog supports meta-data both for the administrator and for the end user. End-user oriented meta-data is made available through an interface tailored specially to end users, including the ability to navigate and search using business terms, to present data lineage and currency information, and to automatically launch applications associated with the data. Additionally, the Visual Warehouse Information Catalog spans a breadth of informational objects allowing web pages, spreadsheets, presentations, and other objects to be represented along with information about data in the datamart or warehouse.

Visual Warehouse Information Models
Interchange of Business Intelligence meta-data is significantly enhanced if a common interchange information model is used to avoid private interchanges between pairs of tools.

IBM provides externally published information models (used by the Visual Warehouse Information Catalog) for relational tables, file records (including DL/I segments), multidimensional cubes, reports, spreadsheets, pictures as well as a process and lineage model. The Visual Warehouse Information Catalog metamodel allows easy creation of additional information models. Using this extensibility feature, IBM has developed support of the Meta-data Interchange Specification (MDIS) models defined by the Meta-data Coalition. See http://www.MDCinfo.com for more information about the Meta-data Coalition.

A metamodel consists of the constructs used to develop information models. The Visual Warehouse Information Catalog uses its own generalized metamodel to allow administrators to describe new information models. Once defined, the Visual Warehouse Information Catalog will create the necessary tables used to store the new objects.

Visual Warehouse Support of Open Interfaces and APIs for Meta-data Interchange
Interchange is significantly enhanced if a common interchange syntax is used to avoid private interchanges between pairs of tools.

IBM's Meta-data Interchange Language, the Meta-data Interchange Specification, and IBM's VisualAge Exchange product
The Visual Warehouse Information Catalog is designed to integrate with a wide variety of products. It comes with extraction technology for a variety of database management systems and end-user tools. Source and target meta-data can be imported directly from RDBMS catalogs. Additionally, Visual Warehouse can exchange meta-data with any system that conforms to IBM's Meta-data Interchange Language or the Meta-data Interchange Specification (MDIS) adopted by the Meta-data Coalition. See Appendix A for a list of products with which the Visual Warehouse Information Catalog can exchange meta-data. Also, the Visual Warehouse Information Catalog has an externalized C type functional API which is mapped to a series of relational tables. Upon request, IBM will provide the model of these relational tables so they can also be accessed via SQL.

Figure 1 illustrates the meta-data flows just discussed.

UML and XML
UML or Unified Modeling Language is designed to give application developers a common language for specifying, visualizing, constructing, and documenting distributed objects and business models. Data Warehouse meta-data models can be designed and visually represented in UML. For example models could be defined for warehouse constructs such as a data transformation, an OLAP schema, or an extract process.

XML or Extensible Markup Language is an open standard of the World Wide Web Consortium (W3C) designed for defining, validating, and sharing document formats on the Web. In a data warehousing context, one could exchange instances of UML models using XML as the interchange language.

As these standards gain widespread usage, IBM can be expected to use UML for representing warehouse meta-data models and to use XML for exchanging instances of meta-data represented in those models between tools. For example, IBM could enhance IBM's Team Connection repository to store a warehouse meta-data model and support exchange of instances of warehouse meta-data using XML. Visual Warehouse could be enhanced to exchange meta-data instances with any

Figure 1

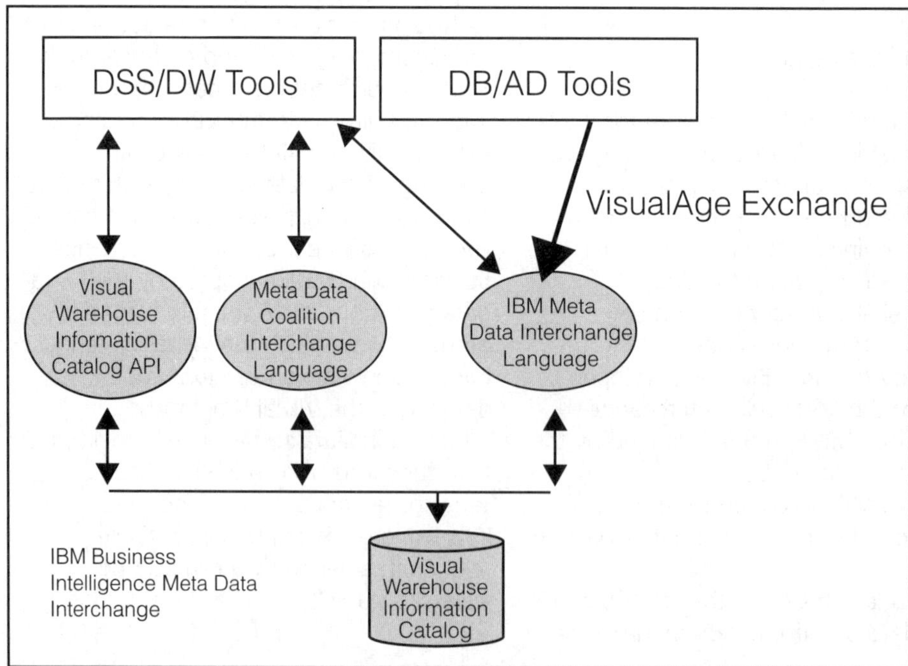

source that supports XML interchange via a common data type definition.

OMG Committee for Common Warehouse Meta-data
IBM is leading an OMG (Open Management Group) subcommittee for the standardization of Common Warehouse Meta-data. The group members include Hyperion, NCR, Oracle and Unisys. The objectives of this committee are to establish an industry standard for common warehouse meta-data interchange and to provide a generic mechanism that can be used to transfer a wide variety of warehouse meta-data. The intent is to define a rich set of warehouse models to facilitate the sharing of meta-data, to adopt open API's (Java and Corba) for direct tool access to meta-data repositories, and to adopt XML as the standard mechanism for exchanging meta-data between tools. The subcommittee, chaired by IBM, submitted a proposal on September 1999. Additional information can be found at www.omg.org.

OMG Committee for XML/XMI
A related OMG subcommittee was formed to standardize XML Meta-data Interchange (XMI). IBM, Unisys and other industry leaders are also involved in this work. The proposal for an XML Meta-data Interchange Format specifies an open information interchange model that is intended to give developers working with object technology the ability to easily interchange meta-data between modeling tools and between tools and meta-data repositories. The standard was approved in May 1999. In a data warehousing context, the proposal defines a stream-based interchange format for exchanging instances of UML models.

Visual Warehouse Automation of Meta-data Interchange
Maintaining independent meta-data stores introduces the risks that the meta-data stores will become inconsistent. IBM addresses this problem by automating meta-data interchange within IBM's Visual Warehouse solution. For example, Visual Warehouse can automate the scheduling of updates for:

- Definitional meta-data such as the addition of a new column to a table
- Operational meta-data such as time stamp information about the refresh of warehouse data
- OLAP meta-data such as information about a multidimensional database

NOTE: See "Meta-data Integration Between IBM's Visual Warehouse and Partner Products" for more details on meta-data interchange between IBM's Visual Warehouse and partner products from Evolutionary Technologies International, Inc., Vality Technology Inc., Brio Technology, Business Objects, Cognos, and Hyperion Solutions.

Visual Warehouse as a Meta-data Integration Hub
Although meta-data interchange can occur directly between pairs of tools, the interchange is significantly enhanced if the interchange goes through a meta-data integration hub. The primary role of the of the hub is to parse and validate the meta-data being interchanged, reconcile it with other meta-data, and detect name

collisions. The hub also provides export/import functions from/to itself in a similar fashion as the participating tools do. In general, the hub assumes the role of "master" for the shareable objects being interchanged. The ideal choice for a meta-data integration hub is Visual Warehouse as it fulfills the requirements just discussed.

Visual Warehouse Meta-data Interchange with DB2 OLAP Server
The Meta-data Hub from Visual Warehouse can also work with DB2 OLAP Server. The operational data can be enhanced by:

1. The Visual Warehouse Information Catalog can extract meta-data about the multidimensional model from the DB2 OLAP Server or Hyperion Essbase.
2. Visual Warehouse can schedule automatic updates for changes to the meta-data extracted from the DB2 OLAP Server or Hyperion Essbase.

Meta-data integration Between IBM's Visual Warehouse and Partner Products

IBM has partnered with several companies with the objective of providing an integrated and scaleable environment for Business Intelligence solutions. At the core of these partnerships are development projects to provide integration between Visual Warehouse and partner products. These partnerships cover two principal areas -- ETML (Extract, Transformation, Move and Load) tools and Analysis tools.

Integrating ETML Tools for Building and Managing Business Intelligence environments
To prepare data for analysis, it is usually extracted from a variety of sources, transformed (e.g., summarized, derived, cleansed, etc.), then moved and loaded into a data store suitable for analysis. IBM's Visual Warehouse has specific integration points with products from Evolutionary Technologies International Inc. And Vality Technology Inc.

ETI
ETI Extract, a tool suite from Evolutionary Technologies International, Inc. extends Visual Warehouse capabilities in the area of data extract and transformation generation.

ETI and IBM jointly developed a new utility software, which offers integration between the ETI Extract Tool Suite, ETI's data integration product, and Visual Warehouse (VW), IBM's easy-to-use data mart and data warehouse solution. The ETI Extract Tool Suite provides data extraction, transformation, movement and load capabilities while IBM's VW offerings combine scheduling or information catalog; and query and reporting capabilities.

The MetaTransport Utility allows businesses to use VW to schedule, manage and monitor the execution of the data conversion programs ETI Extract generates. The utility also enables meta-data captures by ETI Extract to be sent to VW, where it can be displayed, analyzed and queried.

Table 1:Meta-data Interchange between ETI and VW Manager

ETI	VW Manager
Programs	Business Views
Programs	Programs
I-files	Sources

Table 2: Meta-data interchange between ETI and VW Information Catalog

ETI	VW Information Catalog
Plan	Business Subject Area
I-Files	Databases
Program	Transformation

Vality

Vality Integrity, a data re-engineering tool from Vality Technology Inc., extends Visual Warehouse in the area of data quality.

The Integrity Data Re-engineering Environment transforms data from any source into high-quality input data for data warehouse-based business intelligence applications and large-scale production applications. It facilitates an automated and integrated process with the IBM VW

Table 3: Meta-data Interchange between Vality and VW

Vality	VW Manager
Procedures	Business Views
Procedures	Program
Project	Subject
Data Files	Source

Manager and provides customers a high-quality solution to their needs.

Table 4: Meta-data Interchange between VW and the Information Catalog

VW Manager	VW Information Catalog
Business Views	Transformation
Program	Transformation
Subject	Business Views
Sources	Files

Figure 2 shows an administrator's view of flows of information between Visual Warehouse, ETI Extract, and Vality Integrity.

Note: there are several possible scenarios using Visual Warehouse, ETI Extract, and Vality Integrity. In the scenario depicted above, several meta-data related activities occur:

- A1 - a data conversion specialist using ETI Extract registers the "stage 1" data conversions with Visual Warehouse. As each data conversion is registered, meta-data is imported into Visual Warehouse that defines business views which will invoke the data conversion programs. Also imported into Visual Warehouse is meta-data that describes the data conversion source(s) and target(s), and transformations. (i.e., the ETI data conversion targets).
- A2 - the Integrity programmer imports, from Visual Warehouse, the meta-data that defines the input files.
- A3 - the Integrity programmer registers the Integrity process with Visual

Figure 2

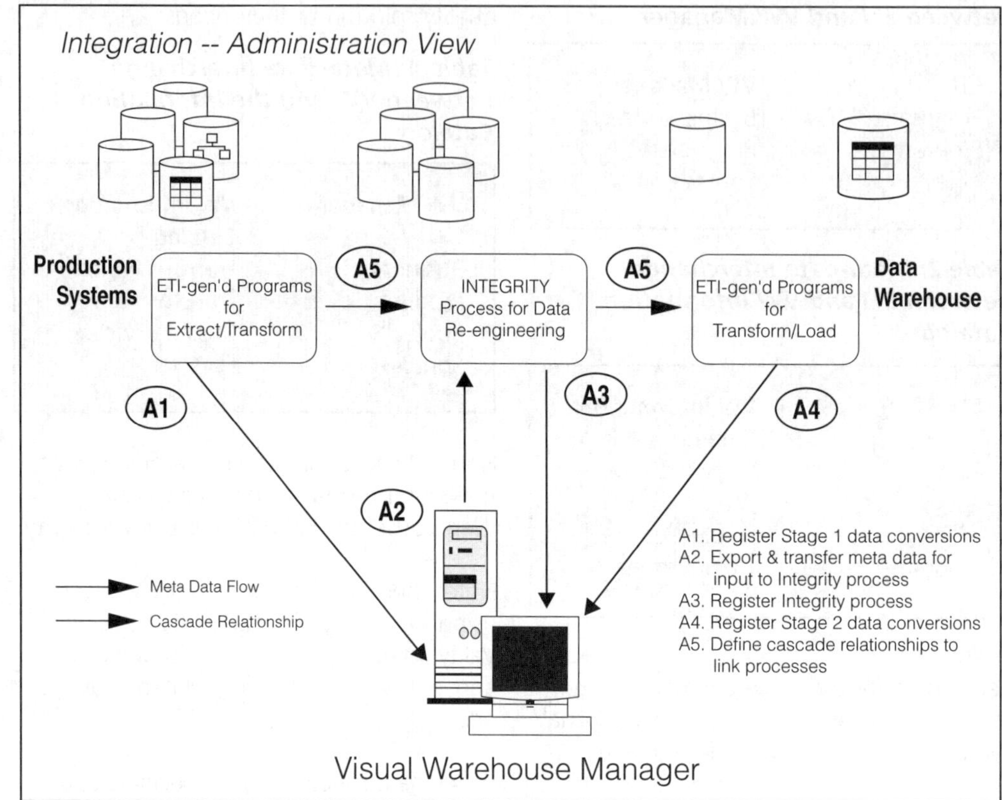

Warehouse. The Integrity registration process automatically transfers meta-data that defines a single business view that will invoke the Integrity process as well as meta-data that describes the input and output files and the relationship of the input and output files to the Integrity business view.

- A4 - a data conversion specialists using ETI Extract registers the "stage 2" data conversions with Visual Warehouse. As in step A1, meta-data is imported into Visual Warehouse.
- A5 - the Visual Warehouse administrator defines cascading relationships between the last business view in the "stage 1" extract process to the Integrity business view and from the Integrity business view to the first business view of the "stage 2" data conversions. To schedule the entire sequence, the Visual Warehouse administrator defines a schedule for the first business view in the "stage 1" extract process.

Integrating Tools for Analyzing Information
Once data is prepared for decision-marketing, there are a variety of analysis tools that can be used. IBM has partnered with Brio Technology, Business Objects, Coglin Mill, Cognos and Hyperion Solutions to provide meta-data integration between respective partner products and the IBM Visual Warehouse solution. Figure 3 and the following descriptions characterize the meta-data flows:

Brio Technology
Brio Enterprise does currently not export meta-data to the VW Information Catalog. Brio Enterprise is able to read meta-data about database tables and columns, which are stored in the Visual Warehouse Information catalog. Brio Technology provides SQL-driven facility that dynamically reads meta-data stored in database tables.

Business Objects
IBM's Visual Warehouse Business Objects Version allows users to access business-critical information through the internet BusinessObjects is fully integrated with IBM Visual Warehouse and Visual Warehouse OLAP server and delivers integrated query and reporting

1. Technical and business meta-data can be extracted from the Visual Warehouse Information Catalog and used to build a BusinessObjects Universe.
2. The Visual Warehouse Information Catalog can extract meta-data about

Figure 3

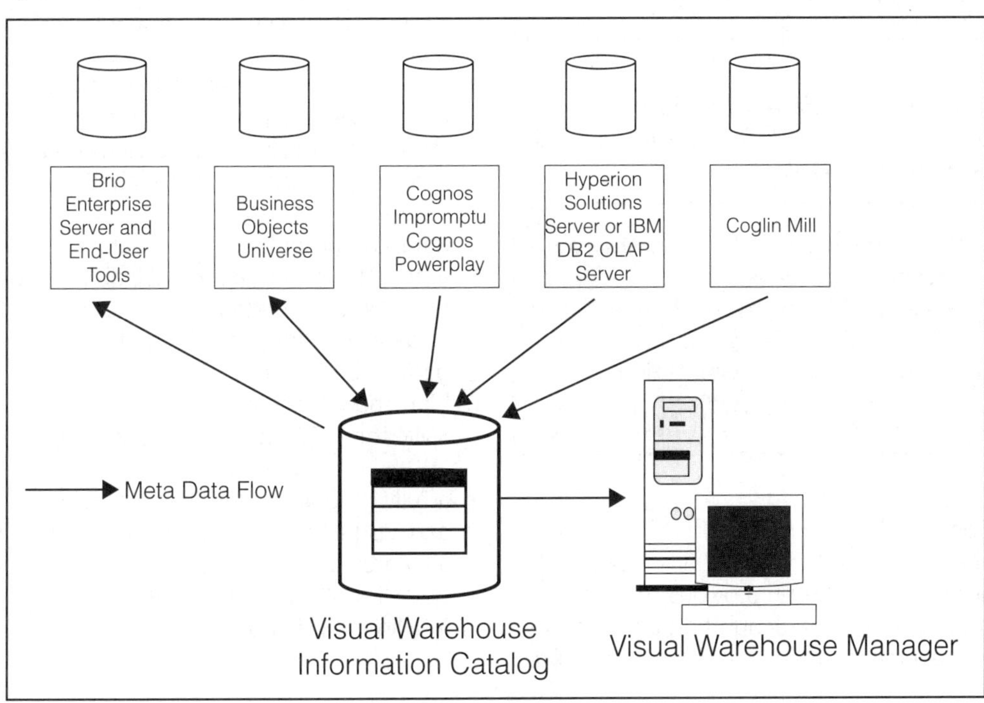

BusinessObjects Universe, Classes, Objects, and Report types
3. BusinessObjects reports or queries can be launched from within the Visual Warehouse Information Catalog

The tables below show the meta-data interchange between Business Objects and the VW Information Catalog.

Table 5: Meta-data interchange between Business Objects and the VW Information Catalog

Business Objects	VW Information Catalog
Universe	Database
Class	Table
Object (BO Object)	Column
BO Report	Document*

**All documents grouped into a Business Subjects Area*

Table 6: Meta-data interchange between the VW Information Catalog and Business Objects

VW Information Catalog	Business Objects
Database	Universe
Table	Class
Column	Object (BO Object)

Coglin Mill
The new release of RODIN (i.e. V3R1 available April 1999) provides the most sophisticated data acquisition and data management capabilities of any automated tool available on any platform. It runs on the AS/400 and leverages DB2/400 as the underlying database technology as well as integrates into the above mentioned IBM data management products. Facilities provided by RODIN include :

1. sophisticated data extraction, validation, transformation and processing logic not possible with SQL loading tools including temporal database support, automatic management of "generalized" keys and "many to many" load capabilities in a single pass of the source data,
2. automated error detection, correction and reject handling, including reporting, holding and reprocessing of rejects,
3. flexible data warehouse and data mart structures including time series arrays integrated into user-definable calendars to support all forms of comparative analyses,
4. an integrated server-based report writer that utilizes the power of the active metadata to deliver simple-to-use but highly sophisticated data analysis and reporting, with paper, screen and database output,
5. automatic generation of HLL object code from "active" metadata to deliver unparalleled functionality and performance levels,
6. high speed parallel processing in both SMP and MPP environments with almost 100% linear scaling,
7. a fully graphical interface to all RODIN and Visual Warehouse functions that also provides a single secured access point for all tools used in the business intelligence environment, and

8. an open architecture that allows integration with all other industry standard compliant tools.

RODIN is 100% metadata active, meaning it generates 100% of the code required to fulfill the functions the user defines in the metadata. It also uses the metadata during processing to manage the flow of data from the operational systems to the informational systems, without the customer needing to write any program code.

Customers can implement RODIN, Visual Warehouse, DataPropagator and DataJoiner in any combination and any sequence, to suit their exact requirements. Many configurations and options exists to ensure only the required components need be licensed.

The integration of RODIN with IBM's leading data management middleware products means customers can now utilize the very best technology available on any platform to meet their entire data warehousing needs on the AS/400, regardless of the sources of data and the complexity of the environment.

With the open architecture of the resultant data warehouse and dependant data marts, any industry standard data mart, data analysis or data visualization tool can be easily added to and integrated into the overall business intelligence environment. This provides the easy integration of a "solution oriented architecture" required to drive modern successful businesses of all sizes and complexities.

Cognos

Cognos provides a data query and reporting tool – Cognos Impromptu, and an OLAP tool for multidimensional analysis -- Cognos PowerPlay.

1. Mappings can occur between business descriptions in the Visual Warehouse Information Catalog and Cognos Impromptu.
2. Mappings can occur between business descriptions in Cognos Impromptu and the Visual Warehouse Information Catalog.
3. Visual Warehouse subject areas can be mapped to Cognos Impromptu folders.
4. Cognos Impromptu and PowerPlay reports and cubes can be registered in the Visual Warehouse Information Catalog with program association.

Table 7: Meta-data interchange between Cognos and the VW Information Catalog

Cognos	**VW Information Catalog***
Impromptu Catalog	Impromptu Catalog
Folder	Business Subject Area
Column	Column
Impromptu Report	Impromptu Report
Power Play Report	Power Play Report
Power Play Cube	Power Play Cube

Table 8: Meta-data interchange between and the VW Information Catalog and Cognos

VW Information Catalog	Cognos
Business Subject Area	All Objects from Impromptu Catalog*
Impromptu Catalog	Catalog
Business Subject Area	Folder
Column	Column
Impromptu Report	Impromptu Report
Power Play Report	Power Play Report
Power Play Cube	Power Play Cube

** Everything gets grouped into a Business Subject Area*

5. Meta-data synchronization can be scheduled and automated by Visual Warehouse or initiated from Cognos Impromptu.

Hyperion Solutions

Hyperion Essbase OLAP Server is a strategic platform optimized for enterprise management reporting, analysis and planning applications. It supports multi-user read/write access, large-scale data-capacity, robust analytical calculation and sophisticated OLAP queries.

Note: See "Visual Warehouse Meta-data Interchange with DB2 OLAP Server" above.

Summary

IBM advocates a decentralized approach to the exchange of technical and end-user meta-data for Business Intelligence solutions. Today, IBM's Visual Warehouse supports integrated and automated meta-data management in conjunction with products from key partners (Brio Technology, Business Objects, Cognos, Evolutionary Technologies International, Hyperion Solutions, and Vality Technology). In addition, the Visual Warehouse Information Catalog can interchange meta-data with dozens of sources using IBM's Meta-data Interchange Language and/or the MDIS Interchange Language. Even more sources can be accessed through bridges in IBM's VisualAge Exchange product.

IBM firmly believes that widely-adopted industry standards are necessary to address warehouse meta-data issues. IBM is leading work with other industry vendors on OMG standards for Common Warehouse Meta-data and standards for interchanging meta-data.

Currently available IBM solutions, combined with IBM's sponsorship of evolving meta-data standards, clearly position IBM as the data warehouse meta-data leader.

Appendix A

The IBM Meta-data Interchange Language provides the ability to exchange meta-data between the Visual Warehouse Information Catalog and:

Hyperion Essbase	Business Objects
Computer Associates ERWIN	CorelDraw!
IBM DB2 Family Catalogs	Harvard Graphics
IBM DataJoiner	IBM QMF
ODBC Sources	Lotus 1-2-3
Oracle RDBMS Catalogs	Lotus Approach
Sybase RDBMS Catalogs	Microsoft Excel
Sterling: Cool	Microsoft Word
	Quatro Pro
	Word Perfect

The Meta-data Coalition Interchange Language is supported by the Visual Warehouse Information Catalog as depicted earlier in the paper. For more information about the Meta-data Coalition go to: http://www.MDCinfo.com

Universal Data Exchange: An Enterprise-Wide Solution

Title: *Universal Data Exchange: An Enterprise Wide Solution*
Author: *Hummingbird*
Abstract: *This paper provides a summary of the fundamental technologies and concepts involved with universal data exchange. It discusses data extraction, transformation, and loading (ETL) tools, widely used in such information technology initiatives as data marts and warehouse projects, online analytical processing (OLAP) cubes, enterprise resource planning (ERP) data sharing, and other distributed data applications.*

Biography: see end article

Introduction

It is widely accepted that information represents the newest opportunity to generate business advantage. However, realizing this advantage is far easier imagined than executed. Getting at the mountains of raw data generated by most modern organizations by a variety of different hardware platforms, databases, and applications is a difficult task. Consolidating vast amounts of data from a variety of departments, branches, and autonomous business units in data marts, warehouses, or other decision support systems is another issue. Harder still is the job of converting that data into useful information conducive to end user query, analysis, and decision-making activities.

There are many sound reasons for transferring data between systems on an enterprise wide basis. Business intelligence solutions, data sharing, application data integration, legacy system migration, and data consolidation for projects like information portals are some of the valuable business applications for what is known as universal data exchange. As opposed to building stovepipe solutions that may serve the needs of one department, one office, or even an entire solution, universal data exchange is capable of handling the requirements of several data movement and transformation solutions simultaneously. In other words, while there are standalone solutions like data marts, data warehouses, and data integration projects, combined they represent what is called a universal data exchange solution.

Universal data exchange solutions include a suite of tools that can manage data across the entire information supply chain. This involves extracting data from a variety of systems and applications, transforming it, standardizing it if necessary, transporting it to where it needs to be, and loading it in database tables in desired formats. The combination of these tools, and the resultant enterprise solution, represents a truly valuable business benefit with rapid and significant return on investment.

The Evolution of Data Exchange Technology

Alternative Technologies

In the past, several alternatives to modern data exchange tools have been used. In fact, many companies still rely on traditional methods for extracting, moving, enhancing, and sharing corporate data throughout the enterprise. While these techniques manage to meet the most basic requirement of data exchange (in that they can transport data from one place to another), they certainly fall short of anything that would be considered robust. The simple truth is that these methods were suitable for the applications of the time they were developed, but are outdated and inappropriate for the requirements of today.

Prior to the advent of pure data extract, transform, and load tools, IT professionals had few options. They could either use basic file transport methods or produce in-house solutions. Tools of this generation included media transfer, FTP file transfer, and code generators, all of which, while serving the requirements of their day, have drawbacks.

Media Transfer

Not that long ago, companies had little choice but to batch copy entire database files to media (tape, disk, etc.) and physically transport them to other machines. Handling data of dissimilar types involved tedious manual re-keying which, as can be imagined, still resulted in a high rate of errors. Additionally, media transfers took an extremely long time and could not be carried out with the required frequency of today's complex data exchange applications. Needless to say, this method quickly became outdated and far too unworkable and costly to be of any practical use in high volume environments.

File and Data Transfer via Communication Line

Similar to media transfer, fi le transfer via communication line was another tool that was commonly used. FTP and other communication line fi le transfer methods are still widely used today for the movement of fi les across wide areas. However, for the more advanced requirements of data sharing, application integration, and other universal data exchange applications, fi le transfer is far too costly a method for data transport.

Code Generators

As the name suggests, code generators use hard coded routines to perform data transformation. Essentially involving two distinct processes — compiling and executing — code generation transformation tools are primarily external programs. That is, all work is done outside of the native application or database. Users must manually fix, recompile, and return to the native program or database. No steps in the exchange process are carried out automatically.

While useful for simple point-to-point data exchange, code generators become unmanageable when disparate systems or databases are added to the mix. That is, code generators can be useful in consolidating data in a data warehouse environment, but become hard to administer and manage if dissimilar systems are introduced or new projects, like departmental data marts, are desired.

Technological Catalysts for Change
Several technological factors rapidly brought about the need for reliable, robust, and efficient tools capable of handling the complex requirements of moving vast amounts of data among disparate corporate systems. These included the high cost of unreliable information, stale data, legacy systems that still held valuable data, high development costs of data warehouses and other data stores for business intelligence, and the proliferation of heterogeneous computing environments.

All of these conditions represent significant technological obstacles in themselves, however most organizations looking to implement data exchange applications, are faced with at least two of them, thereby compounding the challenge. A brief discussion of each issue and how currently available data exchange software tools address them is beneficial.

The Cost of Unreliable Business Information
Data warehouses and other business intelligence systems offer significant competitive advantages to those companies that successfully implement them. The theory behind these modern-day corporate panaceas is that decision-makers and knowledge workers will be able to make better decisions based on timely, accurate, and consistent data. However, for the majority of implementations the reality is far from this. Many organizations have data warehouses and other decision support applications that contain a good deal of stale, unreliable, and oftentimes "sick" data. Sick data is the result of the inability of many tools to convert, concatenate, translate, or otherwise manipulate data during the exchange process. Sick data returns false results, is incomplete, incomprehensible, inaccurate, or anything else that renders it substandard.

It is hard to lay blame on anyone in particular. First, moving data between systems in not easy. Senior IT professionals with knowledge of database structures, numerous programming languages, and other essential skills are required to create the customized interfaces to make data exchange possible. Moreover, unless there is an information policy in place that clearly states how certain values such as revenue, margins, and inventory are arrived at, there will be conflicts. Not many organizations clearly define the calculations of margins, for instance. What a margin is to the CFO may be completely in contrast with what it means to the vice president of sales.

Tools available today solve both problems. ETL software automates the extraction, cleansing, transformation, and loading of data from system to system. Depending on the quality of the tool, companies can exchange data among heterogeneous hardware platforms and databases with a single piece of software. It is easy to see the savings in time, resources, and money that modern ETL software delivers when it comes to validating, ensuring timeliness, and maintaining the consistency of data.

Stale Data
Stale data could really be seen as part of the above section, "The cost of Unreliable Business Information," but deserves special attention. Today's global economy generates data 24 hours a day, seven days a week. Companies wanting to make the most effective use of their data put it to work by distributing it throughout the enterprise. But how can they do it in a timely, efficient, and reliable manner? Critical information changes rapidly. Inventory levels might be adequate one day and depleted the next. The fact is, for many applications, weekly updates, and oftentimes daily replenishing of data repositories is insufficient. Basing decisions on stale, or outdated, data has potentially devastating effects on business.

Data exchange software is capable of loading and replenishing data based on user-defined schedules. This means if an organization requires bi-daily or daily updates, they can now have them. Knowledge workers have access to fresh data, thereby eliminating one cause of damaging decisions.

Legacy Systems
Companies, especially larger or longstanding entities, can have a great deal of information locked away in legacy systems. This does not mean that the data stored on these machines is useless. In fact, quite the opposite is true. Valuable data on customers, financials, legacy demographics, and other historic information is buried in older, and often obscure, data stores.

How can companies take advantage of this stockpile of helpful facts? Previously, IT departments have custom programmed solutions to extract and load legacy data directly into database tables or transferred fl at fi les into temporary data stages for processing. With data exchange software, it doesn't have to be that tough. Data exchange tools can extract and load legacy formatted data into modern relational or multidimensional structures with minimal setup. More advanced tools enable organizations to manage both modern and legacy data exchange through a centralized interface. This avoids the necessity of having specialized tools for handling legacy data.

High Development Costs
Analysts state that close to 80 percent of data warehouse implementation costs can be spent on addressing the problems of data quality and loading. Add to this the cost of maintaining support and compatibility for new versions of database and other software as well as building any new functionality that may be required and the costs continue to mount. Another problem is the high turnover rate in the development field. A developer may build the most robust and functional exchange tool imaginable, but if they decide to move on to another opportunity, the organization may be left with a wonderful but unusable tool as no one understands how it was built or how to modify it.

There are certainly other arguments to support the "buy vs. build" strategy, but suffice to say that it is clearly a sound option. Organizations won't have to worry about supporting the next release of their database or enterprise planning applications. Support is relatively straightforward, and, in many cases, financially sound, publicly traded companies offer the solutions, so users don't have to worry about fly-by-night vendors who may not be around a month or two down the road. Packaged data exchange solutions, such as Hummingbird Genio Suite, can drastically reduce the costs associated with development of in-house tools. Packaged tools have a rapid return on investment (ROI) as opposed to the seemingly endless costs typically generated by homegrown code. In short, buying data exchange solutions can ensure that companies are taking advantage of the latest technologies and are harnessing the power of the most robust and efficient tools available.

Proliferation of Mixed-System Environments
By design, or for a host of other reasons, most corporations have mixed-system computing environments. That is, they rely on different databases, often on separate hardware platforms, for a variety of critical functions. Corporate mergers or acquisitions, lower cost technologies, performance, and user demands for certain software are several of the reasons that lead to mixed-system environments. In order for organizations to implement an effective series of data marts or a data warehouse, they must find a way to consolidate the information gathered on these disparate technologies. Moreover, companies began employing enterprise resource planning systems (ERP) that added

Figure 1: Point-to-point Chaos

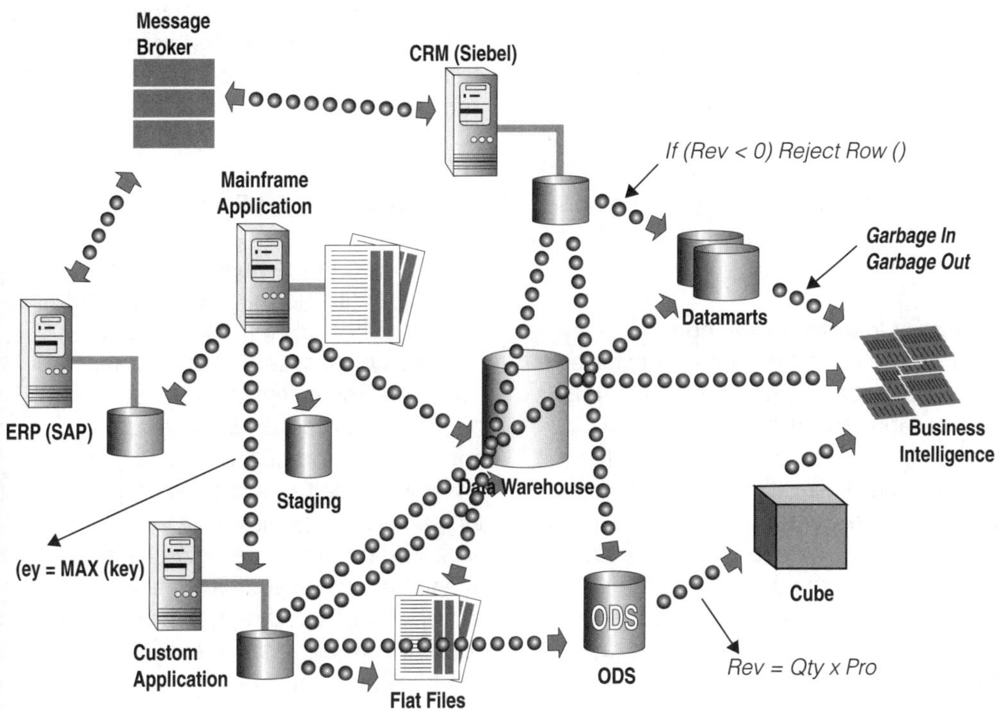

an additional layer of incompatible data. In short, chaos reigned as technology began to take hold. While helping organizations with individual applications and solutions, the promise of consolidated, standardized data – and the decision support enabled by it — would never be realized without a sound, integrated solution.

Data exchange solutions offer companies an effective, high performance, and reliable way to integrate and share data across the enterprise. While varying widely in their ability to handle data transformation and transport requirements of users, most have the ability to handle different platforms and database technologies. Some tools include intuitive user interfaces and graphical languages that enable easy to develop, reusable exchange processes.

Regardless of what tools or methods companies elect to employ when implementing data exchange solutions, it is imperative that they realize and understand what makes for a good solution. Another important element is that there are non-technological considerations in addition to the above noted issues.

Business Catalysts for Change

On top of these technological obstacles, the emergence of several human catalysts also brought about change. The way people use data and the way they think about it has drastically changed in an extremely short period of time. The most important to remember is that, when all is said and done, the development of universal data exchange solutions spawned not from technological issues but rather from the demands of end users.

Knowledge workers and decision makers, over time, realized that having to wait inordinate amounts of time for reports and other information was affecting their performance. CEOs and presidents began seeing the harmful effects of decisions based on stale data. Overall, business started to see the great benefits that data could deliver. More specifically, it began to see the benefits of managing data better. Rather than simply using it as a means to control and keep track of things in a company, data could be harnessed to analyze unit performance, predict trends, identify business pains, and assist in other important tasks.

With this important qualifi er stated, we can now move on to the concept of universal data exchange, the fundamental ideas, processes, and technologies involved with it, what elements and features embody a sound solution, and other useful information.

What is Universal Data Exchange?

As discussed in the previous section, there are several factors that have contributed to the need for tools that extract data, manipulate, cleanse, transform, and otherwise enhance it, and transport it between operational data stores, applications, and business intelligence systems. While there are a variety of techniques companies have employed to achieve data exchange, few qualify as adequate solutions for what is known as universal data exchange. In order to be considered a universal data exchange solution, tools must be able to carry out all vital data exchange operations regardless of data format, syntax, data source, or target. The entire universal data exchange process involves data extraction, data transformation, and heterogeneous data delivery.

Data Extraction

Vast amounts of data are collected by corporate entities; however all of it is not appropriate for decision support systems. This means the tools that simply copy entire database tables or files between systems are unsuitable for data exchange solutions. The ability to easily select and filter which data is loaded into data marts or a data warehouse is essential to building an effective solution. Users should be easily able to choose what data they want to go where and in what format. No programming or complex modifications to existing systems should be necessary and any business rules or other user-defined conditions should also be simple to define and apply.

Data Transformation

The way companies think about data, and the way it is represented in databases, has changed significantly over time. Obscure naming conventions, dissimilar coding for the same item (i.e. numeric representation

Figure 2: Hub-and-Spoke Architecture

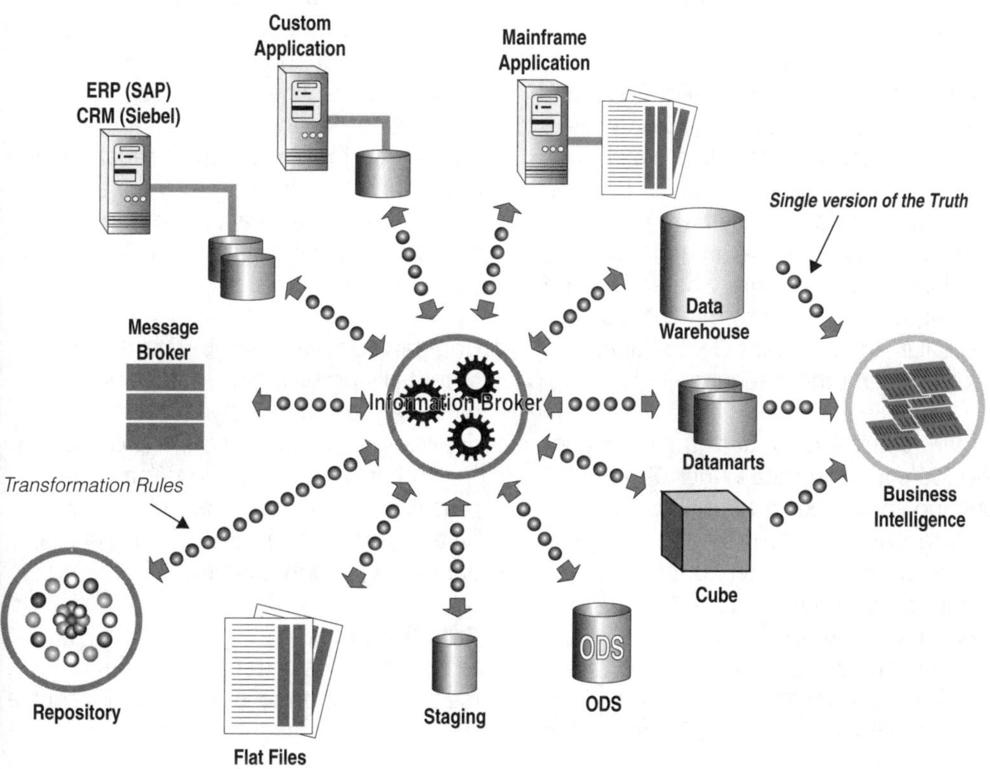

as well as character based codes or acronyms), and separate architectures are all commonplace. Transformation routines, applied as part of the universal data exchange process, remedy these problems while consolidating the information in data marts and warehouses or distributing the data to remote systems.

For example, companies are beginning to realize the benefits of sharing data between enterprise resource planning systems (ERP) and relational data stores housed in Oracle, Sybase, DB2 or other databases. The problem is that ERP systems use proprietary data structures that need to be cleansed and reformatted to fi t conventional database architectures. Rows and columns may have to be split or merged depending on the database format. For instance, an ERP system may require that street address, Zip Code, and state be part of the same column while a company's Oracle-based data warehouse may have a separate column for each item. Similarly, a company may have product type and model number in an inventory database as one column whereas the ERP system requires them to be split. Software tools like Hummingbird Genio Suite, accommodate these requirements.

Other applications of data transformation include changing data values (British Sterling converted to US dollars, Euro conversions, metric to standard weights and measures, character columns to numeric, abbreviations to full text descriptions, number codes to text, etc.), and preparation for loading multidimensional databases such as Hyperion Essbase or Oracle Express. All of these functions allow for code conversion, removal of ambiguity and confusion associated with data, standardization, measurement conversions, and consolidating dissimilar data structures for data consistency.

Data Cleansing

As the amount of data entered in production systems grows, so does the chance that some of that data is corrupt, or otherwise "dirty". A common example that helps to illustrate the problem can be found in a customer database.

Today, businesses realize the benefit of understanding their customer base. To help them with this mission, organizations load contact information, customer buying patterns and other consumer oriented data into decision support systems. However, what happens when a manager comes across Janet Smith, Jan Smith, and J. Smith? Are the three records separate? Is one duplicated? What if they are all the same person? Being able to determine such things means better decisions base on pure, or "clean", data.

Companies have to scrub data that is potentially problematic. In this case, tools must be used to identify and remedy duplication, concatenation, truncated text, spelling errors, abbreviations, and other problems. With such tools, records would be analyzed through the use of low-level data investigation engines.

Data Transport

Quite simply, data transport is the mechanism that moves data from a source to target environment during the data exchange process. Sources and targets may be application systems or operating environments. In a data exchange solution, the transport mechanism is responsible for loading and replenishing data marts or warehouses with fresh data. Essentially, the transport element is the communications layer of the data exchange process.

What to Look for in a Data Exchange Solution

With the basic architecture of universal data exchange covered, outlining some specific features and functions to look for when evaluating tools is useful. As mentioned, there are several ways that companies capture, manipulate and move operational data. However, few meet the complex requirements of effective data exchange. Companies looking to implement universal data exchange solutions should first identify what their specific needs are and look for tools that offer as many of those functions as possible. After all, having to buy a separate tool (often from a completely different vendor) to perform one or two functions is hard to justify. Some of the features and capabilities organizations should look for in quality data exchange software include metadata management, scalability, extensive and flexible data transformation, ease of use, administration and implementation, the ability to reuse defined transformations, and support for heterogeneous platforms and databases.

Metadata Management

Metadata is information about data. It allows business users as well as technical administrators to track the "lineage" of the data they are using. That is, information about where the data came from, when it was delivered, what happened to it during transport, and other descriptions can all be tracked by examining the metadata.

It is widely held that there are two types of metadata: technical, or administrative metadata, and business metadata. Both types are essential to a successful data mart or warehouse solution. Administrative metadata includes information about such things as data source, update times and any extraction rules and cleansing routines performed on the data. Business metadata, on the other hand, allows users to get a more clear understanding of the data on which their decisions are based. Information about calculations performed on the data, date and time stamps, as well as metadata about the graphic elements of data analysis generated by front-end query tools.

Essentially, examining metadata enhances the end user's understanding of the data they are using. For administrators, metadata helps them ensure data accuracy, integrity and consistency.

As far as what to look for in a data exchange solutions, companies should seek out tools that offer an open, extensible repository. That is, users should have the freedom to choose which database technologies store their critical metadata rather than being forced by vendors to store it in a particular database.

Metadata Sharing
From the discussion above, it is evident that effective use of metadata offers significant benefit to both administrators and knowledge workers alike. The trouble is, many tools manage metadata in a restrictive manner. That is, the metadata is locked away in distinct formats that don't readily enable the sharing of the valuable information. Moreover, some tools use proprietary metadata to perform certain tasks. If a company uses identical products throughout the enterprise, then everything will work out just fine. However, as illustrated earlier, not too many IT shops enjoy a completely homogeneous environment.

For one of many reasons, the vast majority of companies will have to share metadata across dissimilar technologies. This is where the ability to provide metadata in an open, extensible format really pays off. Some data exchange solutions store metadata in local database tables or repositories, enabling easy access. Further to this, due to the ability to reformat and share data across platforms that certain tools offer, the metadata can be shared across dissimilar technologies. The idea of freely distributing metadata across heterogeneous platforms is one form of metadata sharing. Essentially, if the data exchange solution has the right capabilities, metadata can be shared, regardless of platform or database technology, thereby ensuring that administrators and users will enjoy access to critical data about their data.

Scalability
Companies pursuing data exchange initiatives would greatly benefit from selecting tools that can handle future growth. As demands on applications grow, due to increased users, complexity and variety of task, and other factors, it is critical that the data exchange solution be able to easily ramp up. That is, the ability to distribute workload and scale tasks over multiple physical servers is important. Additionally, as discussed previously, it is crucial that companies have the ability to easily integrate heterogeneous systems. Suffice to say, when implementing data exchange solutions, organizations must consider the future — particularly a future that could force them to deal with dissimilar computer systems and applications.

Extensive and Flexible Data Transformation
Manipulating, cleansing, enhancing, and transforming data is perhaps the most significant step in the data exchange process. Needless to say, companies implementing data exchange solutions should ensure that the required transformations are readily supported by the tools they choose. Additionally, data exchange software should not require users to learn complex programming or scripting languages in order to define data manipulations. Some tools offer graphical mapping interfaces to simplify the definition process. So what is an adequate level of data transformation support? The only acceptable level of transformation support accommodates any required transformation. That is, such transformations as joins, aggregation, distinction, filtering, and sorting should all

be natively supported while stored procedures, and external expressions, as well as exit facilities should all be provided for.

Adaptable Scheduling and Distribution
Some data exchange tools force users to move data in a constricted manner. Bulk copy transfers, no plotting interface, one way distribution, and inflexible operational controls are some of the impediments to the smooth scheduling and distribution mapping involved with data exchange solutions. There is really no need for any of these obstacles. Tools available today feature intuitive interfaces for scheduling data exchange as well as flexible and adaptable options for the distribution of data.

Good data exchange solutions provide for event-driven scheduling, fixed-time, and periodic (daily, weekly, monthly) modes. Additionally, flexible extraction methods (time-stamp, database log driven, and trigger-based) should be made available.

Ease of Use and Administration
While most software products today make claims of "quick and painless" or "fast and simple" installation, use, and administration, there are some solutions that are definitely easier than others are. Sound data exchange solutions install with no custom programming or changes to existing database structures or applications.

As mentioned, data exchange tools should provide a familiar user interface for the definition and management of the process. The alternative to this is a complex series of code and line commands, which are prone to input errors and require a significant investment of time to conduct. Administration should be facilitated via a central interface, thereby greatly reducing the time required to manage the data exchange process. Some tools require certain administration functions associated with the data exchange solution to be carried out at each "node", or separate system. Not only is this extremely inefficient, but it requires that organizations retain trained personnel at each site which means increased training and staffing costs.

Companies looking to implement data exchange solutions must ensure that the selected tools provide for centralized administration, ease of use features, and minimized ramp-up time.

The Genio Suite Universal Data Exchange Solution

So far, this paper has focused on the concepts and technologies involved with data exchange solutions. It has outlined some of the critical components that assist in the successful implementation of data exchange projects and offered advice regarding some features to consider when looking for superior solutions. With this important prerequisite information covered, we can now shift focus and discuss Hummingbird Genio Suite, the unique broker-based universal data exchange solution.

Genio Suite enables IT professionals to implement data exchange and information sharing across enterprise-wide decision support and operational systems. Offering more functionality than current data transformation tools and greater productivity than point-to-point and hard-coded data exchange routines, Genio helps eliminate the difficulties associated with mixed-system computing environments and inconsistent data nightmares. Genio's single platform, component-based architecture addresses simple and complex data exchange processes within a procedure-driven graphical environment. Genio automates many data exchange tasks that normally require tedious programming. This allows IT professionals to rapidly develop data transformation routines for an immediate return on investment.

Hummingbird Genio Suite is comprised of a tightly integrated set of components including: Engine, Designer, Repository, Scheduler, Met@Data Studio, Met@Data Explorer, Met@Data Web Server, Data Links, and MetaLink.

Genio Engine

Genio Engine is a scalable, multi-threaded transformation engine that brokers information between source and target systems. The scalable architecture supports the distribution and synchronization of data transformation and exchange processes over multiple Genio Engines. This is critical as data volumes increase in size and transformation processes grow in complexity. Additionally, this scalability enables Genio to leverage the power of existing distributed computing resources within user environments.

Genio Designer

Genio Designer provides a graphical scripting environment, enabling users to easily create and administer data transformation and exchange processes. Data structures can be imported directly from source and target systems. User defined business rules, functions, and procedures created in Designer are stored as objects within the Genio Repository and are completely reusable. The unique graphical scripting environment provides a complete and powerful procedural language to design complex data transformation processes. Genio processes can be triggered by external events such as file modifications or table updates. Conversely, Genio processes can trigger external events such as file transfers or e-mail. Essentially, Genio Designer is the nerve center for the data exchange solution, enabling the efficient and effective design of transformation and exchange processes within a familiar and intuitive environment.

Genio Repository

The Genio Repository stores all aspects of data transformation and exchange processing metadata. Housed in any RDBMS, Repository treats and stores each component as an object. Genio automatically identifi es any change made to metadata, provides an impact analysis report, and requires every object affected by the change to be addressed before the next data transformation and exchange process is executed. This ensures information quality and consistency across the entire universal data exchange solution.

Figure 3: The Comprehensive Integrated Genio Toolset

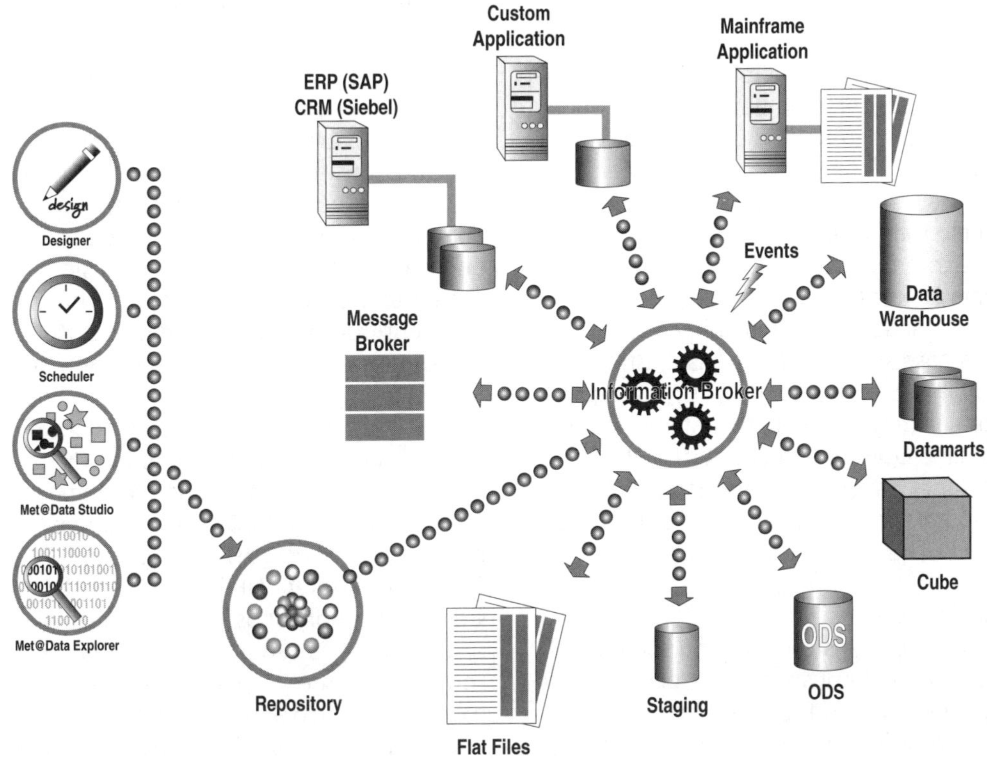

Genio Scheduler

Genio Scheduler is the control center of the universal data exchange solution. Administrators schedule, deploy, and manage Genio processes using Scheduler. Processes can be scheduled to execute on an event or calendar basis. Process scheduling may also include dependencies. Genio Scheduler provides real-time control and monitoring of process executions, full history and audit trail reporting, and detailed log file analysis.

Genio Met@Data Studio, Met@Data Web Server and Genio Met@Data Explorer

Genio Met@Data Studio allows users to create customized views of metadata residing in the Genio Repository. The open Genio repository, storable in any relational database, is employed by Met@Data Studio, allowing users to enrich the metadata model that exists in Genio by adding new metadata objects or by defining new relationships. Met@Data Web Server allows for true thin-client browsing of metadata while Genio Met@Data Explorer, the "fl at client" web browser, allows users to navigate through the customized views designed with Studio.

Fully compatible with Microsoft Internet Explorer and Netscape, Explorer tailored views allow business analysts and power users to navigate the relationships between systems, understand data transformation processes, and trace the lineage of their data.

Genio Data Links
The communications layer of Genio Suite, Data Links provide native connectivity to most relational and multidimensional database systems, as well as flat files. Optimized ODBC connectivity is available for a variety of database systems and generic ODBC connectivity is available for all other data sources and targets. Genio is also able to access complex flat files such as EBCDIC.

Genio MetaLink
Extracting, transforming, and sharing data between enterprise resource planning (ERP) applications and metadata repositories such as Microsoft Repository is critical to successfully maintaining an organization's operational effectiveness. Genio MetaLinks are connectivity bridges that enable the extraction and transformation of data and metadata from ERP applications and repositories. Currently, this gives organizations the ability to access information stored in SAP/R3, combine it with data from other sources, and then share it with systems throughout the enterprise. Future MetaLinks for other ERP systems are in development.

Key Features of Genio Suite

Hub and Spoke Architecture
The thrust of universal data exchange is obviously to address the need for a solution capable of handling the many good reasons for moving data throughout the modern business enterprise. Genio Suite is designed with this premise in mind and is built around the cornerstones of speed, efficiency, and ease of use. This is apparent from examining the product's fundamental architecture — the "Hub and Spoke".

Genio Repository can be housed in databases, such as Microsoft SQL Server, Oracle, Sybase, IBM UDB, and Informix, residing on Windows NT Server, Sun Solaris, IBM AIX, or HP-UX systems. The Genio Repository housed on any hub system acts as a central storage area for source and target ("spoke" system) metadata, source and target interface mappings, business rules, transformation rules, data validation rules, scheduling, and other information about the data exchange process. A spoke can be thought of as a single system interacting with the hub. Genio spoke systems can be midrange systems, mainframes, Windows NT based servers, or even proprietary file systems.

As opposed to point-to-point data transfer architectures, the Genio Suite hub and spoke design connects source and target systems to a central hub. This greatly reduces the number of required nodes in the data exchange network and also greatly increases overall performance. Additionally, the hub and spoke architecture allows for greater flexibility, scalability, and reliability as hubs can be mirrored to provide fault tolerance and system availability.

Distributed Data Transformation Environment

Genio incorporates a unique hybrid architecture that provides the ability to centrally manage all enterprise data exchange requirements. Genio also easily exploits the power of any relational database, leveraging native transformation capabilities for utmost flexibility and efficiency. Regardless of the mode chosen for performing transformations, no data staging is required. This maximizes the efficiency of the transformation process. The following transformation models are available to users:

Transformation performed exclusively by Genio Engine

Genio extracts data from any source database, transforms it using Engine, and then loads it into target database tables. This model is suitable whenever data sources and targets are heterogeneous or whenever the required transformations cannot be performed natively by the source or target databases.

Transformation performed partially by Genio Engine and remote databases

In this model, Genio takes advantage of relational database features by offloading some of the transformation directly to a data source or target. Transformed data is extracted from the source database, brokered through the Genio Engine –

Figure 4: Data Access Method On

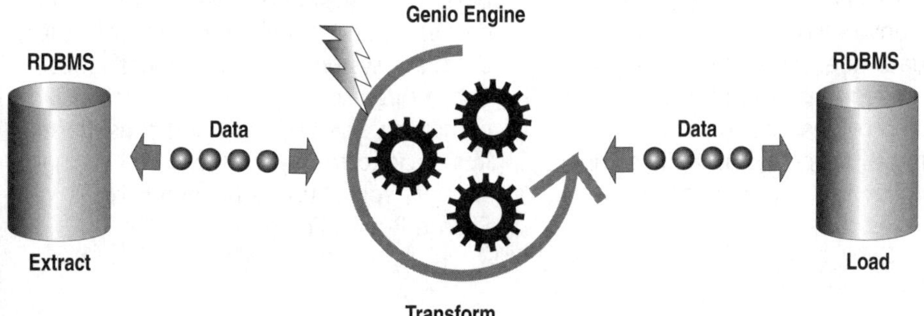

Figure 5: Data Access Method Two

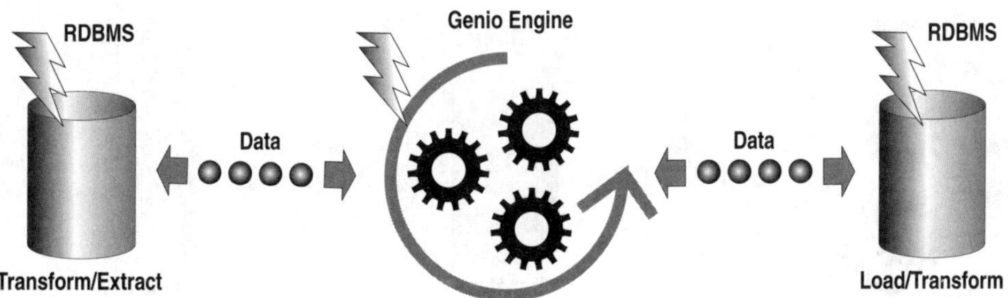

where additional transformation may occur – and loaded into target database tables, where, again, further transformation may be conducted. Typically in this case, aggregations and consolidations are processed at the source, reducing the network bandwidth required to transport data.

Transformation Performed Exclusively by Remote Databases
When a data source and target are on the same server, or are accessible from one another through a gateway, it is unnecessary for data to leave the server and transit through the Genio Engine. In this model, Engine only brokers the SQL instructions between sources and targets, with the RDBMS performing the extraction, transformation, and loading or update of database tables. This model outperforms the other available models as it does not consume any network bandwidth. Even though data does not transit through Genio Engine when using this mode, Genio still provides tracking and monitoring of processes as well as impact analysis following any changes or discrepancies.

Efficient Extraction Across Heterogeneous Systems
Genio Suite is capable of extracting source data using native SQL grammars, optimizing the use of source database functionality and minimizing network traffic. This is achieved by accessing only the source rows required to perform data transformations and avoiding the loading of unnecessary data into staging areas. When working with text sources, Genio has a variety of tools to help work with complex structures like hierarchical data dumps from mainframes or EDI fi les. Regardless of what type of fies Genio works with, full functionality is maintained and no performance loss experienced.

Incremental Data Extraction
Genio has several effective methods for incremental data extraction: selection limits based on timestamps, use of logs from the database, and installing triggers into the database system to provide timestamps. These three strategies are those most commonly used by tools and consultants. If it is decided to use log fi les, an external support application is needed such as Sybase Replication Server.

Figure 6: Data Access Method Three

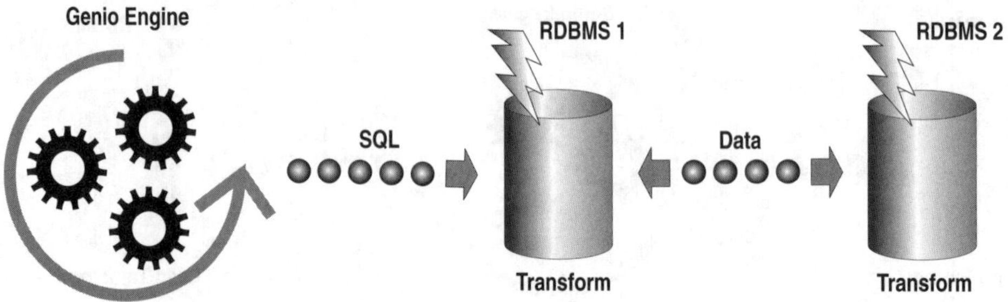

Flexible Scheduling
Genio Suite includes a complete and fl exible scheduling facility making it possible to plan processes on fixed time, periodically (daily, weekly, monthly), triggered by outside events or from the polling service (based on fi les or certain location). Combining these functions, administrators can build as complex scheduling rules as necessary. Addition-ally, the Scheduler interface shows logs for each process, providing for a single point of administration for scheduling the entire universal data exchange solution.

Powerful Data Transformation Capabilities
Hummingbird Genio Suite includes a comprehensive set of data transformation functions. Using Genio Designer, users design data transformations – from the most simple to the most complex – via the product's extremely intuitive interface and graphical procedural language. Genio does mappings in three ways: simple graphical mappings from source to target, text/ graphics based mapping, and mapping visible along with script. Some of the powerful transformations that Genio is capable of include database joins (both internal and external), aggregation, distinction, filtering, sorting, complex expressions (IF, THEN, ELSE, CASE, etc.), and can build custom functions. Genio supports stored procedures and, in the event that highly customized data transformation is required, can call external programs or "exits" to perform complex data manipulation on external tables and draw results back into the Genio data exchange routine. Currently, Genio includes more than 100 built-in data transformations, making it one of the most comprehensive tools on the market.

Reliable Handling of Transactional Data
Genio uses the traditional transactional mechanisms of relational databases (commit/rollback) for one or more databases. Committal or rollback calls can be made at any time during the data exchange, providing for the highest level of customization. For example, commit/rollback can be triggered automatically with each change to a target table, or conditionally, based on data test results from previous data exchange events.

Efficient, Flexible Data Loading Across Heterogeneous Systems and Databases
Genio Suite offers users the choice of several data loading methods – single row, packet loading, and bulk loading — with certain benefits for each. Error control is paramount with single row loading, but a tradeoff is made with speed. Bulk loading, on the other hand, compromises error control but is extremely fast. Packet loading provides a good balance between speed and quality control. As with source data, Genio Suite is capable of loading virtually any target database.

Advanced Performance Measurement
Genio Suite includes a unique performance meter. All tasks are timed including the module coherence tests and SQL statement performance as well as the load processes. As a result, administrators will know the transformed volume and any possible performance issues.

Genio is capable of automatically sending performance reports to administrators after each execution as well as keeping it in the repository making it possible to analyze and track historic performance.

System Requirements and Supported Platforms

Genio Engine

- Windows NT Server 4.0
- Sun Solaris 2.5.1, 2.6
- IBM AIX 4.2.1
- HP-UX 10.20

Genio Metadata Repository Platforms

- Informix 7.22
- Microsoft SQL Server 6.5, 7.0
- Oracle 7.3, 8.0
- Sybase SQL Anywhere
- Sybase SQL Server 11
- Sybase Adaptive Server 11.5
- IBM Universal Database (UDB) Version 5

Bi-directional Connectivity with RDBMS

- Microsoft SQL Server 6.x, 7.0
- Microsoft Access (native, ODBC)
- Oracle 7.x (native, ODBC)
- Oracle 8.0 (native, ODBC)
- Informix 7.x (ODBC)
- Generic ODBC
- Sybase 11.x (native)
- Sybase SQL Anywhere (ODBC)
- Teradata (ODBC)
- IBM DB2 AS/400 (ODBC)
- IBC DB2 CS (ODBC)
- IBM DB2 MVS (ODBC)

Bi-directional Connectivity with Flat File Formats

- Delimited text files
- Fixed text files
- AS/400 fl at files
- Standard fl at files

Native, Direct Population of Multidimensional Databases

- Hyperion Essbase 4.x, 5.0
- Oracle Express 5.x, 6.x

Met@Data Explorer Requirements

- Microsoft Internet Explorer 4.01 SP1 or later
- Netscape Communicator 4.5 or later

MetaLink Support

- SAP R/3 3,4 under Oracle

Conclusion

As stated, data just might represent one of the last great competitive advantage for today's businesses. If this is true, then those companies taking advantage of the most robust, flexible, and fully functional data solutions are going to be industry leaders. Because they address the often complex requirements of several distributed data applications simultaneously, data exchange solutions are going to be at the technological forefront for many organizations. Its advanced hub and spoke architecture, support for the most complete range of database and hardware systems, comprehensive built-in data transformations, and other elements, give Hummingbird Genio Suite what is perhaps the most rich feature set offered to date.

From this paper, three summary findings about universal data exchange can be drawn:

Think About the Future
When selecting tools for any data distribution, transformation, or sharing application, it is important to consider future developments. Are the tools used today going to be the same as next year? Next month? Tomorrow? Will the company be merging with other entities or involved in a buyout or takeover? If so, the new organization will have to merge computing environments. Are new projects going to emerge as corporate requirements? Are data marts going to expand into an enterprise warehouse? Will the need to integrate ERP application data with other operational systems arise?

There are many factors that can contribute to rapid deterioration of the usefulness of certain tools within the organization. When new needs come about, old technologies can make IT departments look bad. On the other hand, if rich, robust, and leading edge tools from forward thinking vendors are selected, companies can really extend their budgets. No one can predict the future with unwavering certainty, but by selecting the tools that are most likely to meet the data exchange needs of today and down the road, companies can build in a cushion against technology obsolescence and extend their investment in computing systems.

As discussed, Hummingbird Genio Suite covers the most complete range of hardware platforms and database technologies. Additionally, industry leading ERP packages from vendors like Oracle and SAP are seamlessly handled for any application integration requirements that users may have.

Minimize Headaches
It is easy to see how a universal data solution can get out of hand from a "variety of tools" standpoint. That is, there are a good number of different software and middleware components that make up an enterprise-wide data exchange solution. A company could easily select tools from fi ve or more vendors. If businesses get caught in this "niche tool trap" they will be contributing to the problem, not solving it. After all, the purpose of universal data exchange solutions is to integrate diverse data from dissimilar systems and applications. Additionally, vendors who do not integrate well with other products tend to blame those other products. This leads to technical support nightmares if an issue arises. Moreover, what happens when the organization decides to upgrade to a new database version or application suite? Do all the vendors support the latest database versions, or only a couple? The question is this: why add more products and applications to the mix when there are integrated product suites that handle the majority of data exchange and transformation processes from a central administration interface?

Hummingbird Genio Suite offers users a complete and integrated solution for universal data exchange. Customers don't have to worry about who to turn to for support and can trust in the fact that Hummingbird stands by its products.

Build a Lasting Relationship

Today's software industry is rife with fl y-by-night startups and players "in it for the quick buck". They don't offer quality service and hang their customers out to dry when issues arise. Companies looking to implement a universal data exchange solution should partner with reputable organizations.

Hummingbird Communications not only offers quality tool suites like Genio but also provides a full range of consulting and education services to ensure that its customers get the most out of the relationship. Hummingbird Professional Services helps customers maximize return on investment in their data warehouse or data mart initiatives, and other data exchange applications. With extensive knowledge and years of experience in designing, building, and deploying universal data exchange solutions, as well as in the training of administrators and end users, Hummingbird Professional Services can greatly enhance business performance by improving the way information is managed within customer organizations.

Biography: Hummingbird is a leader in the development of enterprise software solutions that provide access to all business-critical information and resources. The Hummingbird EIP™ (Enterprise Information Portal) leverages the company's core strengths in network connectivity, data integration & reporting, and document & knowledge management to connect users to all the business information they need, aggregated and categorized through a single user interface. With a diverse product portfolio, Hummingbird offers complete global enterprise solutions from advanced host connectivity, through sophisticated data exchange, business intelligence and analytic applications, to powerful information management at the desktop or on the Web. Headquartered in Toronto, Canada, the company offers its products, along with related consulting, education, and support services, in more than 50 countries around the world.

Database Solutions

Title: *Database Solutions*
Author: *Palo Alto Management Group, Inc.*
Abstract: *The advent of reliable, affordable and highly scaleable servers, coupled with the growing popularity of the client/server paradigm and software that can scale with the hardware, is driving the rapid growth of an allied group of database-oriented applications. These are variously known as Data Warehousing, Data Marts, Decision Support (or DSS), OnLine Analytical Processing (or OLAP) and various other terms. We call them, collectively, Database Solutions.*

While applications definitions often vary from one vendor to another, and there may be functional differences between them, in practice these applications frequently overlap. Nonetheless, the context of Database Solutions as used herein refers to the process of aggregating databases of information and efficiently extracting and and/or analyzing the data in order to support one or more business operations. Fourteen months ago, PAMG completed a landmark study focused on the high end of the business (i.e., >100 GB of useful data) entitled Large-scale Database Solutions (LDBS). The present study covers applications based on as little as 10 GB of useful data and is called Database Solutions II to indicate that it is the second in the study series.

Regardless of the terminology, the industry has embraced this market as one that offers a very large and growing market opportunity. In the course of our work in the field, we identified more than 200 companies offering systems, software or services aimed at exploiting this opportunity. The majority of these companies are less than five years old.

Although Data Solutions is already a large market - roughly $15 billion in calendar 1997 - , it is still in a relatively early stage of development. The market continues to be plagued with confusing claims and counterclaims so that the true nature of the market's development and the relative position of the vendors is practically obscured from vendors and customers alike.

The primary objectives of the research conducted for Data Solutions II were to:

- Assess user perceptions of the major competitors
- Define user procurement decision processes and implementation plans
- Bring the definition of the market into clear focus
- Forecast the worldwide market in detail through the year 2002 for systems, software and services

- Furnish the market shares of the major competitors

The research for the study focused on three things:

- An in-depth Market Forecast through the year 2002, based on a formal I/O (Input/Output) econometric model
- Competitive Analysis focused on those companies having a 10% or greater share of the systems, services or packaged software market segments.
- An in-depth web-based user survey addressing subjects such as future plans and budgets, issues concerning procurement, implementation and technology, and perceptions of vendors.

The scope of the study is worldwide, and original, primary research was carried out in North America, Europe and Japan.

MARKET TRENDS

The worldwide market for Database Solutions expenditures is forecast to grow at an AAGR (Average Annual Growth Rate) of 51% over the period 1997-2002 to more than $113B as shown in figure 1. This forecast is consistent with the findings reached in last year's study that considered only those systems having at least 100 GB of useful data. Thus, we continue to believe that this sector will become one of the most important application markets in the computer industry, particularly in the segment that relies on high-end server-class platforms and large-scale DBMS software.

The view of the market taken in this study is from a user/customer (not end user) perspective. We view the market as made up of four segments which we call . The sum total of the markets for these four categories is equal to the amount of money spent by customers on solutions,

Figure 1: Worldwide Database Solutions Market

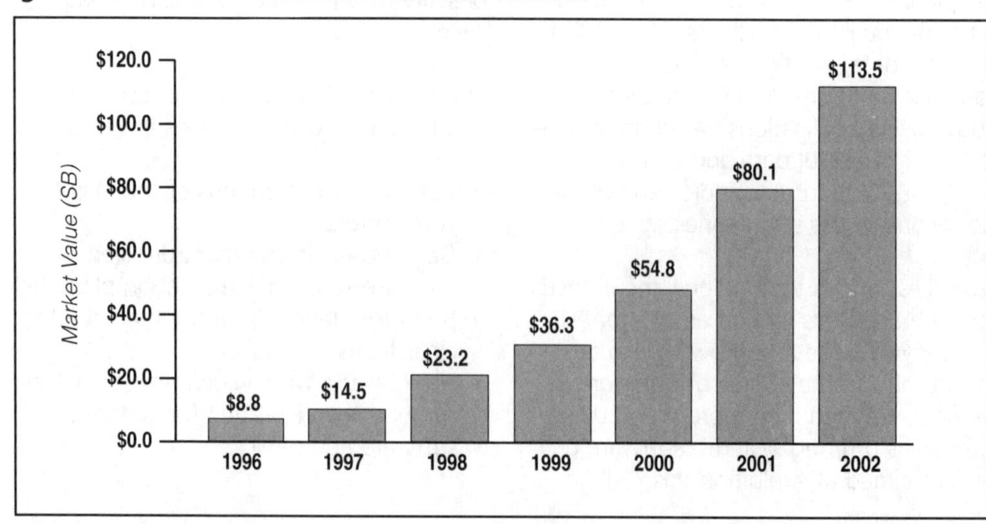

not including the money spent on end users' equipment, interface or time. The four categories are:

1. Systems including platform hardware and operating system.
2. Packaged Software including DBMSs, Query tools such as SQL, OLAP, ROLAP and Data Mining tools, backend tools for tasks such as data cleansing, extraction and transformation, and Vertical Applications software. The latter category frequently includes packages from the other categories wrapped in an industry- or function-specific front end.
3. Services including business consulting, design and implementation (software development), technical support consulting including customer training and education and systems integration services including installation.
4. In-house expenditures , which may also represent a service, market opportunity.

Figure 2: Worldwide Data Solutions Market by Product Type, 2002

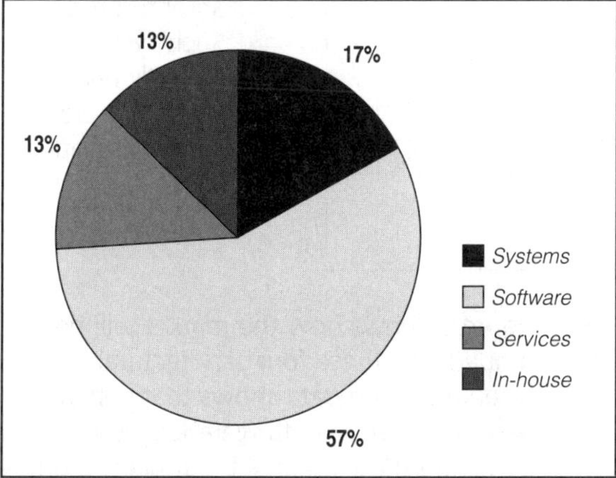

Figure 3: Worldwide Database Solution Market Distribution by Geographic Region, 2002

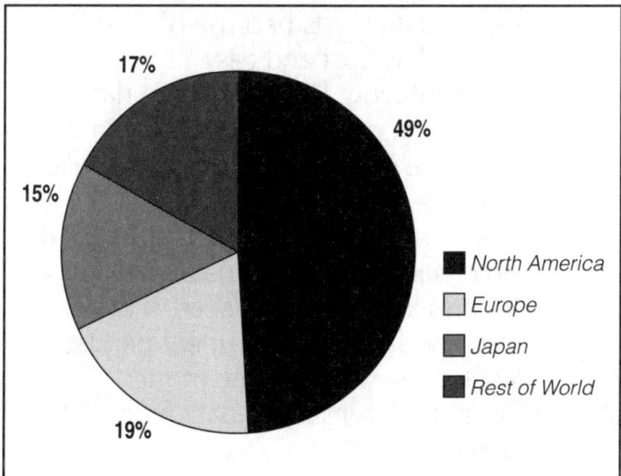

Figure 2 shows how we forecast the relative value of these segments to be distributed in 2002. Software will be the largest, followed by systems and services. The services share could be substantially larger if services vendors succeed in displacing more in-house activity than we project, or smaller if customers decide not to outsource as much as we think they will.

Figure 3 contains the forecast breakdown by geographic region projected for the year

Figure 4 is a market breakout by industry sector. This breakout varies, of course, by region and even within countries depending on the economic mix.

Figure 4: Data Solutions Market by Industry Sector, 2002

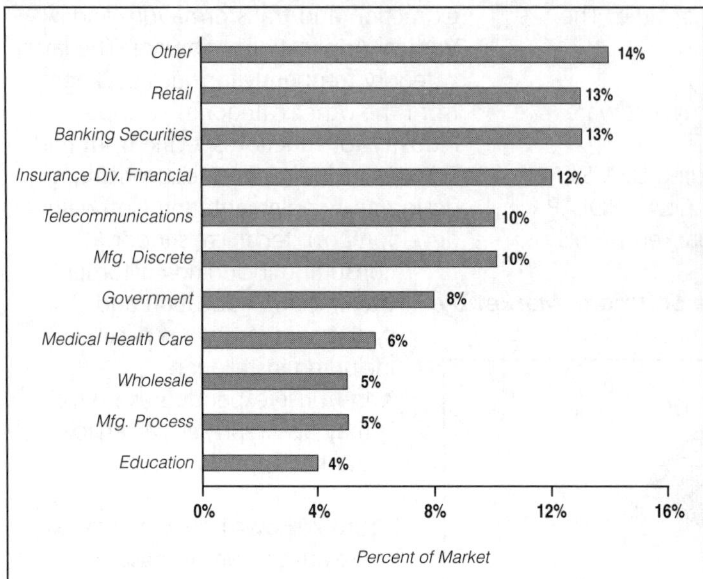

The total market is broken out by system architecture into the following four categories.

- Central Data Warehouse . Sometimes called an "Enterprise Data Warehouse," this configuration contains a large data warehouse that typically contains data from several operational database sources and serves the needs of a broad spectrum of users.
- Distributed System. The data warehouse is distributed across multiple platforms often remotely located from one another.
- Data Warehouse + Data Marts. Data from a Central Data Warehouse is extracted, transformed and fed into smaller systems called Data Marts, each designed to serve a single user or small subset of users, typically a single department or function.
- Single Warehouse or Data Mart. A system usually fed by a single source of operational data and designed to serve the needs of a single department or function within an enterprise. Such systems are typically relatively small, but are sometimes quite large.

Figure 5 shows how the market will be divided into these four architectural categories. The data shows that systems based on central data warehouses will dominate the market. At first glance, one may think that this flies in the face of what seems to be an increasingly popular notion; namely, that much of the market is moving to small data marts because of their relatively low cost and easy implementation. However, while data marts might cost, say $500,000, big data warehouse installations cost many millions, sometimes as much as $100,000,000. It takes a lot of little data marts to equal the market value of one big data warehouse. Furthermore, with experience, it will get easier and faster to implement big data warehouses, so that some of the motivation for installing data marts will diminish.

Figure 5: Worldwide Data Solutions Market by Architecture, 2002

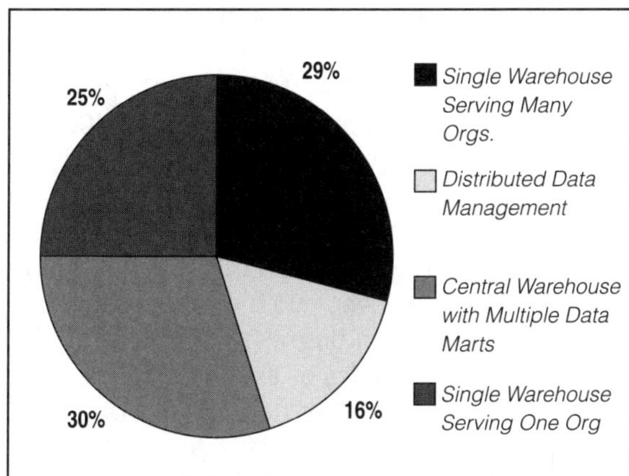

Figure 6: Marts vs. Warehouses, 2002

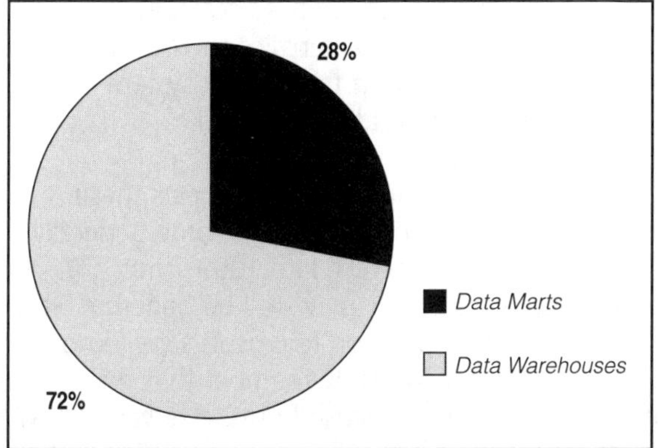

The trade press in general and some of the vendors in particular has made much of the "phenomenon" of the data mart. An impression is often created that marts are easy to implement, while data warehouses take a long time to implement, are expensive, and, are at best risky propositions. These arguments are most often self-serving and have little basis in hard facts. In fact, we view the expression "Data Mart" as a marketing term without any technological basis to distinguish it from a data warehouse.

If we use the definition of a mart as a single-purpose warehouse serving a single allied group of users, however, we can make some estimates as to the relative sizes of these two markets. The data is presented in Figure 6. It shows that, even at the end of the forecast period, marts will account for only a little over a quarter of the market.

The market is cut by operating system platform into the following four categories:

1. Mainframe (principally MVS and plug- compatible variants)
2. UNIX
3. Windows NT
4. Other

Articles in the trade press and speeches at trade conferences would have one believe that the Database Solutions market is today basically a UNIX-based business with Windows NT to come on strong in the next couple of years. The forecast presented in Figure 7 strongly refutes those notions. The data shows that mainframes currently have nearly one-quarter of the market, and, even by 2002, will still account for about 20% of the market!

Figure 7: Worldwide Database Solutions Market by Operating System, 2002

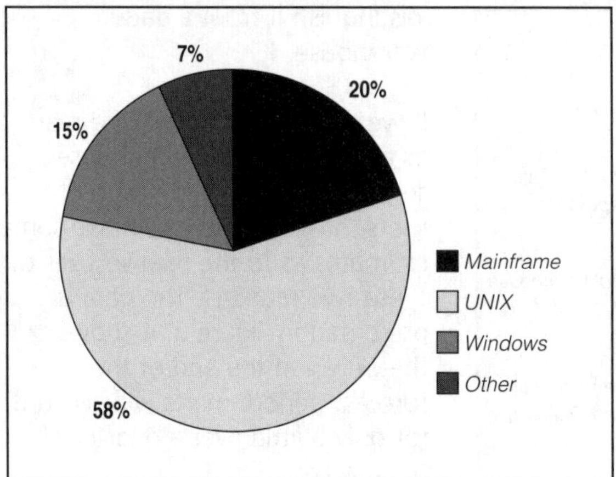

- The market is mostly big-system based, and mainframes still dominate the big system market.
- It is a path of least resistance for many existing mainframe sites to add a processor complex or two rather than to bring in a new technology.
- Mainframes address the availability issue better than any other platforms except fault tolerant systems, and availability is a key purchase criterion.
- The Price/performance and scalability of mainframes is approaching that of other high-end architectures
- The cost of the hardware platform is less than 25% of the total solution cost. Thus, even if the hardware/OS cost of a mainframe solution is twice that of an alternative solution, the impact on total cost will only be in the 10-15% range, and the cost of retraining personnel might well offset that difference.

Nonetheless, UNIX is the single largest OS platform, accounting for 59% of the value of 1997 expenditures. That share is projected to decrease only slightly to 58% by 2002.

"Other" systems, e.g., Tandem, Teradata, White Cross, AS/400, etc., currently account for 13% of the Database Solutions market. That share will gradually decline to about 6% by 2002. By that time, however, much of the proprietary system business will consist of upgrades of existing systems as opposed to new installations.

Windows NT will capture 15% of the market by 2002. This forecast presumes that NT will soon be much improved in its ability to scale, in availability characteristics such as fault resilience and in the area of system management/administration.

The prevailing wisdom suggests these enhancements will not become generally deployable before late 1999. Thus, the forecast for NT may well be generous. It is based, in part, on Microsoft's well-known marketing skills. Remember that this discussion is focused on the server side. NT will, of course, be the major player on the client side.

Figure 8 contains the packaged software expenditure distribution forecast for the year 2002. The DBMS category leads with a 40% share followed by Frontend Tools (29%), Backend Tools (20%) and Vertical Applications (11%). This split is based on data from the user survey.

Figure 8: Worldwide Database Solutions Packaged Software Expenditures Distribution, 2002

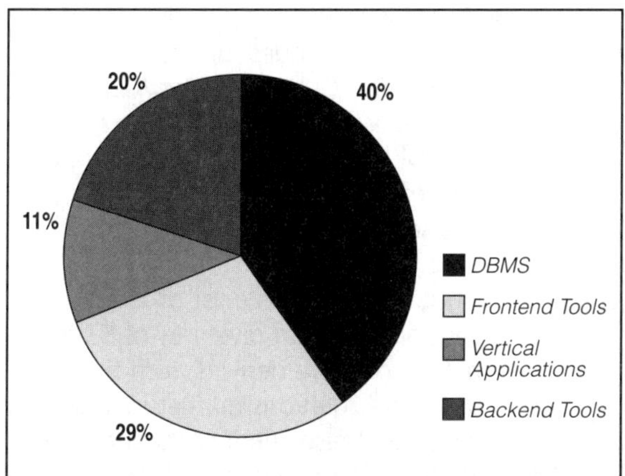

Figure 9: Worldwide Database Solutions Services Market

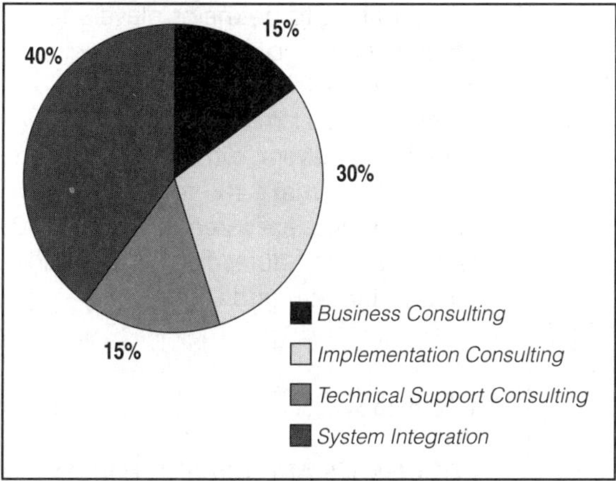

This said, the forecast for Vertical Applications is probably quite conservative. The reason is that business solutions are nearly always become more function-specific and "verticalized" over time. One can see this happening from the responses of some of the leading system and DBMS vendors which have formed solutions groups to support specific industries and or cross-industry functional areas, and by the leading services vendors, many of which have formed industry-specific "practices."

The software product segment will become the largest product segment in market terms by the end of 1998. It is the fastest growing segment and is expected to exceed $60B by the end of the forecast period.

Figure 9 is the forecast breakout for four categories of services. System Integration is the leading category, accounting for 40% of revenues - $7.4B in 2002. This position is comparable to the one that the category occupies in other areas of large system and network deployment, and reflects the current trend toward outsourcing.

The second largest category is Implementation Consulting. This area is driven by several factors, including:

- System complexity
- The need to accommodate an existing operational data infrastructure
- Complications in the data cleansing, extracting and transformation processes
- Moving to new platforms; e.g., a site with its operational data in a mainframe environment and its data warehouse in a UNIX environment.

The Technical Support and Business Consulting categories each hold a 15% share of the forecast services revenues.

Figure 10 shows how the market breaks out by application. It shows that the largest applications fall into the financial and marketing areas.

Figure 10: Worldwide Database Solution Markets by Application, 2002

APPLICATION	PERCENT OF MARKET (%)
Financial Analysis	11
Customer Marketing	10
Product Performance	8
Sales Force Analysis	8
Quality	8
Promotion/Marketing Campaings	7
Risk Management	6
Vendor Performance	6
Churn Analysis	6
Category Management	6
Market Basket Analysis	6
Supply Chain Analysis	6
Fraud Detection	5
Other	3
Yield Analysis	3
Network/Traffic Pattern Analysis	2

There are literally hundreds of vendors vying for a piece of the Database Solutions market. In 1997, the leading vendor worldwide was IBM with an estimated $2.4 billion in revenues, up from $1.3 billion in 1996. Oracle, HP and NCR, each with revenues in the $750-800M range, follow IBM. These companies participate in the systems, packaged software and services segments.

Figure 11 contains a list of eight vendors that had revenues of $300 million or more derived from the Database Solutions market in 1997. Put together, these vendors accounted for 46% of user expenditures for Database Solutions, and 64% of all user expenditures excluding the in-house category. It is likely that these vendors will continue to be major players for several years to come.
Nonetheless, there are many other companies that might become significant players in the market, even if they don't make the top player list. These vendors are listed in Figure II-12. Note that the figures for Compaq include Tandem and Digital.

USER ISSUES

COST ISSUES AND DRIVING FORCES

The average annual cost of a DW/DSS solution is $1.8 million. The figure is higher in North America and Japan and lower in Europe.

Expenditures for all product types are expected to increase during the forecast period, but a significant

Figure 11: Leading Database Solution Vendors, 1997

VENDOR	ESTIMATED 1997 DATABASE SOLUTION REVENUE ($Millions)			
	TOTAL	SYSTEMS	SOFTWARE	SERVICES
IBM	2400	1800	360	240
Oracle	800		600	200
NCR	750	300	150	300
HP	750	600		150
Compaq (inc. Tandem DEC)	700	450	50	200
Sun	450	350		100
SASI	400		400	
Andersen Consulting	400			400
Total Lenders	6650	3500	1560	1590
1997 Worldwide Market Value	14460	4125	3485	2790
% held by leaders	46	85	45	57

number of users stated that they expected that expenditures for outside services would stay relatively flat. With roughly 30% of user expenditures currently allocated to in-house expenditures, this finding has to be taken in context; i.e., many users are concerned about having their in-house personnel displaced by outside service providers and so tend to minimize the importance of outside services.

Driving much of the anticipated growth in expenditures is the anticipated growth in the size of the systems that will be required to meet future needs. For example, although the average size of the database reported by respondents was 272 GBytes, respondents reported that they expected the size of that database to increase by an average factor of 24 in three years! If they are right, the average data warehouse size at the end of the year 2000 will be 6.5 TBytes! (A July '98 news item wherein NCR announced that over forty of its customers have TByte+ size databases.) gives this statement some credibility.

This same group of respondents reported expecting that the average number of users accessing their data warehouse would increase by a factor of 42 over three years from 2176 to 91,392, and the average number of users concurrently accessing the warehouse would increase by a factor of 17 from 779 to 13,243. The reason is that many users see the warehouse as a focal point of information distribution for employees, customers and suppliers, in addition to the "knowledge

Figure II-12: Vendors That Could Become Top Tier Data Solutions Vendors

VENDOR	SYSTEMS	SOFTWARE	SERVICES
Arbor Software		✔	
Brio technology		✔	
Business Objects		✔	
Cognos		✔	
Computer Associates		✔	
Coopers & Lybrand			✔
CSC			✔
Data General	✔		
Deloitte & Touche			✔
EDS			✔
Ernst & Young			✔
Fujitsu/ICI/Amdahl	✔		✔
Hitachi/HDS	✔		
Informix Software		✔	
KPMG Peat Marwick			✔
Microsoft		✔	
Microstrategy		✔	
NEC	✔		
Perot Systems			✔
Pilot Software		✔	
Platinum Technology		✔	
Price Waterhouse		✔	✔
Red Brick Systems		✔	
Sequent Computer	✔		✔
SHL Systemhouse			✔
Silicon Graphics	✔	✔	✔
SNI	✔		✔
Sybase		✔	
Unisys	✔		✔

workers" who are today's most frequent users of Database Solutions. These numbers are up considerably from those obtained in our first survey.

The highest rated driving forces for investing in Database Solutions are:

- Improve decision or management processes
- Improve customer service
- Need to keep ahead of competition
- Corporate strategy initiative
- Reduce cost of operations
- Retain customers
- Identify new customers

PURCHASING ISSUES

In contrast to many other large-scale system procurements, Database Solutions system procurements are most heavily influenced by the departments that will use the system or by line-of-business management rather than by an IT organization. Typically, the IT organization was attributed to have only about a 30% influence rating on purchase decisions.

Respondents were presented with a list of twenty-three purchase criteria and asked to rate them on a 1-5 scale. The six highest rated criteria in order of descending importance are:

- Data Integrity
- System reliability
- Query Capability
- Scalability
- Availability
- Price/performance

With one exception, this list would be very close to that for any application considered as mission-critical. That Database Solutions have or will become mission-critical is something that all vendors must take into account.
In a similar manner, respondents were asked to rate nine vendor characteristics as purchase criteria. The criteria singled out as the most important is the amount of data warehouse experience the vendor could demonstrate.

IMPLEMENTATION ISSUES

Much to-do has been made in the press and by vendor pronouncements about the provision of complete solutions. Many would have us believe that it is the Holy Grail of the Database Solutions market. It turns out that only about half the market is interested in a packaged solution, and of the half that are interested, many don't believe it is possible to buy a packaged solution that will meet their needs. The main reason for interest in packaged solutions is faster deployment followed by lower risk.

The average elapsed time reported from when the business case for a Database Solution is completed to full production status is 25 months. This is the same number obtained in last year's survey.

More than a third of the respondents have implemented or plan to implement at least part of their Database Solution on platforms used for other applications. Most of those replying in this vein were existing large mainframe users, reinforcing the claim that mainframes constitute a major portion of the Database Solution market. The majority of users, however, thought they were better off dedicating systems to Database Solutions. Management control, cost, and compatibility are cited as the main reasons for not sharing a Database Solution platform with other applications.

SOME FUTURE DIRECTIONS

Respondents were asked which technologies they deployed today and which they anticipated would be deployed in three years. Most technology categories were expected to increase anywhere from 100% to 500% over the three-year time span. These included:

- Intranet enablement
- Extranet enablement
- The ability to do data mining directly on operational data
- The ability to handle multimedia data
- Direct linkage of decision support application to operational application

Both the Internet and the Intranet are expected to have a significant impact on Database Solutions. Both are seen as the vehicles for increasing data distribution. On the input side, the Internet and Intranet are seen as vehicles for improving data collection, and, for the Internet, providing access to external information that would otherwise be difficult to collect. On the output side, both are seen as vehicles for dramatically expanding user, customer and supplier access to data. In fact, many companies see Internet/Intranet browsers as the standard front end for distributing information. Some also see the Internet as the repository for software tools, permitting users to select from a variety of simple and complex query facilities just like users today can select from a variety of Web-based search tools.

An important issue in many organizations is the question of permitting a decision issued by a DSS system to be implemented without human intervention. For example, if the system says "double the inventory," should it be allowed to automatically order the merchandise without that decision being reviewed by management? A surprising 58% of the respondents stated that this would become a future requirement.

Another issue confronting some organizations is whether or not to permit data mining directly against operational databases. Some 67% of the respondents said they planned to do this in the future. Unfortunately, this question was not pursued further, so we don't know if this is just wishful thinking or, if plans to that effect are in place, how they will be accomplished.

A final futures question dealt with the application of multimedia data. In last year's survey, most users said they would need to support multimedia data in the future, but few had any ideas about what they would do with it! This year's survey respondents were much better prepared to address this question. In fact, two-thirds of the respondents said they planned to use it for document management. Other applications mentioned frequently are marketing material, training, product displays, mapping, and sales presentations.

Business Intelligence in Half the Time (With Less Cost And Risk)

Title: *Business Intelligence in Half the Time (With Less Cost And Risk)*
Author: *Sybase, Inc.*
Abstract: *Welcome to Sybase's Business Intelligence in Half the Time Solutions Showcase, featuring a variety of customers who have used their Industry Warehouse Studio technology to build highly successful data warehousing solutions. If you are seriously considering a data warehousing project, we invite you to review this "at-a-glance" showcase of Sybase real-world implementations. You'll see how you can significantly reduce your overall implementation time and business risk, and achieve a significant competitive advantage.*

Biography: see end article

"Data warehousing has captured the attention of organizations worldwide. Despite this growing interest, data warehouse development remains one of the riskiest IT projects an organization can undertake."
Curt Hall, Editor, "Business Intelligence Advisor"; from the 1999 Cutter Consortium report, "Data Warehousing for Business Intelligence".
http://www.cutter.com/itgroup/reports/dwissues.html

"Sybase's idea of a packaged data warehouse application infrastructure is certainly valuable. It is very useful for people implementing data warehouses or data marts to have a framework which guides development. There is often a disconnect between user needs and developers during the first iteration of development. Sybase Industry Warehouse Studios help avoid this scenario."
David Wells, Principal Analyst, Ovum

"What we needed was a data warehouse consolidating all of our customer information but what we lacked was specific data warehouse expertise.... We were concerned that we would be spending years designing the system without getting any tangible results. Without a doubt, a major benefit of the retail banking models [contained in Industry Warehouse Studio] is that we were able to significantly reduce the time and effort spent in the design phase, possibly even a whole man-year was saved....The models took a great deal of the complexity and risk out of designing our decision support system, and I expect they will pay for themselves in a matter of months."
Paul Verjans, Project Manager, IT Development, Allied Irish Bank

What You Don't Know Can Put Your Business At Risk

But Building Business Intelligence Applications Can Be Risky Business Too
They say knowledge is power. But in today's cutthroat marketplace, it's a lot more than that—it's survival. With long-

time competitors relentlessly trying to chip away at your business and with upstart competitors coming full tilt at your customers with innovative promotions, products and services, you need to maintain your edge. You need up-to-the-minute information on market trends. You need to know what's going on in the minds of your customers and prospects. You need feedback on the effectiveness of your marketing, sales and customer care activities. You need all of this...today!

This urgent need for business intelligence is fueling the growth of the data warehousing market. But even as this market grows and matures, data warehouse projects continue to be complex, costly, time-consuming and risky. It's still common for projects to take 18 to 24 months from conception to completion and to cost millions of dollars. And it's still all too common for projects to end in failure.

With so much at stake—staff and budget resources and the very future of your business —you've got to create and deploy business intelligence applications quickly, cost-effectively and successfully.

Starting From Scratch: A Losing Proposition

If there's a single lesson to be learned from the experiences of the past decade, it's that building data warehouses from scratch is a losing proposition. It means pouring enormous amounts of time and money into up-front activities, including gathering requirements; understanding the particular line of business; designing schema; creating extraction, transformation and loading templates; and building queries for analysis.

The Meta Group reports that 20% of warehouse projects are "abject failures," while another 50% are only partly successful. Other industry estimates place the overall failure rate even higher. In a great majority of cases, failure is due to organizations' lack of data warehousing expertise and the use of traditional transaction-oriented development techniques and data models.

Given the strategic importance of data warehousing, however, and the ever-increasing demands from sales, marketing and other managers, organizations have had little choice but to plunge ahead, hoping for the best.

But what if there was a way to tap into the experience of data warehousing experts, to leverage the lessons learned in dozens of data warehousing projects, to have access to proven industry-specific methods, applications and data models?

Now, thanks to Sybase Industry Warehouse Studio (IWS), there is!

Our Experience Ensures Your Success

Since the early days of data warehousing in the late 1980s, Sybase has been a pioneer and innovator in this field. Our development and professional services teams have designed and implemented data warehouses and data marts for companies in virtually every major industry around the globe. We know what works. We know how to minimize risk, reduce implementation time and increase return on investment.

Over the past five years, we've studied the factors that make the development of analytical applications such a lengthy, costly and risky process. We found that in every industry, there are common elements — workflow, measurements, reporting requirements, terminology and data types—that need not be recreated for each new project. We packaged these common elements in our IWSs to enable you to deliver business intelligence applications that address the different but related aspects of customer behavior, value and potential across your entire enterprise. Quickly. And with minimum cost and risk.

IWS's modular architecture provides the flexibility you need to compete in a constantly changing business environment, while ensuring the seamless integration of your entire data architecture. Recognizing today's business and marketplace realities, we also designed our IWS data models and applications to facilitate integration across applications and industries throughout your enterprise.

Sybase IWS is a proven business intelligence framework that allows you to reduce overall implementation time and business risk, and achieve a significant competitive advantage. With IWS, your warehouse can be up and running in as little as three to six months, enabling your users to access, analyze and act upon critical company, customer and competitive data.

Sybase IWS supports every major database including Oracle, Microsoft, IBM, Informix and, of course, Sybase.

The bottom line is simple: You need to solve real business problems today, not create new IT problems that sap resources from core business activities. With IWS, you will realize a rapid and significant return on your data warehousing investment.

Industry Warehouse Studios Deliver Results

"A Fast Track To A Decision Support Data Model And Strategy That Specifically Supported Our Industry"

It's no wonder Sybase IWSs have created such a buzz among leading businesses and industry analysts. After all, who has time to recreate the wheel when legions of business users are screaming for information—information that can make the difference between winning and losing in today's ultra-competitive marketplace? And who can afford to commit finite budget and IT resources when the chances of success are no better than a flip of a coin? Sybase IWSs are the products of five years of successful data warehouse deployments around the globe. They enable you to:

- minimize your risk
- reduce time to deployment
- reduce project costs
- increase your return on investment
- put critically important customer and marketplace information in the hands of business users

As you'll read in the following profiles:

- Matáv, Hungary's largest telecommunications company, needed to become a more customer-centric organization to grow its market share against increasing competition. It required a consolidated view of its customers to evaluate their needs and potential. Using Sybase IWS for Telecommunications, Matáv was able to provide access to its data warehouse in just four months. The company's customer-focused strategy has paid off with an increase in market penetration of 12% and revenue growth of over 25%.
- Scottish Widows Group, one of the largest and strongest life insurance, pension and investment providers in the UK with over £32.5 billion under management, was facing ambitious growth targets in a very competitive market. It had 30 years worth of customer data stored in its transaction systems but no easy way to use it in marketing and sales efforts. Nor did the company have in-house data warehousing expertise. Using Sybase IWS for Insurance, Scottish Widows successfully created a data warehouse on its existing IBM OS/390 mainframe, increasing the effectiveness of its marketing programs. "By choosing to work with the methodology and models for insurance, we achieved a fast track to a decision support data model and strategy that specifically supported our industry."
- Voluntary Health Insurance (VHI), one of Europe's most efficiently run medical insurance organizations, was facing the millennium with legacy systems that couldn't meet user demands for information. To continue delivering the best possible value and service to its 1.46 million members, VHI used Sybase IWS for Insurance to create a data warehouse providing complex forecasting and cost containment capabilities. By using IWS's built-in insurance-focused data models, VHI was able to deploy phase one of the warehouse in just six months.
- Allied Irish Bank (AIB), Ireland's leading banking and financial services organization, with assets of over IR £42 billion, needed to obtain an integrated customer view for marketing and sales analysis. With no in-house data warehousing experience, AIB was able to implement the retail banking models to create a 150-gigabyte enterprise data warehouse on NCR Teradata, enabling it to evaluate opportunities, analyze results of sales and marketing campaigns, improve customer relationship management and achieve its targeted return on investment.

"With the telco-focused data warehousing models, we were able to really accelerate the process of building an enterprisewide, customer-focused data warehouse and do so with our existing resources."
Eva Bernat, Project Manager, Matáv

Matav, Inc.

Hungary's Largest Telecommunications Company Ready For Competition

Formed 10 years ago, Matáv came from monopolized beginnings as the original Post and Telephone Company for all of Hungary. Today, Matáv is Hungary's largest telecommunications company and the first central or eastern European company to have its initial public offering on the New York Stock Exchange.

Recognizing Hungary's need for a modern telecommunications infrastructure, Matáv has endeavored to provide the highest quality fixed line, mobile, Internet and commercial telecommunication services. Today, Matáv provides over 68% of the digital services in an area that just 10 years ago, had limited telephone lines and long waiting lists for telephone services.
Not only has the quality and availability of services changed, but so has the overall telecommunications market. No longer the only telco provider in Hungary, Matáv now operates in a growing competitive market. To keep and increase its market share, Matáv decided to focus on the customer and name 1998 the "year of the customer."

Becoming a customer-centric organization made it critical for Matáv to carefully gather and analyze information about its customers. Matáv had isolated data marts, but no way to get a single consolidated view of the customer to evaluate customer need and potential. Eva Bernat, project manager for Matáv, was responsible for building an enterprise data warehouse to meet the needs of the company's new customer focus. "We knew that a good deal of the success of a data warehouse depended on the quality of the data structures it was built on," said Bernat. "We wanted to build it right the first time. We could have done this ourselves but we decided to take advantage of the information found in the data models. With the telco-focused data warehousing models, we were able to really accelerate the process of building an enterprisewide, customer-focused data warehouse and do so with our existing resources. We only wish all aspects of the project went this smoothly."

First phase access to the data warehouse was available only 4 months after the start of the project, and full production is anticipated to follow shortly. The resulting applications provide accurate and valuable decision-support information on the network, marketing and finance areas of the business. Previously impossible to get this kind of information, upon completion of the project, Matáv will have immediate access to billable traffic analysis, unbillable traffic analysis, customer profitability analysis, churn analysis, promotion and campaign analysis information.

By focusing on its customers and providing high quality products and services at competitive prices, Matáv has undergone incredible gains in 1998. Revenues grew by over 25%, while total fixed lines increased nearly 11% to almost 2.7 million lines and market penetration rose by almost 12%. Through market, product and information leadership, Matáv will continue to advance the telecommunications infrastructure of Eastern and Central Europe, accelerating Hungary into a new modern European economy.

Business Issues

- Needed a management and decision support system for analyzing financial, budgeting, traffic, network, billing, customer and market information.
- Traditional analysis simply regurgitated what had already been assumed—no new insights were provided.

Technical Issues

- Analyzing existing isolated data proved time consuming, expensive and in some cases, impossible.
- The transaction systems could not respond adequately to decision support interrogation.

Business Results

- Accurate and valuable decision-support information on billable traffic analysis, unbillable traffic analysis, customer profitability analysis, churn analysis, promotion and campaign analysis.

Technical Results

- Creation of a 3-terabyte data warehouse, on Oracle and HP, utilizing Cognos front-end tools for analysis.
- Applications built using methodology and prepackaged telecommunications warehouse model, available within months of starting the project.
- Once isolated data is now consolidated, providing an enterprise view of the customer.

"*By choosing to work with the methodology and models for insurance, we achieved a fast track to a decision support data model and strategy that specifically supported our industry.*"
Robert Wyllie, Group Database Marketing Manager Scottish Widows

Scottish Widows Group

International Financial Services Provider Selects Sybase Business Intelligence Solution

Scottish Widows' Fund and Life Assurance Society opened for business in 1815 during the Napoleonic Wars, offering a general fund for securing provision to widows, sisters and other women. Today it is one of the best-known companies of its kind in the UK and one of the largest and strongest life insurance, pensions and investment providers. Overseeing pensions and investments for over 2.2 million people and 21,000 employers, Scottish Widows now manages over £32.5 billion in funds. New business in 1998 was in excess of £2.5 billion with further growth planned for 1999.

The goal of Scottish Widows' business strategy is the desire to meet the needs of its customers by providing competitive products, supported by quality service and sound investment performance. In recent years, Scottish Widows has developed from being a traditional life and pensions provider into a more broadly diversified financial services group offering a wide range of products to its customers. By adopting a "customer-centric view," Scottish Widows was looking to grow—quickly and in a very competitive environment. To accomplish this, it knew it had a very valuable asset to tap into—up to 30 years of loyal customer data.

The data was not only isolated for day-to-day transactions but also stored in a multitude of different complex systems. It was perfect for isolated transactions, but all wrong for providing one integrated seamless view of the customer for sales and marketing activity. Like other companies, Scottish Widows sent its data out to an external marketing support bureau, but eventually outgrew that solution.
It needed to have control, to have all the data together, up-to-date and stored in-house.

"We understood our challenges since senior management visits to the US had given us an insight into how leading-edge companies were developing their business intelligence capabilities. We are experts in transactional systems, not data warehousing," said Robert Wyllie, group database marketing manager, Scottish Widows. "Our choice was to either figure it out ourselves and run the risk of not getting it right, or lever-age a tried and tested approach. By choosing to work with the methodology and models for insurance, we achieved a fast track to a decision support data model and strategy that specifically supported our industry."

Scottish Widows ended up with a data warehouse containing up-to-date, complete customer data and a new customer analysis unit. The new group is able to supply a range of valuable support for both direct marketing and sales. Armed with a whole suite of tools for decision analysis, the new unit will provide propensity models, segmentation, profiling as well as support for campaign execution and analysis. "We are now able to undertake more informed marketing activity than was previously possible," said Gordon Drysdale, direct marketing manager. "We always had really great products and a brand that is the envy of our competitors. Now we have the information that will enable us to do an even better job at providing our customers with high quality services and relevant products."

Business Issues

- Inability to effectively leverage the existing customer base and obtain an integrated seamless view of the customer from a marketing perspective.

Technical Issues

- Data in isolated diverse systems, some as much as 30 years old.

Business Results

- A new customer analysis unit providing a range of valuable support for both direct marketing and sales.

Technical Results

- Creation of large data warehouse on S390 platform and implementation of key decision support technology covering statistical analysis, ROLAP, campaign management and GIS tools.
- Deployment of a range of decision support tools to leverage customer data in data warehousing.

"By bringing in the insurance-focused models and methodology, we were able to say with confidence that our data warehouse is built on a solid, best-practices-based architecture."
Damien Purcell, Information Services Manager, VHI

Voluntary Health Insurance, Ireland

Turns Y2K into a Real Opportunity for Advancements in its IT Infrastructure

Founded in 1957, Voluntary Health Insurance (VHI) has grown to 1.46 million members, nearly 40% of the population of Ireland, including a record increase of 64,000 new members in 1998. VHI remains one of the most efficiently run medical insurance organizations in Europe: Its administration costs stand at 6% of turnover, which is less than half of the industry norm.

VHI provides private healthcare coverage allowing members to get immediate access to private healthcare. Although the public healthcare system in Ireland is among the best in the world, it is often fraught with long waiting lists for surgical procedures. VHI members are insured against the financial costs of hospitalization, professional care and a range of primary/out-patient treatments.

To maintain its advantage, VHI made a strategic decision to capitalize on one of its most valuable resources: its customer data. Through daily interaction with its members, VHI has accumulated vast amounts of information that it knows can be used to drive the organization on to even higher levels of customer care and continue to provide the best possible value for money service to its members.

Healthcare companies like VHI rely heavily on information. Unlike almost any other industry, insurance companies are constantly making decisions based on statistics and analysis. Facts and figures are their lifeblood. As you can imagine, the approaching millennium was weighing heavily on the minds of the IT systems group at VHI. As VHI approached the new millennium, its lifeblood was under threat on two fronts: existing legacy and information systems were no longer able to keep up with growing user demands and, of course, the issue of Y2K itself.

Like many forward thinking information services providers, the VHI Information Systems Group was looking at Y2K as an opportunity to create real advancements in its IT systems. Besides replacing non-Y2K-compliant systems, VHI saw this as a chance to move from a traditional transaction and reporting system focus to a more modern data warehousing and decision support focus. Having identified the Y2K implications and with real business-focused IT goals, VHI set off in early 1998.

Faced with the usual challenges—lack of people with data warehousing specific skills and transactional data that was not suitable for direct analysis, VHI Information Services manager Damien Purcell knew VHI was going to need some help. "Our data was set up to support transactions and of course our skill sets were tuned for managing data for just that purpose," said Purcell. "Our biggest challenge was what was this data warehouse going to look like, what data did we need and how would we use it? We had a pretty good idea but the specifics of laying out the models for a data warehouse were quite new to us. By bringing in the insurance-focused models and methodology, we were able to say with confidence that our data warehouse is built on a solid, best-practices-based architecture. With the knowledge of our data and users' needs married to the data warehouse models, we were able to quickly tackle a rather large project."

The first phase of the data warehouse was deployed after only six months. Now users have direct access to data and no longer have to wait for MIS to run or create the needed reports. "We also plan to integrate the system with our new, balanced scorecard reporting system, which will result in much more focused and meaningful business reporting," said Purcell. "So far, everyone is very pleased. It is still too early to come up with hard numbers, but the indications are that this project will produce a significant return on investment."

Business Issues
- Needed to move from slower, limited reporting systems to modern, decision-support systems.
- Address Y2K issues for information systems.

Technical Issues
- Existing resources were limited in their knowledge of deploying data warehousing systems.
- Existing data was not suitable for direct information analysis.

Business Results
- Complex forecasting.
- Cost containment/medical budget monitoring.
- Feeds balanced scorecard reporting.

Technical Architecture
- Server: Data warehouse on Compaq Alpha 4100 and OpenVMS 7.1 systems running Oracle 8.
- Front End: Pentium 400, 64MB RAM, Windows NT, Microstrategy's DSS Agent.

"*Without a doubt, a major benefit of the retail banking models is that we were able to significantly reduce the time and effort spent in the design phase, possibly even a whole year was saved.*"
Paul Verjans, IT Development, Project Manager, Allied Irish Bank

Allied Irish Bank

Allied Irish Bank (AIB) Group is Ireland's leading banking and financial services organization providing commercial banking, leasing, life insurance and pension, trust, consulting and insurance brokerage services. It also offers trading and commercial treasury services, corporate and venture capital financing, and stock brokerage. Operating principally in Ireland, Britain, the United States of America, Central Europe and Asia, AIB employs over 23,000 people worldwide in over approximately 900 offices and has assets of over IR £42 billion.

AIB is at the leading edge in its use of innovative technology and is constantly seeking new ways of utilizing the latest technological developments to enhance the services it offers its customers. From mobile banking where mobile phone users can check their account balances and transaction details on the screens of their mobile phones to new re-loadable Visa cash cards, AIB is committed to providing its customers the products and services they desire. The AIB IT Development Group also has that same sense of commitment when it comes to supporting its employees ensuring that they have the technology-driven tools they need to be successful. When its Sales and Marketing Group needed a solution for designing, managing and analyzing its sales and marketing campaigns, AIB IT went to work.

"What we needed was a data warehouse consolidating all of our customer information but what we lacked was specific data ware-house expertise," said Paul Verjans, project manager, IT Development. "We knew how to build operational architectures, but when it came to designing systems specifically for querying and analysis, we needed some assistance. We were concerned that we would be spending years designing the system without getting any tangible results. Without a doubt, a major benefit of the retail banking models is that we were able to significantly reduce the time and effort spent in the design phase, possibly even a whole year was saved. By merging the prebuilt models specifically for retail banking with our own models, knowledge of the operational systems and business requirements, we were able to quickly design the target data architecture needed. This shortened the whole design process and helped us meet an aggressive development schedule. The models took a great deal of the complexity and risk out of designing our decision support system and I expect they will pay for themselves in a matter of months."

By using the prebuilt models and a planned phased approach, AIB IT was able to immediately deliver needed decision support tools to its Sales and Marketing Business Analysis Group. "Now we can look for opportunities within our customer base as well as analyze the results of our sales and marketing activities. Before this, we had limited tools to determine the success of our campaigns. Now we can really demonstrate tangible results from our efforts," said Jim O'Keeffe, manager of Sales and Marketing Information, AIB. "Our whole marketing business model is changing – we are moving to very targeted, efficient programs and seeing a much higher return."

Business Issues
- Inability to see an integrated customer profile.
- Need for more sophisticated marketing campaigns.
- Need for rapid implementation of warehouse technology.

Technical Issues
- Lack of data warehouse expertise.
- Organizing large volumes of data for easy and efficient query and access.

Business Results
- Ability to evaluate opportunity and analyze results in sales and marketing campaigns.
- Ability to improve customer relationship management.
- Targeted return on investment achieved.

Technical Results
- Data warehouse on NCR teradata built on target.
- Target data architecture implemented.

To Beat the Competition, You Need Business Intelligence. . .

Now That's Why You Need Sybase IWS

Your customers aren't going to wait for you to figure out what they want. Your business users can't afford to wait months or years to get the customer and market information they need to meet revenue, profitability and productivity objectives. Meanwhile, your competitors have you and your customers in their sights. They'd love to see you take a year or more to build and deploy your data warehouse.

With Sybase IWS, you can explode out of the starting gate and have your data warehouse up and running in as little as three to six months. Forget about starting from scratch. Don't worry if you don't have data warehousing expertise. Sybase has done all the up-front work for you and pack-aged it in IWS—a proven framework for data warehousing success.

Call us today at 1-800-8-SYBASE to find out how IWS can help you retain and grow existing customer relationships, create new customer relationships, increase productivity and profitability and more. Or visit our Web site at http://www.sybase.com/bid/technology/

Biography: Sybase, Inc is one of the largest global independent software companies. Sybase helps businesses integrate, manage and deliver applications, content and data anywhere they are needed. With a commitment to distributed, open, and end-to-end computing, Sybase Inc. is helping companies build advanced data warehouse solutions. The company is also leveraging core enterprise product strengths to capitalize on the emerging enterprise information portal market to provide dependable solutions that deliver on the promise of e-Business. http://www.sybase.com/bi.

Business Issues

Technical Issues

Business Issues

Building an Active Data Warehouse Using High Performance AS/400 Technology

Title: *Building an Active Data Warehouse Using High Performance AS/400 Technology*

Author: *DataMirror Corporation*

Abstract: *This paper discusses the concept of the Active Data Warehouse and what it offers businesses that implement it. This paper also examines the "layered" or "tiered" view of data warehousing. Combined, these two ideas offer the reader an understanding of the growing trend of warehousing data and an introduction to one aspect of the future of the warehouse as a tool for business.*

Introduction

In today's information driven economy, fast access to business data used for decision making is critical if a company is to attain a competitive advantage. However, several obstacles exist that prevent businesses from achieving this goal.

Information that assists in sound decision making is often locked up in the data that a corporation collects and stores for product orders, shipments, inventory, product costing and other elements. Getting at that data is a time consuming, often hopeless, task. Even if a company can collect the massive amount of information required, converting that raw data into a useful format is unworkable. Data warehousing, the central storage of an enhanced copy of critical business information, simplifies the job.

Data warehousing provides more than end user query access to raw production files. It involves centrally storing important business information in a form (and with associated tools) that lets nonprogrammers examine relationships and trends in the data. Many kinds of businesses can use warehousing. "Who Uses Data Warehousing?" later in this paper outlines the organizations that can profit from its use.

As mentioned, the ability to manage and store such large volumes of data is a necessity for today's business managers. Companies are using data warehouses to store information for marketing, sales and manufacturing to help managers run the organization more effectively. The ability to manage and effectively present the volume of data tracked in today's business is the cornerstone of data warehousing. Advances in IBM AS/400 technology such as RISC architecture and parallel processing are re-positioning the AS/400 as an effective data warehousing platform.

But how does the warehouse operate? After all, it isn't a physical structure; so what are the data warehouse counterparts to aisles, shelves, boxes, forklifts and other storage facility components?

The warehousing solution that most AS/400 customers need can be divided into three fundamental tiers with data flows between them. The three layers are:

- Data Access/Query Presentation Layer
- Database Structure, Content/Meaning Architecture Layer
- Interfaces and Replenishment Middleware Layer

Presentation Layer

The presentation layer manages the flow of information from the warehouse to the analyst, providing an interface that makes it easier for the analyst to work with the data.

This layer is where graphical user interface (GUI) tools are most important. Front-end query tools should provide an easy and efficient way to visually represent data for decision making in two or more dimensions. Expert systems, pattern recognition and analytic algorithms can highlight areas for close human analysis, but in the end humans still have an edge in improvisation, gut feel and trend forecasting. Warehousing assists users in the analysis of sales data so they can make informed decisions that have real-time impact on company performance.

The presentation layer's ability to store and present multidimensional views or summaries of data is one reason multidimensional databases and query tools are popular at this level of the warehouse.

Architecture Layer (Structure, Content/Meaning)

The architecture layer describes the structure of the data in the warehouse. An important component of the architecture layer is flexibility. The level of flexibility is measured in terms of how easy it is for the analyst to break out of the standard representation of information offered by the warehouse in order to do custom analysis. Custom analysis is where semantic thickness (content and meaning of how data is stored in the warehouse) becomes important.

Semantic thickness is the degree of clear business meaning imbedded in both the database structure and the content of the data itself. Field names such as "F001" for customer number and obscure numbers such as "01" to indicate "Backorder" status are considered semantically thin, or ambiguous and difficult to understand. In contrast, field naming standards such as "Customer_Name" containing the full customer name and "Order_Status" containing the complete description "Backorder& are semantically thick, or clear, meaningful and easily understood.

In other words, data structure and content need to be clear to the analyst at the presentation layer of the data warehouse. The underlying data schema for the warehouse should be simple and easily understood by the end user of the data.

AS/400-based data warehouses should be designed to be SQL compliant. This means the warehouse should not make use of proprietary native AS/400 file formats such as multi-member files. While the underlying production data may be stored in multi-member files, warehouse data will need to be easily accessed using a variety of tools, front-end packages and workstations. SQL compliance will make Open Database Connectivity (ODBC) and other SQL gateway access paths viable. SQL formats will also give your warehouse longevity, offer the flexibility to make changes in the future and even move data to other computers or databases as needed.

Middleware Layer (Interfaces and Replenishment)

The middleware layer is the glue that holds the data warehouse together. It integrates your warehouse to production and operational systems. Data needed for warehouse applications often must be copied to and from computers in different locations and of different types. Warehousing often implies transformational data replication. Production data needs to be secure and is frequently not in the format needed for warehousing. Middleware tools that help you deal with the data management issues of implementing a data warehouse can add real value.

As data volume increases, the challenge of implementing a data warehouse grows significantly. Simple file transfers to replenish the warehouse and to move the data where it is needed most become impractical-. Re-keying data is unrealistic because of the enormous workload and the likelihood of introducing errors.

Intelligent transformational data replication has proven to be an effective middleware layer solution to help AS/400 shops implement data warehousing. The essence of intelligent replication involves automatically copying data from one system to another, or within one computer from one file set to another. With the right middleware or replication architecture, warehouse data can be copied selectively and filtered based on criteria such as row or column characteristics. Intelligent replication can also transform and enhance warehouse data. Field values can be re-mapped to new warehouse data standards. A good replication tool for data warehousing must provide the ability to choose which segments of existing production databases will be replicated. To improve the semantic content of warehouse data, the tool should provide enhancement features such as derived field calculations, value translations, column mapping and data type conversions.

The replenishment tool should be flexible and support real-time, continuous replenishment or periodic replication so data synchronization can be scheduled for off-peak periods. Data changes should be applied to warehouse copies when both the network and CPU cycles are available. The tool should also provide the ability to apply a wide variety of data type transformations including NULL and date type transforms as well as derived field calculations.

Transformational replication software provides a simple solution to many data warehousing issues. Replication provides the warehouse with its own copy of data and can significantly reduce network traffic. Replication improves data access by helping create warehouse databases that can be maintained in real-time on separate AS/400 computers, or as secondary copies on a single AS/400. Some replenishment tools, like DataMirror's Transformation Server for AS/400, support warehousing of AS/400 data into Oracle, Sybase, Microsoft SQL Server and other relational databases.

The Active Data Warehouse

Prevailing data warehousing wisdom claims that a warehouse should contain a snap shot of production data at a given point in time. For example, the warehouse should contain an end of day, end of week or end of month "picture" of production data. In addition, changes to data in the warehouse should have no effect on production systems. If analysis of warehouse data indicates invoice payment delays with certain customers -- while payment terms may be modified in the data warehouse -- these changes would have no immediate impact on payment terms in production systems.

This popular wisdom is based more on the operational constraints of past approaches to replenishing the data warehouse. Best practices have been hampered by problems with introducing production systems to the data warehouse. Historically, it has been impossible to get real-time data warehouse feeds from AS/400 production systems. The snap shot approach was deemed "right" because most data warehouses were maintained by periodically replenishing the warehouse with full copies of production data. File transfers would typically occur at the end of the day, week or month. Since query tools were relatively unsophisticated and complex to debug, it was also difficult to get consistent, reliable results from query analyses if warehouse data was constantly changing.

Who Uses Data Warehousing?

Companies use data warehouses to store information for marketing, sales and manufacturing to help managers get a feel for the data and run the business more effectively. Managers use sales data to improve forecasting and planning for brands, product lines and business areas. Retail purchasing managers use warehouses to track fast-moving lines and to ensure an adequate supply of high-demand products. Financial analysts use warehouses to manage currency and exchange exposures, oversee cash flow and monitor capital expenditures. Warehousing generally provides the greatest benefit to the following types of companies:

Companies with multiple products and locations. For example, consumer-oriented manufacturers or product distributors, such as pharmaceutical, beverage, food, toy and cosmetic firms, often have the depth and complexity of product data that can benefit from warehousing. Data warehousing lets market analysts drill down into data to clearly understand and forecast product demand trends and changes. Multi-location or division companies that use a distributed systems model. Frequently, remote offices or locations have computers that capture customer, sales, shipment, and order information. These companies can warehouse critical data from the remote locations into central processors for detailed analysis.

Companies that operate on a portfolio management approach. In these companies, each division or department is autonomous, but central procurement, asset allocation or financial analysis offers benefits. Such companies can capture operating data remotely from each division and warehouse it.

Conclusion: Warehouse Data Where It's Needed

With IBM's significant investment in new server models and multi-processor architecture, it is clear that the AS/400 has a promising future as a high performance data warehouse engine. It is being "opened up" with improved TCP/IP and POSIX compliant operating system services. The new warehouse role of the AS/400 will be more diverse and will require it to run seamlessly beside a wide variety of mixed hardware and database platforms.

The three tiered data warehouse architecture outlined here offers significant benefits to AS/400 shops undertaking the complex task of implementing a high value added active data warehouse based on AS/400 technology. It can help set up an AS/400-based business for data warehousing and put a company's data into the users' hands when they need it, where they need it and in the form they need it.

Data Warehousing Concepts for AS/400

Title: *Data Warehousing Concepts for AS/400*
Author: *IBM*

Abstract: *Data warehousing is an increasingly popular and powerful concept of applying information technology to solve business problems. Meta Group, Inc., a leading consultant in the data warehousing environment, suggests that over 900f the Fortune 2000 businesses will put into place a data warehouse by the end of 1996. But what is data warehousing, and why is it so important to so many businesses? How can IBM help move your company into the data warehousing environment? Why does AS/400 Advanced Series make an excellent data warehousing platform? This paper focuses on answers to these questions and describes the products and components that make up AS/400 data warehousing solutions.*

What is a data warehouse?

Data warehousing is a concept. It is not a product that you can buy off the shelf. It is a set of hardware and software components that can be used to better analyze the massive amounts of data that companies are accumulating to make better business decisions. The data you use to operate your business represents a wealth of knowledge that you may not be fully tapping into. It is an asset that is probably not being used to its fullest potential. Data warehousing can help you take advantage of the knowledge base you've created over time--your data!

Benefits
The data warehouse can be used to:

- Understand business trends and make better forecasting decisions
- Bring better products to market in a more timely manner
- Analyze daily sales information and make quick decisions that can significantly affect your company's performance

In short, data warehousing can be a solution for maintaining your company's competitive edge.

A data warehouse customer example
One AS/400 customer, a large supplier of consumer goods, found that their sales force lacked the kind of information needed to expand their business. Monthly sales reports simply were not timely or detailed enough to be very useful. To help make strategic business decisions, the company needed to analyze historical information to be able to spot trends. Furthermore, the company needed this analysis to be fast and on-demand. Their existing applications could not meet either of these requirements.

With their new AS/400 data warehouse, the company's salespeople can formulate sales strategies based on the information the warehouse provides. This includes information about the success of previous promotions, regional trends, product profitability, and the effect of product packaging. Salespeople have access to immediate information in order to make on-the-spot decisions that are customized to particular clients.

Other company departments, such as finance and operations, are also using the warehouse to identify and analyze product successes across regions, salespeople, and time. Personnel and machinery resources can be shifted based on demand or projections, to ensure that those resources are optimized for production purposes.

Data warehousing can be a key differentiator in many different industries. Data warehouse applications include:

- sales and marketing analysis across all industries
- inventory turn and product tracking in manufacturing
- category management, vendor analysis, and marketing program effectiveness analysis in retail
- profitable lane or driver risk analysis in transportation
- profitability analysis or risk assessment in banking
- claims analysis or fraud detection in insurance

Data warehousing concepts and terms

Operational versus informational data

Operational data is the data you use to run your business. This data is what is typically stored, retrieved, and updated by your Online Transactional Processing (OLTP) system. An OLTP system may be, for example, a reservations system, an accounting application, or an order entry application.

Operational data is typically stored in a relational database, but may be stored in legacy hierarchical or flat file formats as well. Some of the characteristics of operational data include:

- Updated often and through online transactions
- Non-historical data (not more than three to six months old)
- Optimized for transactional processing
- Highly normalized in the relational database for easy update, maintenance, and integrity

Informational data is typically stored in a format that makes analysis much easier. Analysis can be in the form of decision support (queries), report generation, executive information systems, and more in-depth statistical analysis.

Informational data is created from the wealth of operational data that exists in your business. Informational data is what makes up a data warehouse.

Informational data is typically:

- Summarized operational data
- De-normalized and replicated data
- Infrequently updated from the operational systems
- Optimized for decision support applications
- Possibly "read only" (no updates allowed)
- Stored on separate systems to lessen impact on operational systems

Transforming operational data into informational data

Creating the informational data, that is, the data warehouse, from the operational systems is a key part of the overall data warehousing solution. Building the informational database is done with the use of transformation or propagation tools. These tools not only move the data from multiple operational systems, but often manipulate the data into a more appropriate format for the warehouse. This could mean:

- The creation of new fields that are derived from existing operational data
- Summarizing data to the most appropriate level needed for analysis
- Denormalizing the data for performance purposes
- Cleansing of the data to ensure that integrity is preserved.

Why is this transformation necessary? Consider operational data that contains every detail about every purchase made in a retail outlet. This data holds the answers to the questions:

- what items were purchased?
- what store did the transaction take place in?
- how was it paid for?
- and who was the consumer?

But because the data is stored in a format appropriate for recording these transactions, querying this data to analyze it can be a very time consuming effort and can adversely affect the performance of the transactional system.

A business analyst tracking sales may want to review data collected from every store by product to forecast inventories, determine profit margins, or track revenues compared to last year. The ability to generate summary level informational data from the operational data provides the performance benefits the analyst can take advantage of to quickly view the trends and problem areas affecting the business.

Figure 1

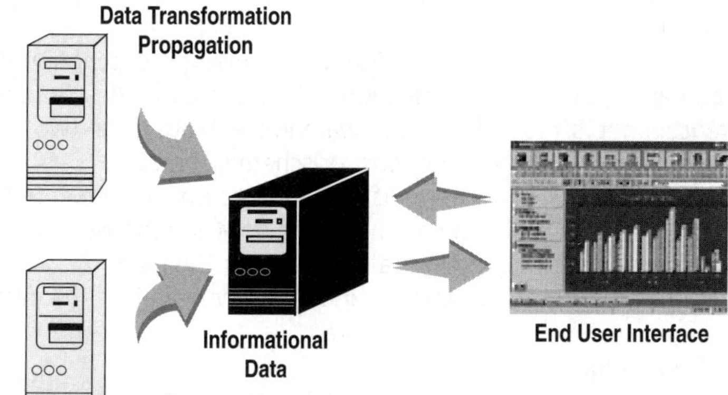

Multi-dimensional analysis and OLAP

Relational databases store data in a two dimensional format: tables of data represented by rows and columns. Multi-dimensional analysis solutions, commonly referred to as On-Line Analytical Processing (OLAP) solutions, offer an extension to the relational model to provide a multi-dimensional view of the data. For example, in multi-dimensional analysis, data entities such as products, geographies, time periods, and sales channels may all represent different dimensions. Actual sales revenues and forecasted revenues may represent measurements to analyze.

Multi-dimensional data structures provide both a mechanism to store the data and a way for a business analyst to, for example, view actual sales versus forecast numbers across the different dimensions in a very timely, very powerful fashion. The power of the data is given to the users who need it most, without the need for users to wait for complex reports to be generated.

Multi-dimensional solutions provide the ability to:

- analyze potentially large amounts of data with very fast response times
- "slice and dice" through the data, and drill down or roll up through various dimensions as defined by the data structure
- quickly identify trends or problem areas that would otherwise be missed

Multi-dimensional data structures can be implemented in many different manners. Relational databases can support this structure through:

- specific database designs (schema), such as "star-schema", intended for multi-dimensional analysis
- highly indexed or summarized designs

These structures are sometimes referred to as relational OLAP (ROLAP)-based structures.

Another method of providing multi-dimensional analysis is through the use of specialized databases that form a "cube"-like structure for achieving high performance analysis.

Data marts
Data marts are workgroup or departmental warehouses, which are small in size, typically 1-10GB. The data mart contains informational data that is departmentalized, tailored to the needs of the specific departmental work group. Multi-dimensional data structures are one way of defining a data structure that can be used for data marts.

Metadata
Information about the data warehouse and the data that is contained in the data warehouse comes in two basic parts. There is technical data the warehouse administrator uses, and there is business data that is of use to the warehouse users. All of this data is referred to as metadata, data about the data.

The technical data contains a description of the operational database and a description of the data warehouse. From these two descriptions, or schema, the data movement operation can be implemented. This data helps the data warehouse administrators maintain the data warehouse and know where all of the data is coming from.

The business data helps users find information in the data warehouse without knowing the underlying implementation of the database. This information is presented in business terms, instead of the terms used by the programmers when the database was built. The business data also gives the user information about:

- When the data was moved into the warehouse (how current it is)
- Where the data came from (which operational database)
- Other information that lets the user know how reliable the data is

Business intelligence software and data mining

Business intelligence software is a fairly new term referring to the tools that are used to analyze the data. This software can consist of:

- Decision support systems (DSS) tools, which allow you to build ad hoc queries and generate reports
- Executive information systems (EIS), which combine decision support with extended analysis capabilities and access to outside resources (such as Dow Jones News services)
- Data mining tools, which allow automation of the analysis of your data to find patterns or rules that you can use to tailor business operations

These tools are typically easy to use and graphically oriented, with point-and-click functionality. The tools often can present the data to the user in tabular or graphical format, in a report, or with key performance indicators highlighted. A significant benefit of today's analysis tools is the ability to quickly and easily put the power of the data in the hands of the people who can best use it.

Data mining

Data mining tools, such as Intelligent Miner from IBM, can find potential gold mines of valuable information in the massive amounts of data that a company accumulates. These tools take decision support and executive information systems to a new level. With traditional DSS and EIS systems, the user forms a hypothesis and uses the query tools to verify or reject the hypothesis. With data mining, the system researches the data and determines patterns, classifications, and associations, while the analyst determines what to do with the results.

Data mining has been quite useful in the retail industry to analyze consumer buying patterns and form marketing programs to take advantage of the analysis results. For instance, data mining can find patterns in your data to answer questions like:

- what item purchased in a given transaction triggers the purchase of additional related items?
- how do purchasing patterns change with store location?
- what items tend to be purchased using credit cards, cash, or check?
- how would the typical customer likely to purchase these items be described?
- did the same customer purchase related items at another time?

Once the buying patterns have been discovered, the retailer can use this information to tailor a marketing strategy that appeals to each type of buyer, thereby maximizing profits or minimizing costs by optimizing inventory management.

But the retail industry is not the only industry to take advantage of data mining. Other uses for data mining include: risk assessment and portfolio management in the finance industry; fraud detection and policy assessments in health and insurance; and optimization, scheduling, and visual inspection systems in manufacturing and process control.

AS/400 information warehouse architecture and components

IBM's approach to data warehousing is to provide solutions for building the warehouse and to assist the decision-making process through a set of products and services. This set of products and services, or components, defines the AS/400 information warehouse architecture.

Figure 2

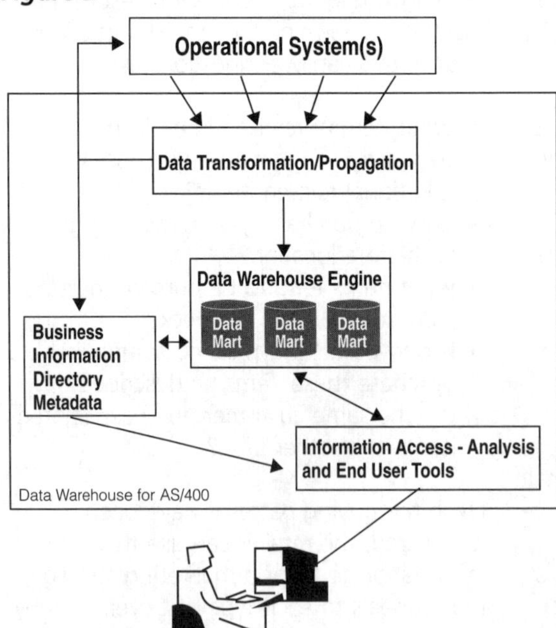

The information warehouse architecture provides the means to change raw data into information for making effective business decisions--the emphasis on information, not data. This architecture provides the overall structure for a comprehensive, flexible, and integrated data warehouse solution.

Components

There are four main components of the AS/400 information warehouse architecture. These are:

- Transformation/propagation tools to load the data warehouse
- Data warehouse database server
- Analysis/end-user tools
- Tools to manage information about the warehouse (metadata)

Transformation/propagation tools

A key component of the warehouse implementation is the loading of the warehouse. This component consists of building the informational database from the operational data in the format optimized for decision support. It also includes regularly updating the informational database as additional transactions to the operational system(s) occur.

The complexity of loading the warehouse can vary depending on a number of factors, including compatibility of operational and informational systems, amount of data massaging that must occur, and timing requirements of the data. Moving data between homogeneous systems is always easier than moving data between heterogeneous systems, because of different database support, differences in (or lack of) support of industry standards for database and/or networks, different security implementations, and so on. Special programming may be required to ensure that the integrity of data is maintained in a heterogeneous environment.

Product examples

- DataPropagator Relational Capture and Apply for OS/400 is an IBM solution for moving data into the data warehouse. DataPropagator moves data from DB2 for OS/400 operational systems as well as from any other DB2 family database. DataPropagator allows you full SQL capability as you move the data--an important feature for creating summarized data, derived fields, and multiple summarized data marts.

  Being able to capture the data from the operational systems and to propagate it on a timed basis is another benefit of DataPropagator. Your business will dictate how often the data warehouse needs to be refreshed: once a day, once a week, or every five minutes. The automated apply process handles this so you need only configure DataPropagator once, and the data warehouse is refreshed automatically.

- Other IBM products that can extract data from non-DB2 data sources include DataJoiner, DataPropagator Non-Relational, and Data Refresher. These products can be used in conjunction with DataPropagator to pull data from IMS, VSAM, and non-IBM relational databases.

- The DB2 for OS/400 SQL client integration exit program interface can be used to provide seamless access to many different database systems. Vendor-supplied application requestor driver programs can be snapped into OS/400. Then, an AS/400 program (such as DataPropagator) that uses SQL for database access can read from or write directly to databases supported by the driver code. With this function, direct access to non-IBM relational databases can be achieved without the need for an intermediate database gateway. Benefits include application portability, higher reliability in distributed data environments, and data access in a heterogeneous network.

- Several IBM Business Partners offer data transformation/propagation products as well. Specific requirements will dictate which product best fits any particular situation. See Table 1 for a list of Business Partner solutions.

Data warehouse database servers--the heart of the warehouse

There are at least five requirements of a data warehouse server:

1. Performance

The performance of the database server must be good enough to support the user's performance expectations during analysis. The warehouse may be very big; it is not uncommon that a warehouse could be over 100GB of data, with fairly complex analysis tasks being executed against the database.

Parallel computing technologies, although not a requirement, become quite important once the warehouse solution grows to a large size.

2. Capacity

The capacity of the server and hardware must be enough to store your entire data warehouse. Data warehouses may be partitioned or split over multiple systems, but the server must support a view of the data that hides where the data is physically stored. In addition to the overall storage capacity requirements of the warehouse, the server and hardware must be able to support very large file or table sizes.

3. Scalability

The scalability of the server must be such that your choice of server can handle the requirements of an ever-growing amount of data in the data warehouse. The typical data warehouse implementation starts out at the data mart level--that is, a small, departmental data warehouse that will grow over time into an enterprise-wide warehouse.

4. Open interfaces

Availability of open interfaces to support the analysis tool of choice is another requirement. Support of open industry standard interfaces allows the solution to utilize the end-user analysis tool of choice. Without this, you may be locking yourself into proprietary interfaces that could cause major expenses to be incurred to support new analytical tools as the business changes.

5. Multiple data structures

Multiple data structures, both relational and multi-dimensional, must be supported.

Product examples

The AS/400 Advanced Server models, with 64-bit PowerPC technology, provide an excellent data warehouse solution. This line of AS/400 servers combined with the most widely installed multi-user database in the industry, DB2 for OS/400, provide the basis for meeting the five requirements noted above. Let's take a look at some of these individually.

Server models

The AS/400 Advanced Server models are specifically tuned for the type of work loads used in data warehousing applications. For example, the DSS or EIS tools used to access the warehouse utilize a client/server database serving workload. The loading of the data warehouse, massaging of the data, and additional analysis tools take advantage of the high performance batch mode on the server models.

Scalability within the server models provides data mart type systems, low-end servers that can handle 10 to 25 users, all the way to enterprise-wide warehouses supporting very large databases and large numbers of users. The PowerPC based server models, combined with the clustering technologies described in reference #1, provide an almost unlimited growth path for data warehouse implementations.

Parallel processing techniques
Storing and analyzing very large amounts of data require the database to take full advantage of the hardware it runs on, in order to get the most performance out of the system and meet the user's expectations. Several advances in the area of parallel computing have been announced for AS/400 and DB2 for OS/400, available in three stages.

Parallel I/O processing: The first stage of the parallel technologies is parallel I/O processing. This feature, available in Version 3 Release 1 and subsequent releases of OS/400, provides parallel computing to occur at the I/O processor level for a single job.

AS/400 business computing systems consist of multiple processors: the main CPU(s) and multiple I/O processors

Figure 3

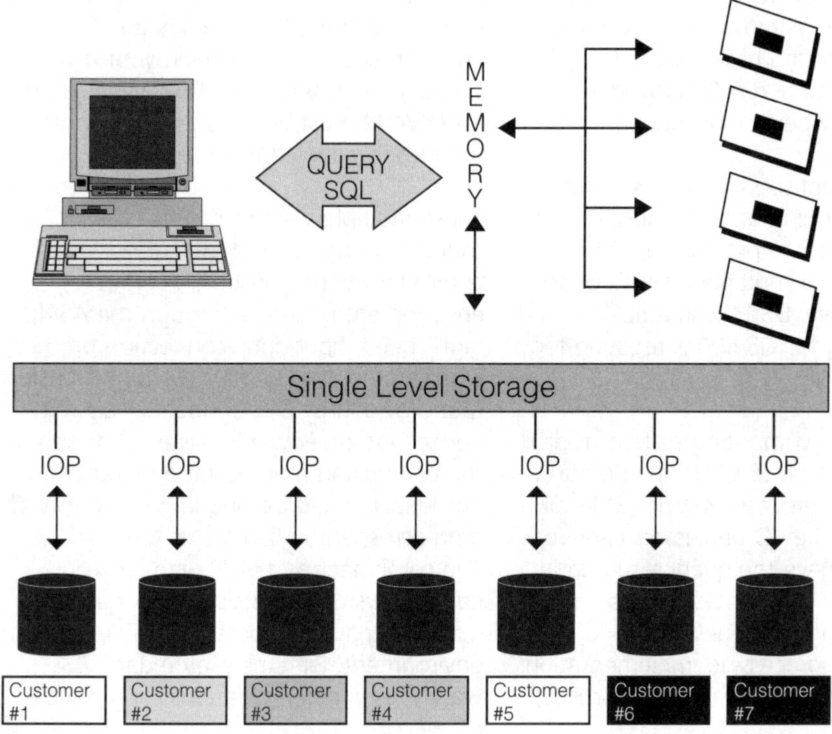

(microprocessor-based adapters) on which to offload the main processors and create a more efficient system. This has been an inherent feature of the AS/400 architecture since its inception.

Parallel I/O processing also takes advantage of another inherent architectural feature of the AS/400: single level storage. Single level storage allows the system to automatically spread data across all available disk drives in the system for more efficient processing. No manual "data striping" is required on an AS/400 system.

Parallel I/O processing means that a single user can submit a query operation against the database, and multiple I/O processor tasks are initiated internally to process the request. This capability to have multiple resources in the system working to retrieve the query result data has produced, in some cases, up to a 700 0mprovement in I/O bound query performance.

Symmetric multiprocessing: The second stage is symmetric multiprocessing, or SMP. Similar to parallel I/O processing, SMP will take advantage of multiple main CPUs for a single job/query. DB2 Symmetric Multiprocessing for OS/400 is required for this function.

AS/400 business computing systems today can contain up to four CPUs, in addition to the multiple I/O processors. With SMP, all four CPUs and the I/O processors can work together to retrieve the query result data for a single job. DB2 for OS/400 uses industry-leading techniques in its symmetric multiprocessing implementation to actually break down the query (or SQL) statement across the multiple processors. SMP has resulted in performance increases of over 400 0.000000or certain queries. Even single processor configurations can make use of the SMP feature, and have shown significant performance improvements through enhanced optimization techniques.

Loosely Coupled systems: The third stage provides an almost unlimited scalability option. Loosely coupled systems will provide the capability to attach multiple (up to 32) systems together in a "Shared Nothing" cluster. Once connected, those loosely coupled systems appear as a single database to the users; the database can be spread across the storage unit on each coupled system. Whereas there is a limit of 520 gigabytes on the high end server models, with the loosely coupled environment you can expand your disk capacity to 16 terabytes. DB2 Multisystem for OS/400 must be installed to support the loosely coupled technology.

These multiple systems can be coupled together using any form of communications transport. A typical environment might be through the AS/400 high-speed, fiber-optic connection product, OptiConnect for OS/400. The high transfer rate provided by OptiConnect (1 gigabit per second on PowerPC systems) prevents the connection method from being a bottleneck when passing large amounts of data across a coupled set of systems.
The combination of SMP with loosely coupled systems effectively provides a massively parallel processing (MPP) environment. Extremely large data warehouse implementations can now be

achieved. In a single query, it is feasible that you could have as many as 128 (32 coupled systems times four CPUs in each system) CPUs all working together with potentially hundreds of I/O processors to retrieve the query result data.

Openness
A major focus area for AS/400 development has been to ensure compliance with industry and de facto standards for database access. Providing support for open standards allows AS/400 customers the most flexibility in choosing tools and inter-operating with non-AS/400 platforms and databases. Some of these standards include:

- ANSI X.3.135.1992, ISO 9075-1992 and FIPS 127-2 Structured Query Language
- IBM Distributed Relational Database Architecture (DRDA) Distributed Unit of Work--Application Directed
- Microsoft Open Database Connection (ODBC)
- X/Open SQL Call Level Interface (CLI)
- Apple Data Access Language (DAL)

The benefit of this is that client/server tools that also support these standards can very easily use DB2 for OS/400 as their database server. Many decision support and EIS front-end tools have been successfully tested with the new AS/400 ODBC driver that is included in the Client Access product. For an extensive list of client/ server tools, refer to the AS/400 Client/ Server Applications Directory, G325-6202.

Internet access and Lotus Notes: The Internet and collaborative computing are important components of today's information technology departments. AS/400 support of the Internet and the leading collaborative groupware solution, Lotus Notes, enhances AS/400 data warehouse capabilities.

All that is needed to access the data warehouse by way of the Internet is a standard web browser on the client PC to allow the AS/400 HTTP World Wide Web server to access your data.

One way to access the data warehouse using the Internet is through server-based applications. Any AS/400 application can be accessed through the Internet using the 5250/HTML Workstation Gateway. The Workstation Gateway enables the web browser to act as an AS/400 workstation by converting text-based data streams into HTML (hyper-text markup language) documents as the application runs. Therefore, an existing AS/400 application that accesses your data warehouse can be accessed through the Internet, and new applications can be created quickly with existing tools, libraries, and procedures.

A second way to access your data through the Internet is by using the DB2 World Wide Web (WWW) offering that is part of Internet Connection for AS/400. DB2 WWW is a program that works from SQL and HTML macro files to set up DB2 for OS/400 queries, with no programming required. You use HTML forms on web browser displays to specify input values for the query. The input values are sent back to the server to query the data warehouse using SQL statements.

Figure 4

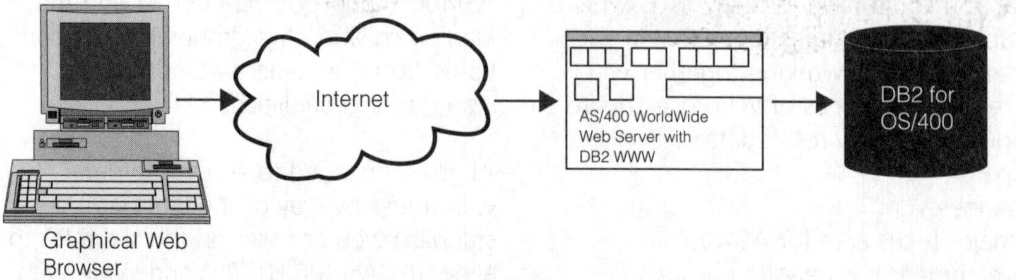

Graphical Web Browser → Internet → AS/400 WorldWide Web Server with DB2 WWW → DB2 for OS/400

As a third option, you can write a program, using the Internet standard Common Gateway Interface (CGI), to collect input from the user with a web browser and to run a DB2 for OS/400 query. This provides the maximum flexibility for creating dialogs with the user to gather input and to display the results, perhaps using graphs and charts to show the information.

The AS/400 World Wide Web server simplifies the accessibility of your data warehouse data to your company, customers, and potential markets.

Lotus Notes is an industry leading groupware product. Its powerful collaborative computing and data replication features can be seamlessly integrated with the AS/400 data warehouse. Built-in replication technology is provided with the Lotus Notes implementation on AS/400, providing the ability to share information from a DB2 for OS/400-based warehouse and Notes applications.

Support for multiple data structures
AS/400 supports many different data structures appropriate for analytical processing. DB2 for OS/400 provides a leading edge relational database management system, with multiple interfaces for defining, loading, accessing, and managing the data warehouse. OLAP data structures are supported through IBM Business Partner products that take advantage of the scalability and performance that AS/400 provides. See Table 1 for a list of Business Partner solutions.

Data analysis and end-user tools

The open interfaces of DB2 for OS/400, combined with the high performance programming interfaces in Client Access, give you the base with which you can select any number of tools for analysis purposes. These are typically PC-based tools that access the AS/400 data warehouse through the Client Access product. The choice of tools includes report writers, query tools, EIS tools, spreadsheets, and client/server programming tools for highly customized implementations. The wealth of tools does not seem to be a problem; picking one from the hundreds on the market is not as easy!

Product examples
IBM and its Business Partners offer a wide range of end-user products to choose from for analyzing the data warehouse from the desktop. IBM can assist you in determining the right tool for you, based on your specific requirements. The IBM Client Series program defines a selected set of leading-edge products to help you through the selection process. These products include IBM Visualizer and Lotus Approach. The IBM Client Series end-user certified products are included in Table 1.

- IBM and its Business Partners offer a wide range of client/server development tools specifically designed for building your own executive information system. For papers and a directory differentiating the many development tools in the market, refer to the AS/400 Application Development Handbook, G325-6249.
- Intelligent Miner, from IBM, provides a powerful set of data mining tools for finding patterns and relationships in your data. The Intelligent Miner tools include neural network and statistical algorithms to create leading-edge data mining solutions. Data mining techniques included in this product are:

Association
This technique allows you to discover which items are related. For example, you can discover what items are purchased in a retail store at the same time. The output from this type of data mining is a rule such as: "If a customer buys product X, then he will also buy product Y 75 percent of the time."

Sequential pattern
This technique allows you to discover associations over some period of time. For example, it can be used to determine the likelihood that a person will buy a product next week if he buys a related one today. This information could be used to determine what items a retail store should put on sale together in order to make both related sales, or which items should be stocked in the same aisle. The output from this type of data mining is a rule such as: "If a customer buys product X, then 75 percent of the time he will also buy product Y within a week."

Classification
Historical data frequently consists of a set of values and a classification for those values. Mining data that has already been classified allows you to discover which attributes and values contributed to the classification. For example, you could mine a database of currently insured customers and previous customers who allowed their insurance to lapse. You could then use the resulting classification model to predict which current customers are likely to lapse in the future. Results can also be viewed in a decision tree format.

Clustering
This technique places records into groups with similar characteristics. For example, the customer database has information about customers and how much money they have spent in the past. Clustering techniques be applied to this information to find out which customers have similar attributes and would be likely to spend more money if they became targeted with a marketing campaign. Another important

use of clustering is to learn why the items (in this case, customers) fall into particular groups.

Prediction
Also known as scoring, this technique involves mapping a set of input values to a single output value. An example is an application that determines real estate market values. The application receives a set of input values such as location, number of bedrooms, square footage, and so on. The output of the application is the value of the property.

Combined with these state-of-the-art techniques are data preprocessing functions for transformation and cleansing, and a graphical administration facility that makes data mining easy to set up and run. Each technique provided includes appropriate graphical visualization to make it easy to understand the mining results.

In addition to allowing you to discover new information, the models developed from your data can be used in applications using an extensive set of APIs. For example, the Intelligent Miner can tell you what attributes make a loan applicant a credit risk. Discovered from past loan history, this information can then be imbedded in an application that can screen future applicants.

Managing information about the warehouse--metadata
Factors such as the number of operational systems, diversity of platforms, and consistency and size of data across the platform can affect the need for metadata. Metadata can be found in database catalogs, data dictionaries, and repositories. Anything that contains information about the operational and data warehouse databases can be used to supplement this information. By far the largest source of this information, especially the business information, is the person who created it. The correlations between business terms and the data warehouse structure do not exist in any online facility and must be created by hand.

Product examples
With Version 3 of OS/400, the enhancements to the system-wide catalog may mean that all the metadata you need is already in the AS/400. The DB2 for OS/400 system-wide catalog contains information about your files--independent of whether they were created with data description specifications or using SQL. Information about tables, fields, referential integrity constraints, and cross-reference information are kept in the system-wide catalog.

The IBM DataGuide set of products provide a more extensive information catalog that can include data from multiple platforms. Extraction utilities allow object descriptions of tables, columns, queries, spreadsheets, and so on to be gathered from a wide range of sources. The DataGuide administrator function provides a common point of control for gathering and organizing information for the catalog for all end-user environments. Business views allow users to access the data warehouse while shielding them from the complexities of the database.

Many IBM Business Partner products offer their own layer of metadata for use with their product sets. For example, IBM Visualizer includes an administrative function that can provide descriptions of files or tables and fields or columns, and can even control join processing.

Putting it all together (or where to start)

Up until now we've addressed the various components that make up a data warehouse implementation. Particular requirements will dictate which components are appropriate for each individual situation. Do you need a multi-dimensional data structure? Is 80 percent of your operational data in legacy flat files? How sophisticated should the desktop presentation be for the users of the warehouse? Has someone already built the transformation programs to extract data from the software package that you run your business with today? Do you have the tools you need to help you manage the warehouse?

Selecting the data warehouse platform is just one piece to the puzzle. Defining requirements, selecting the right components, and implementing the solution completes the process. Whether you build your own solution, or choose to have the solution built for you, IBM can help.

Product examples
On the next page is a list of IBM and Business Partner solutions and their appropriate solution areas (table 1).

Consulting services
IBM offers an extensive set of consulting services specializing in data warehouse and data mining solutions. Expert consultants can help in the planning, design, systems integration, product installation, and testing of a data warehouse implementation, as well as provide the follow-on support for managing and automating the data warehouse processes.

Summary

Data warehousing implementations need not be complex. The AS/400 Advanced Server models can meet the demands of data warehousing while letting you focus your energies on running your business, and not on running your computer. These models build on the strengths of AS/400 business computing systems: ease of use, advanced architecture, open interfaces, scalability, and investment protection.

IDC has completed a number of studies on cost of ownership showing AS/400 business computing systems as the least expensive system compared to LANs and UNIX environments. Recent benchmarks by Client/Server Labs, an independent bench-marking firm, shows AS/400 beating 15 other competitive systems by at least 52%.

The affinity you have with your operational systems make the AS/400 Advanced Server models the most logical choice for the data warehouse. Not only is data transformation made simpler, but systems administration is significantly easier as well. You'll have the same backup procedures, security, and operations as your existing system, but also

Solution area	Product	Provider	Features
Warehouse management	RODIN	Coglin Mill	Build, administer, secure and describe the data warehouse. Extract data to data marts or presentation tools.
Warehouse management	ShowCase Strategy	ShowCase Corp.	Data distribution, administration, and tightly integrated analysis tools.
Data mart management	Visual Warehouse	IBM	Data mart administration and analysis tools in a packaged offering
Data propagation and transformation	DataPropagator	IBM	Data replication across all IBM DB2 platforms
Data propagation and transformation	DataMirror	DataMirror	AS/400 to AS/400 data propagation including S/36 files and bidirectional support.
Metadata	Data Guide	IBM	Information catalog tool for database administrator and end users.
Parallel database	DB2 Symmetric Multiprocessing for OS/400	IBM	Turbo-query feature to significantly enhance performance of query applications.
Parallel database	DB2 Multisystem for OS/400	IBM	Database functionality to take advantage of coupled AS/400 systems providing almost unlimited growth.
OLAP, data mart	AMIS/400	Hoskyns Group PLC, IBM	Multi-dimensional analysis tools.
OLAP, data mart	MIT/400	SAMAC	Multi-dimensional analysis tools.
OLAP, data mart	ShowCase Strategy with ESSBASE/400	ShowCase Corp.	Multi-dimensional analysis tools.
OLAP, data mart	Sales Tracker	Silvon Software, Inc.	Multi-dimensional analysis applications for manufacturing and distribution.
Executive information system	InfoManager	Ferguson Inf. System (U.S.) InfoManager O.Y. (Europe)	Health and banking industry multi-dimensional executive information system applications.
Decision supp. tools	Visualizer	IBM	Query, report writing, graphics.
Decision supp. tools	ShowCase Strategy with VistaPro	ShowCase Corp.	Integrated query, report writing, graphics.
Decision supp. tools	Impromptu, PowerPlay	Cognos	Query, report writing, and desktop OLAP
Decision supp. tools	BrioQuery	Brio Technologies	Query, report writing, and desktop OLAP
Decision supp. tools	Lotus Approach	Lotus	PC-based database management
Data mining tools	Neural Network Utility	IBM	Visual development environment for mining data with neural networks; includes graphical training monitor, training language, data translation.
Data mining tools	Intelligent Miner	IBM	Decision support tool for mining data; includes neural network, decision tree, statistical algorithms, graphical interface, and data translation functions

the ability to use the AS/400 server for operations such as batch offload, application development, or communications.

What customers say

One customer had this to say about an AS/400 warehouse solution: "It has allowed our users to analyze and spot trends we simply could not do previously. By implementing a data warehousing solution with the AS/400, we projected an improvement in our merchandising and category management areas by ten percent."

Another: "I believe that it has changed our style of management throughout the whole company, since managers at all levels are getting the information they need at the right time and in the right format!"

And still another: "We measure the performance of each SKU relative to plans, historical trends, and forecasts. This in turn helps us make management decisions--taking advantage of the more profitable business and controlling the less profitable."

Transformational Data Replication

Title: *Transformational Data Replication*

Author: *DataMirror Corporation*

Abstract: *This document outlines the terms and concepts associated with one method of moving, sharing, enhancing, and integrating enterprise data - transformational data replication. Additionally, this paper discusses technology available today from DataMirror that enables bi-directional cross-platform, cross-database replication between heterogeneous platforms and database technologies.*

Market Snapshot

Companies use data replication and transformation for a variety of applications. Whether companies need nightly backups of day-to-day activity or more advanced requirements such as loading and replenishing data marts and warehouses or content delivery for electronic business applications, there is a replication solution that accommodates the need. But how did companies become so dependent on the ability to move data throughout the organization?

There are several driving factors behind the growth of data replication software. First, an expanded user base has contributed significantly to the need for a data replication strategy. The rapid introduction of powerful personal computers has enabled users to perform complex data query, analysis and reporting from their desktop rather than filing requests with IT departments. Professionals from accounting, knowledge workers from sales and marketing, and decision makers like CEO executive management all make use of local or network-accessible databases for personal use.

Next, dispersed data has increased the need for replication software. Many companies have expanded from single site operations to regional, international and global organizations. The collection of data at remote sites necessitates movement of that data to central locations for decision support systems and business applications like data marts and warehouses.

A shift in application models from centralized mainframe systems to client/server architecture and distributed systems has also impacted the market growth of replication software. With users depending on local servers for access to applications and data, many companies turn to replication software for enterprise-wide data distribution and consolidation requirements.

Figure 1: Simple replication from source system to target

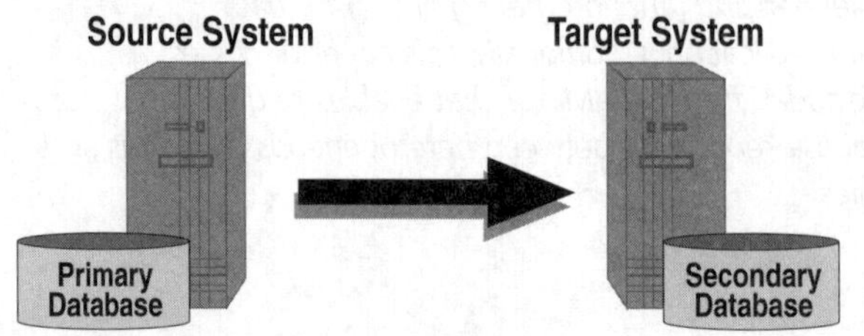

Data Replication Defined

The concept of straight data replication is not a difficult one. In its simplest form, replication is the capture and movement of data from one database at a source system to another database at the target machine.

Evolution of Data Replication

Data replication is a relatively new technology. Prior to data copy, mirroring, and replication capabilities, and still in use today, users accessed data via dumb terminals, or computer stations that had no local processor or storage capabilities. Dumb terminals linked to a mainframe or high end servers that stored corporate data and allowed users to make changes to data, run reports and queries, and facilitate any data entry requirements.

With the proliferation of powerful personal computers, end users are now able to do more, faster, and more efficiently. However, with the growth of PC-based organizations, the need to share data between relatively local areas (a branch office, regional headquarters and even desktop to desktop) also grows. To accommodate this, several methods were developed.

First, companies simply copied flat files to physical media storage devices such as tape, or disk and transported them between machines. This method is limited by capacity, efficiency and time. Most organizations can not take nightly captures of their data, copy it to physical media, and transport and load it on all remote servers in their organization.

The prospect of doing this -- the time consuming, costly and resource intensive task of physical flat file copies -- lead companies to develop in-house applications to carry out data replication tasks. These early programs involve a good deal of expense, resources and time to develop and are often outdated before final implementation.

Commercial software became available that addressed the immediate need for data movement. These database copy tools took entire databases and moved them on a full-refresh, or overwrite, basis. As databases grow, the time to refresh the target machine increases. Even if the database has relatively few changes since the last update, the tool sends the entire database. That is, there was no selection or filtering capabilities and the tools did not replicate on a net change basis.

Database snapshots are another method of transferring data between systems. Basically, a "picture" of a source database is sent at a given point in time. This differs

from database copies in that snapshots do not involve entire database movement but simple captures of parts of database files (e.g. specified columns).
The growing number of users requiring access to data and the increasingly diverse ways in which companies used data generated a need for more sophisticated replication tools. The answer was synchronous and asynchronous replication tools.

Synchronous Vs. Asynchronous Data Replication

Data replication tools used today are based on either synchronous or asynchronous architectures. The most advanced data replication software uses an asynchronous architecture; meaning that synchronization can occur while other processes continue on the source machine. This is in contrast with the two-phase commit logic inherent in synchronous distributed database management systems (DBMS). Distributed DBMSs involve placing pieces of a database on different systems and accessing data as though it exists on one system.
Two-phase commit architecture guarantees that all database copies are synchronized, regardless of location, but any update failure can cause a transaction to be rolled back. This necessitates a complete database refresh, or resynchronization, which can be extremely time consuming. Moreover, as the number of nodes within a DBMS increases, two-phase commit logic becomes unworkable as all subsequent updates are frozen until the commit process is completed for the current transaction.
Essentially, system usage comes to a halt each time an update occurs.

Asynchronous replication, on the other hand, provides reliable delivery of data while preventing any possible transaction deadlock between multiple database engines. Asynchronous architecture also allows data recovery in case of communication failure and offers replication on a predetermined schedule to avoid network or resource interruption.

Figure 2: Contrasts between synchronous and asynchronous replication

Synchronous

* All targets updated before source transaction complete
* Uses two-phase commit
* Not Practical
  - *update response times*
  - *join performance*
  - *network traffic*

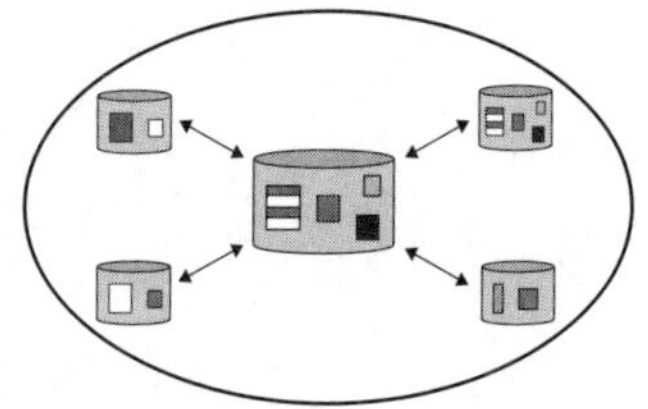

Asynchronous

* Source transaction complete when source database updated
* Target databases updated at a later time
* Transparant to usres and applications
  - *no change in source transaction response*
  - *no additional application code*

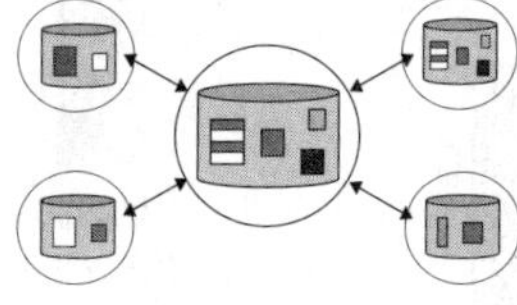

Transformational Data Replication Defined

Whereas straight data replication involves simply copying database tables between two or more systems, transformational data replication is capable of the enterprise-wide data movement requirements of today's dynamic computing environment. Transformational data replication involves moving data between systems regardless of hardware platform or database. Transformational replication tools are capable of reformatting database schema, filtering, cleansing, and enhancing data, and moving it to where it needs to be.

For example, many companies rely on a variety of computing systems and databases to manage the massive amount of data collected today. The occurrence of rapid corporate mergers and acquisitions also leads to mixed-system computing environments Sharing access throughout the organization has been problematic in the past. A high performance transformational replication tool can handle the heterogeneous replication needs of global organizations.

There are several key features to look for in data transformation and replication software; the following section outlines several of them.

Figure 3: Illustrates mixed-system environment and replication requirements of a sample data warehouse application

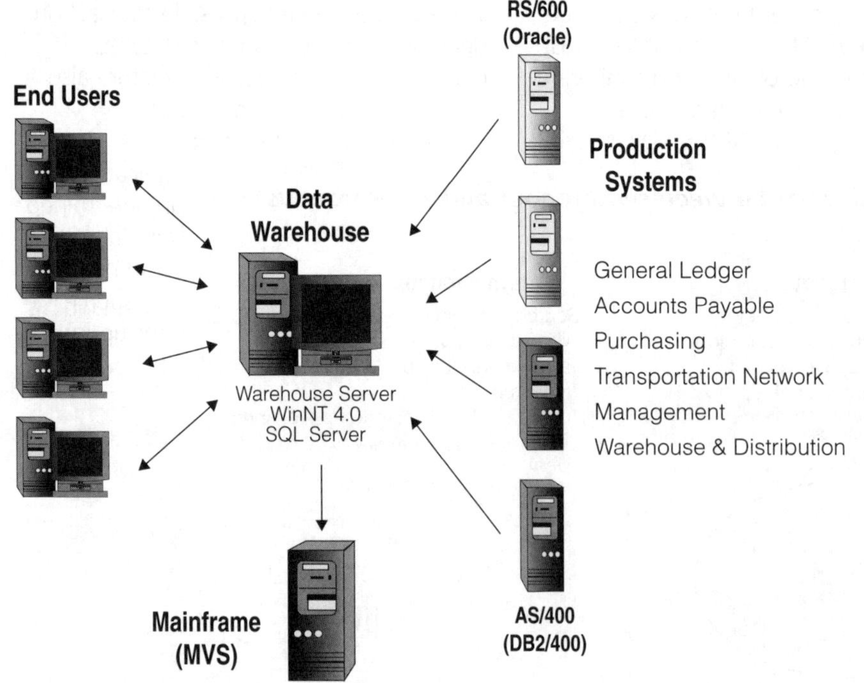

Advanced Functions of Replication Software

Many data replication utilities and software packages are capable of straight database copies, unidirectional replication, or database snapshots. They do not enable delivery of meaningful information to target systems, movement among heterogeneous platforms and databases, or the ability to select and filter what data is transmitted.

Selectivity

Business solutions like data marts and warehouses, distributed require the ability to select and filter which data is moved throughout the organization. With transformational replication software, source data can be selectively filtered by row and/or record for specific target.

For example, a company planning to implement a data warehouse may want to filter out information about salary, sick time, or vacation, while allowing access to hire date, salary range, and department. Transformation Server software from DataMirror includes built-in data filtering and selection functions in addition to data enhancement and transformation capabilities.

Data Transformation

The way companies think about data, and the way it is represented in databases, has changed significantly over time. Obscure naming conventions, dissimilar coding for the same item (e.g. number representation as well as character based codes), and separate architectures are all commonplace. Transformational data replication software can remedy these problems while consolidating the information in data marts and warehouses or distributing the data to remote locations.

Figure 4: Illustrates row/column selection capability. Certain applications require data, like salary information in a human resources database, to be filtered out of the replication process or other columns, first and last name fields for example, to be combined

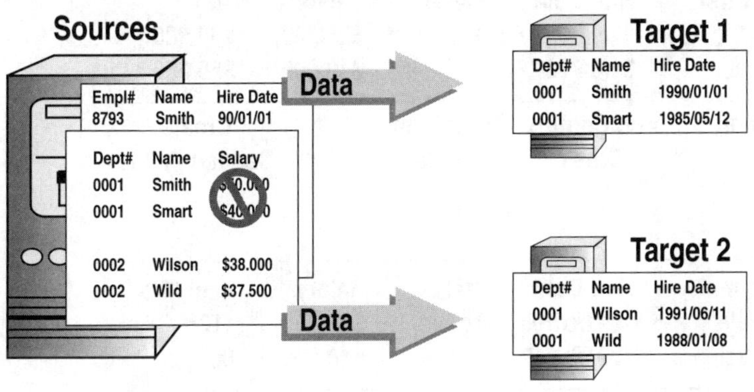

For instance, some companies are beginning to see the benefit of sharing data between enterprise resource planning systems (ERP) and relational data stores housed in Oracle, Sybase, DB/2 or other database. The problem is that ERP systems use proprietary data structures that need to be cleansed and reformatted to fit conventional database architectures. Rows and Columns may have to be split or merged depending on the database format. For example, an ERP system may require that Zip Code and state be part of the same column while a company's data structure in Oracle may have the two columns separated. Similarly, a company may have product type and model number in an inventory database as one columns whereas the ERP system requires them to be split. Data transformation and replication software, like that from DataMirror, accommodates these requirements.

Other applications of data transformation software include changing data representation (US dollars converted to British Sterling, metric to standard, character columns to numeric, abbreviations to full text, number codes to text), visualization (aggregate, consolidate, summarize data values), and preparation for loading multidimensional databases. All of these functions allow for code conversion, removal of ambiguity and confusion associated with data, standardization, measurement conversions, and consolidating dissimilar data structures for data consistency.

Support for Heterogeneous Environments
Most data replication solutions focus on moving data between homogeneous systems and database software. Users today want the ability to choose what technology drives their application. Also, corporate mergers and acquisitions often lead to mixed system computing environments. Some replication tools, like DataMirror Transformation Server, are capable of moving data among a wide range of systems and databases. For example, companies use Transformation Server to share data between Microsoft SQL Server databases on Digital Alpha-Server systems with Oracle databases housed on Intel based servers. Others

Figure 5: Examples of data transformations. Applications, particularly data warehousing projects, require data to be reformatted, enhanced, standardized, or otherwise made more useful and meaningful

Empl#	Last	First	Hire Date	Status	Salary	Max
1234	Moreiro	Nicole	91/01/05	A	$55.000	$50.000
2345	Ellis-Dixon	Val	91/04/12	A	$40.000	$50.000

Increase Field Size → Concatenation → Add Century Dates → Transform Fields → Create Derived Fields

Empl#	Employee Name	Hire Date	Status	Salary	% of Max
001234	Moreiro, Nicole	1991/01/05	Active	$55.000	110%
002345	Ellis-Dixon, Val	1991/04/12	Active	$40.000	80%

consolidate IBM AS/400 data from regional offices in Sybase data marts and warehouses.

Bi-directional Replication
With some transformational data replication software, users can freely move data between systems, enabling true data sharing applications. Bi-directional data movement facilitates an "update anywhere" architecture for fully distributed business solutions.

Ease of Implementation
Some replication software can be awkward to install and set up. A serious consideration when evaluating replication tools is the work required to set up and initiate the data replication. Organizations should ensure that no programming changes to existing applications are required and that coding must be done to get the process initiated. A good thing to keep in mind is that replication software is meant to avoid time-consuming, resource intensive, and costly custom programming, not necessitate it.

Implementation Alternatives

There are several methods for replicating data. The major alternatives are master/ slave, broadcast, staging, consolidation, cascading, bi-directional, and subset.

Master/Slave
Simply, a system that houses data is a master while the system(s) that connect to and access data from it are said to be the slave(s). Also referred to as client/server where the server is the "master" and clients "slaves".

Broadcast
The method of replication involves a one to many relationship where a server will transmit, or broadcast, data to one or more systems.

Staging
This involves replicating data from an operational system to a temporary holding area on either the same system or, more commonly, to a separate system. Usually implemented in data warehousing applications, data stages are where transformation, cleansing, and enhancement routines are performed on the data.

Consolidation
In contrast with broadcast replication, consolidation involves moving data from many systems to a central computer. Data warehousing involves consolidation of data from several operational systems, branch offices, or regional data centers in a central database.

Cascading
This replication method enables the most efficient movement of data throughout an organization. Particularly useful for national or global companies, cascading replication involves a source system transmitting data to a target which, in turn, serves as the source for the system in the chain of replication.

For example, let's say a company has 12 branch offices and a head office. If we assume that for each site to send it's nightly data update to head office it takes an average of 15 minutes, the total replication time will be three hours. In a

Figure 6

Without Cascading

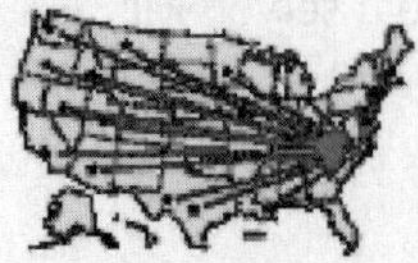

With Cascading

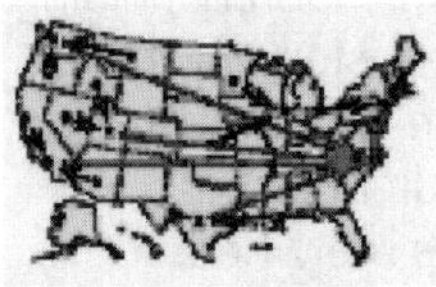

Cascading replication streamlines the replication process by enabling organizations to select regional cascade 'points' for neighboring sites to replicate to. In turn, these points replicate to a central system, usually a data warehouse.

cascading replication environment, this time can be cut significantly. If three of the remote sites served as cascade points for three systems each (the three offices closest to them), the process could be reduced drastically. In this case, each cascade point would require the same 15 minutes, but the remote sites replicating to the points will require significantly less time than 15 minutes. Given this, the time would be reduced to 45 minutes rather than three hours.

Bi-directional

Replication between two or more systems is referred to as bi-directional replication. Some data replication software is capable of simple one-way copying of data. Robust, high performance, bi-directional replication is required by organizations implementing enterprise-wide data sharing applications. Bi-directional replication enables replication among all systems in a company -- the ability to share data in real-time and, with some tools, across heterogeneous platforms and databases. The most common use for bi-directional replication is in data synchronization applications. Centrally administered inventory systems, for example, can have changes in product levels reflected in real-time from all branch sites.

Subset

This method allows users to move portions of databases to and from other systems. Often used in data mart or data warehouse implementations, subset replication provides for efficient movement of appropriate data. That is, data which is not suitable or appropriate for the application is not transmitted.

Other Considerations

Administration

There are two types of setup and administration methods that replication tools follow. The first involves custom programming of the replication process. This means code must be written to have the replication software understand what data has to be moved, and when. Any changes in the replication schema must be programmed.

Mapping-based tools, on the other hand, involve built-in administration utilities that provide quick and easy definition of the replication process. Changes in the replication schema are simply re-mapped using the same front-end that defined the original process.

Operating Modes

Good data replication tools will allow for flexibility with respect to the replication "mode". There are three modes: continuous mirroring, periodic net-change, and full copy refresh.

Continuous Mirroring: Also known as real-time replication, continuous mirroring enables organizations to update databases as changes (adds, updates, deletes) occur and reflect those changes to target systems.

Periodic Net Change: This mode involves capturing changes to databases as they occur and storing them until a predetermined replication time. Usually scheduled for nightly or hourly transmission, only those records that have changed since the last update are sent to target databases.

Full Copy Refresh: Sometimes it is necessary or desirable to replicate an entire database copy to target systems. Full copy refreshes are done to resynchronize databases after an outage, for example, or upon initial synchronization.

Initiation Schemes
There are several techniques used by data replication software to move data. Essentially, replication tools either push or pull data on an event driven or polling basis.

Push Vs. Pull Replication
Push replication is initiated at the source for each subscribed target. This means that as changes occur, they are captured and sent, or "pushed" across to each target. Pull replication is initiated at the target by each subscribed target. In other words, the target system extracts the captured changes and "pulls" them down to the local database. Push replication is more efficient as it can better manage system resources. As the number of targets increases, pull replication becomes resource draining on the source system, especially if that machine is a production machine that may already be overworked.

Event Driven Vs. Polling
Event driven replication is a technique that involves events at the source initiating capture and transmission of changes. Polling involves a monitoring process that polls the status to initiate capture and application of database changes. Event driven replication conserves system resources as replication only occurs after preset events whereas polling requires continuous resource utilization by a monitoring utility.

Replication Solutions

There are many applications that data replication software enables. High systems availability, data warehousing, data distribution, workload balancing, development and test environments, and electronic business are all solutions that data replication is used for.

High Systems Availability
The reliance on data as a competitive tool and, in many cases, the ability to conduct business, few companies can afford even a few hours of total system downtime, let alone days or a week. Without access to production data, business loses momentum or, worse still, ceases. Even if companies can avoid disaster, they still have scheduled downtime for hardware and software upgrades and routine maintenance. To avoid the loss of data, or the loss of access to that data, companies implement high availability solutions.

Figure 7: High Systems Availability Diagram for the IBM AS/400

● High Availabilty

In most cases, companies elect to transfer business critical applications and data to a failsafe system located off-site. The ideal situation is to switch to the failsafe site when needed and have any changes that occur during downtime replicated back to the production machine when it is brought back online. That is, if the main system is down for two hours, and none of the original data was lost, then only the changes should be transmitted back from the failsafe site -- not the entire database. However, if data is lost on the production machine as a result of system failure or other disaster, then companies should have the ability to resynchronize it with data from the failsafe machine. Bi-directional data replication software, capable of real-time data delivery, meets the needs of organizations looking to implement high systems availability solutions.

Data Distribution

Data distribution allows companies to move data from one source system to multiple targets -- regardless of computer hardware or database. Organizations can replicate entire databases from the source machine to targets or replicate location specific data, such as daily price updates, to branch offices or retail sites. For example, parts of centrally administered database files can be replicated to remote locations for local query and analysis purposes. Transformational data replication software satisfies the data selection, filtering, enhancement and movement requirements of data distribution projects.

Data Warehousing

Data warehousing as a tool for business intelligence is widely implemented. Undoubtedly, the data warehouse offers businesses a significant competitive advantage with key benefits enabling companies to:

- Monitor sales activity in order to make fast, informed decisions based on up-to-the-minute information
- Deliver product to market faster using inventory and manufacturing elements of the data warehouse
- Predict and understand business trends to make better business decisions

Perhaps the most important element of the data warehouse is loading and replenishing the data. This involves selecting the appropriate data and constructing an informational database in a format that is beneficial to users. It also includes regularly updating the warehouse database with new transactions. Transformational data replication software is ideal for performing these critical data warehousing tasks.

Workload Distribution

Companies suffer from strained system resources as transaction levels rise and query and analysis activity increases. Replication software is well suited for improving system performance and reliability by distributing batch jobs and query and analysis activity to a replica server. This allows business users to manipulate data on a secondary machine

Figure 8: Workload balancing between operational system and system supporting query and analysis activity

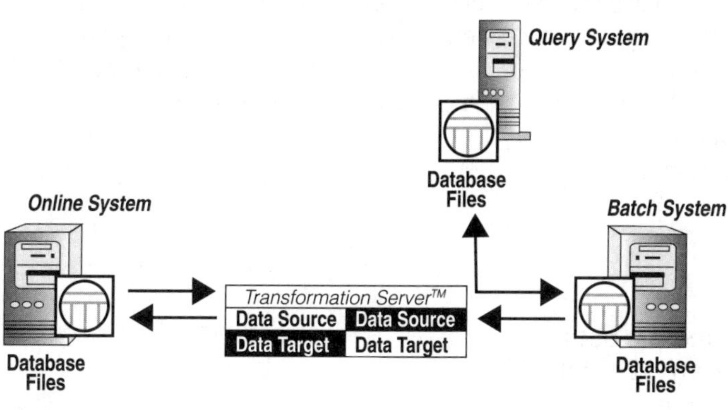

Figure 9

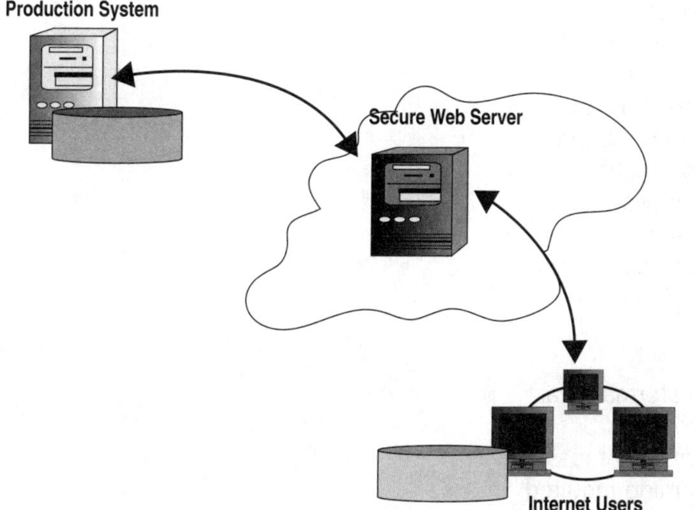

business models, streamlining supply chains, increasing efficiency and productivity, and bringing collaborative applications to unprecedented levels. Data replication software meets the data transformation and movement needs of many e-business solutions.

A recent study by Information Week (May 18, 1998) found that 20% of respondents listed "integration of diverse platforms" as the major obstacle to the growth of e-business in their organization. This was second only to security or transactions as a technical limitation. Replication software is capable of

without affecting performance on operational systems.

Electronic Business

Electronic business is changing the way companies interact with suppliers, alliances, and customers. It is changing

feeding secure web servers with operational data for electronic business applications. For example, a company selling computers on the Internet will require a good deal of data movement to have the process run as efficient as possible. For each transaction, a credit card database must be queried, inventory levels reflected, shipping and receiving database updated, and perhaps a customer database loaded. Replication software is capable of meeting all the data movement requirements of these types of electronic commerce applications, even across dissimilar hardware and software.

Summary

Today's computing environment is both dynamic and volatile. Concerns about the Year 2000, trends toward e-business solutions, and the proliferation of mixed system computing environments are placing strain on already pressed IT resources within many organizations. Many applications require the movement of data between both similar and heterogeneous systems and databases. Transformational data replication software can simplify development of business solutions that require data sharing, distribution and consolidation -- like electronic commerce applications, data warehouses, and data distribution projects.

The advantages of using transformational data replication software are many: support for cross-platform, cross-database data movement, no programming required, bi-directional replication, high performance, secure data movement, and rapid installation are just a few. The alternative, in many cases, is costly and time-consuming custom programming that requires utilization of seasoned application developers who are familiar in a broad range of both current and legacy systems and technologies.

If your organization is considering any of the applications discussed in this paper, evaluation of transformational data replication software like DataMirror Transformation Server may be the first step in overcoming the obstacles.

Ten Mistakes to Avoid

Title: *Ten Mistakes to Avoid*

Author: *The Data Warehousing Institute*

Abstract: *The staff of The Data Warehousing Institute has called upon experts across the industry, and conducted meetings in several cities with active data warehousing project managers and IS executives to assist us in developing a compendium of the "ten mistakes to avoid for data warehousing managers." This article contains about 65 percent of the complete document.*

1. Starting With The Wrong Sponsorship Chain

The right sponsorship chain includes two key individuals above the data warehousing manager. At the top is an executive sponsor with a great deal of money to invest in effective use of information. A good sponsor, however, is not the only person required in the reporting chain above the warehousing manager. When a data warehousing project craters, the cause can sometimes be traced to the lack of a key individual between the sponsor and the data warehousing manager. That person is often called the project "driver" because he or she keeps the project moving in the right direction and ensures the schedule is kept. A good driver is a business person with three essential characteristics: (1) s/he has already earned the respect of the other executives, (2) s/he has a healthy skepticism about technology, and (3) s/he is decisive but flexible.

2. Setting Expectations That You Cannot Meet And Frustrating Executives At The Moment Of Truth

Data warehousing projects have at least two phases: (1) the selling phase in which you attempt to persuade people that they can expect to get wonderful access to the right data through simple, graphical delivery tools, (2) the struggle to meet the expectations you have raised in phase one. Data warehouses do not give users all the information they need. All data warehousing is, by necessity, domain specific, which means it focuses on a particular set of business information. Worse still, many warehouses are loaded with summary information - not detail. If a question asked by an executive requires more detail or requires information from outside the domain, the answer is often, "we haven't loaded that information, but we can, it will just cost (a bunch) and take (many) weeks." Executives focus their frustration on the person who made the promises.

3. Engaging in Politically-Naive Behavior. (e.g. Saying "This Will Help Managers Make Better Decisions")

A foolish error made by many data warehousing managers is promoting the value of their data warehouse with arguments to the effect of, "This will help managers make better decisions." When a self-respecting manager hears those words, the natural reaction is "This person thinks we have not been making good decisions and that his/her system is going to 'fix' us." From that point on, that manager is very, very hard to please.

Most experienced CIOs know that the objective of data warehousing is the same one that fueled the fourth generation language boom of the late seventies, and the EIS craze of the late eighties - giving end users better access to important information. Fourth generation languages have had a long and useful life, but EIS had a quick rise and a quicker fall. Why? One possible answer is that 4GLs were sold as tools to get data while EIS were promoted as change agents that would improve business and enable better management decisions. That raised political issues, and made enemies out of potential supporters.

4. Loading The Warehouse With Information "Just Because It Was Available."

Some inexperienced data warehousing managers send a list of tables and data elements to end users along with a request asking, "which of these elements should be included in the warehouse?" Sometimes they ask for categories such as 'essential', 'important', and 'nice-to-have'. They get back long lists of marginally useful information that radically expand the data warehouse storage requirements and, more importantly, slow responsiveness. Extraneous data buries important information. Faced with the need to dig through long guides to find the right field name, and having to deal with multiple versions of the same information, users quickly grow frustrated and may even give up entirely.

5. Believing That Data Warehousing Database Design Is The Same As Transactional Database Design

Data warehousing is fundamentally different from transaction processing. The goal here is to access aggregates - sums, averages, trends, and more. Another difference is the user. In transaction processing, a programmer develops a query that will be used tens of thousands of times. In data warehousing, an end-user develops the query and may use it only one time. Data warehousing databases are often denormalized to make them easier to navigate for infrequent users.
An even more fundamental difference is in content. Where transactional systems usually contain only the basic data, data warehousing users increasingly expect to find aggregates and time-series information already calculated for them and ready for immediate display. That's the impetus behind the multi-dimensional database market.

6. Choosing A Data Warehousing Manager Who Is Technology-Oriented Rather Than User-Oriented

"The biggest mistake I ever made was putting that propeller-head in as the manager of the project." Those are the exact words from the driver at a large oil company, explaining how the user-hostile project manager had made so many people angry that the entire project was in danger of being scrapped.

Do not let his words tar all technologists. Some make excellent project managers and can serve as effective data warehousing managers; however, many cannot. Data warehousing is a service business-not a storage business-and making clients angry is a near perfect method of destroying a service business.

7. Focusing On Traditional Internal Record-Oriented Data and Ignoring The Potential Value of External Data and of Text, Images, and - Potentially - Sound And Video

A White House study of commerical executives showed that the very highest executives rely on outside data (news, telephone calls from associates, etc.) for more than 95 percent of all the information they use. Because of their focus on external sources of information, senior executives sometimes see data warehouses as irrelevant. Therefore, it's valuable to extend the project focus to include external information.

In addition, consider expanding the forms of information available through the warehouse. Users are starting to ask, "Where's the copy of the contract (image) that explains the information behind the data? And where's the ad (image) that ran in that magazine? Where's the tape (audio or video) of the key competitor at a recent conference talking about its business strategy? Where's the recent product launch (video)?" This is the age of television. Traditional alphanumeric data is two generations behind the current technology.

8. Delivering Data With Overlapping And Confusing Definitions

The Achilles heel of data warehousing is the requirement to gain consensus on data definitions. Conflicting definitions each have champions, and they are not easily reconciled. Many of the most stubborn definitions have been constructed by managers to reflect data in a way that makes their department look effective. To the finance manager, sales means the net of revenue less returns. Sales to the distribution people is what needs to be delivered. Sales to the sales organization is the amount committed by clients. One organization reported twenty-seven different definitions of sales.
Executives do not give up their definitions without a fight, and few data warehousing managers are in a position to bully executives into agreement. Solving this problem is one of the most important tasks of the data warehousing driver. If it is not solved, users will not have confidence in the information they are getting. Worse,

they may embarrass themselves by using the wrong data - in which case, they will inevitably blame the data warehouse.

9. Believing The Performance, Capacity, And Scalability Promises

At a recent conference, CIOs from three companies-a manufacturer, a retailer, and a service company-described their data warehousing efforts. Although the three data warehouses were very different, all three ran into an identical problem. Within four months of getting started, each of the CIOs unexpectedly had to purchase at least one additional processor of a size equal to or larger than the largest computer that they had originally purchased for data warehousing. They simply ran out of power. Two of the three had failed to budget for the addition, and found themselves with a serious problem. The third had budgeted for unforeseen difficulties, and was able to adapt.

A very common capacity problem arises in networking. One company reported that it sized a network to support an image warehouse, but discovered that the network was soon overwhelmed The surprise was that the images were not at fault. The problem turned out to be network traffic for data transfer between the end-user application and the database of indices on the server. The images moved fast, but the process of finding the right one clogged the network. Network overloads are a very common surprise in client/server systems in general and in data warehousing systems in particular.

10. Believing that Once The Data Warehouse Is Up and Running, Your Problems Are Finished

Each happy data warehouse user asks for new data and tells others about the 'great new tool.' And they, too, ask for more data to be added. And all of them want it immediately. At the same time, each performance or delivery problem results in a high-pressure search for additional technology or a new process.

Thus the data warehousing project team needs to maintain high energy over long periods of time. A common error is to place data warehousing in the hands of project-oriented people who believe that they will be able to set it up once and have it run itself. Data warehousing is a journey, not a destination.

11. Focusing On Ad Hoc Data Mining And Periodic Reporting.*

This is a subtle error, but an important one. Fixing it may transform a data warehousing manager from a data librarian into a hero. The natural progression of information in a data warehouse is (1) extract the data from legacy systems, clean it, and feed it to the warehouse, (2) support ad hoc reporting until you learn what people want, and then (3) convert the ad hoc reports into regularly scheduled reports. That's the natural progression, but it isn't the best progression. It ignores the fact that managers are busy and that reports are liabilities rather than assets unless the recipients have time to read the reports.

Alert systems can be a better approach and they can make a data warehouse mission-critical. Alert systems monitor the data flowing into the warehouse and inform all key people with a need to know, as soon as a critical event takes place. Harris Semiconductor's industry-leading manufacturing alert server, for example, monitors patterns in semi-conductor test data, and screams loudly (via email) when wafer characteristics anywhere in the world (Malaysia, Singapore, or three US sites) creep too far from the ideal. Rethink the manager's need: Does he or she really want reports? Or would an alert system be better?

** You'll find eleven "mistakes" on our list. Believing there are only ten mistakes to avoid is also a mistake, so we've given you eleven to keep you on your toes.*